# REFUGEE CRISIS IN INTERNATIONAL POLICY

## VOLUME IV

## REFUGEES AND INTERNATIONAL CHALLENGES

# REFUGEE CRISIS IN INTERNATIONAL POLICY

## VOLUME IV

### REFUGEES AND INTERNATIONAL CHALLENGES

Edited by

Hasret Çomak, Burak Şakir Şeker, Mehlika Özlem Ultan,
Yaprak Civelek, Çağla Arslan Bozkuş

TRANSNATIONAL PRESS LONDON

2021

MIGRATION SERIES: 31

Refugee Crisis in International Policy

Volume IV - Refugees and International Challenges

Edited by Hasret Çomak, Burak Şakir Şeker, Mehlika Özlem Ultan, Yaprak Civelek, Çağla Arslan Bozkuş



First Published in 2021 by TRANSNATIONAL PRESS LONDON in the United Kingdom, 12 Ridgeway Gardens, London, N6 5XR, UK.
www.tplondon.com



Paperback
ISBN: 978-1-80135-016-7
Digital
ISBN: 978-1-80135-017-4

Cover Design: Nihal Yazgan
Cover Photo by pixpoetry on Unsplash.com

CONTENTS

# PREFACE

Every day, in many parts of the world people are giving the hardest decisions of their lives. With these decisions, they have to leave their homes behind for a better and safer life. Many people in the world, by giving the decision to leave where they grew up, move to a close settlement. Some have to leave their country for a short period of time or for a lifetime.

In many parts of the world, there are many reasons why people try to re-establish their lives in other countries. Some leave their home country to find a job or for education. Others are forced to escape from human rights violations such as inhuman treatment and torture. Millions run away from armed conflicts or violence. These people who do not feel safe; might be targeted due to their characteristics that establish their identity or faith such as their ethnic origin, religious beliefs, gender, and political thoughts.

These journeys that have begun in pursuit of a better future, might be full of danger and fear; some might fall into the trap of human traffickers or other forms of exploitation. Also, some are taken into custody by authorities as soon as they arrive in a country. Many, who settle in a country and start a new life face racism, xenophobia, and discrimination almost every day. They may feel lonely and isolated.

There are many reasons which make it difficult and dangerous for people to stay in their country of origin. Violence, war, hunger, and poverty are the most important ones. Sexual preferences and sexual identity also take an important place. People may also have to leave their home country because of climate change and natural disasters. Mostly, it is possible to encounter many of these difficult conditions all at once.

Fleeing danger is not the only reason people leave their country. Some think of becoming a part of a qualified workforce or gain capital in another country. Moreover, they suppose there is a higher possibility of finding a job in a foreign country. Others seek to live with their relatives and friends currently living abroad. Also, there might be those who aim to begin and continue their education in another country. Therefore, there are many reasons why people might start out to establish a new life in another country.

It is noteworthy to mention the words "refugee", "asylum seeker" and "migrant" in terms of International Law. The refugee is the person who leaves his home country due to the threat of being subjected to grave human rights violations and persecution. These people have to leave their home country and seek asylum in another country due to security threats and threats against their lives. As they have no other choice and they feel their governments cannot or will not protect them against these threats, they are forced to take this decision.

According to the provisions of the "United Nations Convention Relating to the Status of Refugees", adopted on 28 July 1951 by the United Nations Conference of Plenipotentiaries on the Status of Refugees and Stateless Persons convened under General Assembly resolution 429 (V) of 14 December 1950 and entered into force on 22 April 1954, refugees have "the right for international protection".

An asylum seeker is a person who has left his home country to seek asylum in another country to be protected from persecution and grave human rights violations. However, in this case, one only has the status of asylum applicants and legally has not yet been accepted as a refugee. Seeking an asylum application is a human right. This means everyone should be given permission to enter a country to seek asylum.

Migrants, on the other hand, are those who live outside their home country thus who are not asylum seekers or refugees. Migrants in general, leave their home countries to work, to have an education, or to live with their family members in another country. Some feel the need to leave their home country for the reasons of poverty, political turmoil, natural disasters, or other difficult conditions.

The issue that should be emphasized here is the situation that many people who do not fit into the "refugee" definition might get be in danger once they are returned to their home country. Even if they may not be escaping from persecution, no matter what their legal status is in the country they established themselves, migrants' human rights must be protected, and these rights must be respected.

States must protect all migrants against violence based on racism and xenophobia, exploitation, and forced labor. Migrants should not be detained without legitimate reasons or forcefully send back to their home country.

Human rights have become both a subject and a legitimate instrument of international politics. Therefore, the human rights of refugees, asylum seekers and migrants must always be protected at the international level. States must fulfill their joint responsibility to protect the rights of refugees, asylum seekers and migrants.

People are not the source of the problem. The main problem is the reasons that force families and individuals to cross borders. Those who cause these reasons have responsibilities. The attitude of authorities who are trying far-sighted and unrealistic approaches matters in the creation of this problem.

States must ensure that refugees, asylum seekers and immigrants are safe, not subject to torture, discrimination and living in poverty.

States should assess the applications of asylum seekers according to international rules except for those who;

- has committed a crime against peace, a war crime, or a crime against humanity, as defined in the international instruments drawn up to make provision in respect of such crimes;
- has committed a serious non-political crime outside the country of refuge prior to his admission to that country as a refugee;
- has been guilty or suspicious of acts contrary to the purposes and principles of the United Nations.

The situation of asylum seekers should not be left in a state of uncertainty for years. Unlawful detention practices should not be carried out and the necessary diligence should be taken in this regard. Also, international regulations must be made in order to protect migrants against the exploitation of employers or human traffickers and abuse.

States must take responsibility for and fulfill these responsibilities meticulously for refugees, asylum seekers and immigrants to be able to rebuild their lives safely against serious dangers. Sharing responsibility for global problems is fair in the 21st century.

Welcoming people from other countries might empower host communities by making them more diverse and more flexible in a rapidly changing world. Some of the successful, impactful, and productive people in the field of arts, politics, and technology can be refugees, asylum seekers, or migrants. There are very successful people in the international community who have been given the opportunity to start a new life in another country and become a member of a new community.

In the 21st century, leaders, by showing sufficient political will, should produce and develop new projects to relocate people fleeing conflict and persecution in their countries.

Furthermore, the practice of other safe approaches should be implemented to enable refugees to start a new life. Providing the necessary financial support for refugee families to come to the country and granting them a study or work visa might be considered as an appropriate method for them to establish a new life.

States should not force anybody to return to a country where they might be subjected to human rights violations. Instead, states should ensure a safe place for refugees and asylum seekers, and migrants to live, a job, access to education, and health services.

Refugees, asylum seekers, and immigrants should be treated with dignity without being deprived of their freedom as stated in the United Nations Universal Declaration of Human Rights. Under all the circumstances which require detention and retention, refugees, asylum seekers, and immigrants should be informed about their current rights as well as their fundamental rights. Their detention conditions should comply with international standards in terms of rights and freedoms.

Comprehensive programs should be prepared with the United Nations Member States and the United Nations High Commissioner for Refugees on the provision of social and legal assistance to refugees, asylum seekers and migrants. For this purpose, a valid and secure "country of origin information system" should be established. This system should be targeted to be structured as an "international joint system".

All these developments have revealed the necessity of preparing a multidimensional, original, up-to-date, original and rich content about refugees, asylum seekers and immigrants in the international community and presenting it to science.

This six volume book series is titled "Refugee Crisis in International Politics" are prepared with the aim of clarifying the above-mentioned issues and enriching the content, context, and depth to the field of science.

The fourth volume in this series contains insightful analyses on a variety of international problems within the context of refugee issue. Contributions in this volume are as follows: Ahmet Sapmaz "Refugees and Security"; Saadat Demirci "Refugees, Migration and Security Threats"; Hüsmen Akdeniz "The Impact of Irregular Migration on Security in the Framework of Changing Security Context"; Mehmet Emin Erendor "Refugees and Terrorism"; Burak Şakir Şeker and Hasret Çomak "Mena Versus Europe: Arising Dimensions of Mediterranean Maritime Security"; Cem Oğultürk "The Impact of Food Insecurity on Migration and Conflict in the Horn of Africa"; Burak Şakir Şeker and Hasret Çomak "Migration by Sea: Libyan Case and EU Approach"; Neziha Musaoğlu "Demografic, Economic, Political and Legal Dimensions of the Russian Federation's Migration Policy"; Ainur Nogayeva "Central Asian Fighters and their Families in Syria: Refugees or Terrorists?"; Murat Pinar and Soyalp Tamçelik "Determining the Socio-Economic and Security Impacts of Rohingya Refugees on Neighbouring Countries: Bangladesh and India"; Ferdi Güçyetmez "Immigration and Belonging Issue on the American - Mexico Border"; Zekeriya Alperen Bedirhan "The Deferred Action for Childhood Arrivals (Daca)"; Akın Sağıroğlu and İlhan Aras "The Issue of Immigration in the United States Elections: A Look at Trump-Era"; Saadet Çalişkan Ciğer "An Alternative Solution to Problems Arising in Refugee Crises: Humanitarian Space and Humanitarian System"; Murat Koray "Developing Effective Resilience Based Strategies for Refugees"; Tarık Demir "Enclavity and Refugees"; and Sezin İba Gürsoy "Refugee and Climate Change".

We would like to thank all the contributing and researching colleagues who supported us with their research and findings.

We would like to express our gratitude to Prof. Dr. İbrahim SİRKECİ who made the publication of "Refugee Crisis in International Politics" possible.

Special thanks should be given to the staff of Transnational Press London (TPLondon) for their valuable guidance and technical support on this process, for preparing our books for publication, and for designing the covers.

We sincerely hope that the work will be useful and useful to the world of science.

Hasret Çomak, Burak Şakir Şeker, Mehlika Özlem Ultan, Yaprak Civelek, Çağla Arslan Bozkuş

ISTANBUL, MARCH / 2021

# CHAPTER I

## REFUGEES AND SECURITY

Ahmet Sapmaz[*]

### Introduction

Refugee flows and refugee crisis are the most used terms in the international arena lately. The United Nations High Commissioner for Refugees (UNHCR) defined the 20th century as the "refugee century". The number of refugees, which was 2.1 million in 1950, 1.5 million in 1960, 2.5 million in 1970, 8.9 million in 1980, 17.2 million in 1990, 15.2 in 2009[1] increased to 26 million in 2020. Today, millions of people are refugees on every continent. Most of these refugees originated from conflict and war-torn countries from Africa and the Middle East. Again, according to the UNHCR data, as of 2019, 79.5 million people around the world, that is 1% of the world population, have been forcibly displaced. Of these, 26 million are refugees, 45.7 million are internally displaced and 4.2 million are asylum seekers. 73% of the refugees are in neighboring countries, and 68% originate from only 5 countries.[2] As can be seen from the numbers and percentages given above, refugees are an increasingly important reality in both national and international systems. The relationship between the expanding and deepening understanding of security and the refugees has recently attracted the attention of the society, statesmen and academics.[3] This attention often addresses the impact of refugees on security. In this study, the relationship between refugees and security and the effects of refugees on national, international, social and human security are discussed.

### Who is a Refugee?

According to the Convention Relating to the Legal Status of Refugees signed in 1951, a refugee is a person who has a well-founded fear of persecution because of his / her race, religion, nationality, membership in a particular social group or political opinion; and is unable or unwilling to avail himself / herself of the protection of that country, or to return there, for fear

---


[*] Dr., e-mail: ahmet_sapmaz@yahoo.com


[1] Edward Mogire, Victim as Security Threats: Refugee Impact on Host State Security in Africa, New York, Routledge, 2016, p. 1.

[2] https://www.unhcr.org/figures-at-a-glance.html (Access 25.06.2020).

[3] Joanne Hopkins, R. Gerald Hughes, "Refugees, Migration and Security: States, Intelligence Agencies and the Perpetual Global Crisis", **Intelligence and National Security**, Vol. 34, No. 5, 2019, p. 1.

of persecution.[4] It should be emphasized that becoming a refugee is the result of the forced displacement of people. An asylum-seeker is a person who applies to the relevant government to obtain refugee status and awaits a decision. Until their legal status are defined as a refugee, these persons are considered as asylum-seeker and will not be repatriated.

Under normal circumstances, it is not possible for individuals or societies to leave their homeland without a serious threat to their life and freedom. The formation of refugees is a manifestation of both internal disorder, instability and violation of human rights and humanitarian standards. The most important complaint of refugees is the poor security conditions in their country.[5] Within this framework, it is possible to state that refugee movements are the result of political problems going beyond national borders.[6]

The most important international regulation regarding refugees is the 1951 Convention Relating to the Status of Refugees. In 1967, a protocol (New York Protocol) was drawn up in addition to the Geneva Convention. The essence of the convention is the non-refoulment principle. That is, a refugee should not be repatriated to a country where there is a serious threat to his/her life and freedom. This principle has become a part of international customary law at present.[7]

Refugee movements have occurred at different times in history. The refugee problem, which came up with World War I in the recent past, grew with World War II and reached high numbers during the Cold War. After the World War I, as a result of the dissolution of multinational empires, refugee flows were experienced in Europe and the Middle East. Europe has encountered around 800.000 refugees from Russia alone. Besides, the Russian civil war, the Soviet-Polish War and the Soviet famine in 1921 went down in history as events that generated refugees. When the refugee crises that occurred reached the bounds of a single state or international organization, the first refugee regime was established under the umbrella of the League of Nations in 1921. France received a total of 400.000 refugees in just ten days due to the Spanish Civil War. World War II created a total of 12 million refugees in Central and Eastern Europe and the Soviet Union. About 500.000 Europeans lived in refugee camps in Western Europe until the mid-1960s, although most of them returned to their home countries.[8]

---

[4] https://www.unhcr.org/3b66c2aa10 (Access 28.07.2020).
[5] Gil Loescher, "The Victim: Refugees and Global Security", **Bulletin of the Atomic Science**, Vol. 58, No. 6, 2002, p. 47.
[6] Reg Whitaker, "Refugees: The Security Dimension", **Citizenship Studies**, Vol. 2, No. 3, 1998, p. 414.
[7] https://www.unhcr.org/1951-refugee-convention.html (Access 10.05.2020).
[8] Gil Loescher, James Milner, "Security Implication of Protracted Refugee Situations", **The Adelphi Papers**, Vol. 45, No. 375, 2005, p. 23.

Many reasons cause the refugee flow. However, in general, inter-state and civil wars, ethnic and separatist conflicts that occur due to land or right claims, class and ideological internal conflicts, terrorism, repressive authoritarian and revolutionary regimes, interventions of global and regional powers, natural disasters and environmental problems cause the formation of refugees.[9] The Syrian civil war, whose effects are being felt intensely today, has created the biggest refugee crisis since the World War II.[10] The protests against the Bashar Assad government that started in 2011 in Syria turned into a large-scale and long-term civil war between government forces, moderate opponents and terrorist organizations. 5.6 million Syrians have fled to Turkey, Jordan and Lebanon for security reasons. 6.6 million Syrians are internally displaced.[11] In Europe, after the Cold War, the Yugoslavia War resulted in an influx of refugees, and with the enlargement of the EU in 2004, an inland migration flow was experienced. Arab Spring has led to large refugee flows in the last decade. Mass migration movements do not occur only in Europe, Africa or the Middle East. 3.6 million people from Venezuela have immigrated to the Caribbean and Latin America[12] and since 2017, 742,000 Rohingya people fled from Myanmar to Bangladesh.[13]

## What is Security?

There is no consensus on a definition of security for everything and everyone. However, security in general is the protection of values owned. Security objectively refers to the situation that there is no threat to the values owned. In a subjective sense, it means that there is no fear of attack on the values owned.[14] Historically, security has been considered primarily in terms of states. They guaranteed their security by protecting their borders against other states with the military force they created. Especially in the post-cold war period, it was thought that not only states but also society and individuals could be under threat. In this context, threat perceptions have expanded and covered many subjects and areas. Such a security problem is tried to be defined by searching for answers on very important questions. These questions are "What is the meaning of security?", "Whose security?" and "How is the security built?".[15]

---

[9] Oğuzhan Türkoğlu, "Refugees and National/International Security", **Uludağ Journal of Economy and Society**, Vol. 30, No. 2, 2011, pp. 105-109.

[10] Elena Tilovska-Kechedji, "The Refugee Crisis Affecting EU Foreign and Security Policy", **International E-Journal of Advances in Social Sciences**, Vol. 2, No. 4, 2016, p. 269.

[11] https://www.unhcr.org/syria-emergency.html (Access 19.07.2020).

[12] Ebru Canan Sokullu, "Mülteciler ve Güvenlik", https://trguvenlikportali.com/wp-content/uploads/2019/11/MultecilerveGuvenlik_EbruCananSokullu_v.1.pdf (Access 26.08.2020).

[13] https://www.unhcr.org/rohingya-emergency.html (Access 15.08.2020).

[14] Arnold Wolfers, "National Security as an Ambiguous Symbol", **Political Science Quarterly**, Vol. 67, No. 4, 1952, pp. 484-485.

[15] Özlem Özdemir, Emrah Özdemir, "Syrian Refugee Women and Human Security", **Security Strategies**

A brief overview of security within the scope of international relations theories reveals the expansion and deepening process of security. Realism is the tradition that emphasizes that states must pursue a power policy for their national interests.[16] According to classical realism, states are selfish and driven by self-interest just like people. In this context, states are constantly in conflict with each other to increase their power.[17] Classical realism is based on a state-centric understanding as the referent object of security and defines the international system as an anarchic environment. Military deterrence and allied control are of paramount importance. According to the neorealism approach embodied in Kenneth Waltz's work titled "Theory of International Politics", the international system is analyzed through the structure. The structure consists of states that are in contact with each other and regulates international relations. In Neorealism, power is not the goal, but a tool that states use to exist in the international system.[18]

In the post-cold war period, it has been observed that security approaches based on the protection of territorial integrity of the nation state were insufficient. In the security environment, where non-state and supranational actors and regimes are increasingly important, neoliberal and critical approaches have emerged. According to neoliberals, mutual economic dependence determines the power of states. States tend to cooperate with the principle of mutual dependency in their international relations. This approach is closely related to structuralism. According to structuralism, institutions and structures are in a mutual interaction. In this framework, norms, identity and ideas play a central role in the formation of world politics. According to the structuralism, security is a social construction. In this context, norms, identities and ideas affect the states' decisions regarding security.[19] Buzan, Waever and Wilde explained the center of security with the military, political, economic, social and environmental sectors and the concept of regional security complexes[20] and securitization. Securitization, one of the prominent concepts of the Copenhagen School, provides a theoretical tool for analyzing security policies. [21] The threat, which has an important place in security according to the concept of securitization, is discursively constructed by

---

**Journal**, Vol. 14, No. 27, pp. 116-120.

[16] Jack Donnely, "Realism", **Theories of International Relations**, Scott Burchill (Ed.), New York, Palgrave Macmillan, 2005, p. 29.

[17] Colin Elman, "Realism", **Security Studies: An Introduction**, Paul D. Williams (Ed.), New York, Routledge, 2008, pp. 17-18.

[18] Kenneth N. Waltz, **Theory of International Politics**, California, Addison-Wesley Publishing Company, 1979.

[19] Özdemir, Özdemir, ibid, pp. 116-120.

[20] The Regional Security Complex Theory points out that most threats reach short distances more easily and that security interdependence has a regional dimension. Barry Buzan, Ole Waever, **Regions and Powers**, New York, Cambridge University Press, 2003, p. 4.

[21] Ole Wæver, 'Securitization and Desecuritization', **On Security**, Ronny D. Lipschutz (Ed.), New York, Columbia University Press, 1995, p. 55.

political elites. It is claimed that something within the political community threatens the existence of the referent object and that urgent and exceptional measures must be taken to combat this threat. While political elites perceive some issues as threats with their speech act and take them into the scope of security, they leave some issues out of the scope of security. [22]

Ken Booth, with his article titled "Security and Emancipation" published in 1991, led to the emergence of a different critical security approach. Booth, putting human security at the center, argued that, in order to be free, there should not be things that prevent people from what they want to do. In this context, all kinds of physical and humanitarian threats such as war, poverty, poor educational conditions, political pressure, environmental pollution and natural disasters limit what people want to do.[23] As it is seen, while classical, liberal and structuralism approaches develop a more state-centric security approach, the critical approach exhibits a society and human-centric approach.

States faced with transboundary security threats in the post-cold war era. In the new world order, an insecure situation has arisen due to civil wars, ethnic wars and terrorism. The individual and society, who are the referent object of the new security understanding, started to reach security less, especially in the global south. In new wars, identities clashed instead of ideologies, civilians became military targets, ethnic cleansing became a method of war, and non-state actors began to fight. This situation has accelerated mass and illegal migration flows.[24] Refugees emerged as one of the new threats identified in non-state threats during this period.[25]

## Refugees and Security

High flows of refugees have always had significant security repercussions. It is not possible to think of refugee movements independently of the economic, political, cultural and ideological policies of the sending and receiving country. The refugee problem does not occur automatically; it is created by the sending state. The sending state causes forced migration and creates refugees in order to achieve cultural homogeneity, ensure the superiority of one ethnic group over another, get rid of opposition and

---

[22] Barry Buzan, Ole Waever, Jaap de Wilde, **Security: A New Framework for Analysis**, London, Lynne Rienner, 1998, pp. 7-27.

[23] Ken Booth, "Security and Emancipation", **Review of International Relations**, Vol. 17, No. 4, 1991, p.319.

[24] Sokullu, ibid. (Access 26.08.2020).

[25] Matthew J. Gibney, "Security and the Ethics of Asylum after 11 September", **Forced Migration Review**, https://www.fmreview.org/sites/fmr/files/FMRdownloads/en/september-11th-has-anything-changed/gibney.pdf (Access 10.06.2020).

achieve foreign policy goals.[26]

Security threats posed by refugees are classified in various ways. The first of these is economic and non-economic. The second classification is based on the struggle for power over economic and political power, limited resources, work and land, between the people of the host country and newly arrived refugees. Countries that were adversely affected by the 2008 economic crisis, such as Portugal, Spain, Italy and Greece, blame refugees for this. Refugees in these countries have been accused of not paying taxes and negatively affecting the economy by sending their earnings to their origin countries.[27] It is possible to specify the third classification of security threats posed by refugees as threats to security and other threats. Threats to security are the stability of the country, crimes, social conflicts and terrorism. Other threats include increased taxes, decreased wages, jobs seized by refugees, and social cohesion problems.[28]

During the Cold War, refugees were seen as part of the global struggle between the West and the East. Refugees fleeing communism have been described as "voting with their feet". The West has taken a generous approach towards refugees to take advantage of its ideological and propaganda benefits.[29] During this period from the 1940s to the mid-1970s, it was defined as the "golden age" for refugees and refugees became a tool for the Cold War security and propaganda policies.[30] Refugees were not one of the main threats to security in the Cold War environment. Because during the Cold War, security was mostly handled in a geopolitical framework and it was considered that threats against states could be military threats from outside the country.[31]

After the Cold War, the link between refugees and security has become more evident. In this period, the refugee movements originating from the Third World and former Communist bloc countries led the West to reorient its refugee policy.[32] A large number of refugee movements were perceived not only as the emergence of an insecure situation, but also as a threat to international peace and security with the sending country, receiving country and region, and a "closing doors" policy was implemented against refugees. The situation of refugees, which occurred as a result of conflicts in various regions during this period, became the agenda of the United Nations Security

---

[26] Myron Weiner, "Security, Stability, and International Migration", **International Security**, Vol. 17, No. 3, 1992-1993, pp. 98-101.

[27] Vilmante Kumpikate-Valiuniene, Eugene T. Agoh, Ineta Zickute, "Refugees as a Security Threat: Case of Lithunia", **Public Security and Public Order**, No. 18, 2017, pp. 236-237.

[28] Valiuniene, Agoh, Zickute, ibid., pp. 238-239.

[29] Loescher, Milner, ibid., p. 24.

[30] Whitaker, ibid., p. 413.

[31] Loescher, Milner, ibid., p. 24.

[32] Whitaker, ibid., p. 413.

Council (UNSC), NATO and other international security organizations and caused political developments. Refugees have created more agenda in the field of international security, and international reactions such as the imposition of sanctions and military intervention against the countries that produce refugees have been revealed by UNSC resolutions. During this period, sensitivity towards refugees turned to sending countries. [33] During the 1990s, the UNSC's resolutions no. 688 for Iraq, no. 733 and 794 for Somalia, no. 841 for Haiti, no. 929 for Rwanda and no. 1199 for Kosovo focused on human movements that threaten international peace and security as a result of internal instability.[34] Iraq, Somalia, Yugoslavia and Haiti witnessed international intervention due to refugee flows in line with UNSC resolutions.[35]

During this period, the UN and the great powers tried to solve the refugee problem with conflict resolution, peacemaking and peacekeeping activities. In this context, by focusing on the countries and regions that produce refugees, prevention, containment and return of refugee flow has been achieved. In this direction, UNSC and UNHCR carried out joint activities.[36]

Refugee movements affect security at three levels. First of all, refugees are perceived by receiving and transit countries as a threat to economic and social order, cultural and religious values, and political stability. Second, cross-border refugee mobility affects the balance of international and regional relations. Third, and finally, the irregular refugee flow raises the issue of human security of refugees and turns them into an international actor.[37]

Today, the understanding of security is expanding from the state-centric understanding that protects states from other states to a human-centric approach that tries to prevent social, economic and physical threats against individuals. In this context, refugees are perceived as both individuals whose security needs to be protected and as danger, threat and uncertainty by the states. Refugees who leave their country in order to ensure their own safety are faced with various dangers, risks and threats in transit and / or receiving country. Therefore, both ensuring the security of refugees and transit or receiving countries come to the fore as phenomena that should be carried out simultaneously. In this context, refugees are both the consequence and source of insecurity. While refugees are victims of insecurity, they are also

---

[33] Kohki Abe, "Are You Good Refugee or Bad Refugee?: Security Concerns and Dehumanization of Immigration Policies in Japan", **Asia Rights**, No. 6, 2006, http://archives.cap.anu.edu.au/asiarights journal/Abe.pdf (Access 10.06.2020).
[34] Gill Guy S. Goodwin, "Refugees and Security", **International Journal of Refugee Law**, Vol. 11, No. 1, 1999, p.2, https://doi.org/10.1093/ijrl/11.1.1 (Access 10.07.2020).
[35] ibid., p.2.
[36] Loescher, Milner, ibid., p. 27.
[37] Türkoğlu, ibid., p. 110.

seen as a potential threat to national and international security. [38] Refugees affect security both as threat and referent object. While refugees are evaluated within the scope of human security in terms of referent object, refugees as threat are evaluated in terms of their effects on the national, economic, social and cultural security of the host country and international security. [39]

While the initial studies with a security approach on refugees focused on the high politics dimension of refugees based on the sending and receiving country and the physical security of the region and the globe, recent studies focused on the indirect low politics security threats created by refugees, especially in socio-economically underdeveloped receiving countries. In a particularly European context, refugees are securitized and associated with social identity and problems. With the attacks of September 11, 2001, the perception of threat against refugees increased and refugees and asylum-seekers were associated with insecurity. In this context, refugee admission procedures have been updated, border controls have been increased, and the fight against illegal migration and smuggling has been considered as priority policies.[40] International migration and refugees have been positioned as a threat to national and international security by the western developed states.[41]

Refugees can create international and regional conflicts. Because refugees have the potential to create instability in neighboring countries.[42] Refugees leave their countries due to compulsory reasons and sometimes go directly to neighboring countries, and in some cases they reach the receiving country by using neighboring countries as transit countries. A country that accepts a refugee recognizes that the country that created the refugee is a place that cannot be lived for its own citizen. This can create problems between the sending and the receiving country.

Weiner states that generally there is an impression that the migration takes place on the east-west and south-north axis, but this is misleading. Most of the refugee flows are from developing countries to developing countries.[43] 95% of the people who had to flee from their country have taken refuge in developing countries. Because developed countries set very strict conditions for the admission of refugees, so they accept fewer refugees. For example, Japan, one of the most developed countries in the world, granted refugee

---

[38] Alice Edwards, "Human Security and the Rights of Refugees: Transcending Territorial and Disciplinary Borders", **Michigan Journal of International Law**, Vol. 30, No. 3, 2009, p. 774, https://repository.law.umich.edu/cgi/viewcontent.cgi?article=1133&context=mjil (Access 10.06.2020).
[39] Loescher, "The Victim: Refugees and Global Security", p. 47.
[40] Loescher, Milner, ibid., p. 29.
[41] Bülent Şener, "Soğuk Savaş Sonrası Dönemde Uluslararası Göç Olgusu ve Ulusal Güvenlik Üzerindeki Etkileri Üzerine Bir Değerlendirme", **Güvenlik Bilimleri Dergisi**, Vol. 6, No. 1, 2017, p. 25.
[42] Federico Donelli, "Syrian Refugees in Turkey: A Security Perspective", **New England Journal of Public Policy**, Vol. 30, No. 2, 2018, p. 2.
[43] Weiner, ibid., p. 93.

status to only 106 people between 1995 and 2004. This figure is less than the number of refugee status granted by smaller states such as Luxembourg and Malta during the same period. [44] Developed countries generally accept refugees with high educational, cultural and financial opportunities. This further increases the security problems in underdeveloped or developing countries, which are not sufficient in terms of national power elements.

Developed countries and regions want to limit the possible refugee flow to their regions with various political, military and economic measures. The European continent has recently witnessed a large influx of refugees. Refugee influx to Europe is from three regions. These regions include Middle East countries such as Algeria, Iraq, Libya, Morocco and Syria, North Africa and African countries such as Eritrea, Gambia, Guinea and Nigeria, and South Asian countries such as Afghanistan, Bangladesh and Pakistan[45]. For refugees, the Mediterranean route is one of the most popular ways to reach Europe. Italy started operation "Mare Nostrum" in 2013 to assist refugees crossing the Mediterranean[46]. However, the said naval operation was terminated in 2014 as it caused more refugees to come. After the Mare Nostrum operation, the EU Border Agency (Frontex) started the operations Triton (Greece), Poseidon (Italy), Hera, Indalo and Minerva (Spain). NATO, in accordance with the request of Turkey, Germany and Greece, conducts intelligence, reconnaissance and surveillance enforcement activities in order to provide support to the fight against illegal migration and trafficking at Aegean Sea and Turkey-Syria border since 2016.[47]

German Chancellor Angela Merkel announced in August 2015 the "Open Door Policy" based on providing protection to refugees from Syria or other countries in order to escape conflict and war. This policy has brought concerns about the abuse of refugee status by terrorists. Frontex officials announced in 2016 that ISIL terrorists use unorganized border controls to infiltrate Europe as migrants. [48] In a survey conducted in 2016, 59% of European citizens stated that they believe that the refugee influx will increase the terrorist acts in their country. The European Union tries to prevent illegal immigrants from entering the European continent. In this context, people who may be refugees are prevented from entering the continent with the understanding of "preventative protection".[49] Asylum seekers are kept away

---

[44] Abe, ibid.
[45] Nikolaos Lampas, "Why Greeks Perceive Refugee Flows as a Security Threat", **Mediterranean Quarterly**, Vol. 29, No. 4, 2008, pp. 77-78.
[46] Kechedji, ibid., p. 270.
[47]https://www.nato.int/cps/en/natohq/topics_128746.htm (Access 10.05.2020).
[48] Joao Ricardo Faria, Andreas Novak, Aniruddha Bagchi, Timothy Mathews, "The Refugee Game: The Relationship Between Individual Security Expenditure and Collective Security", **Games**, Vol. 11. No. 24, 2020, p. 1.
[49] Lampas, ibid., pp. 77-78.

from EU member states by opening processing centers for refugees in third countries or by establishing regional protection zones close to refugee producing countries.[50] The EU and Turkey signed Readmission Agreement for refugees. Only 5-7% of Syrians in Turkey were able to reach Europe due to measures taken by Turkey.[51]

The European Migration Agenda, adopted in 2015, includes the issues of saving immigrants' lives at sea through search and rescue operations, targeting criminal smuggling networks, responding to high-scale arrivals to the EU, providing protection to those in need with a common approach and resettlement. Likewise, it includes issues such as bringing solutions to the migration problem in partnership with third countries, making EU instruments available to the member states located at the borders.[52]

It is feared that refugees may form armed groups and be radicalized. Situations brought up by Palestinian armed groups in Lebanon and Jordan in the past support this fear. However, it is difficult for refugees to form armed groups with their own potential. Refugees who could form armed groups have been able to achieve this with external support. Egypt and Syria supported Palestinian armed groups against Israel.[53] Host countries sometimes covertly support refugees for terrorist and armed attacks against countries of origin.

At the present time, states that create refugees have to implement policies based on the return and adaptation of refugees in order to get rid of various international political and military pressures and to benefit from financial assistance. The situation of being an origin country by creating immigration and exile and not facing any sanctions as a result, which was observed in the past, is not in question today. International military forces such as peacekeepers created to protect refugees from war and conflict can be deployed on the territory of the origin country.[54] Refugee movements can constitute a legitimate justification for humanitarian intervention against the origin country due to their international dimensions.[55]

---

[50] Aramide Odutayo, "Human Security and the International Refugee Crisis", **Journal of Global Ethics**, Vol. 12, No. 3, 2016, p. 369.

[51] Ünal Acar, "Şartlı Mülteciler ve Ulusal Güvenlik", **Atatürk Üniversitesi Sosyal Bilimler Enstitüsü Dergisi**, Vol. 23, No. 3, 2019, p. 1223.

[52] https://ec.europa.eu/home-affairs/sites/homeaffairs/files/what-we-do/policies/european-agenda-migration/background-information/docs/communication_on_the_european_agenda_on_migration_en.pdf (Access 10.08.2020).

[53] Doris Carrion, "Are Syrian Refugees a Security Threat to the Middle East?", http://blogs.reuters.com/great-debate/2015/09/15/are-syrian-refugees-a-security-threat-to-the-middle-east/#:~:text=However%2C%20history%20also%20provides%20examples,itself%20create%20a%20security%20threat., (Access 01.06.2020)

[54] Nurcan Özgür Baklacıoğlu, Dış Politika ve Göç: Yugoslavya'dan Türkiye'ye Göçlerde Arnavutlar (1920-1990), İstanbul, Derin Yayınları, 2010, pp. 73-74.

[55] Baklacıoğlu, ibid., pp. 73-74.

There are various specialized organizations dealing with the refugee problem in the international arena. The most important one is the UNHCR which was established in 1950 and is under the UN umbrella. UNHCR's duty is to protect refugees, facilitate bureaucratic procedures and ensure their integration into society. International organizations such as UNHCR have great importance in creating pressure on states to solve the refugee problem, focusing on human rights and human security.[56] UNHCR emphasizes that state security and protection of refugees are not separate concepts, and sacrificing one for the other will prevent the desired result.[57]

The refugee crisis is a phenomenon that the international community can find a solution together. It is not possible to find a solution with the efforts of only one state or region. Powerful countries of the global north are accused of trying to get rid of their responsibilities in solving the problem by putting forward their national security while causing the formation of the global refugee problem. [58] The continuation of problems producing refugees in the country of origin prevents refugees from returning to their countries. If the host country is not given sufficient political, economic and social support, the deficiencies of international security actors are tried to be compensated by international agencies such as UNHCR.[59] However, the refugee problem is not a problem that can be overcome only by providing humanitarian aid to refugees. Long-term development investments should be made in countries hosting refugees, and foreign investments should be encouraged in this direction.[60]

When the relationship between refugees and security is presented by the media and politicians, the security of the receiving state and its citizens is generally mentioned. Refugees have become the most important national security issue for some states. Turkey is the country that hosts the most forced displaced foreign nationals around the world with 3.6 million. Turkey is followed with Colombia with 1.8 million, Pakistan and Uganda with 1.4 million and Germany with 1.1 million. The country that created the highest number of refugees is Syria with 6.6 million. Syria is followed by Venezuela with 3.7 million, Afghanistan with 2.7 million, South Sudan with 2.2 million

---

[56] Gonca Oğuz Gök, "Kimin Güvenliği? Uluslararası Göç-Güvenlik İlişkisi ve Uluslararası Örgütlerin Rolü", Kocaeli Üniversitesi Sosyal Bilimler Dergisi, No. 31, 2016, p. 79.

[57] "Addressing Security Concerns without Undermining Refugee Protection: UNHCR's Perspective", https://www.refworld.org/docid/5672aed34.html (Access 10.08.2020).

[58] Sarah Pedigo Kulzer, Ryan Philips, "Those Who Must Die: Syrian Refugees in the Age of National Security", Human Rights Review, No. 21, 2020, p. 142, https://doi.or/10.1007/s12142-020-00582-1 (Access 20.08.2020).

[59] James Milner, Gil Loescher, "Responding to Protracted Refugee Situations Lessons From A Decade of Discussion", Refugee Studies Centre Oxford Department of International Development, 2011, p. 4, https://www.refworld.org/pdfid/4da83a682.pdf (Access 03.09.2020).

[60] Shiva Pedram, "Syrian Refugee Crisis Threatens Stability in the Middle East", https://www.americanprogress.org/issues/security/news/2014/08/12/95595/syrian-refugee-crisis-threatens-stability-in-the-middle-east/ (Access 10.09.2020).

and Myanmar with 1.1 million.[61]

Protecting its borders is one of the most fundamental responsibilities of a state. Irregular and illegal migration is a security problem for the state and society. Because the borders and territorial integrity of a state are violated without its consent. States apply visa regimes to ensure border security and regulate entry into their countries. Entries contrary to the visa regimes determined by the countries are within the scope of illegal migration and are carried out by human smugglers.[62] However, as a paradox, states' restrictive measures against refugees cause an increase in irregular and illegal migration.

States have a say on the identity of those living in their country with the citizenship status.[63] They regulate and control who can and cannot be situated in their country. However, refugees impose various restrictions on the sovereignty of states. Refugees have international rights that go beyond national regulations of states. It is the sovereign right of a state to grant a person migration status or not. However, whether or not to grant refugee status to a person is not the sovereign right of a state.[64] 149 states are party to the 1951 Refugee Convention and / or the 1967 Protocol.[65] This disturbs the states in the high number of refugee movements.

Refugees are perceived by states as a direct and indirect threat to their security. The first direct threat is relocation of conflict and the armed groups to the host country. Refugees are victims of violence, but in some cases, they also export conflict and instability to the host country. Because refugees mostly emerge as a result of a conflict. As a result, combatants, weapons, and ideologies come from the country of origin to the host country.[66] Wars and conflicts in third world countries produce "refugee combatants" as well as refugees.[67] Refugee movements are produced or driven by one or more parties to the conflict to achieve their political, military and strategic goals. Refugees can engage in terrorist attacks by cooperating with opponents in their countries. Choi and Salehyan analyzed 154 countries in terms of the relationship between refugees and terrorism, covering the period 1970 to 2007. Their study revealed that countries with more refugees are exposed to more local and international terrorism.[68] However, the data provided from

---

[61] https://www.unhcr.org/figures-at-a-glance.html (Access 23.09.2020).

[62] Sokullu, ibid.

[63] Benjamin Muller, "Globalization, Security, Paradox: Towards a Refugee Biopolitics", **Refugee**, Vol. 22, No. 1, 2004, p. 50.

[64] Whitaker, ibid., pp. 414-415.

[65] https://www.unhcr.org/1951-refugee-convention.html (Access 10.08.2020).

[66] Idean Salehyan, Kristian Skrede Gleditsch, "Refugee Flows and the Spread of Civil War", **International Organization**, Vol. 60, No. 2, 2006, p. 342.

[67] Gil Loescher, Beyond Charity: International Cooperation and the Global Refugee Crisis, New York, Oxford University Press, 1993, p. 13.

[68] Seung-Whan Choi, Idean Salehyan, "No Good Deed Goes Unpunished: Refugees, Humanitarian Aid, and Terrorism", Conflict Management and Peace Science, Vol. 30, No. 1, p. 55.

the USA is of a nature that will strain the relationship established between refugees and terrorism. The USA accepted 784,000 people as refugees from September 11, 2001 until 2015, and only 3 of them were arrested for terrorism.[69] Similarly, from 1975 to 2015, 3.252.493 people were accepted to the USA with refugee status and 20 of them were found to be terrorists.[70]

Secondly, the use of refugee camps by combatants involves refugees in cross-border conflicts and causes instability in the host country. Refugees can act against the interests of the country of origin in the host country with or without the support of the host country. The combatants use the refugee camps as a safe base for their attacks on the origin country. In such cases, food, health and other aid materials delivered to refugee camps may be used outside of their original purpose. One of the factors leading to this is that refugee camps are generally established in border regions close to the country of origin.[71] On the other hand, the long-term dense presence of refugees creates problems such as arms trafficking, drug trafficking, human trafficking and the source of combatants.

Indirect threats are related to the situations created by long-term refugee flows in the host country. Developing countries bear the bulk of the social and economic burden of the refugee flow. For developing countries, refugees are both a result of internal disorder and a source of new instability and problems. Refugees can increase inter-communal conflicts and exacerbate existing ones. If the differences are evident in the host country, the economic and social situation is fragile and there are hostile neighboring countries, the refugee problem leads to more complex and severe negative consequences. The government and the public of the host country often perceive refugees negatively, seeing them as a security issue, a source of violence and crime, a threat to social cohesion and job opportunities.[72] The incoming refugees are uneducated, have a bad economic situation and have no profession, which increases security concerns in the host country.

Refugee movements are perceived as a greater threat in countries with homogeneous communities than in countries with heterogeneous communities. The size of the refugee movement is also of great importance for states' perception of threat. Small movements of refugees are not perceived as threats, while large movements of refugees are perceived as threats. Another issue is the ethnic affiliation of the refugees. Ethnic

---

[69] Kathleen Newland, "The U.S. Record Shows Refugees Are Not a Threat", https://www.migrationpolicy.org/news/us-record-shows-refugees-are-not-threat?gclid= Cj0KCQiAnb 79BRDgARIsAOVbhRoZM9v91xwbqIf9xrlEuCF9SanxidMSwXOVHZtfVRkMiPeSw7AxDnIaAhfBE ALw_wcB (Access 10.06.2020).

[70] Alex Nowrasteh, "Terrorism and Immigration: A Risk Analysis", https://www.cato.org/sites/cato.org/ files/pubs/pdf/pa798_2.pdf (Access 10.06.2020).

[71] Gil Loescher, "The Victim: Refugees and Global Security", p. 49.

[72] Ibid.

affiliation facilitates the admission of refugees in the host country.[73] However, refugees defined as "others" can easily be perceived as a threat.

Refugees mostly target countries that are neighbors to the country they have to leave. Refugees head towards neighboring countries primarily for security concerns. These destination countries are sometimes used as a transit route to reach another country, and sometimes they can be the end point for refugees. Some of the refugees who are relieved from their security concerns want to reach the developed Western countries for better social and economic needs.

Refugees change the demographic structure in the host country, and this may be perceived as a threat by the host country. For example, the number of Syrians who found temporary protection was under 14.237 in 2012. Turkey reached 3,618,918 as of 16/09/2020.[74] Syrians under temporary protection has changed Turkey's demographic structure significantly in some provinces. As of 16.09.2020, 76% of Kilis, 26.77% of Hatay, 21.81% of Gaziantep and 20.33% of Şanlıurfa are Syrians under temporary protection.[75] In addition, the high birth rate seen in Syrians coming to Turkey will further affect the demographic balance with second-generation Syrians in the future.[76] Changes in the demographic structure may cause various security problems by affecting the social structure. Although some part of the society in Turkey is concerned, social acceptance of Syrians under temporary protection is high. However, there is a potential for increased reactions towards Syrians under temporary protection. The said Syrians creating cheap labor, causing a decrease in wages, benefiting from free health services, etc. tend to increase reactions in society. While a segment of Turkish society is against granting citizenship to Syrians and want Syrians to return to their country as soon as possible, the majority of Syrians constantly tend to stay in the temporary protection status in Turkey.[77]

States are considering some criteria for admission to refugees. The economic situation of the countries, understanding of foreign policy, ethnic origin and number of refugees are some of these criteria.[78] For example, Turkey, at the beginning of the Syria civil war followed a morality-oriented open-door policy. Turkey, however, in later stage followed a security-oriented closed door policy because of increase in the number of people crossing the border, exceeding the capacity of the Turkey, and prolonging of civil war.[79]

---

[73] Weiner, "Security, Stability, and International Migration", **International Security**, Vol. 17, No. 3, 1992-1993, pp. 103-105.

[74] https://www.goc.gov.tr/gecici-koruma5638 (Access 27.09.2020).

[75] https://www.goc.gov.tr/gecici-koruma5638 (Access 27.09.2020).

[76] Donelli, ibid., p. 5.

[77] Acar, ibid., pp. 1218-1219.

[78] Türkoğlu, ibid., p. 110.

[79] Donelli, ibid., p. 3.

In this context, Turkey have expressed the demand of no-fly zone or a buffer zone in the north of Syria in international arena for the purpose to stop the flow of refugees and to ensure the protection of people from the Syria.[80]

There is a general belief in Western countries and societies that border control has been lost and refugees are harming the national identity and economy. Western countries take measures to restrict entry to their countries in order to provide security. These are strict visa practices, sanctions on airlines and other means of transport that do not have the required documentation, deployment of migration-related officers abroad, arresting asylum seekers before they reach their national borders, and threatening to cease economic and development aid to countries that do not re-accept refugees who are rejected by them. The aforementioned policies implemented by states can turn into violations of refugee rights. This leads to practices contrary to the spirit of the 1951 Refugee Convention.[81]

For example, Australia detained everyone who entered country without a visa in      1993-1994, and imprisoned or deported those who sought asylum until the process was concluded. [82] Australia developed a so called "off shore processing" in 2013 against the refugee flow from the sea. [83] In this context, the task of controlling the refugees and keeping them until the end of the process has been transferred to small and poor states close to Australia such as Papua New Guinea and Nauru. Australia established detention centers in these countries within the framework of the agreements it has drawn with Papua New Guinea and Nauru. On the other hand, Australia tries to get rid of asylum claims by towing refugee boats to Indonesia, which is not a member of the 1951 Refugee Convention. Many international organizations, including the UNHRC, have condemned the Australian Government's practices as violating a number of international agreements.[84]

In the face of the refugee flow, states expel refugees within the framework of security concerns, sign readmission agreements with the origin country and try to find a solution by bringing the refugee problem to the agenda of international organizations.[85] On the other hand, states also make national legal arrangements in the face of refugee pressure. For example, Kenya made an amendment to the Security Laws Act 2014, limiting the number of refugees and asylum seekers in the country to 150,000 and requiring refugees

---


[80] Donelli, ibid., p. 6.

[81] Loescher, "The Victim: Refugees and Global Security", ibid., p. 52.

[82] Odutayo, ibid., pp. 367-368.

[83] https://www.unhcr.org/news/briefing/2018/10/5bc059d24/unhcr-urges-australia-evacuate-off-shore-facilities-health-situation-deteriorates.html (Access 21.09.2020).

[84] Odutayo, ibid., pp. 367-368.

[85] Baklacıoğlu, ibid., pp. 95-96.

to be in only two camps.[86]

Especially after the terrorist attacks in the USA on September 11, 2001, the refugees started to be perceived as a source of the international terrorism threat. After the terrorist attacks of September 11, 2001, states started effective migration and border control practices in order to ensure their national security. [87] For example, in the USA, all migration and border control units were linked to the newly established Department of Homeland Security, whose main task is security. [88] To obtain refugee status in the USA, a difficult and lengthy process is required. After the refugees apply, they are examined before arriving in the USA. All refugees are subjected to security screening by numerous intelligences, security and public security agencies. People applying for refugee status undergo biometric and biographical controls. Specially trained government officials interview and question each asylum-seeker about whether they are real refugees in their particular circumstances and whether they will pose a security threat to the USA. 1% of asylum seekers can usually pass this process which takes about two years. However, it is not enough to pass all these processes, it is necessary to be within the upper limit of the annual refugee admission within the framework of the Refugee Act of 1980 of the USA, which is 70,000.[89]

There is a direct link between refugees and social security. Social security is a security that includes identity, social segments and sometimes the whole society that perceive threats to their existence as a result of state policies. As a result of mass migration movements, the economic, social, cultural, demographic and political structure of the host country's society may change. Refugees can disturb the balance of power between communities in the host country. The ethnic and religious affiliation of the refugees to the community in the host country is an important issue. If the refugees coming to the country are perceived as "from us", this creates a positive situation and the incoming refugees are treated and accepted more hospitably.[90] However, refugees can also be defined as "others", their places separate from the main society can be built socially.[91]

---

[86] Neil James Wilson, **"Kenya's Harsh New Security Laws Put Hundreds of Thousands of Refugees at Risk",** https://theconversation.com/kenyas-harsh-new-security-laws-put-hundreds-of-thousands-of-refugees-at-risk-35789 (Access 20.07.2020).

[87] Hopkins, Hughes, ibid., p. 1.

[88] Sara McElmurry, Juliana Kerr, Theresa Cardinal Brown, Lazaro Zamora, "Balancing Priorities: Immigration, National Security, and Public Safety", https://www.thechicagocouncil.org/sites/default/files/oct16_immigrationandnationalsecurty_report.pdf (Access 10.07.2020).

[89] Ehsan Zaffar, "Do Syrian Refugees Really Pose a National Security Risk?" https://www.pacificcouncil.org/newsroom/do-syrian-refugees-really-pose-national-security-risk (Access 10.09.2020).

[90] Loescher, Milner, "Security Implication of Protracted Refugee Situations", p. 33.

[91] Sarah Pedigo Kulzer, Ryan Philips, "Those Who Must Die: Syrian Refugees in the Age of National Security", **Human Rights Review**, No.21, 2020, p.142, https://doi.or/10.1007/s12142-020-00582-1 (Access 20.08.2020).

Socially, the negative dimension of migration is anti-immigration. Anti-immigration includes issues such as anti-immigrant prejudice, xenophobia, and ethnic prejudice. Xenophobia which aims to separate refugees from the people of the host country can be seen as expelling refugees from the host country, holding them in specific regions or camps in the country, and closing borders to refugees.[92] Although immigrants are accepted humanely in the host society, their impact on social security varies depending on variables such as their cultural affiliation, number and reasons for arrival. In addition, refugees do not always negatively affect security. Refugees can contribute economically, demographically and culturally to the host country and society, as well as to meeting the economic need for employment, socio-cultural multiculturalism and cultural enrichment.[93]

On the other hand, there is a strong tendency that the refugee crisis should be seen as a human security problem rather than a national and international security issue. The security impacts of refugees fleeing domestic or inter-state conflict, war and terrorism, should also be evaluated within the scope of human security in their origin, host and transit countries.[94]

Human security considers people within the scope of international law as those who must be protected from war, conflict and genocide. Human security is based on the protection of individuals' freedoms. In this context, human security aims to protect people from threats. Human security is generally the creation of political, social, environmental, economic, military and cultural systems that ensure the survival, life and dignity of people.[95]

Human security is human-centric, its threats are transnational and diverse, its elements are inseparable, and it requires cooperation and early prevention mechanisms. In migration studies, human security is based on the migrant individual and society as a human security analysis unit. According to human security, the security of immigrants is threatened by the state of their citizenship, human trafficking, and cross-border criminal organizations, host state and society.[96] Between 2014 and 2019, 2,081,779 asylum-seekers reached Italy, Cyprus Island and Malta by sea, Greece and Spain by sea and land. 19,140 people either died or disappeared on the way.[97] Refugees need to be protected legally, physically and psychologically, provided with shelter, health and education opportunities, and have a job. This causes refugees to

---

[92] Robert Mandel, "Perceived Security Threat and the Global Refugee Crisis", **Armed Forces & Society**, Vol. 24, No. 1, 1997, pp. 84-85.

[93] Sokullu, ibid.

[94] Özdemir, Özdemir, ibid., p. 115.

[95] Ibid., pp. 121-122.

[96] Sokullu, ibid.

[97] http://data2.unhcr.org/en/situations/mediterranean#_ga=2.229413594.791185886.1605766030-514745803.1603536565 (Access 17.11.2020).

adapt by integrating with the host society.

Human security and national and international security are closely related. For example, greater respect for human rights, social and economic development and the establishment of democracy both prevent refugee formation and lead to a more stable and secure national and international order.[98] When the concept of human rights fell short of protecting asylum seekers, refugee rights defenders started to emphasize the concept of human security. In this way, it is aimed to shift the security discourse from the state to the people and to bring the refugee rights to the fore. Although human security is tried to be brought to the fore, its effect of protecting asylum seekers and refugees against the concept of national security is at a limited level. When human security conflicts with national and citizen security, it is often overlooked.[99]

## Conclusion

Refugees are a security issue for themselves, the country of origin, the host country and its citizens, as well as the transit country and its citizens. In this context, refugees affect all levels of security directly or indirectly. The refugee problem is no longer a national problem that can be solved solely based on interests or only can be solved from a humanitarian perspective.

The reaction of the international community to the refugee crises contains two basic elements from the national and international security perspective and the human security perspective. Instead of looking at the refugee problem from one of these two perspectives, it should be viewed from a holistic perspective. Giving weight to one of these points of view against the other may aggravate the problem.

Refugees who have security problems are heading towards places where security is available. The best way to deal with the refugee problem is to eliminate the problems in the refugee-producing country or region. Efforts within this scope should be at national, regional and international levels. These efforts should include military, political, economic and social dimensions. On the other hand, when refugee formation continues despite all efforts, it is necessary to protect refugees within the framework of international law and to make them productive and useful by ensuring their harmony with the host society. Seeing refugees as a security threat and following a policy based on protecting national borders will not only reduce but rather increase the security threats posed by refugees.

---

[98] Loescher, "The Victim: Refugees and Global Security", p. 47.
[99] Odutayo, ibid., p. 377.

# CHAPTER 2

# REFUGEES, MIGRATION AND SECURITY THREATS

Saadat Demirci[*]

## Introduction

In the 21st century, where states place more and more importance on the concept of protecting their borders, the concept of immigration is seen as an important phenomenon that poses a security threat to these borders. Due to the "Arab Spring" and the Syrian civil war that started in the Middle East in 2015, a large migration movement started. 244 million people were immigrated. Asylum movement creates security weaknesses for refugees as well as states. Refugees are seen as a threat to the social order of the state they migrated to. Many European countries have seen the political solution as closing their borders to refugees. However, the security threat is not a phenomenon that frightens a single state. Refugees' avoidance of threats such as falling into the network of radical terrorist organizations and human traffickers during migration has become more difficult with the closing of the borders of the states where they seek asylum.

The stereotypical fear that refugees will create security threats causes the societies to support regimes that claim the necessity of strict measures against migrants. According to the data of the Global Terrorism Database, 20. 975 terrorist attacks were carried out in Europe from 1970 to 2015. Most of the attacks were organized in response to the rejection of the extremist groups in Europe by the local population. Only 2% of the attacks were made for religious and ideological reasons. The perpetrators of the attack are second-third generation immigrants who have previously moved to Europe. The fact that a generation, most of whom were born and raised in Europe, is not accepted by the society in which they live, reveals itself with reactions. Demands for recognition and respect sometimes turn into radical acts of violence. The problem of terrorism has developed internally, not externally as feared. In this context, the study evaluates the concept of refugee, migration and the security problems they create in the light of different findings. Refugees claim that this problem is the result of the wrong policies implemented by Europe in the near and Middle East regions, despite the belief that it constitutes a suitable platform for the development of terrorism. The evaluation for this determination is discussed in the first part of the

---

[*] Assoc. Prof., Çankırı Karatekin University.

study.

The security and terrorism threats in the countries that accept refugees and immigration develop as a result of the rejection and exclusion of migrants by the society of the country they live in. The issue of "marginalization" in society includes not only their personal selves but also the characteristics of religion, language and culture, which are identity elements.

The movement to protect these values and to impose their identities, which constitute their characteristics, to the Society they live in, is sometimes carried out with violent methods. The issue of social approach that causes radical violence to escalate is dealt with in the second part of the study.

The extremely harsh and repressive policy of the states against the refugees may cause this problem to continue with the newly arrived migrants. Migration is not always a negative movement, it can often be an important factor in solving economic and demographic problems. As a result of the correct orientation of the refugee flow by the societies and the implementation of appropriate integration policies, refugees can constitute an important resource element for the development of the country and multifaceted economy growth.

## Security Threats from Refugees

The Migration and Refugee issue is one of the global problems of the 21st century after terrorism and civil war. The challenge of this difficult to define phenomenon is that it is constantly variable. In addition to the reasons that occur according to today's conditions, it emerges in different dimensions in the light of developments. Migration develops due to political, economic, geopolitical and social problems.

In 2019-2020, the refugee crisis came before all other problems, especially for European countries. For Europe, migration and refugee flow is a serious burden associated with economic and demographic problems. When it realized that it could not bear this burden alone, it had to reconsider its relations with other countries[1]. The serious refugee crisis it experienced in 2016 showed the fact that Europe should redesign its foreign policy and reconsider its relations of alliance. The EU's support for anti-government forces in Syria and Lebanon along with the United States has led to the escalation of conflicts in these regions. The conflicts have forcibly displaced and forced local people to migrate[2]. The wrong politics of Europe in the Middle East countries is one of the important reasons that triggered the

---

[1] Koutsoliakos and Filntisis, " Refugees, Smugglers anad Terrorists", Perncordiam, October 24, 2016, https://perconcordiam.com/refugees-smugglers-and-terrorists/, 05.11.2020
[2] Kharlamov Anton Alekseevich, " The Migration Factor İn The European Security System İn The Context Of The Arab Spring", …

refugee flow. The leaders of the government, which were described as dictatorial regime against democracy and human rights in the Middle East region, Iraq, Lebanon, Tunisia and Egypt, were overthrown with the initiatives of Europe and America. The welfare and the spring of democracy expected after these revolutions were replaced by the Arab Spring chain strengthened by civil war. The ongoing Arab Spring in Syria caused the war in this region to last 9 years and to give the most immigration. Martin Edward Dempsey, the former US Chief of Staff, while evaluating the EU's refugee problem, said: "Europe should have dealt with this problem before the refugees come to the country"[3].

The wrong policy of Europe in the Middle East exposed it to the 2016 migration crisis. For a long time, Libya served as a shield preventing illegal immigration from Africa from infiltrating into EU countries. Gaddafi's visa policy for those coming from the East and Africa prevented illegal immigration and prevented the asylum movement from coming to the EU threshold. In line with the agreements with France and Italy, refugee camps were established in Libya against illegal immigration. Libya, as a rich and developed country, was directing the migration flow towards this region. Gaddafi's era has removed the shield that stopped immigration to European countries, and turned the people of his country into refugees escaping from civil war and post-revolution irregularities[4]. ISIS's temporary domination in Iraq and some parts of Syria in 2014 has increased the wave of refugees escaping from Syria and Iraq. Refugees crossed borders and turned towards the borders of Europe. Thus, by overthrowing the authoritarian regimes that dominated the Middle and Near Eastern countries, Europe led to an immigration flow with its own politics.

The first refugee flow started after the "Tunisian (Jasmine) Revolution" that started in Tunisia and before the Gaddafi era in Libya. The coasts of Greece and Italy, which are exposed to refugee flows, are the first countries to be exposed to the migration crisis. The crisis started on these coasts and covered all European regions. The flow of migration has added security and economic problems to the agenda. The possibility of terrorist organization members' infiltration to the borders of Europe along with the refugees caused fear and anxiety in the region. Another element of the security problem is illegal immigration. Thousands of immigrants escaping from conflict zones were transported with dangerous ways to European coasts by human traffickers and caused a migration crisis in Europe[5].

EU security forces took action together with Italy and Greece within the

---

[3] Ria Novosti, https://ria.ru/20150915/1253118704.html, 05.11.2020
[4] Kharlamov, ….
[5] Koutsoliakos and Filntisis, https://perconcordiam.com/refugees-smugglers-and-terrorists/, 05.11.2020

scope of combating illegal immigration from Tunisia and Libya. When the Mare Nostrum operation created a heavy burden for Italy struggling with the economic crisis, the EU Organization expanded the scope of the operation and took it under its own management. In this context, it continued with the Triton operation. The Triton operation was conducted with the participation of 19 EU countries except Italy. These operations were enough to stop the flow to the Italian coast, but caused the migration to be diverted to the eastern Mediterranean and Balkan region. Refugees from Aegean and Mediterranean seas located within Turkey was trying to reach Europe6. In 2015, this resulted in some EU member states closing their borders to refugees. The announced figures summarize Europe's refugee crisis. It is known that 600,000 immigrants crossed into European borders in 2014. In the first half of only 2015, 500.000 more migrants crossed the European borders. According to the figures reported by the international migration organization, the number of refugees in Europe reached 3,877,000 people in 20167. To solve the crisis EU was signed "Refugee Convention" with Turkey. "Refugee Consensus" signed between Turkey and European Union on 18 March 2016 includes returning of immigrants who arrive to European Countries illegally to Turkey and acceptance of Syrians who are legally remain in Turkey as refugees in Europe against this. It has been promised against the Refugee Convention that 6 Billion Euro financial support from EU aid fund shall be given to Turkey and visa facilitation for Turkey citizens to EU countries and acceleration of Turkey to the EU accession period shall be ensured8.

Increasing unemployment along with the refugee crisis has deeply caused the economic crisis in some European countries. The cheap labor market, filled with immigrants from Syria, Iraq and Libya, has caused unemployment among the locals and the population who have previously migrated. This situation has led to social conflicts from time to time between locals and refugees. Migration manifested itself with the developments that caused social problems besides the economy. Although most of the refugees who reach Europe do not want to return, they are far from trying to keep up with the order of the country they live in. Most of them refuse to learn the language and culture of the country they took refuge in, and those who are up to 20% of the locals want their cultural behavior to be accepted in the new country. Local people must accept this situation or fight against it. The

---

[6] Yahya M., "Refugees and the making of an Arab regional disorder", Carnegie Middle East Center. 2015. [9] November, http://carnegie-mec.org/2015/11/09/refugees-and-making-of-arab-regional-disorder-pub-61901, 05.11.2020

[7] Migration flows, http://migration.iom.int/europe/, 05.11.2020

[8] https://tr.euronews.com/2018/03/26/ab-turkiye-multeci-anlasmasi-ab-fonlari-nereye-ve-nasil-harcaniyor-, 05.11.2020

second situation leads to the conflict of the locals with the immigrants[9]. Unlike previous immigrants, newly arrived refugees have more information about asylum conditions and are aware of the advantageous social rights Europe offers them. Most immigrants prefer to live on social assistance rather than work. The void created by living without work can increase security threats. Refugees facilitate the search for new members of terrorist and illegal members. It is possible that refugees can be used by terrorist organizations as an auxiliary resource for new networking and attack. Armed and bomb attacks were carried out at 7 different points in a row in Paris, the capital of France on 13 November 2015. One of the attacks was against young people, the hostages taken to the concert hall were later set on fire by terrorists and killed. More than 100 young people died in this attack It was reported that a total of 300 people, 80 of which were seriously injured, and 129 people died in the attack. ISIS claimed responsibility for the attack with a statement made in French and Arabic[10]. One of the attackers had a fake Syrian passport. According to the records, the terrorist holding a passport entered Europe from the Greek island of Leros on October 3, 2015 and proceeded to Serbia. In line with this information, it has been revealed that there are members of ISIS and other radical terrorist organizations among those who infiltrated Europe as refugees. According to the statements made by Rob Wainwright, the chief of the European police organization Europol, it is known that 3000 to 5000 jihadists have infiltrated Europe along with the refugees[11]. Similar information came from other parts of Europe. In October 2014, RT News reported that US intelligence had seized encrypted correspondence containing information about agents tasked with moving ISIS members with refugees to European borders[12]. Hungarian TV channel M1 reported through photos posted on social media that two terrorists among the refugees were discovered[13]. In line with this news, the USA, which previously stated that it would accept 10,000 refugees, decided to reconsider its refugee policy. The US National Security Committee stated that among the asylum seekers who will enter the USA, there may be members of the terrorist organization and they will pose a great threat to the security of the country. The 2015 Paris and 2016 Belgian attacks justified these fears of the United States.

These attacks have also caused European society to feel unsafe in their country and to regard migrants as terrorists. According to the data provided

---

[9] Апанович М., "Мигранты «топят» Евросоюз", http://old.mgimo.ru/news/experts/document27692 9.phtml, 05.11.2020

[10] https://onedio.com/haber/paris-te-isid-teroru-127-olu-tum-gelismeler-624080, 05.11.2020

[11] https://www.amerikaninsesi.com/a/fransa-yi-sarsan-cihatci-saldirilar/3281211.html, 05.11.2020

[12] Mullins, S., "Terrorists Rarely Exploit Refugee Networks To Conduct Attacks, https://perconcordiam. com/terrorism-and-mass-migration/, 06.11.2020

[13] https://russian.rt.com/article/114040, 06.11.2020

by the survey studies conducted by the EU Commission, while 48% of the local people are concerned about the refugee flow, 39% of them live with the fear of terrorist attacks[14]. Due to these conditions, right-wing parties against refugees and immigration are gaining increasing popularity among the people in Europe. The Alternative for Germany (AFD) party, which is the political equivalent of the PEGIDA movement (Patriotic Europeans Against the Islamisation of the Occident) in Germany, has won the most votes in its history thanks to its anti-refugee propaganda[15]. Islamophobia, which started after the September 11 attacks, started to become more unpleasant with the increase of immigration. This view formed in European society towards Muslim immigrants has developed with the reflection of the media more than its own opinion. The British news newspaper "The Guardian" has confirmed that 3/2 of the local people in Britain formed their thoughts about Muslim immigrants through the media[16].

Several factors play a role in the development of Islamophobia. These are can be listed as follows:

1. The most important of these is the media. Media coverage of the news and spreading negative news about Islamic culture spreads Islamophobia.

2. Increasing the effectiveness of radical extremist groups in European regions and especially the increase in the Muslim population due to immigration triggered this situation.

3. The attacks that police and security forces prevented before the attack was carried out with the 2015-2016 Paris and Belgium attacks.[17]

The attitude taken against immigrants in France is not different from the rest of Europe. Especially after the 2015 Paris attack, although there is no comprehensive evidence that the attack was carried out by the refugees, the French are sure that the terrorists entered their country under the guise of refugees[18]. The files of the perpetrators of the terrorist attacks show that they are long-term European citizens, not newly arrived refugees. In fact, according to information provided by the Belgian prosecutor's office, Ibrahim al Bakrav who was the 27-years-old perpetrator of bombing held in Brussels subway in 2016 was arrested in Turkey in 2015 and was returned to

---

[14] https://ncpti.su/aricles/719/, 06.11.2020

[15] http://www.aljazeera.com.tr/haber/multeci-karsiti-propaganda-ve-asiri-sag, 06.11.2020

[16] Britain after September 11: Special reports Guardian Unlimited] // guardian.co.uk, http://www.guardian.co.uk/ukresponse/archive/0,,583504,00.html, 06.11.2020

[17] Kupchinskaya S.D., " Osvesheniye Problemı İntegratsiyi Migrantov v Evrope İzdaniyem " Daily Mail", **Mediaprostranstvo Mnogopolyarnogo Mira**, Moskva RUDN 2017, s.281

[18] Fawn R. "The Temelín nuclear power plant and the European Union in Austrian–Czech Relations" **Communist and Post-Communist Studies**, №. 1, 2006, p. 101–119.

Belgium as the information that he is foreign fighter as being organization member of ISIS. The terrorist, who was released despite the warnings, was hidden in Belgium until the attack, along with the members of the ISIS organization, using a false identity. The 2015 Paris assault suspects, brothers Salah Abdeslam and İbrahim Abdeslam, are French citizens. They are the perpetrators of the attacks on 13 November and claimed by ISIS. Another terrorist activist, Abdulhamid Abaaoud, is a 28-year-old Belgian citizen. He was one of the terrorists involved in the Paris attack and was killed as a result of the conflict during the operation. It has been claimed that he was one of the planners of the attack that he fought in Syria in 2014 and was wanted to be organized an attack for a train traveling between France and Belgium with the attack on the Jewish Museum, but was blocked at the last minute.[19]. As it can be seen, terrorist attacks have little relation with the 2016 refugee crisis, with exceptions. Therefore, it is possible to say that terrorism was brought up in Europe, not from the Middle East along with the refugees. In this context, it can be said that the increase in the radical terrorist threat depends on the increase in the number of refugees.

The link between radical terrorism and refugees has its roots in deeper history. After the withdrawal of the Soviet army from Afghanistan in the 1990s, when jihadists from the Near East and North Africa could not return to their countries, they turned to the borders of Europe and the USA for jihad actions. Terrorists who have gained jihad experience in Afghanistan have expanded their network of organizations through propaganda in order to expand the terrorist network and recruit new members by establishing active terrorist groups in their countries of residence. These terrorists, who have obtained citizenship and have been settled, have established appropriate financial mechanisms for terrorist networks and enlarged their network cells without revealing their identity for a long time.

For example, Abu Qatada – is known as Europe's most influential radical Islamic preacher man. He came to England from Jordan as a refugee in 1993. The British Security agency believes that Abu Qatada poses a major threat to society because of his radical-minded preachers, so his imprisonment continues.[20]

Sheikh Anwar Shabaan enabled terrorists to reach Europe via Bosnia in İslamic Center established in Bosnia by establishing jihad training center in an area 50 km from Milan. It is known that he has close relationships with al-Qaeda and Usama bin Laden.[21]

---

[19] https://www.dw.com/tr/br%C3%BCksel-ve-paris-zanl%C4%B1lar%C4%B1-kimler/a-19140868, 06.11.2020

[20] https://www.bbc.com/russian/uk/2012/02/120207_abu_qatada_still_wanted_deported, 06.11.2020

[21] Engald.U., "Svyashennıye Voinı Zapadnogo Mira", https://mybook.ru/author/uilyam-engdal/

Remzi Ahmet Yusuf has been successfully completed the radiotechnology department studied in England and consolidated all his science and experience in Al Qaeda terror training centers in Pakistan. He infiltrated America in 1993 by requesting political asylum. After long-term preparations, he organized a bomb attack in New York World Trade Center in 1993, causing 6 deaths and hundreds of injuries. After the attack, he fled to Pakistan and took refuge in the rest camp that Al Qaeda created for terrorists. He made preparations for other attack action plans in the camp. One of his actions was the assassination attempt against Pakistan Prime Minister Benazir Bhutto[22]. In this context, it can be said that terrorist attacks are linked to the phenomenon of immigration. It is clear that the refugee movement has contributed to the spread of jihad and radical terrorist movements partially. Immigrants are used by terrorist organizations to explore new regions and to organize attacks and organizations. However, for a clearer determination, the level of participation of new migrants and refugees in terrorist attacks should be compared with the figures. Until 1990, there were a small number of immigrants from Algeria in England. According to the data of the UK refugee and asylum association, their number increased by 25.000 to 30 000 in 2014. Until 1980 and 2013, 44 Algerian immigrants participated in terrorist acts in England. This explains that they are less than 0.2% of British citizens living in the UK from Algeria. After the census conducted in the USA, it was announced that there were 85,000 American citizens from Somalia. Until 2013, only 36 immigrants were accused of any illegal or terrorist acts. Most of these criminals are from Somalia and they constitute 0.04% of the immigrants. Based on this research, it can be said that refugees may pose less than 1% risk of terrorism.[23]

Most of the terrorists in Europe came from legal means. Most of their asylum and visa requests have been met. Another part was born there or settled when he/she was very young. For example, the brothers Dzhokhar and Tamerlan Tsarnaev were ethnic Chechens from Central Asia. In 2003 and 2004, they came to the USA separately for training and sports competitions. They lived in America for 10 years before organizing the attack. In 2013, they organized a bomb attack at the end point of the Boston Marathon, causing 3 deaths and more than 200 injuries[24]. Most of the perpetrators of terrorist attacks agreed with radical terror advice in the countries where they lived. It is seen that the number of those who come to these countries with the intention of attack is very low. The low number does

---


svyashennye-vojny-zapadnogo-mira/read/, 06.11.2020

[22] https://antiterrortoday.com/baza-dannykh/litsa-terrora/3409-ramzi-akhmed-yusef, 06.11.2020

[23] Mullins, S., " Terrorism and Mass Migration", Marshall Center, pril 28, 2016, https://perconcordiam. com/terrorism-and-mass-migration/,

[24] https://www.nbcnews.com/news/crime-courts/boston-marathon-bomber-told-fbi-agents-he-his-brother-acted-n923556, 06.11.2020

not mean that there is no possibility of this threat. There are examples, albeit exceptional. Qatar citizen Ali Saleh Kahlah al-Marri came to the USA on a student visa and was arrested by the FBI as an important witness for the September 11 attack. Apart from credit card fraud, he is still in imprisonment in the US, accused of providing financial support to radical Islamic terrorist organizations and being linked to Mustafa al-Havsavi, the financial supporter of al-Qaeda.[25]

Not only Syrian internal conflicts are triggering the refugee crisis but also it has facilitated the infiltration of members of terrorist organizations to Europe and Turkey. Removal of ISIS from Syria and Iraq via the power of US, Turkey, Russia and Europe has led to greater danger for Europe. Members, who travel from European countries to Syria, join ISIS and similar terrorist organizations and fight in these regions and gain experience of terrorism, return to their homes. The possibility that these terrorists, who have the opportunity to enter the countries of their citizenship legally, will be able to apply their knowledge and experience about terrorist attacks in conflict zones in Europe and the USA worries these countries. Despite the strict security measures taken between countries, the refugee flow and migration crisis make these controls difficult in many ways. It is possible for terrorists who take advantage of the chaos to enter the borders with false identities despite being searched. Cooperation agreements initiated by states on intelligence and identity control are important measures to prevent terrorists from easily crossing borders.

According to estimated data, it is expected that between 15,000 and 20,000 foreign terrorists can return to their countries[26]. The data prepared by the Republic of Turkey Ministry of Foreign Affairs within the framework of the report confirms these determinations. Approximately 22,000 foreign were controlled by Risk Analysis Groups established in various airport terminals and bus stations, almost 13,000 were interviewed and it was not allowed to enter Turkey more than 6,000 foreigners.[27]

Despite taking the strict security measures in many countries, as in the case of Turkey, it is a potential possibility that experienced terrorist fighters can infiltrate to countries by illegal means or refugees. Well-trained terrorists in military camps can cause major disasters in areas where they infiltrate. Apart from planning and organizing attacks by terrorists, it is possible for their organizations to propagate to recruit members. The success of its activities increases with the presence of significant numbers of ISIS

---

[25] https://www.brennancenter.org/our-work/court-cases/ali-saleh-kahlah-al-marri, 06.11.2020

[26] Vallance Ch. Collapse of IS will lead to attacks, say EU officials / BBC. –L., 2016. – 18.10. – Mode of access: http://www.bbc.com/news/world-europe-37691490, 21.11.2019

[27] http://www.mfa.gov.tr/turkiye_nin-yabanci-terorist-savascilarla-mucadelesi.tr.mfa, 21.11.2019

sympathizers in many countries. According to research conducted by the "ICM Research" research group for the Daily Mirror in 2015, for example, there are 1.5 million people who are sympathizers of ISIS just in the UK[28]. As of the beginning of 2016, estimates for the number of ISIS foreign fighters showed a figure of around 30,000[29]. The reasons for terrorists' return vary. Some are disappointed in the conflict and want to return and others return with the intention of carrying out a terrorist attack in their country of residence. The Paris attack, in which 214 people died in 2015[30] and Brussels attacks in which 300 people were killed on March 22, 2016[31] are the result of those who returned for this reason.

There are also denunciations that Jihadists returning from war zones have used refugees for terrorist attacks. There have been 3 incidents involving immigrants in 2015. In May 2015, Italian police caught Tunisian Abdel Macit Tuili and arrested him as one of the suspects for the attack on the Tunisian Bardo national museum[32]. The Italian police caught Tuil, whom he has been thought was the perpetrator of the attack, after he crossed the sea route to Italy via Libya. During the investigation, when it was announced that Tuli was in Italy during the attack, he was released. This incident brings into doubt on two other incidents where refugees are cited as perpetrators.

In 2015, the Spanish and German police forces arrested Ayub Mucho from Tunisia. It has been suggested that suspect gained new members for ISIS in Spain and was one of the Europe representatives of terrorist network which has been in Syria, Iraq and Turkey. However, the news that Mucho has just entered Spain as a refugee has not been confirmed. The third incident is about the Tunisian Mahdi Ben Nasr. In April 2014, he was arrested and deported in Italy on charges of being a member of a terrorist organization. Ben Nasr, who appeared among the refugees in Lampedusa island of Italy on October 4, 2015, was arrested again and deported[33].

These incidents do not clearly explain the terrorist link of the refugees. However, as stated above, the Syrian civil war, the dissolution of ISIS and the continuing activities of many radical terrorist organizations by infiltrating different regions increase the possibility of the refugees to contact terrorist

---

[28] Harris D. UK poll shows up to 1.5 million ISIS supporters in Britain /Clarion Project. – Wash., D.C., 2015. – 08.07. – Mode of access: https://web.archive.org/web/20170420095526/https://clarionproject.org/uk-pollshows-15-million-isis-supporters-britain-4/, 21.11.2019

[29] Haldun Yalçınkaya, "İŞİD'in Yabancı Savaşçıları ve Yarattığı Tehdit: Türkiye'nin Tecrübesi (2014-2016)," Orsam Raporu No 210, p.17

[30] https://www.bbc.com/turkce/haberler/2015/11/151113_paris_saldiri, 21.11.2019

[31] https://www.bbc.com/turkce/haberler/2016/03/160323_bruksel_agir_yaralilar, 21.11.2019

[32] Tunus'un en prestijli Milli Müzesi Bardo'ya 2013 yılında silahlı sldırı düzenlenmiştir. Teröristler müzede bulunan turistlere ateş açarak 17'si yabancı 19 kişiyi öldürmüşlerdir: https://www.bbc.com/turkce/haberler/ 2015/03/150318_tunus_muze_saldiri, 06.11.2020

[33] Mullins, S., https://perconcordiam.com/terrorism-and-mass-migration/, 06.12.2020

organizations.

In July 2015, Michele Coninsx, Executive Director of the UN Anti-Terrorism Committee, reported that human traffickers brought ISIS terrorists to Europe along with the refugees via ships. The "The Telegraph" newspaper announced that it has conducted 10 incident investigations by the police forces in Germany regarding the membership of refugees in a terrorist organization and their attacks. Upon this news, the identities of the refugees were checked and several refugees were arrested in European countries[34].

## Radicalism in Europe and Reasons

In 2016, Europe experienced the biggest wave of immigration after World War II. 160,000 refugees arriving at the European gate could not be distributed within the quotas specified within the EU. Although the arrival of refugees to Europe causes the greatest uneasiness in terms of security, the connection of newly arrived refugees with terrorism has not been clearly determined yet. Most of the terrorist attacks in Europe and America were not made by "newcomers" but by second generation immigrants who had previously settled in these countries. It is tried to explain why the citizens born and raised in Europe carry out terrorist attacks against the countries they see as their country with different theories. Each of them deals with the problem in different dimensions. Some studies approach the problem of immigrants not being integrated into the country they live in. Another theory focuses on religious ideological conspiracy theories. Studies show that radical movements should be handled not unilaterally but with a sociological, political and psychological dimension.

The starting point of radicalism depends on many conditions. All of them have political, economic, environmental, ideological and religious factors. Four important facts that support radical violence are:

1. Discontentment

2. Relationships that nurture the hate feelings of the second person

3. Political and religious ideologies

4. The appropriate condition for nurturing and growing these ideologies. It is possible for the individual to become radicalized with the combination of these four factors.

As a result of surveys conducted among immigrants from other nationalities living in the UK in 2001-2011, 90% of immigrants identified themselves with England. Although this is a good result, the remaining 10%

---

[34] Mullins, S., https://perconcordiam.com/terrorism-and-mass-migration/, 06.12.2020

is sufficient to cause the terror and radicalization we are experiencing today. The fact that the individual does not see himself/herself on the same side with the society in which he/she lives may be the first factor for the development of radical feelings. The rate of participation of Muslims originating from Europe in terrorist organizations is three times higher than that of the countries they live in. Uncovering the factors that caused his/her to fight against his/her country, rather than fighting for the country where he/she grew up and perhaps was born, is an important condition for telling the origin of radical terrorism.

Every nation has a desire to be met with dignity in their society. This respect should be directed not only to his/her person but to his/her identity and values. The values that he/she reflects as identity are religious belief, cultural habits and traditions. The feeling of owning them is more pronounced, especially in those who live far from their homeland. Religion and language element are the most important value of their national identity. The desire to impose them on the society they live in is mostly suppressed by the nationalist appeals of the local people. European countries have experimented with a multicultural policy model for the integration of immigrants according to the American and Canadian models between 209-2010. Despite the assimilation policy, the multiculturalism model stipulates that immigrants adapt to the local society order, provided that they protect their identity and values. German Chancellor Angela Merkel stated in her speech at the congress organized by the youth branch of the Christian-Democratic party on October 16, 2010, that the West has failed in multiculturalism politics[35]. Merkel reflected the attitude of all European countries towards multiculturalism policy with this statement. The Prime Minister of Hungary, Viktor Orban, declared that he was against the policy of multiculturalism in his country. He stated that the refugee and migration flow will cause Europe to struggle with various crises and problems, and announced that the borders of Hungary will be closed to the wave of immigration.[36] The European leaders' comparison of the immigration problem with all the disasters Europe may cause the European society to have negative feelings towards immigrants.

Migration was not always a problematic phenomenon for Europe. Although the 2016 crisis is considered to be the cause of social and economic crises for Europe, refugees have an important role in the European economy and demographic structuring. In Europe, the birth rate has been decreasing for 200 years. Birth reform was defeated to demographic decline in the last 20 years. It shows that there is a serious demographic crisis in this region and

---

[35] https://www.bbc.com/russian/international/2010/10/101016_merkel_multiculturalism_failed, 07.11.2020
[36] https://www.dw.com/ru, 07.11.2020

the real nation of Europe is gave out. On the other hand, the Muslim population has increased in the last 25 years. It increased from 1.5 billion in 1972 to 1.7 billion in 1999. The rapid growth of the Muslim population in Europe and the fact that the 2016 refugee migration is largely composed of the Muslim population could make Europe the new center of Islam[37].

The growth of the Muslim population in Europe along with the migration increases the effectiveness of the Muslim diaspora. The young strata of immigrants adopt a different approach from their fathers based on the confidence of growing up in this region. Previously, immigrants who came with a business migration were trying to hold on to the job market and support their families. Since they lived with the intention of returning to their country at any moment, they had no intention of revealing their religious feelings and keeping their culture alive in these lands. Religion was maintained within the family as part of their culture and identity. By the 70's, with the increase of the Muslim population, mosques, associations and non-governmental organizations started to be established as a part of their culture. Thus, the formation of local Islamic culture started in Europe[38]. The new generation was not afraid to openly express their problems with their identity and cultural values. On the one hand, young European Muslims are seen to be identified with the society in which they live. They can have a command of the local language and mentality of the country, on the other hand, their interest in religion may be deeper and often at the level of fanaticism. The new generation of Muslims want to take an effective place in the formation of the intellectual and social fund in Europe, but they desire to do so with their Muslim identity. As one of the active participants of the civil society operation whose feelings live in France explained: "I want to be respected as a Muslim in France"[39]

Three factors are important for immigrants to protect themselves in the social environment of nations:

1.  Growth and protecting their values,

2.  Respect,

3.  Maintaining a positive social life.

Apart from these three factors, there is a constant comparison of themselves with the society they live in. It is important for measuring comparison values. They must make sure that they share the same rights and

---

[37] Chetverikova O, " İslam v Sovremennoy Evrope: Strategia " Dobrovolnogo Getto" Protv politiki İntegratsiyi, **Evropeyskiye Paraleli**, https://mgimo.ru/files/144983/144983.pdf, 06.12.2020

[38] Chetverikova O, https://mgimo.ru/files/144983/144983.pdf, 06.12.2020

[39] Lathion S. La jeunesse musulmane européenne vers une «identité commune»? // CEMOTI. 2002. №33. P.110, cited by : Chetverikova O, https://mgimo.ru/files/144983/144983.pdf, 06.12.2020

obligations. Thus, they can understand that they are "equal" and respected in the society they live in. If they lack the "respect" or "equality" factor during the comparison, they may turn to the group that looks at them more positively. D. Brennan and A. Srtindberg highlight three measures of emotion when examining the types of behavior of immigrants in a foreign society:

1. Cognitive (the formation of perception and thinking in daily life).

2. Value measurement.

3. Emotional behavior.

The individual sees himself/herself as a certain part of the society in which he/she lives. For example, if he/she is a Muslim, he/she feels that he/she belongs to this group. In the second stage, he/she measures the prestige of the group he/she sees as belonging. As stated before, each individual wants his/her group to have a weight and activity in the society. The group's effectiveness and dignity in society determines his/her behavior towards society. He/she has positive or negative feelings towards the group he/she belongs to. In both cases, he/she must form a behavior towards the group to which he/she belongs. In the first case, he/she becomes ready to protect the values of the group to which he/she belongs and to fight for these values. In the second case, he/she wants to leave this group and join another group, so he/she completely get free from this group and joins another cultural group. In another situation, he/she goes into a struggle to increase the dignity and effectiveness of his/her group[40]. If these attempts are fed by fanatical beliefs, it leads to his/her radicalization.

When it seemed like integrating Muslims would be a solution to many problems in Europe, Europe tried to do this in different ways. The acceptance of Islam as an official religion in European countries is located at the center of this policy. This idea was supported by the idea of initiating a new Islamic trend, called European Islam or Euro-Islam, which is thought to be developed for Muslims born in Europe. In this new type of modern Islamic flow, the duties of Islam and Sharia laws should be developed in accordance with liberal thought and supporting human rights. It was envisaged to combine with the values of rule of law, democracy and sexual equality. Manuel Castells evaluates the development of Islam in Europe in his work called "Muslim Europe or Euro-Islam"[41]. Regarding the issue of religion in Europe, while the number of citizens who determined themselves as believers in 1981 was 85%, in 1999 this number decreased by 75%. The

---

[40] Lorand Bodo, "A sense of nonbelonging fuels violent radicalization in the United Kingdom", **Perconcordiam,** https://perconcordiam.com/excluded/, 07.12.2020

[41] Castels, M., Müslüman Avrupa yada Avro İslam (Muslim Europe Or Euro-Islam Politics , Culture and Citizenship in The Age Of Globalization, Çev. Z.Savan, Everest yayınları 2004

belief of the European society, which had been in economic prosperity for a long time, was replaced by the consumption habit. The important thing that is forgotten in the Europeanization policy of Islam is that Islam is a way of life and culture rather than a different faith from other religions. The religion of Islam, which understands all aspects of daily life, determines its laws by sharia. The belief that no son of Adam can change what is written in its holy book, the Qur'an, is the deep belief of all Muslims. For this reason, efforts to reform Islam in any society have always been reacted by Muslims. The Islamic strands in Europe also supports the diversity of different sects and strands of Islam.[42]

Although immigrants changed two generations in Europe, the problem of not being integrated into society caused them to live in isolation from society. The problem that unites immigrants is that although they speak the same language with Europeans and live with the knowledge that they adopt the social order, they can never be a part of this society. As stated in the above research, if the group to which it belongs does not have any value in society, the group member will struggle to gain this dignity. Most of the time, this struggle takes a radical shape and generates terrorism.[43]

In Europe, the number of young Muslim women who cover their heads and young people who grow beards and wear skullcaps is increasing. This is a form of negative attitude towards Islam in Europe and a form of protest against some racist movements developing in societies. This kind of behavior makes them feel unique. If the European community imposes its own social order on immigrants but disregards their values, it throws them out of society. This situation can have disastrous consequences in terms of their radicalization. The deprivation of European Muslims from the sense of belonging to the society they live in leads to their complete integration with the Muslim group. Marginalized feeling pushes them to the search for the group that is their own. In this way, young people can easily become victims of radical extremist terrorist organizations. It is easy for those who seek identity lost in the networks of terrorist organizations.

Mosques serve as a shelter for immigrants in foreign countries. Mosques and prayer halls are places where they can live their beliefs that are a part of their identity and make them feel safe. Therefore, these places should give confidence to the visitors and provide the belief that they are a part of this culture. Otherwise, it is possible for young Muslims to turn to places that they think they understand better and fall into the hands of organizations making radical terrorist propaganda. The Muslim young generation is the target group

---

[42] Chetverikova O, https://mgimo.ru/files/144983/144983.pdf, 06.12.2020

[43] Demirci, S., " Küreselleşme Şartlarında Radikal İslami Terörizmin Gelişimi", **Güvenliğin Gündeminden: Ayrılıkçı Ayaklanmalar ve Terörizm**, Nobel Yayını 2015, p.112.

that terrorist organizations particularly hunt. The fact that the mosques are not understood by them causes them to be dismissed from such mosques. Imran Suleyman is a man of god who was born in England and is an imam in mosques all over the country. In a statement gave to British radio, İmran stated that especially the old generation imams insisted that the mosque's functioning was just like their homeland. The fact that most of the Imams do not have a command of the native language makes it difficult for them to be understood by young people.[44] Radical organizations claim that they understand young people's problems and are ready to answer their questions. The most important thing is that they can speak in the language they understand. The apolitical behavior and lack of integration of mosques cause the loss of young Muslims. The destructiveness of this type of mosque culture is that it causes the young generation to turn to radical organizations. Young people need places where they can speak openly without fear of being kicked out of the mosque and being accused of irreligion. If the mosques do not support the open-mindedness of the youth, then radical organizations fill this gap.

However, it would be wrong to say that radicalism is linked to religious fanaticism. Radical violence is a calculated reaction to existing conditions. Individuals' use of violence is often an option for strategic and political reasons. The presence and direction of a radical political group is generally at the center of terrorist and violent activities. This group has values that they determine collectively and they prefer to apply to terrorism as an alternative. It is not the legitimacy of the method chosen here, but its effectiveness.[45]

The individual adopts the values of the group that he / she feels to belong to, and the group chooses the method he / she considers effective. This choice consists of methods with or without violence as the individual determines his/her preferred group, he/she may have to accept the methods of the group. The group selection of the individual determines the way he/she preserves his/her political stance and cultural values.

## Conclusion

International migration movement can be evaluated in several periods. At the beginning of the 20th century, the wave of immigration did not create a huge movement, but it gradually grew and caused a change in the demographic map of Europe in particular. After the Second World War, the biggest migration wave in history was experienced. After the war, the worn-out states needed new labor, so the migration movement was encouraged. In

---

[44] Lorand Bodo, https://perconcordiam.com/excluded/, 07.12.2020

[45] Küçükcan T., "Terörün Sosyolojisi: Toplumsal Kökenleri Anlama imkanı", **Uluslararası İlişkilerde Çatışmadan Güvenliğe**, Ed. M. Aydın, İstanbul Bilgi Üniversitesi Yayınları 2012, p.103

the 1960s, cheap labor and the associated migration movement became a necessary permanent factor to revive Europe's economy. Most of those who migrated to Europe were from the former colonies of these countries. Demographic structure change started with the majority of the population being Muslim. When economic growth came to a stop in the 1970s, migration became a major hump for states. When the excessive workforce increased unemployment, strict management began to be applied to stop the migration movement. Immigrants have made efforts to stay in these countries by bringing their families for fear of deportation. Thus, the refugee management policy has enabled immigrants to take root in Europe.

During the Balkan war, which emerged with the destruction of the Soviet Union and Yugoslavia in the 1990s, the second wave of migration began. In essence, migration movement is not a danger to states and is an important growth factor, especially for developing countries. During these periods, Europe's "open door" policy against the immigration movement caused not only economic but also demographic problems. Europe has been one of the states with the lowest birth rate for the last 20 years. Europe has recognized that it is experiencing a demographic crisis. However, the birth rate of Muslims in Europe has doubled in the last 25 years. Europe needs a young population formed by immigrants to fill the demographic gap and to operate and grow some factors of the economy. With the increase in the number of immigrants, serious changes have taken place within the Muslim society settled in Europe. In 20-30 years, second-third generation young people of immigrants have grown up and have formed the new society members of Europe. The younger generation was born and raised in these lands, unlike older immigrants. Based on this, they feel different from their fathers. While former immigrants were dealing with their social problems, they did not have any demands regarding their cultural and religious needs. The new generation of Muslims have no other homeland than the country where they were born. Their historical lands are far away and they are strangers to the culture they belong to. Although they identify with the country of their birth, they are aware that they have their own privileges different from the locals. As part of this society, they have the self-confidence to express openly their demand for their values to be accepted and respected by society. The problem that they are experiencing is due to the inability of societies to absorb cultural values apart from their historical order. While European countries demand recognition of their own order and values, they tend to reject the values of immigrants who form the other part of society. Huntington's "Clash of Civilizations" theory was rejected and the multiculturalism policy applied for the integration of refugees was deemed unsuccessful by European leaders in 2016. Right-wing politicians strongly opposed the policy of multiculturalism and identified the refugee flow with the worst disasters Europe could face. This propaganda, which caused the natives to have negative feelings towards immigrants, was met with different reactions by the immigrants. It has manifested itself in different movements, from the popularity of the appearance that highlight their religious characteristics to the more radical reactions among the youth. In the light of these reactions in Europe, the movements of returning to the essence of identity and the rebirth of Islam in these lands started. Due to the Arab Spring and the Syrian civil war, Europe's exposure to the largest immigration movement after the Second World War increased the Muslim population.

The terrorist attacks in France and Belgium in 2015 and 2016 showed that radical terrorist organizations use the refugee channel as a corridor to Europe for their members. These attacks have raised fears that the refugee crisis poses the greatest threat to European security. Although there is no clear evidence that refugees are linked to terrorism, it cannot be said that this possibility does not exist. There is always the possibility that new refugees, who have to deal with all kinds of difficulties in immigrant cities, fall into the network of radical terrorist organizations and act with them in search of a better life. Europe's fast integrated and refugee aid program will prevent migrants from turning to solve their problems in different ways. As the security problem is a global problem that threatens not only the countries that accept but also mostly immigrants.

CHAPTER 3

# THE IMPACT OF IRREGULAR MIGRATION ON SECURITY IN THE FRAMEWORK OF CHANGING SECURITY CONTEXT

Hüsmen Akdeniz[*]

## Introduction

One of the biggest effects of globalization, which gained momentum with the end of the Cold War and the disappearance of the bipolar world order, has shown itself in the field of security. In this context, while the classical defense and security mindset is based on military issues, threats, dangers, risks and problems with a wider framework other than military issues (economic, political, environmental, social, etc.) have started to be included in the scope of security. In other words, security, which is considered to be a high politics issue in traditional international relations theories, began to be considered together with low political issues. Today, this stance of dealing with security issues in an extended way continues.

While security was considered to be about external threats within the scope of national or strategic security when it was under the responsibility of the state, nowadays, it includes internal threats, dangers and risks. The level of security has also been reduced to the individual domain, and has gained depth within the scope of securitization concept. Along with the social security between the state and the individual, the understanding of international security has also come to the forefront.[1]

With the inclusion of individual to the security sphere, and as a result of the proliferation of actors in the objects to be secured with the participation of non-state actors as well as the state, and the spread of security to economic, political, social and environmental sectors as well as the military sector.

As a result of the increase in actors with the involvement of state along with the non-state actors to the objects to be secured -reference objects- and extending security to economic, political, social and environmental sectors along with the military sector, the concept of extension and deepening of

---

[*] Hüsmen Akdeniz, Beykent University, Department of International Relations, husakdeniz@gmail.com
[1] Beril Dedeoğlu, **International Security and Strategy**, Istanbul, 2014, p. 36 (The level of security is considered to be the security of inrividual, social sub-group, society, state, region and international system.)

security has emerged and security has become "a derived concept".[2] Therefore, the concept of securitization, which found its expression in the thinking of "When a serious threat to the existence of the reference object occurs or the threat is presented in this way, there is a security issue. In order to maintain the existence of the reference object, it is necessary to take measures."[3] occurred.

## The Change in the Security

Security, in its simplest connotation, means "the absence of threat, danger and fear situation and feeling"[4] and all human-based reference objects of security are included in this definition. Objects and things like state, society, individual, regional and international organizations and even environment, ecosystems and liberal values are also included.[5] As is seen, there are elements that include the objective and subjective aspects of security within this concept. Thus, according to Wolfers, in objective-subjective security approach, objective security is defined as "non-existence of a threat towards acquired values (assets)", subjective security is described as "non-existence of the fear of any threats towards values".[6]

The intervention of the North Atlantic Treaty (NATO) in Afghanistan under the umbrella of the United Nations (UN) at the beginning of the 21st century, the environment of insecurity triggered by the intervention of special coalition forces in Iraq in 1990-1991, the US invasion of Iraq in March 2011, the US invasion of Iraq in 2003, NATO's intervention in Libya in March 2011, the Syrian civil war that has been going on since April 2011, the Arab spring in some Arab countries and the colorful revolutions in Russia's immediate vicinity (such as Georgia, Kyrgyzstan and Ukraine) caused a large number of people from Asia, the Middle East and North Africa to be expelled from their homes and a new migration phenomenon. This has created the concept of "irregular migration". Irregular migration has become unmanageable with existing international legislation and system regarding refugees and asylum seekers which were prepared according to migration movements caused by situations threatening security -such as war and conflict-, and a smaller number of migration movements.

---

[2] Hasret Çomak, Caner Sancaktar, Sertif Demir, **International Security, New Policies, Strategies and Approaches**, Beta Publications, Istanbul, 2016, p. 19. See: "Extending, Deepening and Security as a Derived Concept".

[3] Barry Buzan, Ole Waever, Jaap De Wilde, **Security: A New Framework For Analysis**, London, Lynne Rienner, 1998, p. 1

[4] Haydar Çakmak, **European Security**, Akçağ Publications, Ankara, 2003, p. 25

[5] Mustafa Aydın, Hans Günter Brauch, Mitat Çelikpala, Ursula. O. Spring, Necati Polat, **From Conflict to Security in International Relations**, Istanbul Bilgi University Publications, 2012, p. 260

[6] Arnolds Wolfers, "National Security As An Ambiguous Symbol", **Political Science Quarterly,** 67 (4), 1952, pp. 481-507

Irregular migration is defined as "movement of persons that takes place outside the laws, regulations, or international agreements governing the entry into or exit from the State of origin, transit or destination" by International Organization for Migration (IOM). It means the illegal entry to a country or to stay or work illegally in a country for the countries of destination. From the viewpoint of the country of origin, it means that a person leaves the country without a valid passport or travel document to cross an international border or does not fulfill the administrative requirements.[7] And for the countries of transit, it is understood as the people who enter the country legally or illegally to reach the country of destination from the country of origin, and to use the country as a transit country and leave the country border.[8]

At the end of the 20th century and in the first fifteen years of the 21st century, the most important developments concerning security have been in the fields of individual security or human security. In the past, depending on the concept of national security, the security of society and individual, which was under the guarantee of the state, was the object of the political and military sectors.

However, since the boundaries of the state and of society rarely coincide, social security or social security is perceived as "the defense of an identity against a perceived threat" or, more clearly, "the defense of a community against a perceived threat to its identity".[9] In fact, with this definition, the issue has become a part of the "identity politics" as well as a security object, —its victims in a sense— and its actors —and in a sense, the creators of security problems— has increased deeply and extensively. In this context, four different violence structures have emerged, in which the concepts of the US War On Terror Doctrine (Bush Doctrine) and the globalization of securitization, and a framework in which securitization has expanded from the classical state-centered environment to an environment where different reference issues and non-state actors are involved in the military security agenda.

- The state against the state (US declaring North Korea, Iraq and Iran as evil)

- The state against the non-civil society (State protection of its citizens against terrorists, organized crime networks)

---

[7] International Organization for Migration (IOM), **International Glossary on Migration In Turkish**, p. 15 https://www.goc.gov.tr/kurumlar/goc.gov.tr/files/goc_terimleri_sozlugu(1).pdf, (Retrieved: August 17, 2020)

[8] Republic of Turkey Ministry of Interior Directorate General for Migration Management Web Site. https://www.goc.gov.tr/duzensiz-goc-hakkinda (Retrieved: August 17, 2020)

[9] Mustafa Aydın, et al., ibid, p. 260. (Article by Ole Waever titled as **"The Change of Social Security"**)

- The state against the civil society (Examples of Burma, Zimbabwe, Sudan, Rwanda, Indonesia, East Timor)

- Civil and non-civil society against each other (environments where states become incapable, such as Congo, Liberia, Sierra Leone, Somalia and Angola)[10]

As is understood from the examples, individual security has come to the fore between the state and non-state actors, with new conflicts and disagreements with multi-actors and multi-reference objects supported by identity politics, in which they resort to the use of force between each other, in different parts of the world. If the definitions refer to the security of a person instead of an identity, the issue might not be so complex and about securitizing.

At that time, according to Article 3 of the Universal Declaration of Human Rights[11], Articles 2-5 of the European Convention on Human Rights[12] and Article 33 of the 1951 Convention Relating to the Status of Refugees[13], all rights could be expected to be recognized to irregular migrants and are expected to be abided. Identity politics brings along marginalization and the superiority of some and the exclusion of the rest.

Human security, which interacts with almost all security sectors, also placed on the security agenda of the Copenhagen School. Today, human security is defined as the freedom from fear and want. It is accepted that human security will be achieved not only by being exempt from violence and conflict, but also disposing of poverty, hunger, pandemics and ignorance. Human security is multidimensional, including economic, food, health, environment, personal, social and political security, and its implementation for everyone is a necessity recognized by international regulations as it is a universal right.[14]

On the other hand, migration is one of the most important threats to

---

[10] Barry Buzan, et al., ibid, pp. 324-325 (Article by Barry Buzan titled as "The Changing Agenda of Military Security")

[11] The Universal Declaration of Human Rights, **Article 3**: Everyone has the right to life, liberty and security of person.

[12] For the Articles 2-5 of the European Convention of Human Rights, please see: https://www.echr.coe.int/Documents/Convention_ENG.pdf

[13] Article 33 of the 1951 Convention Relating to the Status of Refugees:

1. No Contracting State shall expel or return ("refouler") a refugee in any manner whatsoever to the frontiers of territories where his life or freedom would be threatened on account of his race, religion, nationality, membership of a particular social group or political opinion.

2. The benefit of the present provision may not, however, be claimed by a refugee whom there are reasonable grounds for regarding as a danger to the security of the country in which he is, or who, having been convicted by a final judgment of a particularly serious crime, constitutes a danger to the community of that country.

[14] H. Çomak, et al., ibid, p. 31

social security. According to Waever,

- If the people of one country are invaded by another, the majority of the population will change and the invading people can take over the majority (immigration)

- Life styles of the people will change in terms of culture and language (horizontal competition)

- Increasingly, people will find themselves in either an integration process or a separatist process.[15]

The phenomenon of migration here manifests itself in two ways today: Either the occupation like the examples of Afghanistan, Iraq, Syria, Libya, or the disruption of state order with external interventions, and the migration of people to safer places due to the changing ethnic balances and war, or it takes place in the form of migration of people from South Asia, Central America, China and some African countries to attraction centers where they can find job opportunities for economic reasons. This phenomenon of migration, whose theoretical construct is stated above, is typically seen due to the current Syrian civil war. Due to the civil war that started in Syria in 2011 and has been going on for nine years, the country was evacuated, and more than 5.5 million people, representing around 1/3 of the country's population, were displaced and forced to migrate to other countries.[16]

As of July 2019, 3,622,748 people from these immigrants registered with biometric data are in Turkey under temporary protection.[17] In the beginning, because of the increasing number of people who migrated to neighboring countries such as Turkey, Lebanon, Jordan, Iraq and Egypt, them not staying in the countries they took refuge in and going towards the European countries caused a great humanitarian tragedy.[18] This situation created serious security problems not only in the source country, but also in transit and destination countries. Moreover, this security has become a national, regional and international security problem by exceeding the social and national security of source, transit and destination countries considering the multitude of source, transit and destination countries. Because the protection of the right to life of immigrants who migrate by sea with primitive and unsafe

---

[15] Mustafa Aydın, et al., ibid, p. 264

[16] Refugee Brief by UNHCR dated March 11, 2020 for more recent info: https://www.unhcr.org/refugeebrief/the-refugee-brief-11-march-2020/#:~:text=More%20than%205.5%20million%20Syrians, in%20 the%20last%20three%20months.

[17] Republic of Turkey Ministry of Interior Directorate General for Migration Management Web Site. https://www.goc.gov.tr/gecici-korumamiz-altindaki-suriyeliler (Retrieved: August 18, 2020)

[18] According to the United Nations Refugee Agency (UNHCR), 65% of asylum seekers are in Turkey, 11% in Jordan, 15% in Lebanon, 0.5% in Iraq and 0.2% in Egypt. (Retrieved: August 18, 2020) https://data2.unhcr.org/en/situations/syria?id=224

methods requires serious security, search and rescue activities at sea. This is both a humanitarian duty and a requirement of the 1951 Convention. According to the Ministry of Foreign Affairs' records, between the years 2005-2016, around 900.000 people were counted as irregular immigrates, and the number of irregular migrants in Turkey by the year 2017 is given as 175.752 people.[19]

However, besides these numbers, there are also irregular migrants who are in our country illegally and whose biometric data cannot be obtained[20]. In 2016, there were about 5.5% of Syrians as irregular migrants on temporary protection status in Turkey.[21] Looking at the data in the world, the view is as follows: The United Nations data shows that in 2015, 3.3% of the world population of 7.3 billion, that is, 244 million people, was immigrants, 76 million of them reside in Europe and the second and third countries receiving the most immigrants are Germany and Russia in this continent. Both countries host 12 million immigrants each.[22] As seen, the number of migrants in Turkey constitutes 1,3% of immigrants worldwide and corresponds to 4% of the country's population.[23]

In 2015, the European Union received more than 1.2 Million refugees. 1.1 Million of these refugees were living in Germany and more than 150,000 in Sweden. The USA, on the other hand, only accepted 75,000 asylum seekers a year and still takes very strict security measures.[24] In fact, the most important reason for irregular immigration is the legal regulations implemented by the countries of destination. The difficulties brought by these regulations force people to take illegal ways. On this issue, the critical theory opposes the theses that put the state in the foreground on security. Linklater argues that when countries pursue aggressive and thoughtless

---

[19] Republic of Turkey, Ministry of Foreign Affairs. http://www.mfa.gov.tr/turkiye_de-duzensiz-goc.tr.mfa (Retrieved: August 18, 2020)

[20] https://www.goc.gov.tr/gecici-korumaya-ait-kayit-islemleri. (Retrieved: August 19, 2020)

[21] As of the end of 2015, in Turkey, there were 2,733,784 immigrants. The number of irregular migrants was given as 146,485 people. For further info, please see the statement of the Deputy Prime Minister of the period Yalçın Akdoğan dated March 10, 2016: https://www.sozcu.com.tr/2016/gundem/yalcin-akdogan-turkiyedeki-suriyeli-gocmen-sayisi-2-milyon-733-bin-784-1130888/
According to current data, the number of registered Syrians under temporary protection in Turkey is a total of 3,600,710 people as of July 16, 2020, while the number of Syrians staying in temporary accommodation centers was announced as 62 thousand 133 people. For further info, please see: https://multeciler.org.tr/turkiyedeki-suriyeli-sayisi/ (Retrieved: August 19, 2020)

[22] Martin L. Philip, "Europe's Migration Crisis: An American Perspective" (translated to Turkish), **Göç Dergisi**, Vol: 3, Issue: 1, p. 121, (Translators: İ. Sirkeci, D. Eroğlu)
According to current UN data, in 2019, the number of international migrants reached 272 million and approximately 31% of them reside in Asia, 30% in Europe, 26% in the Americas, 10% in Africa and 3% in Oceania. For further info, please see: https://www.un.org/en/sections/issues-depth/migration/index.html

[23] Turkey's current demographic data was taken from Turkish Statistical Institute (TUIK). http://www.turkstat.gov.tr/HbGetirHTML.do?id=33705 (Retrieved: August 19, 2020)

[24] Ibid, p. 121

foreign policies in the international arena and when these policies end up with war, they are the source of insecurity of their own country's citizens. He also states that although states are not always conscious, they pose a threat to other states while struggling with the security climate.[25] It is necessary to include the states that caused war in a region for whatever purpose in this idea.

On the one hand, countries' approaches to international migration are shaped by security concerns, on the other hand, the inadequacy of considering security as state security alone in explaining the changing world order after the Cold War is emphasized by the critical security school. This situation has led to the emergence of studies that put individual at the center and criticize the migration and security duo.[26]

International migration, which is shown as a threat in many of the studies dealing with the issue of migration and nation-state security, is actually carried out by individuals whose own security is in danger and these people often cannot reach full and complete security even when they arrive in the host country. In other words, the migrant avoids the threat, crosses the most dangerous roads, and once again finds himself under threat because of the protective policies of the countries when he reaches the place he wants to reach.

### Is Irregular Migration a Risk or a Threat? What are Its Effects on Safety ?

Irregular migration creates important security problems for the country/countries of destination as well as the country of origin. Today, the Syrian civil war, which has been going on especially since April 2011, has made the country uninhabitable. In addition to regular state forces and opposition forces, the country has been evacuated due to some groups which are considered as freedom fighters by some and terrorist organizations by others, such as Daesh, Al-Nusra and PYD/YPG.

Fleeing from the country continues due to the veterans of the United States, Russia and some other countries, some of them based on Saddam Hussein's former army, mercenaries and private security agencies, waging a proxy war, and the war of terrorist organizations consisting of radical religious fighters, mostly from Islamic countries and the close circle of the EU and Russia, such as Daesh.[27] (According to UNHCR June 2015 data, a

---

[25] Andrew Linklater, Political Community and Human Security, **Critical Security Studies and World Politics,** 2015, p. 116

[26] Please see: Elspeth Guild, **Security and Migration in the 21ˢᵗ Century**, Cambridge, United Kingdom, 2009.

[27] Assoc. Dr. King Shuk Chatterjee from Calcutta University, in Turkish Military Academy in the

total of 11,925,806 people were displaced due to the Syrian civil war.)

Especially after the Libyan civil war, against the increasing immigration from North Africa to Italy, the migration route shifted from the middle Mediterranean to the Turkish-Greek coast due to Italy's rescue effort adopting a European method that includes the destruction of boats used in smuggling called Triton.[28]

When Germany and Sweden announced that they would accept immigrants to meet the increasing labor need, immigration to the European Union was almost encouraged. On the other hand, it is not possible for irregular migrants to be deported because the country of origin is not known. This situation creates a de facto impossibility in terms of refugee, asylum seeker and immigrant legal status. Migrants who know this destroy their passports, and many of them claim to be Syrians because it increases their chances of asylum.[29]

As a result of these immigrants trying to cross the sea by very primitive means, being the subject of human trafficking and smuggling and the precautions they have been exposed to in transit and destination countries, a large number of lives have been lost, mostly children and women. According to the records of the International Organization for Migration, among the immigrants in the Horn of Africa, 246 lives were lost in the Gulf of Aden and the Red Sea in 2014, 95 in 2015 and 3279 in the Mediterranean in 2014 and 3,771 in 2015.[30] Even the existence of these casualties is a security problem.

United Nations High Commissioner for Refugees describes the humanitarian tragedy experienced by Syrians as "the greatest immigration wave in recent history". The former United Nations High Commissioner for Refugees, António Guterres, who is now serving as the ninth secretary-general of the United Nations, has also described the Syrian Crisis as "the greatest humanitarian emergency of our time".[31]

---

Declaration on **International Relations and Security Symposium on May 26-27, 2016**, Daesh consists of 6,000 foreign fighters from Tunisia, 2,000 from Saudi Arabia, 2,000 from Turkey, 800 from Russia and 2,200 from the European Union (700 from France, 400 from Britain). The total is around 30,000.

[28] Ibid, p. 121

[29] Ibid, p. 123

[30] **"Irregular Migration in Horn of Africa Increases in 2015"**, International Organization for Migration (IOM). http://www.iom.int/news/irregular-migration-horn-africa-increases-2015 (Retrieved: August 27, 2020). Also according to IOM data, 107,546 migrants and refugees have entered Europe by sea through 18 December 2019, 60,363 of them to Greece and 24,976 to Spain. Deaths recorded on the three main Mediterranean Sea routes through 18 December stand at 1,246 individuals. 2,219 deaths confirmed during the same period in 2018. For more info, please see: https://www.iom.int/news/mediterranean-migrant-arrivals-reach-107546-2019-deaths-reach-1246 (Retrieved: August 21, 2020)

[31] Murat Erdoğan, **Syrians in Turkey: Social Acceptance and Adaptation**, Istanbul Bilgi University Press, 1st edition, Istanbul, 2015, pp.1-2.

Legal status of refugees and asylum seekers, the issue of refugees and migration has been handled as a humanitarian approach rather than a security-based approach with the 1951 Convention and the 1967 Protocol that complements it. However, as in the case of Syria, security comes to the fore when large-scale human movements occur due to internal disturbances such as war or terrorism, and because of the dangers to which human life is exposed during the journey. In other words, human safety and saving lives are exactly the human-centered approach.

On the other hand, the security problems and difficulties faced by migrants in transit, whether they are within the scope of irregular migration or not, and destination countries, or in the "first safe country" or "safe third countries" included in the 1990 Dublin Convention, has been following considering the example of Turkey in Syrian Crisis because of the crisis:

- Registration: Registration of irregular immigrants in particular is based on declaration and biometric photographs and fingerprints. Since the persons do not have any identification on them, there is no information, document and Interpol record regarding their previous lives. This situation creates a serious security problem for transit and destination countries. Thus, Turkey, due to the events in Syria, opened its borders for humanitarian purposes starting from 28 April 2011. However, due to the unforeseen developments, the recording process started only in 2013 and as of December 20, 2012 87% of Syrians in Turkey (1,450,000 people) were able to record it.[32]

- Another difficulty encountered here was undoubtedly the fact that a large number of people were treated as irregular migrants due to the fact that those fleeing the war did not have the opportunity to obtain a passport or a passport. It also led to the avoidance of migrants from the records because of temporary protection status has put into practice in Turkey. Thus, instead of pulling the refugee status because of the large number of Syrian immigrants, Turkey has chosen to use the concept of asylum seekers or guests.

- Security problems related to sexual and physical abuse of children: Although there is not enough and uncovered data on this subject, there may be threats to individual security as in the Nizip Camp example.[33]

- The dangers and threats of child marriages and women: There are dangers of preventing marriages of children 13-14 years old, whose

---

[32] Ibid, pp. 63-70

[33] **Birgün Gazetesi**, May 11, 2016, http://www.birgün.net/haber-detay/nizip-mülteci-kampında-30-cocuga-tecavuz-edildi (Retrieved: August 27, 2020)

marriages are common in their own countries, and young girls falling into the hands of prostitution gangs. Despite the occasional news in the press, it is not easy to obtain data due to the fact that the issue is a crime and its sensitivity.[34]

- The kidnapping of unaccompanied minors and their falling into the hands of organ mafia are also a serious danger and threat to children, as the presence of those who are still unregistered raises concerns about the issue.[35]

- Education problems of children: Considering that 74% of the children who were still out of the camps could not go to school, for reasons of providing income for their families by working or begging, it might also cause a serious loss generation problem for the country, given that the return of children may not be possible.[36] This situation carries an important potential danger for the present and future for the host country in terms of fundamental human rights and freedoms.

- Lack of control and security risk threats: The death of 53 people in the explosion that took place in Reyhanlı in 2013 is an example of a serious security threat.[37]

- During periods of mass migration movements, it is not possible to determine the status of immigrants for a long time. For this reason, in situations that force or even exceed the possibilities of the country they are in, newborn children become "stateless" due to the statuses that countries apply or have to apply (difficulties in applying refugee/asylum status, granting long-term temporary protection status, conditional refugee, etc.) It is possible that they may encounter many uncertainties and problems regarding their future. This issue remains sensitive and serious, especially for countries that have not signed the United Nations Convention on the Status of Stateless Persons of 28 September 1954 and the Convention on the Reduction of Statelessness of 30 August 1961, as in the case of Turkey.

- In mass migration movements caused by war and terrorism, the fact that women and children among immigrants are much more than

---

[34] **The Guardian**, https://www.theguardian.com/world/2014/sep/08/syrian-refugee-brides-turkish-husbands-marriage (Retrieved: September 13, 2020)

[35] Ibid, p. 99

[36] Ibid, pp. 86-87

[37] https://www.hurriyet.com.tr/gundem/reyhanli-cehenneme-dondu-23257089 (Retrieved: August 21, 2020)

men causes various problems such as work, employment, security and protection, moral problems (sexual abuse, polygamy), care needs and begging. All these carry potential danger and risk factors for the public order of the host country.

- The fact that the immigrants constitute a majority in some settlements increases the unrest and insecurity by forcing the indigenous people to migrate internally. For example, the presence of 80,000 indigenous and 100,000 Syrians in Kilis forced native population to internal migration.[38] In this case, for the Syrians accepted because they are Muslims in Turkey, it may not be possible for people to allow a similar situation in European countries.

- The threat of epidemic disease from immigrants[39]

- As the influx and numbers of immigrants increased, it has led to a change in countries' attitude towards asylum seekers and their policies from protecting them to protecting their own citizens. In this regard, two events have been effective: first, on 13 November 2015, 8 religious terrorists –two of whom arrived to the country by Turkey-Greece route of European immigrants- killed 130 people in Paris, and secondly, thousands of asylum seekers attacked a German woman at Cologne railway station on New Year's Eve. The Paris attacks have shown that terrorists can hide among immigrants.[40]

With the example of Turkey, it was seen that mass migration can cause economic, social, health, safety and environmental risks for any country, such as employment, work and employment, education, social cohesion, epidemic, accommodation, subsistence and public order problems. Instead of being denied that this issue is a security risk, danger and threat for any reason, it should be the starting point of joint efforts for a solution and constitute the first step.

The greatest danger posed by irregular migrants in terms of security is that, as stated above, terrorists find the opportunity to hide themselves within the same group and commit terrorist acts in the countries they reach. The terrorist attacks on 10 October 2015, 17 February 2016 and 26 March 2016 in Ankara, on 12 January and 19 March 2016 Istanbul, on 13 November 2015 in Paris, on 27 June 2015 in Tunisia and on 22 March 2016 in Brussels have clearly exposed this. Some of the terrorists arrive with the immigrants

---

[38] Murat Erdoğan, ibid, p. 211

[39] The report of the Turkish Medical Association dated August 2, 2013 titled "**The state of health services in Syria and our neighboring countries**". http://www.ttb.org.tr/index.php/haberler/rapor-3969html (Retrieved: June 30, 2014)

[40] Philip L. Martin, ibid, p.125

through Turkey and Greece. This shows irregular migration is not only a risk and danger but also a threat which turned out to be real. The prevention of this threat makes it a necessity to take measures at regional and international level, since it exceeds the capacity of the sending transit and destination country/countries to take measures alone and is at the national level for the countries in question.

In fact, the problem in this regard is not only due to the securitization concept. Deliberate securitization of such an issue does not seem logical, especially for countries exposed to terrorism. Regarding migration, the prevention of marginalization of immigrants, ensuring the safety of their lives in the countries where immigrants stay during migration and until their status is determined, are all security issues. When it comes to irregular migration, it becomes a much more important and urgent security issue when there are no records and the cause of migration is civil war and terrorism.

## What Should be Done?

Since the concept of irregular migration is a new concept, it has not been the subject of international relations theories but has been studied in a small number of articles[41]. It is also rarely involved in the threat issues of countries and international security organizations. For example, it is not included in the threat and danger assessment of countries and international organizations, such as NATO, EU and USA[42]. In Western countries, the term "illegal immigrant" appears only in the UK National Security Strategy Document. On the other hand, in the New National Security Strategy Document of the Russian Federation dated December 31, 2015, it was included as "threats due to illegal and uncontrolled immigration". Last but not least, in Turkey's Disaster Response Action Plan "mass population movements" has been considered one of the Disasters and Emergencies.[43]

It is possible to reach the following conclusion from this: irregular migration was not envisioned, but it emerged de facto as a result of some practices. In other words, although it causes a security problem, there are other reasons causing it. Some of these reasons are terror, conflict, civil war and wars that emerged as a result of the struggle for domination in the geographies where the world's energy and other precious underground

---

[41] Philip L. Martin, ibid, pp. 307-319. Also see for sample study: Nazif Mandacı, Gökay Özerim, "Transformation of International Migration Into a Security Issue: Radical Right-wing Parties in Europe and the Securitization of Migration", **Journal of International Relations**, Vol 10, Issue: 39, Fall 2013, p.105-130

[42] **NATO Strategic Concept 2010**, p.10-12, https://www.nato.int/cps/en/natohq/topics_82705.htm?. Retrieved: September 12, 2020. US FEMA official website, **Make A Plan**, https://www.ready.gov/ Retrieved: September 12, 2020

[43] Recep Sait Arpat, **Emergency and Crisis Management**, Night Library Publications, 2016, pp. 33, 51, 83, 116, 145.

resources are located. Its solution lies in the elimination of these causes. However, there is a current emergency. Irregular migration can be viewed primarily as a crisis management issue because there is not enough regulation in this regard. In the theories dealing with the issue of security in international relations, individual security and social security have come to the fore with globalization and even the importance of the borders between countries has been ignored (with consensi like Schengen Agreement and Frontex border applications). At this point, some people cannot even be entitled to have the most basic human right to life. Therefore, the first thing to do is to include the issue of irregular immigration within the scope of emergency and crisis management and to take the necessary measures within this framework.

For this purpose, by using the Emergency and Crisis Management Organizations of the international organizations such as NATO and the EU, firstly to carry out search and rescue activities at sea and to minimize losses. Afterwards, the implementation of inter-organizational coordination and cooperation with organizations such as the International Organization for Migration (IOM), the United Nations High Commissioner (UNHCR) and the necessary Emergency and Crisis Management and Migration Management Units on the basis of nations is considered as the first measure. Because, according to the statement of "Life, liberty and security of person are the right of every individual." in Article 3 of the United Nations Universal Declaration of Human Rights, and the provisions of Articles 2-5 of the European Convention on Human Rights and Article 33 of the 1951 Convention, it is of great importance that all rights are provided to immigrants, even if they have irregular migration status.

Today, there are flaws in this regard that can be attributed to both the victims of irregular migration, source transit and destination country administrations (actors) for various reasons. In this context, it is a fact that immigrants hide their identities and force all kinds of illegal opportunities. The actors, on the other hand, have created a "securitization" model about irregular migrants being a threat to identity problems, the benefits of the welfare state, or national security, and therefore irregular migration is transformed from a social phenomenon to a threat[44]. Among the methods applied within the scope of the newly emerging hybrid war concept known as the Chief of Staff of the Russian Federation Valery Gerasimov Doctrine, the new methods show the disorder and asymmetry of the war, as in the example of the Green Men practice in Ukraine.[45] In his article titled "The Value of Science In Prediction", Gerasimov states that in a period when the line between war and peace is becoming blurred, for the capture of political

---

[44] Hasret Çomak et al., p. 707
[45] Charles K. Bartles, "Getting Gerasimov Right", **Military Review**, US Army Combined Arms Center, January-February, 2016, p. 30-38

or military objectives, the role of non-military vehicles increased, modern military operations started in peacetime, and the need to use military vehicles including information warfare and special force operations under the guise of Peace Protection and Crisis Management has increased. He also states that internal opposition must be turned into a tool to maintain a permanent front in enemy territory, and that the information environment creates asymmetrical possibilities to reduce the combat effectiveness of the enemy forces by affecting the enemy state ranks and people. The operation carried out in Ukraine and Syria without the use of large-scale military forces is remarkable as it shows that the "Gerasimov Doctrine" has been successfully applied in the field. In fact, the possibility that mass migration can be used as a hybrid warfare method in security and war environments further complicates the problem.

These behaviors are far from a human-oriented approach. The issue of illegal immigration is very susceptible to being associated with terrorism, organized crime, human trafficking and smuggling. Moreover, today, because of the civil war in Syria, Turkey, France and Belgium have experienced suicide attacks causing death and injury to many people. This creates a serious paradox when the subject is viewed from the human perspective. However, after the attacks, it has been stated by official sources that the perpetrators of all these attacks, including those used as suicide bombers, which terrorist organization the perpetrators of all these attacks were from, all kinds of identity information, residence addresses, entry and exit points were known. These perpetrators have always had the opportunity to hide their identities among irregular migrants. Fighting terrorism is difficult. There is a need for mutual determination, understanding and cooperation and the acceptance of joint decisions. If one can be a terrorist for one side and a freedom fighter for the other, terror will always find support.

The solution to the problem of irregular immigration lies in removing its causes. For this, it is necessary to take measures from the beginning of the problem and to establish an environment of peace in the source countries. It is possible to summarize other measures that should be taken as follows:

### a) Struggle and measures at the state level:

As stated above, the most effective struggle for the source country is to restore peace in the country. What is essential for this is that all terrorism, conflict, civil war and wars that cause migration should be ended by the joint decision of all actors. In places where conflict continues, measures such as suspending conflicts and ceasefire can be considered.

One of the most important measures that can be taken in transit or in neighboring countries and in the first overseas countries is the effective control of land and sea borders. However, this is one of the most sensitive issues. The countries in which conflict and war continue and the neighboring countries are the ones that have experienced the humanitarian tragedy most closely. Therefore, closing the borders does not seem possible in humanitarian terms. Therefore, assistance to the countries in this category is to take temporary protection measures in full, to fulfill the regulations stipulated by international conventions (such as refugee status, requests for asylum, prevention of repeated asylum requests, readmission process) as soon as possible. or this, the implementation of emergency and crisis management in these countries and the establishment of an effective fight against irregular migration are priority issues.

The first of the measures to be taken in terms of the target country or countries is to take temporary protection measures, the acceptance of some of the requests for asylum according to the conditions to be provided, and the return of those who want to return to the country of origin or the signatory of readmission agreements by creating readmission conditions. Effective containment of immigration has created a new type of security measure. In particular, internal and external (social and military) security are linked to each other differently. The policy of reducing the visibility of migration has led to the need for transparency and genuine control. The potential impact of this situation is increased monitoring and inspection overall. Thus, the need to monitor immigrants and other dangerous items has become legitimate.[46] In this context, NATO's operation in the Aegean Sea is a first in preventing immigration originating from Syria, and it also sets an example for emergency and crisis management. It is also vital to provide control and surveillance against migrants moving by sea and human traffickers on the high seas.

When the subject is considered as a whole, there may be situations that require the taking of regional and global measures that require the joint efforts of all countries, including source, transit and destination country or countries.

For this reason, in order to open a common migration security umbrella that takes into account the contributions and experiences of international organizations in the world, such as the UN, EU, NATO, ASEAN and APEC, the necessary self-sacrifice and mutual assistance are required and the UN migration law must be implemented by the relevant countries.

Besides, the current UN Migration Legislation needs to be reconsidered and adapted to the current conditions. In addition, a quota application that will meet the needs of refugees, migrants and asylum seekers on a regional or country basis is seen as an urgent solution.

---

[46] Hasret Çomak et al., p. 275

**b) Struggle and measures at the level of international organizations and institutions other than the state:**

In this context, organizations such as the United Nations High Commissioner for Refugees (UNHCR) and the International Organization for Migration (IOM) do not have the capability to formulate direct migration policies. The duty of such organizations is to contribute to the governments of the country with their corporate identity and knowledge in transit and destination countries, to supervise the rights and laws of immigrants, and to provide the necessary emergency first aid from the moment the migrants leave their country. The most important effect of these organizations is to help the affected countries with their experience and technical means and to inform the world about whether the migrants are being treated in accordance with international human rights legislation.

On the other hand, with the decisions of institutions such as the International Criminal Court and the European Court of Human Rights, and the activities of special-purpose organizations such as Journalists Without Borders and Doctors Without Borders in order to identify the issue, keep it on the agenda and provide support for their fields, contribute to the solution of the problem by doing their duties impartially.

**c) Other social reference objects (such as ethnicity, minorities, sects and diaspora):**

The most important reference objects in the social sector in the world system are tribes, clans, nations, ethnic identities defined as minorities, and non-contiguous ethnicities around diasporas, civilizations, religions and race[47]. These groups are one of the most vulnerable groups to irregular migration. Because, when the defense and protection of the rights of a group is formed by referrals against the other group, it can cause more harm than contribution and can be the igniting fuse of conflicts. For this reason, their contribution may be in the form of publicizing the problem and providing material and moral support as much as possible and marginalization or avoiding marginalization.

**Conclusion**

In essence, migration is a social phenomenon that leads people who are not satisfied with the environment and conditions they live in (individual, social, political security), for reasons such as economic and security, to continue their lives in attraction centers that promise prosperity and security. Today, immigration is different from this characteristic, as a result of the inclusion of the individual in the field of security, human security has been

---

[47] Ibid, p. 274

removed from the umbrella of the state in political and military terms under the concept of national security, and has been taken under the umbrella of social security.

The greatest danger posed by irregular migration in terms of security is that terrorists find the opportunity to act within the same group and pose a threat in terms of carrying out terrorist acts in transit and target countries. The prevention of this threat exceeds the capacity of source, transit and target country or countries to fight alone and requires joint efforts, regulations and practices. Terrorism, conflicts, civil wars and conventional warfare, which emerged as a result of the struggle for domination in the field of energy resources and underground resources in the world, are the leading causes of irregular migration. Therefore, the first condition of effective fight against irregular immigration is the establishment of peace in the source countries where the problem started.

In addition, the statement that 80 million people are ready in Africa due to the climate migration is a warning for the urgency of the issue.[48]

Within the scope of other measures to be taken, at the state level, it is important to ensure effective control and governance of the borders, to execute search and rescue activities in the high seas to prevent human losses by implementing emergency and crisis management, to prevent human trafficking and smuggling, to take temporary protection measures for irregular migrants, to evaluate it in a short time and to make it operational with new agreements. At the level of non-state international migration organizations and institutions, it is again important to help the problem with the technical capabilities and human resources they have and to inform the world about whether or not the immigrants are being treated in accordance with the basic human rights legislation, to keep the issue on the agenda and to provide impartial support regarding their interests.

Elements such as minorities, ethnicities, sects and diasporas, which are among other social reference objects, should contribute in the form of announcing the problem and providing material and moral support to immigrants as much as possible, by avoiding acts that ignite the conflict.

---

[48] UN Specialist Nasra Hassan, ACUNS Member, UN and Irregular Immigration, 26-27 May 2016, Turkish War College, **International Relations and Security Symposium**, Istanbul.

CHAPTER 4

REFUGEES AND TERRORISM

Mehmet Emin Erendor[*]

## Introduction

There are many studies on the concepts of refugee and terrorism. These studies often are designed from a perspective leaning towards the experiences of the countries or the international community. At the same time, although there are many studies on the impact of terrorism on migration or refugees, but not many studies focus on the effects of refugees on terrorist incidents in host countries or on their involvement in terrorist activities in host countries. This lack of studies on the effect of refugees on terrorism in host countries or their participation in terrorist organizations in host countries means an opportunity for a unique field of study, while on the other hand, it poses a lot of difficulty in doing research on the subject. While some studies claim that there is a link between refugees and terrorist incidents[1], others disagree[2].

In this study, first of all, the concepts of refugee and terrorism will be defined. The main aim is to analyse the relationship between refugees and terrorism and therefore, this analysis will be detailed in the last section. In this article, it is argued that although refugees are believed to have negative effects on the social, cultural and economic structures of host countries, this does not mean that they increase terrorism or there is no link between refugees and terrorism.

## Conceptual Framework

Refugees and terrorism are two different and powerful concepts effecting the international community. These two strong and complex concepts stand out as the elements that states have long strived to solve. On the other hand, most studies on these two concepts until now have often focused on the effect of terrorism on refugees, but it is important to focus and investigate

---

[*] Assoc. Prof., Visiting Lecturer at the Kyrgyz-Turkey Manas University, International Relations Department. Adana Alparslan Türkeş Science and Technology University, Political Science Faculty, International Relations Deparment.

[1] Seung-Whan Choi & Idean Salehyan, "No Good Deed Goes Unpunished: Refugees, Humanitarian Aid, and Terrorism", **Conflict Management and Peace Science**,Vol. 30, No. 1, 2013, pp. 53-75.

[2] Daniel Milton, Megan Spencer & Michael Findley, "Radicalism of the Hopeless: Refugee Flows and Transnational Terrorism", **International Interactions**, Vol. 39, No. 5, 2013, pp. 621-645, https://www.tandfonline.com/doi/pdf/10.1080/03050629.2013.834256?needAccess=true (Accessed 03.11.2020).

the impact of refugees on terrorism. Although the main purpose of this study is to examine the impact of refugees on terrorism, it is important to primarily examine these concepts. Therefore, in this section, the concepts of refugees and terrorism will be analysed and their historic evolution will be analysed.

## Refugees

Under this heading, attempts to define refugees rather than their political and legal rights will be the focus, because evaluating the political and legal rights of refugees requires a separate study and goes beyond the scope of this chapter.

Millions of people around the world have been forced to leave from their own homes and countries. These people, who were forced to flee from their own countries, were forced to live in other countries and were deprived of support from any state. Especially after the civil war in Syria, the refugee crisis has become more exposed. People fleeing from such countries can survive with international aid or they can hold on to life with the aid provided by the countries where they are received.

Although the concept of refugee has a long history, legal arrangements took place only after the World War II. The concept of refugee is generally defined to refer those who have had to flee their countries due to the fear persecution for political, ethnic, or religious convictions and they have no protection from any other state. Nowadays, there are nearly 80 million forcibly displaced people and 26 million of them are recognized as refugees.[3]

It is a known fact that in history, people were displaced very often, violent incidents were constant, and states persecuted foreigners who were living in their territories even those who were citizens. The holocaust in Germanybefore and during the Second World War and civil wars in other countries are the most striking examples. Thus the refugee problem is not new, it carries a much larger history. In this study, the historical process of the concept of refugee will not be detailed, the concept will be evaluated within the framework of the developments in the international system after the First World War.

The early studies on the protection of refugees in the international system were during the League of Nations period. Especially after the revolution in Russia in 1917, people started to flee to all parts of the world, particularly in Western Europe.[4] As a result of these movements, the League of Nations

---

[3] https://www.unhcr.org/figures-at-a-glance.html (Accessed 04.11.2020)

[4] James C. Hathaway, "The Evolution of Refugee Status in International Law: 1920-1950", The International and **Comparative Law Quarterly**, Vol. 33, No. 2, 1984, pp. 350, https://www.jstor.org/stable/pdf/759064.pdf?refreqid=excelsior%3A994f386706b8b4012ce1adba45b1f90a (Accessed 10.10.2020).

established the first international agency regarding refugees which was called the Office of High Commissioner for Refugees in 1921.[5]

Within the framework of the problems experienced in 1926[6] and 1928[7], the concept of refugee was attempted to be defined, but these definitions did not go beyond ethnic or regional criteria.[8]

The addition of the world economic crisis to the developments experienced especially after the First World War caused the refugee crisis to reach serious levels. Attempts were made to determine the legal status of refugees, and decisions were taken at the League of Nations Intergovernmental Commission in 1933.[9] The first Convention relating to the International Status of Refugees was accepted by the League of Nations in 1933.[10] The non-refoulement principle was, for the first time, accepted by states with this Convention.[11] According to Hathaway, refugees earned mixed absolute and contingent rights after the Convention and they were able to access to work, social welfare and so on.[12] Refugees had some rights after the Convention, but this Convention was accepted by no more than nine states.[13]

Besides, although different commissions were formed and decisions were made regarding refugees, it can be said that more serious steps were taken after the Second World War and the rights of refugees were based on stronger legal grounds.

The international destruction brought about by the Second World War, on the other hand, caused a greater refugee problem to arise. The next important step was taken by the United Nations to establish International Refugee Organization (IRO) in 1946.[14] This organization was established

---

[5] *Ibid.*, p. 351; Louise W. Holborn, "The League of Nations and the Refugee Problem", **The Annals of the American Academy of Political and Social Science** , Vol. 203, 1939, pp. 124-125, https://www.jstor.org/stable/pdf/1021893.pdf?refreqid=excelsior%3A2bb9645fa615f8e269e38857f76 7663e (Accessed 11.10.2020).; Sir John Hope Simpson, **The Refugee Problem**, Oxford, Oxford University Press, 1939, p. 199.

[6] https://www.refworld.org/pdfid/3dd8b5802.pdf (Accessed 10.10.2020)

[7] https://www.refworld.org/docid/42cb8d0a4.html (Accessed 10.10.2020)

[8] Hathaway, *op.cit.*, p. 359

[9] https://biblio-archive.unog.ch/Dateien/CouncilDocs/C-311-1933_EN.pdf (Accessed 10.10.2020)

[10] https://www.refworld.org/docid/3dd8cf374.html (Accessed 10.10.2020); Gilbert Jaeger, "On the History of the International Protection of Refugees", IRRC, Vol. 83, No. 843, September 2001, p. 729, https://www.icrc.org/ar/doc/assets/files/other/727_738_jaeger.pdf (Accessed 12.10.2020).

[11] David Martin, Thomas Aleinikoff, Hiroshi Motomura & Maryellen Fullerton, **Forced Migration Law and Policy**, 2nd Edition, Minnesota, West Academic Publishing, 2001.

[12] James C. Hathaway, **The Rights of Refugees Under International Law**, Cambridge, Cambridge University Press, 2005, p. 88.

[13] Jaeger, *op.cit.*, p. 730.

[14] Arthur Rucker, "The Work of the International Refugee Organization", **International Affairs (Royal Institute of International Affairs 1944-)**, Vol. 25, No. 1, Jan. 1949), p. 66; Dennis Gallagher, "The Evolution of the International Refugee System", **International Migration Review**, Vol. 23, No. 3, Sep. 1989, p. 579, https://journals.sagepub.com/doi/abs/10.1177/019791838902300309 (Accessed 9.10.2020).

under the resolution 62 (I) of the General Assembly of the UN on 15 December 1946. The IRO was known as resettlement agency[15] and relocated more than 1 million Europeans to the Americas, Israel and Oceania[16], but the Second World War refugees more than 1 million and it is expected to say that after the Second World War more than 50 million people displaced and it is not possible to expect an institution established temporarily to work effectively. The IRO completed its activities in 1950.

Before to the termination of the activities of the IRO, the UN have started to work on legal and political protection of refugees by establishing an ad hoc committee in 1949.[17] While the ad hoc committee started its work, the UN General Assembly established the Office of the United Nations High Commissioner for Refugees (UNHCR) instead of the IRO in 1950.[18] The main responsibility of the UNHCR is to protect refugees in terms of legally and reduce the number of refugees who requires protection.[19]

The UNHCR mandate and the Convention Relating the Status of Refugees were adopted by the UN in 1951.[20] With the adoption of the Convention, the international community agreed on the definition of the Refugees.

1951 United Nations Convention Relating the Status of Refugees define the term refugees as; "As a result of events occurring before 1 January 1951 and owing to well-founded fear of persecution for reasons of race, religion, nationality, membership of a particular social group or political opinion, is outside the country of his nationality and is unable or, owing to such fear, is unwilling to avail himself of the protection of that country; or who, not having a nationality and being outside the country of his former habitual residence as a result of such events, is unable or, owing to such fear, is unwilling to return to it".[21]

The main important aspect of this definition was that there was a limitation in terms of time and geography. The Convention was recommending to accept a person who left their country only due to the events took place in Europe and only if these events occurred before 1 January 1951. This definition and limitation cause the concept of refugee to be interpreted in a narrow framework and it has not been effective at the

---

[15] Jaeger, *op.cit.*, p. 732.

[16] Hathaway, *op.cit.*, p. 91.

[17] Göran Melander, "The Protection of Refugees", **Stockholm Institute for Scandinavian Law**, 1974, p. 154, https://scandinavianlaw.se/pdf/18-6.pdf (Accessed 9.10.2020).

[18] https://www.unhcr.org/history-of-unhcr.html (Accessed 11.10.2020).

[19] Gallagher, *op.cit.*, p. 581.

[20] Melander, *op.cit.*, p. 155.

[21] UNHRC, "Convention and Protocol Relating to the Status of Refugees", p. 14, https://www.unhcr.org/3b66c2aa10, (Accessed 11.10.2020).

desired level because it excludes people who face the same problems outside of Europe.

The 1967 Protocol Relating the Status of Refugees was accepted by states and this protocol removed the temporal and geographical limitation of the 1951 Convention.[22]

The 1951 Convention and the 1967 Protocol gives an important and critical obligation to signatory states to protect refuges to accept the principle of non-refoulement. The meaning of is that if a person has left his country in accordance with the Articles of the 1951 Convention and the 1967 Protocol and applied the country which he/she seek asylum, then this state cannot send his/her to their own country. Although the Convention and Protocol have accepted the principle of non-refoulement, today, states are engaged in activities to prevent refugees from coming to their countries. In particular, after the Syrian crisis, serious attempts were made and refugees faced serious difficulties.

On the other side, although the Organization of African Union use the same definition of the 1951 Geneva Convention, it also includes; *"the term "refugee" shall also apply to every person who, owing to external aggression, occupation, foreign domination or events seriously disturbing public order in either part or the whole of his country of origin or nationality, is compelled to leave his place of habitual residence in order to seek refuge in another place outside his country of origin or nationality"*.[23]

According to this additional definition, the African Union includes people who are not included in the definition of the UN, and even people who have to leave their country as a result of natural disasters or the activities of other forces on their own countries, and gives them the status of refugee.

It is a fact that refugees have acquired political and legal rights in the historical process. Developments especially after the Second World War show that states and international organizations have attempted to solve this problem. Although the attempts made before the Second World War were important, they could not be solved completely due to the difficulties brought by the conjuncture, but they led to the developments that would come later.

To sum up, the temporal and geographical restrictions adopted in the 1951 Convention were lifted with the 1967 additional protocol, but no sanctions were imposed on the states that still use this restriction, even though they signed the 1967 protocol.

---

[22] *Ibid.*, p. 46.

[23] African Union, "OAU Convention: Governing the Specific Aspects of Refugee Problems in Africa", p. 6,https://au.int/sites/default/files/treaties/36400-treaty-oau_convention_1963.pdf (Accessed 11.10.2020).

## Terrorism[24]

The concept of terrorism has become one of the most critical issues confronting the international community in terms of the threat to peace and security. It is worth noting that, over time the meaning and use of the term *'terrorism'* has changed. Since the French Revolution in 1789, concepts of terrorism have varied, but the most critical transformation occurred after 9/11. Following these attacks, terrorists began to use technological tools to threaten international peace and security. Details of why 9/11 was important for international security will be given, but before that, it is important to define the concept of terrorism. Given the significance of the threat, it is, perhaps, surprising that there is no common definition of terrorism. States[25] [26] and organisations use their own definitions. Different nations, however, have their own legal definitions which define the concept of terrorism only in their home countries, and which cannot be used in any other country. For example, Turkey has its own terrorism definition like the UK and Turkey. According to Anti-Terror Law number 3713: *"Terrorism is any kind of act done by one or more persons belonging to an organisation with the aim of changing the characteristics of the Republic as specified in the Constitution, its political, legal, social, secular and economic system, damaging the indivisible unity of the State with its territory and nation, endangering the existence of the Turkish state and Republic, weakening or destroying or seizing the authority of the State, eliminating fundamental rights and freedoms, or damaging the internal and external security of the State, public order or general*

---

[24] This section is taken from the PhD dissertation "An Analysis of Threat Perceptions: Combating Cyber Terrorism: The Policies of NATO and Turkey, Evaluated Using Game Theory in The Context of International Law", completed at the University of Southampton.

[25] The United Kingdom Terrorism Act 2000 interprets terrorism in the following way:
(1) In this Act "terrorism" means the use or threat of action where—
(a) the action falls within subsection (2),
(b)the use or threat is designed to influence the government [or an international governmental organisation] or to intimidate the public or a section of the public, and
(c)the use or threat is made for the purpose of advancing a political, religious, racial or ideological cause.
(2) Action falls within this subsection if it—
(a)involves serious violence against a person,
(b)involves serious damage to property,
(c)endangers a person's life, other than that of the person committing the action,
(d)creates a serious risk to the health or safety of the public or a section of the public, or (e) is designed seriously to interfere with or seriously to disrupt an electronic system
"The Terrorism Act 2000", http://www.legislation.gov.uk/ukpga/2000/11/contents (Accessed 18.10.2020).

[26] Title 22 of the U.S. Code, Section 2656f (d) defines terrorism as:
(1) the term "international terrorism" means terrorism involving citizens or the territory of more than one country;
(2) the term "terrorism" means premeditated, politically motivated violence perpetrated against non-combatant targets by subnational groups or clandestine agents; and
(3) the term "terrorist group" means any group practicing, or which has significant subgroups which practice, international terrorism.
"The title 22 of the U.S. Code", http://www.state.gov/documents/organization/65464.pdf (Accessed 18.10.2020).

*health by means of pressure, force and violence, terror, intimidation, oppression or threat."*[27] It seems clear that Turkey defines the concept of terrorism for its own security and the protection of its citizens from this threat. Mariona Llobet Angli states that the concept of terrorism *"is used indistinctly by the contending forces to criminalise their enemies and is manipulated by the different groups in a conflict to favour their own political interests. Al Qaeda or the CIA, Hamas or the Israel Defence Force, the separatists from Chechnya or Russian security forces are terrorists according to some people and freedom fighters or legitimate combatants according to others."*[28] It should be understood that all countries define the concept for their own purposes, and therefore it may not be possible to have a common understanding of terrorism in the international arena. Indeed, as Hoffman quoted from Chinlund *"one person's terrorist is another person's freedom fighter."*[29]

There have been many attempts to define the concept of terrorism in the international arena. For example, Koufa stresses that the concept of terrorism was first used in the framework of the international legal context at the Third Conference for the Unification of Penal Law in Brussels.[30] The act of terrorism was defined at the Third Conference as:

*"[T]he intentional use of means capable of producing a common danger that represents an act of terrorism on the part of anyone making use of crimes against life, liberty or physical integrity of persons or directed against private or state property with the purpose of expressing or executing political or social ideas will be punished."*[31]

Although the concept of terrorism was defined for the first time in the international legal context, it did not have any legal binding on the states.

After these initiatives to define the concept of terrorism in the Conferences for the Unification of Penal Law, the League of Nations' Convention for the Prevention and Punishment of Terrorism in 1937 defined

---

[27] "Anti-Terror Law Number 3713", http://www.masak.gov.tr/userfiles/file/3713.pdf (Accessed 15. 10. 2020).

[28] Mariona L. Angli, "What does 'Terrorism' Mean?", **Counter-Terrorism, Human Rights and the Rule of Law: Crossing Legal Boundaries in Defence of the State**, Aniceto Masferrer & Clive Walker (Eds.), Cheltenham, Edward Elgar, 2013, pp. 18-19.

[29] Paul Hoffman, "Human Rights and Terrorism", **Human Rights Quarterly**, Vol. 26, No. 4, 2004, p. 936, https://muse.jhu.edu/article/174729/pdf (Accessed 18. 10. 2016).

[30] Kalliopi Koufa, "Human Rights and Terrorism in the United Nations", **Justice Pending: Indigenous Peoples and Other Good Causes**, Gudmundur Alfredsson & Maria Stravropoulou (Eds.), The Hague: Martinus Nijhoff Publishers, 2002, p. 205.

[31] Ben Saul, "Attempts to Define 'Terrorism' in International Law", **NILR**, 2005, p. 59, http://www.cicte.oas.org/olat/documents/Defining%20TERRORISM%20in%20International%20Law.pdf (Accessed 18. 10. 2020/07/2016); Reuven Young, "Defining Terrorism: The Evolution of Terrorism as a Legal Concept in International Law and Its Influence on Definitions in Domestic Legislation", **Boston College International and Comparative Law Review**, Vol. 29, No. 1, 2006, p. 35, http://lawdigitalcommons.bc.edu/cgi/viewcontent.cgi?article=1054&context=iclr (Accessed 02.10.2020); Sir Arnold K. Amet, "Terrorism and International Law: Cure the Underlying Problem, Not Just the Symptom", **Annual Survey of International&Comparative Law**, Vol. 19, No. 1, 2013, p. 29, http://digitalcommons.law.ggu.edu/cgi/viewcontent.cgi?article=1168&context=annlsurvey (Accessed 18.10.2020).

the concept of terrorism for the first time at an international level,[32] but this Convention covered only trans-national terrorism,[33] and the Convention never entered into force.[34] The Convention defined the concept of terrorism as: *"Criminal acts directed against a State or intended to create a state of terror in the minds of particular persons, or a group of persons or the general public."*[35]

Although the Convention defined the act of terrorism, it was not explicit in terms of the identification of illegal acts without criminal acts.

Following the League of Nations initiatives to adopt a global definition of terrorism, the Convention on the Suppression of Financing of Terrorism was signed, and for the first time after the League of Nations attempt, sought to define the concept of terrorism.[36] According to Golder and Williams, there are two different limbs in the definition.[37] The first limb of the definition adopts a specific approach to the question by referring to certain acts[38] and the second limb to:

---

[32] Human Rights Council, "Counter-Terrorism and the Protection of Human Rights", 2010, p. 1, http://www.humanrightsadvocates.org/wp-content/uploads/2010/05/HRC13_Counter-terrorism_and_Human-Rights.pdf (Accessed 19.10.2020); Hans-Peter Gasser, "Acts of Terror "Terrorism" and International Humanitarian Law", **International Review of the Red Cross,** Vol. 84, No. 847, 2002, p. 550, https://www.icrc.org/en/doc/assets/files/other/irrc_847_gasser.pdf (Accessed at: 18/07/2016); Young, *op.cit.*, pp. 35-36.

[33] Young, *Ibid.,* pp. 35-36; Gasser, *Ibid.*

[34] Christian Walter, "Defining Terrorism in National and International Law", **Terrorism as a Challenge for National and International Law: Security versus Liberty?,** Christian Walter, Silja Vöneky, Volker Röben, and Frank Schorkopf, (Eds.), London, Springer, 2004, p. 33.

[35] Young, *op.cit.,* p. 36; Gasser, *op.cit.,* p. 552.

[36] Ben Golder and George Williams, "What is 'Terrorism'? Problems of Legal Definition", **UNSW Law Journal,** Vol. 27, No. 2, 2004, p. 274, http://classic.austlii.edu.au/au/journals/UNSWLawJl/2004/22.html (Accessed at: 28. 10. 2020); Young, *Ibid.*, p. 52.

[37] Golder and Williams, *Ibid.*, p. 274

[38] There are 19 universal legal instruments and additional amendments. These are; 1963 Convention on Offences and Certain Other Acts Committed on Board Aircraft; 1970 Convention for the Suppression of Unlawful Seizure of Aircraft; 1971 Convention for the Suppression of Unlawful Acts Against the Safety of Civil Aviation; 1973 Convention on the Prevention and Punishment of Crimes Against Internationally Protected Persons; 1979 International Convention against the Taking of Hostages; 1980 Convention on the Physical Protection of Nuclear Material; 1988 Convention for the Suppression of Unlawful Acts against the Safety of Maritime Navigation; 1988 Protocol for the Suppression of Unlawful Acts Against the Safety of Fixed Platforms Located on the Continental Shelf; 1988 Protocol for the Suppression of Unlawful Acts of Violence at Airports Serving International Civil Aviation, supplementary to the Convention for the Suppression of Unlawful Acts against the Safety of Civil Aviation; 1991 Convention on the Marking of Plastic Explosives for the Purpose of Detection; 1997 International Convention for the Suppression of Terrorist Bombings; 1999 International Convention for the Suppression of the Financing of Terrorism; 2005 Protocol to the Protocol for the Suppression of Unlawful Acts Against the Safety of Fixed Platforms located on the Continental Shelf; 2005 Protocol to the Convention for the Suppression of Unlawful Acts against the Safety of Maritime Navigation; 2005 Amendments to the Convention on the Physical Protection of Nuclear Material; 2005 International Convention for the Suppression of Acts of Nuclear Terrorism; 2010 Convention on the Suppression of Unlawful Acts Relating to International Civil Aviation; 2010 Protocol Supplementary to the Convention for the Suppression of Unlawful Seizure of Aircraft; 2014 Protocol to Amend the Convention on Offences and Certain Acts Committed on Board Aircraft. "International Legal Instruments", http://www.un.org/en/counterterrorism/legal-instruments.shtml (Accessed 26.10.2020).

*"Any other act intended to cause death or serious bodily injury to a civilian, or to any other person not taking an active part in hostilities in a situation of armed conflict, when the purpose of such an act, by its nature or context, is to intimidate a population, or to compel a Government or an international organisation to do or to abstain from doing any act."[39]*

In comparison of this definition with national definitions of terrorism, it can be said that the definition requires physical violence directed at civilians,[40] but on the other hand, the object is not sufficient in national definitions.[41] Also, the definition does not mention any political, ideological or religious motivations.[42] The definition of terrorism by Convention determines the minimum requirements of terrorism, and states use their own definitions according to their national laws.

The main turning point in terrorism was the attacks on the Twin Towers on 9 September 2001. The primary significance of the 9/11 attacks was that the international community had to confront serious international terrorism.[43] Steiner *et al* explain the importance of 9/11 as *"the attacks on 11 September 2001 constituted a turning point in the relationships between international law, global institutions and terrorism."*[44] According to them, 9/11 was a turning point because, international institutions responded to the case immediately, and important resolutions passed by organisations such as the UN Security Council determined that these attacks be evaluated as a threat to international peace and security, with Resolution 1368 of the UN Security Council[45] which recognized the inherent right of individual or collective self-defence in accordance with the Charter.[46] This Resolution was also crucial because, for the first time, a terrorist attack had been evaluated under Article 51 of the UN Charter.[47] Steiner *et al* state that NATO and the Organisation of

---

[39] "International Convention for the Suppression of the Financing of Terrorism", http://www.un.org/law/cod/finterr.htm (Accessed 02.11.2020).

[40] Walter, *op.cit.*, p. 13.

[41] Ibid.

[42] Ibid.

[43] Andrea Gioia, "The UN Conventions on the Prevention and Suppression of International Terrorism", **International Cooperation in Counter-Terrorism: The United Nations and Regional Organisations in the Fight Against Terrorism**, Giuseppe Nesi (Ed.), Aldershot, Ashgate Publishing Limited, 2016, p. 21.

[44] Henry Steiner, Philip Alston, and Ryan Goodman, **International Human Rights In Context: Law, Politics, and Morals**, Oxford, Oxford University Press, 2007, p. 380.

[45] *Ibid.*; The UN Security Council, "Resolution 1368", 2001, https://documents-dds-ny.un.org/doc/UNDOC/GEN/N01/533/82/PDF/N0153382.pdf?OpenElement (Accessed 21.10.2020).

[46] *Ibid.*; Stephen P. Marks, "International Law and the 'War on Terrorism': Post 9/11 Responses by the United States and Asia Pacific Countries", **Asia Pacific Law Review**, Vol. 14, No. 1, 2006, p. 46, https://cdn1.sph.harvard.edu/wp-content/uploads/sites/580/2012/09/spm_Terrorism_and_IL_APLR_2006_vol14.pdf (Accessed 21.10.2020).

[47] *Ibid.*, p. 45; Noelle Quenivet, "The World after September 11: Has It Really Changed?", **The European Journal of International Law**, Vol. 16, No. 3, 2005, p. 569, http://www.ejil.org/pdfs/16/3/309.pdf

American States evaluated 9/11 as an armed attack and invoked the collective self-defence provisions of their treaties.[48] However, this was a different kind of threat, and it was the first time that the problem was understood as an international problem, international organisations accepting this case as an armed attack and threat to international peace and security. According to Palmer:

> *"The threat from the Irish terrorist campaign cannot be compared with the threat from Al Qaeda. The Irish campaign was domestic in nature and operated within a set of reasonably defined parameters using conventional weaponry. Those involved formed tightly knit networks. They avoided capture, had no wish to die and used warnings to restrict casualties. Eventually they were willing to engage in a political process to move forward. In contrast, Al Qaeda is global in its membership and ambition. Its networks are fluid and mobile enabling it to meet its objective of inflicting maximum loss."[49]*

The 9/11 terrorist attack was a physical, social and illegal phenomenon, which expressed itself in two distinct ways. The first is that it highlighted the personal relationship of the citizen with the threat they faced from terrorism, including the risks to public institutions and to public and private property. According to Palmer, *"after the attack any new concept of terrorism must now consider the possibility of serious harm and be sensitive to the potential social impact of a major terrorist attack. The second is the risk that terrorism presents to the values of the state that it seeks to attack"*.[50] The 9/11 terrorists succeeded in their aim of creating fear and threatening policies, because the attack had both sociological and psychological impacts, which created an insecure place for citizens including military, police and public areas.[51]

After these attacks, George W. Bush announced a new strategic plan for the USA. According to the plan, pre-emptive action must be taken by countries. States could not afford to wait for terrorists to strike in their territory; collectively the international community should seek to prevent attacks.[52] The pre-emptive doctrine or Bush's doctrine provides, in a large part, the justification for the USA and its allies to attack Iraq and Afghanistan. In Iraq, the stated aim was to deal with weapons of mass destruction, whilst

---

(Accessed 21.10.2020).

[48] Steiner *et al., op.cit.*; Christine Gray, "The Use of Force and The International Legal Order", **International Law**, Malcolm Evans, M. D. (Ed.), Oxford, Oxford University Press, 2010, p. 629.

[49] Phil Palmer, "Dealing with the Exceptional Pre-Crime Anti-Terrorism Policy and Practice", **Policing and Society**, Vol. 22, No. 4, 2011, p. 11.

[50] *Ibid.*, p. 16.

[51] R. Perl, **Open for Debate: Terrorism**, New York, Benchmark Books, 2004, p.23.

[52] Dale T. Snauwaert, "The Bush Doctrine and Just War Theory", **The Online Journal of Peace and Conflict Resolution**, 2004, http://www.trinstitute.org/ojpcr/6_1snau.pdf (Accessed 20.10.2020); National Security Council, "The National Security Strategy of the United States", 2002, http://www.whitehouse.gov/nsc/nssall.html (Accessed 20.10.2020).

in Afghanistan, it was in order to end Taliban and Al-Qaeda actions and stop terrorist attacks in the international arena.

Following the 9/11 terrorist attacks, the United Nations Security Council adopted Resolution 1373. The importance of this resolution was the first use of Chapter VII of the UN Charter,[53] but it does not define the concept of terrorism.[54] The Convention lays significant obligation on states to fight terrorism, but the lack of at common definition of terrorism has resulted in the avoidance of fighting terrorism, or, as Young says, it masks the human rights abuses in the states.[55]

The CTC was established by Resolution 1373 to monitor human rights abuses, and to:

*"Take appropriate measures in conformity with the relevant provisions of national and international law, including international standards of human rights, before granting refugee status, for the purpose of ensuring that the asylum seeker has not planned, facilitated or participated in the commission of terrorist acts."*[56]

The role of CTC was limited because of the lack of definition of terrorism, but the Security Council tried to resolve this problem in 2004 with Resolution 1566.[57]

According to Resolution 1566 of the Paragraph 3;

*"...criminal acts, including against civilians, committed with the intent to cause death or serious bodily injury, or taking of hostages, with the purpose to provoke a state of terror in the general public or in a group of persons or particular persons, intimidate a population or compel a government or an international organisation to do or to abstain from doing any act, which constitute offences within the scope of and as defined in the international conventions and protocols relating to terrorism, are under no circumstances justifiable by considerations of a political, philosophical, ideological, racial, ethnic, religious or other similar nature, and calls upon all States to prevent such acts and, if not prevented, to ensure that such acts are punished by penalties consistent with their grave nature..."*[58]

The UN General Assembly tried to define the concept of terrorism, and

---

[53] Young, *op.cit.*, p. 42
[54] Alex Conte, Human Rights in the Prevention and Punishment of Terrorism: Commonwealth Approaches: The United Kingdom, Canada, Australia and New Zealand, Berlin, Springer, 2010, p. 20.
[55] Young, *op.cit.*, p. 32
[56] The UN Security Council, "Resolution 1373", 2001, http://www.un.org/en/sc/ctc/specialmeetings/2012/docs/United%20Nations%20Security%20Council%20Resolution%201373%20(2001).pdf (Accessed 18.10.2020).
[57] Ben Saul, "Terrorism in International and Transnational Criminal Law", **Legal Studies Research Paper,** No. 15 (83), 2015, p. 13, http://ssrn.com/abstract=2663890 (Accessed 19.10.2020).
[58] Security Council, "Resolution 1566", 2004, http://www.un.org/ga/search/view_doc.asp?symbol=S/RES/1566%20(2004) (Accessed 18.10.2020).

the Draft Comprehensive Convention on International Terrorism defines the concept of terrorism in Article 2 (1) as:

> *"Any person commits an offence within the meaning of this Convention if that person, by any means, unlawfully and intentionally, causes:*
>
> *• Death or serious bodily injury to any person; or*
>
> *• Serious damage to public or private property, including a place of public use, a State or government facility, a public transportation system, an infrastructure facility or the environment; or*
>
> *• Damage to property, places, facilities, or systems referred to in paragraph1 (b) of this article, resulting or likely to result in major economic loss, when the purpose of the conduct, by its nature or context, is to intimidate a population, or to compel a government or an international organisation to do or abstain from doing any act."*[59]

This Convention also refers to physical violence towards any person, like the International Convention for the Suppression of Financing of Terrorism. The difference between the Draft Convention and the International Convention for the Suppression of Financing of Terrorism is that damage to property and private property is significant.[60] According to Walter, *"there seems to be a tendency in international law to extend the notion of terrorism to destructive violence against objects, which corresponds to the recent development in national legal orders."*[61] Although the Draft Comprehensive Convention defines the concept of terrorism, it is still in debate, and does not have any binding status on states.[62]

On the other hand, international humanitarian law prohibits any form of terrorism committed as international or non-international armed conflict,[63]

> *"including deliberate attacks on civilians or civilian objects, indiscriminate attacks, reprisals, the use of prohibited weapons, attacks on cultural property, objects indispensable to civilian survival, or works containing dangerous forces (including dams, dykes and nuclear facilities); or through illegal detention, torture or inhuman*

---

[59] "Draft Comprehensive Convention Against International Terrorism", https://www.ilsa.org/jessup/jessup08/basicmats/unterrorism.pdf (Accessed 19.10.2020).

[60] Young, *op.cit.*, p. 55.

[61] Walter, op.cit., p. 36.

[62] Golder and Williams, *op.cit.*, p. 274.

[63] Luigi Condorelli and Yasmin Naqvi, "The War Against Terrorism and Jus in Bello: Are the Geneva Conventions Out of Date?", **Enforcing International Law Norms Against Terrorism**, Andrea Bianchi (Ed.), Oxford, Hart Publishing, 2004, p. 30; Hans-Peter Gasser, "Prohibition of terrorist Acts in International Humanitarian Law", **International Review of the Red Cross**, Vol. 26, No. 253, 1986, p. 212; Thomas Weatherall, "The Status of the Prohibition of Terrorism in International Law: Recent Developments", **Georgetown Journal of International Law**, Vol. 46, 2015, https://heinonline.org/HOL/LandingPage?handle=hein.journals/geojintl46&div=23&id=&page= (Accessed 20.10.2020); Gasser (2002), *op.cit.*, p. 549; Saul (2015), *op.cit.*, p. 4.

*treatment."[64]*

Gasser explains the international humanitarian law approach for in two different reasons. According to him;

*"First, the right to use force and commit acts of violence is restricted to the armed forces of each party to an armed conflict. Only members of such armed forces have the "privilege" to use force against other armed forces, but their right to choose methods or means of warfare is not unlimited. On the other hand, only members of armed forces and military objectives may be the target of acts of violence. Second, other categories of persons, in particular the civilian population, or of objects, primarily the civilian infrastructure, are not legitimate targets for military attacks — they are, in the words of the Geneva Conventions, "protected" and must in all circumstances be spared."[65]*

It is clear that international humanitarian law prohibits attacks on civilians during armed conflict, and that if any part of the armed conflict targets the civilian population, the states will be punished. Also Article 33 of the IV Geneva Convention in 1949 states that:

*"No protected person may be punished for an offence he or she has not personally committed. Collective penalties and likewise all measures of intimidation or of terrorism are prohibited.*

*Pillage is prohibited.*

*Reprisals against protected persons and their property are prohibited."[66]*

*Saul mentions that Article 33 of the IV Geneva Convention was a response to the mass intimidation of civilians in the Second World War.[67] Also Protocol 1 Additional to the Geneva Conventions in 1977 protects civilians in international conflict. According to Article 51 (2) of the Protocol 1:*

*"The civilian population as such, as well as individual civilians, shall not be the object of attack. Acts or threats of violence the primary purpose of which is to spread terror among the civilian population are prohibited."[68]*

Additional Protocol 1 also stresses the protection of civilians during armed conflicts, and prohibits the threats of violence against the civilian population. With this Protocol 1, the IV Geneva Convention is expanded in

---

[64] Saul (2015), *Ibid.*

[65] Gasser (2002), *op.cit.,* p. 554.

[66] "Convention IV Relative to the Protection of Civilian Persons in Time of War", https://ihl-databases.icrc.org/ihl/385ec082b509e76c41256739003e636d/6756482d86146898c125641e004aa3c5 (Accessed 21.10.2020).

[67] Saul (2015), *op.cit.,* p. 4.

[68] "Protocol Additional to the Geneva Conventions of 12 August 1949, and Relating to the Protection of Victims of International Armed Conflicts (Protocol 1)", https://ihl-databases.icrc.org/ihl/WebART/ 470-750065 (Accessed 21.10.2020).

terms of intention. The meaning of the Article is, briefly, that intention is the one of the important elements of the definition of acts of terrorism.[69] Protocol 2 also prohibits acts of terror in non-international conflicts.[70]

According to Saul, "the International Criminal Tribunal for the former Yugoslavia (ICTY) was the first international tribunal to recognise 'the crime of terror as a violation of the laws or customs of war' in the Tadic[71] case".[72] It seems clear that international humanitarian law strongly prohibits terror among civilian persons, and the first prosecution was seen in the ICTY. As was stated above, the ICC prosecutes terrorist acts if they threshold to war crimes, crimes against humanity, or genocide and the case of Tadic shows us that terrorist acts can be considered as war crimes.[73]

Although the Conventions and Protocols prohibit acts of terror, there is no definition of terror in these documents, and the ICTY, likewise did not define the concept. The Appeal Chamber of the Special Tribunal for Lebanon (STL) found a definition of terrorism under the customary international law.74 The Appeal Chamber of the STL used the definition of terrorism by the International Convention for the Suppression of the Financing of Terrorism. According to Cohen, the Appeal Chamber was right

---

[69] Gasser (2002), *op.cit.*, p. 556.

[70] Article 4 of the Protocol 2 states that: "Article 4 [ Link ] -- Fundamental guarantees

1. All persons who do not take a direct part or who have ceased to take part in hostilities, whether or not their liberty has been restricted, are entitled to respect for their person, honour and convictions and religious practices. They shall in all circumstances be treated humanely, without any adverse distinction. It is prohibited to order that there shall be no survivors.

2. Without prejudice to the generality of the foregoing, the following acts against the persons referred to in paragraph 1 are and shall remain prohibited at any time and in any place whatsoever:

(a) violence to the life, health and physical or mental well-being of persons, in particular murder as well as cruel treatment such as torture, mutilation or any form of corporal punishment;

(b) collective punishments;

(c) taking of hostages;

(d) acts of terrorism;

(e) outrages upon personal dignity, in particular humiliating and degrading treatment, rape, enforced prostitution and any form of indecent assault;

(f) slavery and the slave trade in all their forms;

(g) pillage;

(h) threats to commit any of the foregoing acts."

Article 13 (2) of the Protocol 2 states that: "The civilian population as such, as well as individual civilians, shall not be the object of attack. Acts or threats of violence the primary purpose of which is to spread terror among the civilian population are prohibited."

"Protocol Additional to the Geneva Conventions of 12 August 1949, and Relating to the Protection of Victims of Non-International Armed Conflicts (Protocol 2)", https://ihl-databases.icrc.org/ihl/INTRO/475?OpenDocument (Accessed 21.10.2020).

[71] This case is not the scope of the research. Therefore, the detail of the case is not given.

[72] Saul (2015), *op.cit.*, pp. 4-5.

[73] Aviv Cohen, "Prosecuting Terrorists at the International Criminal Court: Reevaluating an Unused Legal Tool to Combat Terrorism", **Michigan State International Law Review**, Vol. 20, No. 2, 2012, pp. 247-248, http://digitalcommons.law.msu.edu/cgi/viewcontent.cgi?article=1080&context=ilr (Accessed 20.10.2020).

[74] *Ibid.*, p. 230.

and the Convention's definition of terrorism can be accepted as a de facto internationally acceptable definition.[75]

The above information shows us that the lack of definition of the concept of terrorism has created many problems in the international area in terms of the cooperation between states, human rights and information exchange. This situation also blocked the jurisdiction of the ICC on the terrorism issue and the crimes of terrorism were rejected by the states.

Coming back to pre-emptive doctrine (Bush doctrine), it has failed to prevent terrorism in the international arena. According to Elmas, pre-emptive strategies or doctrines are risk scenarios, and are based on the worst events which could occur in the future to affect the world in terms of security and peace.[76] Pre-emptive doctrines are not based on evidences, but on suspicions.[77] Beck explains this situation as a real *'virtuality'* and he quotes the example of the Second Iraq War as, *"conducted in order to prevent what we cannot know, that is, whether and to what extent chemical and nuclear weapons of mass destruction get into the hands of terrorists."*[78] As stated previously, the invasion of Iraq was to obstruct the use of chemical, biological and nuclear weapons, and, as Williams infers,

> *"while the United States changed reality so that this original risk could never occur, Washington opened the flood gates that turned Iraq into the best terrorist training ground on earth. Furthermore, the United States destabilized the Middle East, which has allowed Tehran to pursue its nuclear programme without check from traditional balance Iraq"*[79].

This scenario lost its position and new risks have emerged in the region. As Heng suggests there was no Al Qaeda presence before the war, but in aftermath of the war, the region attracted terrorists from around the world.[80] Therefore, this policy has failed to prevent terrorist attacks. For example some terrorist attacks occurred after the war such as: in November 2003, bomb attacks were carried out in Istanbul in the buildings of HSBC, the British Consulate, and the Beth Israel and Neve Shalom Synagogues. On 11

---

[75] *Ibid.*, p. 231.

[76] Elmas, *op.cit.*, p. 173.

[77] *Ibid.*, p. 174.

[78] Ulrich Beck, "Living in the World Risk Society", **Economy and Society**, Vol. 35, No. 3, 2006, p. 335,https://edisciplinas.usp.br/pluginfile.php/4095470/mod_resource/content/0/Beck--WorldRisk.pdf (Accessed 22.10.2020).

[79] M. J. Williams, "(In) Security Studies, Reflexive Modernization and the Risk Society", **Cooperation and Conflict: Journal of the Nordic International Studies Association**, Vol. 43, No. 1, 2008, -p. 63.

[80] Yee-Kuang Heng, "The 'Transformation of War' Debate: Through the Looking Glass of -Ulrich Beck's World Risk Society", **International Relations**, Vol. 20, No. 1, 2006, pp. 85-86, http://ire.sagepub.com/content/20/1/69.full.pdf+html?hwshib2=authn%3A1472486035%3A20160828%253Aac9c830f-b0c0-4084-9f42-11b0f3c242a4%3A0%3A0%3A0%3AePN6ZQXBeRR1k%2FrdPv5wMA%3D%3D (Accessed 23.10.2020).

March 2004, terrorists bombed trains in Madrid, Spain. Al-Qaeda attacked London in 2005, when the public transport system was bombed during rush hour.

Although there have been many international agreements, terrorist organisations continue to use violence and technology to achieve their aims.[81] These attacks show us that terrorist organisations can attack at any moment and anywhere in the world coupled with the believe that terrorist groups might acquire biological and nuclear weapons it almost goes without saying that terrorism is now the most influential threat to the international community.

## Refugees and Terrorism

In the previous section, the concepts of refugees and terrorism tried to be defined. In this section, the effects of refugees on national and international terrorism in the countries where they migrated will be examined.

Refugee crises have occurred in almost every period of history and continue to be present today. Although refugees are accepted as victims of violence in the historical process, today this situation has started to reverse and the states that host many refugees have started to hold refugees responsible for the problems of violence in their own territories.[82] Today, the restrictions imposed by the European Union countries on Syrian refugees can also be evaluated within this framework.

The fact that the refugees, who bring great responsibilities to countries in

---

[81] There are 19 universal legal instruments and additional amendments. These are; 1963 Convention on Offences and Certain Other Acts Committed on Board Aircraft; 1970 Convention for the Suppression of Unlawful Seizure of Aircraft; 1971 Convention for the Suppression of Unlawful Acts Against the Safety of Civil Aviation; 1973 Convention on the Prevention and Punishment of Crimes Against Internationally Protected Persons; 1979 International Convention against the Taking of Hostages; 1980 Convention on the Physical Protection of Nuclear Material; 1988 Convention for the Suppression of Unlawful Acts against the Safety of Maritime Navigation; 1988 Protocol for the Suppression of Unlawful Acts Against the Safety of Fixed Platforms Located on the Continental Shelf; 1988 Protocol for the Suppression of Unlawful Acts of Violence at Airports Serving International Civil Aviation, supplementary to the Convention for the Suppression of Unlawful Acts against the Safety of Civil Aviation; 1991 Convention on the Marking of Plastic Explosives for the Purpose of Detection; 1997 International Convention for the Suppression of Terrorist Bombings; 1999 International Convention for the Suppression of the Financing of Terrorism; 2005 Protocol to the Protocol for the Suppression of Unlawful Acts Against the Safety of Fixed Platforms located on the Continental Shelf; 2005 Protocol to the Convention for the Suppression of Unlawful Acts against the Safety of Maritime Navigation; 2005 Amendments to the Convention on the Physical Protection of Nuclear Material; 2005 International Convention for the Suppression of Acts of Nuclear Terrorism; 2010 Convention on the Suppression of Unlawful Acts Relating to International Civil Aviation; 2010 Protocol Supplementary to the Convention for the Suppression of Unlawful Seizure of Aircraft; 2014 Protocol to Amend the Convention on Offences and Certain Acts Committed on Board Aircraft. "International Legal Instruments", http://www.un.org/en/counterterrorism/legal-instruments.shtml (Accessed 26.10.2020).

[82] Seung-Whan Choi and Idean Salehyan, "No Good Deed Goes Unpunished: Refugees, Humanitarian Aid, and Terrorism", **Conflict Management and Peace Science**, Vol. 30, No. 1, 2013, p. 53, https://journals.sagepub.com/doi/pdf/10.1177/0738894212456951 (Accessed 26.10.2020).

social, cultural and economic terms, cause political instability of the countries, stands out as one of the most important problems discussed today. There are not many studies in the literature on the impact of refugees on terrorist incidents or the relationship between terrorism and refugees.[83] In a sense, the fact that there are few studies on this subject in the literature makes it both difficult and necessary to examine this field.

In the literature, there are mostly studies within the framework of the relationship between refugees and security, and it is obvious that there is a perception that especially refugees or migrations create problems for the security of states in the historical process.[84] Especially the perception that the perpetrators of 9/11 terrorist attacks were carried out through immigrants/refugees led to the investigation or examination of the connection of refugees with terrorist incidents.[85]

While big and powerful states may have the capacity to control the relationship between immigration and security, it is very difficult for weak states, or especially states with many internal problems, to balance these two elements. Adamson points out this situation as; *"the world's poorest states host most of its refugees, and the uncontrolled flow of refugees or other migrants across borders produces additional stresses on already weak state institutions, heightens competition over scarce resources, and exacerbates ethnic and sectarian tensions."*[86] This situation increases the possibility of ethnic conflict, if it exists within the state. In addition, as Adamson points out, this situation allows the refugees who

---

[83] David Randhal, "Refugees and Terrorism", **PAX et Bellum Journal**, Vol. 3, 2016, p. 46, http://paxetbellum.org/wp-content/uploads/2015/11/Pax-et-Bellum-Journal-Third-Edition-Spring-2016.pdf#page=50 (Accessed 25.10.2020).

[84] Ahmet İçduygu and E. Fuat Keyman, "Globalization, Security and Migration: The Case of Turkey", **Global Governance**, Vol. 6, Issue 3, 2000, https://brill.com/view/journals/gg/6/3/article-p383_6.xml (Accessed 25.10.2020); Sarah Leonard, "EU border security and migration into the European Union: FRONTEX and securitisation through practices", **European Security**, Vol. 19, Issue 2, 2010, https://www.tandfonline.com/doi/full/10.1080/09662839.2010.526937 (Accessed 25.10.2020); Catherine Dauvergne, "Security and Migration Law in the Less Brave New World", **Social and Legal Studies**, Vol. 16, No. 4, 2007, https://journals.sagepub.com/doi/abs/10.1177/0964663907082734 (Accessed 25.10.2020); Elspeth Guild, **Security and Migration in 21st Century**, Cambridge, Polity Press, 2009.; e, Roxanne Lynn Doty, "Immigration and the Politics of Security," Security Studies, Vol. 8, Nos. 2/3 (Winter 1998/99-Spring 1999), pp. 71-93; Myron Weiner (Ed.), **The Global Migration Crisis: Challenges to States and to Human Rights**, New York,Harper Collins, 1995; Jef Huysmans and Vicki Square, "Migration and Security", **The Routledge Handbook of Security Studies**, Myriam Dunn Cavelty and Victor Mauer (Eds.), Oxon, Routledge, 2010; Myron Weiner, "Security, Stability, and International Migration", **International Security**, Vol. 17, No. 3, Winter 1992-1993, pp. 91-126, https://www.jstor.org/stable/2539131?seq=1#metadata_info_tab_contents (Accessed 25.10.2020).

[85] Fiona B. Adamson, "Crossing Borders: International Migration and National Security", **International Security**, Vol. 31, No. 1, Summer, 2006, p. 165, https://www.jstor.org/stable/pdf/4137542.pdf?refreqid =excelsior%3A89555759a0f86340856d7272517857bf (Accessed 25.10.2020); Cory Eybergen & Martin A. Andresen, "Refugees of Conflict, Casualties of Conjecture: "The Trojan Horse Theory of Terrorism and its Implications for Asylum", **Terrorism and Political Violence**, https://www.tandfonline.com/doi/ pdf/10.1080/09546553.2020.1763962?needAccess=true (Accessed 25.10.2020).

[86] Adamson, *op.cit.*, p. 177.

migrate to such countries to be used as refugee-warriors by non-state actors.[87]

While refugees can cause such problems in weak states, some situations can cause problems in big states. For example, it is possible for people who are members of terrorist organizations to go to the countries that will host them together with the refugees who flee from the violence in their country. In addition, members of these organizations may have the capacity to incite refugees against the host state and cause new security problems for the host states.[88]

Murphy states that most of the terrorist attacks in 2014 were carried out in Iraq, Pakistan, Syria, Afghanistan and Nigeria[89], and in general, the citizens of these countries seek refuge in Europe with refugee status. As it can be understood from here, the instability and civil war in the country cause people to flee from their homeland to different countries and take refuge.[90] It seems almost impossible for people trying to escape from a major problem in their own country, such as the terror problem, to directly contribute to terrorism in the host country, but this situation does not prevent refugees from being targeted by terrorist organizations. The fact that most of the time the refugees search for a safe place and that this situation can be used by terrorist organizations in their own interests does not prove that the refugees have a relationship with terrorist incidents. Emmerson, UN Special Rapporteur, states in his statement that there is no evidence that migration increases terrorist activities.[91] However, UN Secretary-General António Guterres, then-UN High Commissioner for Refugees, points out that *"there is little evidence… that terrorists take advantage of refugee flows to carry out acts of terrorism. Such perceptions are analytically and statistically unfounded, and must change."*[92] This statement clearly shows that the states cannot claim refugees in terms of the increase of terrorist activities in their territories.

On the other side, it is important to mention the radicalization of refugees. As Ladbury states that the refugee camps provide suitable grounds for radicalization.[93] Although it is difficult to measure the level of radicalization

---

[87] Ibid.

[88] Elizabeth Ferris and Kemal Kirişçi, **The Consequences of Chaos: Syria's Humanitarian Crisis and the Failure to Protect**, Washington, Brookings Institution Press, 2016, pp. 40-41.

[89] The list has not changed in 2019 and these five countries have the most of the terrorist attacks. For more detail: https://www.visionofhumanity.org/maps/global-terrorism-index/#/ (Accessed 26.10.2020).

[90] Tom Murphy, "Terrorism and refugees are linked, but not how you might think", **Humanosphere**, 2015, https://www.humanosphere.org/world-politics/2015/11/terrorism-refugees-linked-now-might-think/ (Accessed 26.10.2020).

[91] https://refugeesmigrants.un.org/zh/node/100042568 (Accessed 26.10.2020).

[92] https://en.unesco.org/news/correcting-media-myths-about-terrorism (Accessed 26.10.2020).

[93] Sarah Ladbury, "Why Do Men Join the Taliban and Hizb-i Islami? How Much Do Local Communities Support Them?", **Independent Report for the Department of International Development**, 2009, p. 3.

of the refugees, Milton and *et. al.* mention three different factors. First of all, the experience of the refugees stands out as a great depressing situation for them. The refugees left their homes, belongings, maybe their families behind them and come to the host country, in a sense leaving their real lives. This situation can cause physical as well as mental problems for them. On the other hand, the situation of refugee camps, such as health, cleaning, heating, food and education, can cause radicalization of refugees, but it may be a great mistake to think that this can reach the level of terror.[94] The main reason for the low probability of this may be that people fleeing violence in their own countries do not want to be in a new spiral of violence. The main point to be taken into consideration here is whether the country has a terrorist background or is a target of terrorist organizations, as Milton and *et. al.* stated.[95] Because in such a situation, it is also among the possibilities that terrorist organizations may use these situations of refugees and cause them to radicalize. However, it remains uncertain whether this radicalization will reach the terror dimension. Secondly, the pressure exerted by the host state on refugees can also lead to radicalization. The main point here is that the host state has implemented policies for refugees to leave the country instead of finding solutions to the aforementioned problems. Failure to integrate refugees with the local population can also be seen as a sign that new problems may arise in the host country, as it will have a negative effect.[96] Finally, it is the limitation of the political rights of refugees. In particular, most states are not sufficiently politically represented by refugees, increasing the likelihood of finding individual solutions at later levels.[97]

The radicalization that Milton and *et. al.* have mentioned is not only valid for refugees but also for all ethnic groups living in the country. Because, people who think that their ethnic group is not represented sufficiently can carry out various activities individually. Likewise, it is a fact that terrorist organizations carry out activities within the framework of perception operations on different ethnic groups in the country. In this context, it is considered unlikely that the refugees will radicalize in the host country and carry out terrorist activities.

When evaluated in general terms, it is clear that there is no direct relationship between refugees and terrorism in both the literature and official statements. People fleeing violence in their countries are unlikely to be the triggers of new violence. Although the policies and pressure factors applied to refugees, especially in host countries, allow them to radicalize at certain lower levels, it seems quite difficult to state that the refugees are involved in

---

[94] Milton, Spencer & Findley, *op.cit.*, p. 626
[95] *Ibid.*, p. 626
[96] *Ibid.*, p. 627
[97] *Ibid.*, p. 628

terrorist incidents or engage in terrorist activities in the host country.

## Conclusion

As stated in the study, the concepts of both refugee and terrorism have occupied the agenda of the international community for many years and continue to do so. While the refugees are defined as people who have been forced to migrate from their country, it should also be noted that the terrorism problem is the most at the root of this. Especially, as stated in the study, the fact that the countries with the most terrorist incidents are also the countries that cause the most immigration also proves this situation.

It seems almost impossible to have a direct link between refugees and terrorism, as it seems quite difficult for people fleeing violence in their home countries to engage in a new violence in their host countries. On the other hand, this does not mean that individual radical movements will not emerge from among the refugees. It can also be thought that the possibility of radical movements reaching the terror dimension is difficult on an individual basis.

However, it is also possible that terrorist organizations operating within the borders of the host state pursue these refugees. In particular, taking into account the difficult conditions they live in may cause the sub-groups within the refugees to become radicalized, and there is also the possibility of recruiting new soldiers of terrorist organizations from among the refugees. Failure to improve the poor conditions in refugee camps, and even pressure for these refugees to go, may pave the way for radicalization. This situation may create great opportunities for terrorist organizations. Preventing this situation is of great importance for states and the international community.

When evaluated generally, refugees may cause social, cultural, economic and even political problems in the host country, but this does not mean that they increase terrorist incidents. To be clear, these people who have suffered physical and mental destruction also have the right to live like normal people and states and the international community have to take responsibility to fulfill this duty. Today, the perspective of many states, especially the European Union countries, towards refugees may cause major problems in the future. Although there is no link between the refugees and the increase in terrorism at the moment, there is a possibility that the reactions that may occur in the following years may reach this point.

CHAPTER 5

## MENA VERSUS EUROPE: RISING DIMENSIONS OF MEDITERRANEAN MARITIME SECURITY

Burak Şakir Şeker[*] and Hasret Çomak[**]

**Introduction**

The purpose of this study is to highlight all the problems that create instability in the security of the wider Mediterranean region, highlighting both those that remain unresolved over time, as well as those of asymmetric threats, in order to examine whether there is a possibility to overcome and give a new breath to the aforementioned area where growth and prosperity will prevail. In addition, this research investigates how much and in what ways the coastal states from the post-Cold War period until today contributes to achieving this. It should be noted that no other forces (e.g. NATO) or countries (USA) are considered to be active in the region and which in turn help to curb illegal activities other than the Mediterranean countries.

The study discusses in detail the threats and problems that affect the security of the specific geographical area. In particular, the research contains both interstate and transnational armed conflicts and uprisings, which emerged after the post-Cold War period, including those that traditionally pre-existed and continue to concern the international community. Particular emphasis is placed on the new asymmetric threat of terrorism which lists a number of attacks that have occasionally hit major cities in the Mediterranean. Then the new security challenge is analyzed, namely the rapid increase of irregular migration flows. In addition, the illicit trafficking of drugs, weapons and in many cases human souls is reflected, making the Mediterranean the main gateway for these illegal activities.

Besides, principles of law, democracy and human rights, as well as development and prosperity possibilities for the countries of the southern basin in order to achieve stability and security have also been discussed. Finally, the work concludes with results whether security can be achieved in the wider Mediterranean region, what are the thorns that prevent the achievement of the above goals, as well as how much the coastal states' action contributes to these targets.

---


[*] Assoc. Prof., Ankara Hacı Bayram Veli University
[**] Professor, Istanbul Kent University

## MENA and Uprisings

The Mediterranean since the end of the USSR is a field in which strong uprisings continue to exist. One of them, which remains unresolved to this day, is the Palestinian question within the Arab-Israeli relation which is the most significant one in the duration of the post-war regional conflict. In particular, the two peoples, the Palestinians and the Jews, are claiming the same territory, that of Palestine. It began to take on global proportions in 1917 and from 1948, when the state of Israel was founded, it began to intensify with the outbreak of the First Arab-Israeli War. A few years later in 1956, the president of Egypt, in his attempt to play a leading role in the Arab world of the Middle East as well as in the expulsion of the colonial powers from the region, decided after a series of actions such as the nationalization of the Suez Canal. So the Suez Crisis broke out, a major political turning point in the modern political history of the Middle East, where France and Britain, the two most powerful European powers in cooperation with Israel, intervened in Egypt using military force to overthrow its president, Jamal Abd al-Nasser. The result was that between October 2 and November 7 of the same year, the Israeli army occupied the Sinai Peninsula, while a French-British paratrooper brigade occupied the northern entrance to Suez. At the same time, French-British warships besieged Port Said, while French-British aircraft bombed Egyptian airports. The above-mentioned conflict stopped after a UN decision and intense pressure from both the USA as well as the USSR, additionally bringing 3,000 dead, 5,000 wounded and 20,000 prisoners on the Egyptian side, while for the attackers 258 dead and 1,100 wounded. Although Egypt was defeated, the above result highlighted the rise of Arab nationalism with the Egyptian president playing a leading role while Britain and France suffered a major political and diplomatic defeat, losing even their prestige as the Great Powers.[1]

Then, in 1967, the Palestinian issue would come to the fore again, where another war broke out between Israel and the three Arab countries, Egypt, Syria and Jordan, which lasted only six days. The result allowed Israeli forces to occupy the West Bank, East Jerusalem, the Golan Heights, the Gaza Strip and the Sinai Peninsula (later returned to Egypt after a peace treaty). The Six Day War shown that the Palestinian question is not the result of Arab nationalism, as the cause of its onset was not solely the two peoples, but the sharp confrontation between the two most powerful Arab states in the Middle East, Syria and Egypt with Israel.[2]

This will be followed by another armed conflict between the two countries

---

[1] Fitzsimons, M. A. "The Suez Crisis and the Containment Policy." *The Review of Politics*, vol. 19, no. 4, 1957, pp. 419–445.

[2] Berry, M., & Philo, G., "1967: The Six-Day War." Israel and Palestine: Competing Histories, by Mike Berry and Greg Philo, Pluto Press, London; Ann Arbor, MI, 2006, pp. 43–52.

in 1973 with the Yom Kippur War, where with the agreement at Camp David, Israel manages to consolidate its integrity. The result was the relocation of the Palestine Liberation Organization (PLO) headquarters to Lebanon, where in June 1982 Israeli forces invaded southern Lebanon, bombed the city of Beirut, and carried out hundreds of massacres in Palestine and Satila. Despite the UN Security Council's attempt to find a peaceful solution to the conflict, systematic repression, assassinations, annexation of Israeli forces in the heart of the Palestine resulted in 1987 being the first an Arab uprising also known as the Intifada. The first Intifada, despite intense efforts to suppress Israeli forces, ended in August 1993 with the Oslo Accords.[3]

After the Oslo Accords, although negotiations continued, many issues remained unresolved, such as East Jerusalem and the numerous Jewish settlers in the West Bank. As a result, a second Intifada broke out in September 2003, ended in late 2004 /early 2005 with 5,300 Palestinians dead and 1,000 Israelis. Afterwards 34-day war (July 12, 2006) is emerged between Israeli forces and Hezbollah in Lebanon and northern Israel and the number of civilian casualties and refugees almost quadrupled. This will be followed by a series of military operations by the Israeli side in the Gaza Strip, culminating in Operation "Protective Edge" in the summer of 2014, leaving behind incalculable costs of human losses, refugees and infrastructure. As a result, that can be said that the Palestinian question can be seen as an issue with deep roots in time and an uncertain future.[4]

Another important issue that has occupied the wider Mediterranean region has begun in 2010 after the self-immolation of Tunisian Mohamed Bouazizi as a result of protests against oppression and living conditions which launched a series of kinematic processes aimed at overthrowing authoritarian regimes in the Maghreb and the Middle East. These uprisings were originally called the "Arab Spring" and these uprisings consisted of several factors that were not religious but mainly social. The long stay in power of certain individuals in connection with the oppression and unjust distribution of wealth has resulted in the creation of poverty, impoverishment, oppression and many times the violation of human dignity, which strengthened the voices of protest for the arrival of something new. The "Arab Spring" originally started in Tunisia and within a few weeks spread to Egypt, Yemen, Bahrain, Libya and Syria. In addition, in other countries there were large demonstrations, while in others, there were simply small protest organizations.[5]

---

[3] Falk, R., "Oslo Diplomacy: A Legal Historical Perspective." Palestine's Horizon: Toward a Just Peace, by Richard Falk, Pluto Press, London, 2017, pp. 10–21.
[4] Kattan, Victor. "The Implications of Joining the ICC after Operation Protective Edge." *Journal of Palestine Studies*, vol. 44, no. 1, 2014, pp. 61–73.
[5] Ghanem, H., "Roots of the Arab Spring." The Arab Spring Five Years Later: Toward Greater

As a result, authoritarian leaders who remained in power for years were forced to step down because of these uprisings, such as Hosni Mubarak in Egypt and Zine El Abidine Ben Ali in Tunisia. On the contrary, on October 20, 2011, the civil conflict in Libya resulted with the death of Colonel Muammar al-Gaddafi, who ruled Libya for 42 whole years. Nevertheless, while one would expect the Arab Spring to usher in a new era of democratization in North Africa and the Middle East, the result is disappointing as countries that were previously at least functional before failed. Libya, Syria and Yemen are plagued by anarchy, lawlessness and civil strife. In addition, other countries like Egypt, Bahrain returned to a worse state than before or returned to the previous regime before the uprising. The only exception country that seems to be moving into a relatively new smooth and stable state is Tunisia.[6]

Although the "Arab Spring" ended in most countries relatively soon after its inception, Syria and Yemen continue to occupy world events where they are raging from civil wars. The Syrian issue in particular, while beginning as a political, racial and religious confrontation, has turned into a proxy war where broader geopolitical interests are at stake. In particular, the conflict is between the regime of Bashar al-Assad and substitutes. In terms of religious strife, the predominant religion in Syria is Muslim and predominantly Sunni, but al-Assad's family is Alawite (a Shiite sect) which is a minority. From the earliest stages of the Syrian crisis, many groups arrived on Syrian soil where they began to exert increased military and ideological influence in the scattered camp fighting against government forces.[7]

The fact that Russia, Iran and Iraq, for their own reasons are on the side of the Ba'athist regime, as opposed to the Western powers, which want to overthrow the regime but have not taken any important decisions and initiatives to intervene, shows that the Syrian issue is getting wider. Moreover, the Kurds living in Syria saw it as an opportunity to achieve something similar to what the Kurds had done in Iraq, namely the creation of a quasi-state within the Syrian reality, a fact that comes into conflict with Turkey. The solution to the Syrian drama seems uncertain in the near future, what is certain is that, whatever regime prevails, it will not be able to impose itself on the whole territory, because different ethnic and religious groups live there and it will be even more difficult to reshape it deeply. The result so far is that from March 15, 2011 until today, the death toll has exceeded 400,000 and half of the population has been displaced, leaving the country completely

---

Inclusiveness, by Hafez Ghanem, Brookings Institution Press, Washington, D.C., 2016, pp. 39–64.

[6] Yahya, Maha. *Great Expectations in Tunisia.* Carnegie Endowment for International Peace, 2016, p. 1-44.

[7] Martin, Kevin W. "Syria and Iraq: ISIS and Other Actors in Historical Context." *The Future of ISIS: Regional and International Implications,* edited by Feisal Al-Istrabadi and Sumit Ganguly, Brookings Institution Press, Washington, D.C., 2018, pp. 89–118.

devastated.[8]

## Roots of the Terrorism and Piracy as a threat against the Stability of the Mediterranean

Terrorism is the poisonous fruit of many forces. It can be the weapon of the weak in a classic conflict between states or within a state. In addition, it can be perceived as a product of globalization as it can take on supranational dimensions using a variety of media. A manifestation of modern terrorist activity, which has particularly preoccupied the countries of the northern Mediterranean basin and consequently the EU, is the manifestations of social extremism. The range of organizations that express social violence and which do not lack an ideological background displaying characteristics similar to those of the far right.[9]

In Western Europe, 3 years after the terrorist attack of September 11, 2001 in the heart of New York, an event that changed the page of global security, for the first time suffered a terrorist attack that killed hundreds of civilians. On March 11, 2004, two days before the Spanish elections, 192 people were tragically killed and about 1,800 injured after 10 bombs exploded in three police stations in Madrid. The terrorist attack in the Spanish capital was seen as retaliation for the country's involvement in the Iraq war, which had 1,400 troops. In May of the same year they withdrew after the rise of the anti-war Socialist Party in government.[10]

France has been the target of a number of terrorist attacks in recent years, listing a large number of victims from DAESH. A terrorist group killed more than 130 people and injured another 350 in Paris, including the Bataclan concert hall and the courtyards of many bars and restaurants and the Stade de France on November 13, 2015. The attack was carried out by the Islamic State from members who had returned from Syria. The following year, on July 14, the driver of a truck, drove into a crowd in Nice on the Cote d'Azur, where they had gathered for celebration of Bastille Day. As a result, 86 people lost their lives and more than 400 were injured. The question that arises is why this country in Europe is a pole of attraction from such attacks? The answer could be that French government does not represents a more general set of values especially in the field of religion.[11]

---

[8] Anthony, Ian. Addressing the Threat Posed by Chemical Weapons: Accountability and Disarmament. Stockholm International Peace Research Institute, 2020, in Strengthening Global Regimes: Addressing the Threat Posed by Chemical Weapons, pp. 1–6.

[9] Hutchinson, Jade. "Far-Right Terrorism: The Christchurch Attack and Potential Implications on the Asia Pacific Landscape." *Counter Terrorist Trends and Analyses*, vol. 11, no. 6, 2019, pp. 19–28.

[10] Rose, William, et al. "Does Terrorism Ever Work? The 2004 Madrid Train Bombings." *International Security*, vol. 32, no. 1, 2007, pp. 185–192.

[11] Soliev, Nodirbek, and Mohammed Sinan Siyech. "Terrorist Attacks: The Politics of Claiming

Another terrorist attack that hit a Western European country is Portugal. Specifically, on August 17, 2017, a van crashed at speed on pedestrians where it dragged them for several meters in the Ramblas area in the center of Barcelona. The result was 13 dead and 50 wounded.[12]

On the other hand, the Muslim country that has been targeted many times by terrorists is Turkey. In particular, Istanbul, received dozens of terrorist attacks while more than 200 people for that year, in 2016, lost their lives and hundreds were injured. The targets were mainly areas with a strong human presence of both Turkish nationals and tourists. The following year, with its opening on January 1, a nightclub became the target, leaving 39 dead and 70 injured.[13]

It is noteworthy that some of the members of the DAESH come from European countries, also known as "foreign fighters". Essentially, these are second and third generation immigrants, regardless of gender and social status for the sake of seeking a more radical model of life, they initiate Salafism. The result of the above is Iraq and more Syria to be formed as a jihadist International. From the beginning of the Syrian issue, 20% of the "foreign fighters" come from Western Europe. It is characteristic that the largest representation comes from France and then from Great Britain and Germany, which is even more problematic, as these countries are often the targets of bombings by people who were born, lived and many times educated by them.[14]

Finally, as far as modern piracy is concerned, there is no evidence that countries bordering the Mediterranean are taking such actions. Nevertheless, the sea route from the Mediterranean to Southeast Asia and vice versa, part of which handles 15% of world maritime trade, is being hit by modern pirates as they operate in the Red Sea and especially in Somalia. The main target is mainly merchant ships and fishing vessels as they carry goods, which can be sold directly on the black market. On the other hand, attacks on cruise ships are almost negligible.[15]

---

Responsibility." *Counter Terrorist Trends and Analyses*, vol. 8, no. 8, 2016, pp. 17–21.

[12] Ballesteros, Alberto. "Counter-Terrorism Efforts in Spain." *Counter Terrorist Trends and Analyses*, vol. 10, no. 11, 2018, pp. 9–13.

[13] Soliev, Nodirbek. "The Terrorist Threat in Turkey: A Dangerous New Phase." Counter Terrorist Trends and Analyses, vol. 9, no. 4, 2017, pp. 24–29.

[14] Hamming, Tore. "Is the Islamic State Islamic or Not? The Discursive Struggle to Define the Islamic State." *St Antony's International Review*, vol. 12, no. 1, 2016, pp. 38–52.

[15] Polepalli, Sindhura Natesha. "Floating Armories and Privately Contracted Armed Security Personnel on Board Ships: Balancing Coastal State Security Concerns Against Navigational Freedom." *The Journal of Territorial and Maritime Studies*, vol. 6, no. 2, 2019, pp. 68–93.

## Crisis Definition: Irregular-Illegal Migration, Migrant Smuggling, Human-Drug-Weapon Trafficking

According to the UN High Commissioner for Refugees, 2015 is characterized as global record of people movement. For the Mediterranean region alone, one million people crossed the Mediterranean in 2015, either legally or illegally. After all, the Mediterranean is one of the corridors used by migratory waves to Europe and the rest of the world to survival and a better tomorrow.[16]

Outbreaks appear to be exacerbated in the Middle East (Syria, Iraq, and Yemen), Libya, Eritrea, Somalia, sub-Saharan Africa, and the undoubted war in Syria. Official data from Eurostat (European Statistical Office) show that for the past year it was found that 601,500 people remain illegally in the EU within the EU Member States. Of these Member States, the four countries with the largest number 68.4% (compared to the rest of the EU) are Germany (134,000), France (105,900), Greece (93,400) and Spain (78,300).[17]

In this regard, it should be noted that the specific number of illegal immigrants is reduced by 2.8% compared to 2017 and by 72.1% compared to the record level of 2015. In addition to the above figures it should be emphasized that the number of people who may have entered illegally and not been recorded, the number of those who were prevented from entering illegally at the last minute and the number of people who lost their lives in the attempt to enter illegally, which proves that this phenomenon has larger dimensions. As can be seen from the above, the countries that shoulder the largest wave of irregular influx of migrants are the Mediterranean countries and especially those of the Northern Mediterranean basin, as due to their geopolitical position, it makes them vulnerable to this type of activity.[18]

In addition, in the five years 2013-2018, according to official Eurostat data, we see that most illegal immigrants who are registered as "illegal" in EU Member States and have not been granted refugee or subsidiary protection status come from the following countries: First is Morocco, followed by Ukraine, third is Iraq followed by Albania and in the last five comes Syria. From the above one can see that with the exception of Iraq and more of Syria affected by civil armed conflict, the inhabitants of the other countries who entered illegally seem to have a purely economic purpose and not to protect the integrity of their lives. As for the Syrians, because of the violence of the

---

[16] UNHCR, Worldwide displacement hits all-time high as war and persecution increase. https://www.unhcr.org/news/latest/2015/6/558193896/worldwide-displacement-hits-all-time-high-war-persecution-increase.html (Retrieved 05.01.2021)

[17] EU, Immigration law enforcement in the EU. https://ec.europa.eu/eurostat/web/products-eurostat-news/-/DDN-20190712-1?inheritRedirect=true&redirect=%2Feurostat%2F (Retrieved 03.01.2021)

[18] EU, Enforcement of immigration legislation statistics. https://ec.europa.eu/eurostat/statistics-explained/index.php/Enforcement_of_immigration_legislation_statistics (Retrieved 06.01.2021)

DAESH and the government in imposing its own way of life, they were forced to leave their homes and try to save their lives.[19]

On the one hand, the usually poor living conditions in the refugee camps especially in Greece, which has left many of others at sea to the death, are pushing the Syrians to illegal immigration to EU countries. It should be added that due to the Dublin Regulations, the asylum seeker is "tied" to the country to which he / she has applied, as only in that other Member States may travel for tourism purposes for a period not exceeding six months. More specifically, the asylum application must be submitted to the first EU member state that receives the potential refugee. So if you want to be granted asylum in Sweden, you must first register and identify yourself and, consequently, apply for refugee status within that country and not in another country.[20]

Being unable to obtain a visa, in order to be in the country of his choice for recognition as a refugee, means being illegal for living and passage. A typical example is the "Balkan Corridor" created from April 2015 to March 2016, where many immigrants entered Greece, continued through Northern Macedonia and tried not to be registered until they arrived in the countries of their choice, such as Germany, Austria or Sweden to submit their first formal application.[21]

The followings are illegal immigration corridors used to prevent third-country nationals from entering the EU illegally across the Mediterranean. The first corridor is the so-called Eastern Mediterranean and concerns the passage by sea from Turkey to Europe. Usually the citizens who use the above corridor are from Afghanistan, Syria, Turkey, Iraq and Palestine. The next corridor is the Central Mediterranean and residents from Tunisia, Pakistan, Algeria, Sudan and Cote d'Ivoire, where they try to enter Europe by sea from Libya. The last corridor is from the Western Mediterranean and is used by Moroccans, Guineans, Mali, Algerians and Ivory Coast nationals from Morocco in order to enter EU countries by sea.[22]

Trafficking in human beings is one of the most lucrative forms of organized crime, generating billions of euros for traffickers each year. Most victims of human trafficking come from sub-Saharan Africa, especially from West Africa, Nigeria, Cameroon, Ghana, Guinea, Cote d'Ivoire and Sierra Leone, i.e. poor countries with high unemployment and through the

---

[19] EU, Migration and migrant population statistics. https://ec.europa.eu/eurostat/statistics-explained/index.php/Migration_and_migrant_population_statistics (Retrieved 02.01.2021)

[20] EU, Glossary:Asylum applicant. https://ec.europa.eu/eurostat/statistics-explained/index.php/Glossary:Asylum_applicant (Retrieved 04.01.2021)

[21] Edmonda. A. "Migrations' Changing Scenario: the New Balkan Route and the European Union." *Rivista Di Studi Politici Internazionali*, vol. 85, no. 2 (338), 2018, pp. 189–206.

[22] Rolando, Francesco, and Paolo Naso. "Humanitarian Corridors to Italy" *Harvard International Review*, vol. 39, no. 2, 2018, pp. 64–67.

Mediterranean Sea (West Road, Main Road and East Road) have as final destination one of the EU countries. Especially from Nigeria, a large number of young girls, some of whom are minors supplied for the European sex market, in particular, the victims are sold by poor communities, where families struggle to survive in traffickers or they are approached by being offered a better paid job in an EU country and then promoted to Libya or Morocco. They then move to Italy and to a lesser extent to Spain where they end up in brothels. It is noteworthy that during this whole journey they are either sold to other smugglers or raped, and many times they are brutally beaten in order to force them to accept this particular way of life. Another large group of victims of human trafficking are children. Most of them leave war and conflict, poverty, natural disasters, coercion and recruitment, or are separated from their families, seeking refuge for a better life in an EU country. Upon arrival in Europe, these children are the perfect target for unscrupulous traffickers, as their young age, inexperience, innocence and desire to start work or further education makes them vulnerable and easily manipulated, which exposes them to a serious risk of exploitation.[23]

With regard to the trafficking of illegal weapons, their transit differs from that of human trafficking. The focus of the above action for the Mediterranean Sea is North Africa and in particular Libya. In addition, a large number of illegal weapons and explosive devices are trafficked through the Balkan countries. Especially since 2011 with the fall of the Gaddafi regime, a number of small arms, surface-to-air missiles, RPG launchers, anti-personnel mines, grenades and ammunition have been launched on the black market in the hands of terrorist groups in Syria, Libya, Egypt, Tunisia, Algeria and Lebanon. In Europe, most of the illegal weapons come from the Balkans and have been used in many cases of terrorist attacks.[24]

Finally, in relation to drug trafficking, it is estimated that around 125 tonnes of cocaine, worth of € 27 billion, are consumed in Europe. Most of it comes from Latin America through North and West Africa, where they end up in European countries. The bulk of the volume is transported by sea and in particular by maritime transport containers. An additional 80 tonnes of Afghan heroin is smuggled into Western and Central Europe via the Balkan Corridor and through the Southern Corridor. As for the Southern Corridor, it is a network that extends from Afghanistan through Pakistan, the Persian Gulf, the Indian Ocean and East Africa. It then crosses the Mediterranean

---

[23] Dean, L. "Contrasting Policy Approaches to Human Trafficking in Eurasia." Diffusing Human Trafficking Policy in Eurasia, by Laura A. Dean, 1st ed., Bristol University Press, Bristol, 2020, pp. 23–46.
[24] Clarke, Colin P. Small Arms and Light Weapons (SALW) Trafficking, Smuggling, and Use for Criminality by Terrorists and Insurgents: A Brief Historical Overview. International Centre for Counter-Terrorism, 2020, pp. 3-14.

Sea in various alternative ways and ends up in Europe.[25]

## Progress of The EU's Approach to the Both Regional and Global Challenges

In this regard, when take into consideration all challenges, EU has understood that it should not be left out of the international community, especially when the victims are civilians and the security of the wider region is at stake. Mediterranean region with the Balkans changing, with conflicts in the Middle East remaining unresolved, with illegal immigration and with the rise of terrorism especially after the events of 9/11, the EU fears that the danger is just around the corner and the only solution is joint action by all Member States. The main threats to the EU listed in the European Security Strategy include the proliferation of weapons of mass destruction, terrorism and organized crime, cyber security, energy security and climate change. In addressing these challenges, the EU is using both political and military means in various countries in Europe, Asia and Africa.

European Security Strategy first sought to resolve the Middle East through its role in the Quartet (UN, US, Russia and EU), as well as its cooperation with Israel and the Palestinian Authority, the Arab League and other regional partners. In addition, it was fully involved in the 2007 Annapolis process for a two-state solution, and provided ongoing financial and budgetary support to the Palestinian Authority, as well as support for infrastructure, including the deployment of experts in the field of justice, police and of border management. Finally, the EU participated with the reinforcement of military forces in the operation "UNIFIL", which had the mission of sea and air control outside the territorial waters of Lebanon (12 NM) in the context of a ban on the movement of illegal weapons and related materials to Lebanon. Finally, it should be noted that this strategy was adopted until June 2016 as it succeeded the EU Global Strategy on Foreign and Security Policy.[26]

New strategy, entitled 'Common Vision, Joint Actions: A Stronger Europe', set out and analyzed a strategic vision for the EU's global role. For the Mediterranean and the Middle East in particular, it stressed that the immediate priority is to resolve conflicts and promote development and human rights in order to tackle terrorism, the demographic problem, migration and climate change in the region, as well as the creating the achievement of a common prosperity. It pointed out that the EU will support

---

[25] Mandić, D. "Middle East." Gangsters and Other Statesmen: Mafias, Separatists, and Torn States in a Globalized World, by Danilo Mandić, Princeton University Press, PRINCETON; OXFORD, 2021, pp. 124–145.

[26] Cordesman, Anthony H., and Grace Hwang. *The Military Dynamics of the Arab-Israel Confrontation States.* Center for Strategic and International Studies (CSIS), 2020, pp. 54–80.

cooperation with all regional organizations in Africa and the Middle East. Encourages practical cooperation on issues such as border security, trafficking in human beings, the fight against terrorism, non-proliferation of weapons of mass destruction, food and water security, energy and climate, and the management of infrastructure and natural disasters. It also stressed that EU would step up dialogue and negotiations on regional conflicts in Syria and Libya. With regard to the Palestinian issue, it again aims to resolve it through the Quartet, the Arab League and key stakeholders in order to reach a viable international solution based on the 1967 guidelines. Finally, it seeks to deepen sectoral cooperation (education, energy and transport) with Turkey and to conduct a coherent dialogue on the fight against terrorism, regional security and the refugee issue.[27]

Aiming to have safe and clean seas around it, as it promotes prosperity and peace, the EU has drawn up a plan to maintain a generally satisfactory level of maritime safety and to protect its maritime strategic interests in areas beyond national law enhancing:

* overall security and peace,

* the rule of law and freedom of navigation,

* external border control,

* maritime infrastructure such as ports, coast guard, commercial facilities, submarine pipelines and cables, offshore platforms and scientific equipment,

* common natural resources and environmental health and

* climate change preparedness.[28]

As a result, in June 2014 the European Council approved the European Union Maritime Security Strategy (EUMSS), which covers the entire maritime sector in order to effectively address security challenges at sea through the cooperation of military and civilian authorities at international, European and national levels.In addition, the above strategy links internal and external security, and combines overall European maritime safety with integrated maritime policy. It is essentially a broader maritime safety strategy that covers all the challenges of the global maritime sector (e.g. piracy, illegal immigration, etc.) which could affect individuals, activities or infrastructure in the EU. It will help the EU with its Member States to use all available

---

[27] EU, Shared Vision, Common Action: A Stronger Europe. https://eeas.europa.eu/archives/docs/top_stories/pdf/eugs_review_web.pdf (Retrieved: 03.01.2021)
[28] EU, Maritime security strategy. https://ec.europa.eu/maritimeaffairs/policy/maritime-security_en (Retrieved: 03.01.2021)

resources and join more established international partnerships, in order to defend the above. [29]

The result of the above strategy was the preparation of the EU Maritime Safety Action Plan (EUMSS Action Plan) in December of the same year. In more detail, this Plan consists of a series of 130 actions within time frames. The above actions are categorized into five Areas of Implementation as follows:[30]

* External action where the EU acts to contribute to maritime security by using a range of political, economic and military tools,

* Maritime vigilance Environment (Maritime Security Awareness / MSA),

* Capability Development of the Member States,

* Crisis Management, Infrastructure Protection, Crisis Response,

* Research, Technology, Innovation, Training, Practice.

* Achieving the aforementioned is based on 4 principles:

* Firstly in the intersectoral approach, which is fulfilled through all the competent bodies (Political - Military Authorities) of the Member States.

* The second principle is that of functional integration, which is achieved with the existing regime of sovereignty.

* The third principle is full compliance with and respect for both international law and the United Nations Convention on the Law of the Sea (UNCLOS). In particular, the EU and its Member States argue that any dispute in the maritime space should be settled in accordance with UNCLOS and the relevant International Courts of Justice.

* The last principle is multilateralism, where cooperation and coordination with the UN and NATO is necessary.[31]

In addition, the main naval forces operating in the Central and Eastern Mediterranean, with the possibility of intervention beyond the wider region

---

[29] EU, Responding Together To Global Challenges. https://ec.europa.eu/maritimeaffairs/sites/maritimeaffairs/files/leaflet-european-union-maritime-security-strategy_en.pdf (Retrieved: 02.01.2021)
[30] EU, European Union Maritime Security Strategy (EUMSS) Action Plan. https://ec.europa.eu/maritimeaffairs/sites/maritimeaffairs/files/2018-06-26-eumss-revised-action-plan_en.pdf (Retrieved: 05.01.2021)
[31] Tardy, Thierry, and Gustav Lindstrom, *The Scope of EU-NATO Cooperation*. NATO Defense College, 2019, pp. 5–14.

of the EU Member States, have as their main mission the following:[32]

* Maritime Defense for the purpose of protection of the maritime lines and the sovereign rights of the Member States (e.g. EEZ).

* Maritime security operations (MSO) in order to combat terrorism, the proliferation of weapons of mass destruction (WMD) and to reduce illegal immigration, piracy and criminal cross-border activities,

* Crisis response operations (CRO),

* Maritime diplomacy.

In 2018, the EU voted on the revised Maritime Safety Action Plan to ensure that the maritime strategy meets current and future challenges in the light of ever-changing align with the EU Global Strategy, the renewed EU Internal Security Strategy 2015-2020, the Council Conclusions on Global Maritime Safety and the Joint Communication on International Ocean Governance. More specifically, the revised action plan compared to 2014 focuses more on maritime security in the field of terrorist, hybrid, biological, chemical, nuclear and cyber threats and at the same time seeks to address global challenges through regional peripheral solutions for maritime needs at European level (Mediterranean and Black Sea) as well as internationally (Gulf of Guinea, Horn of Africa - Red Sea or Southeast Asia). In conclusion, one can see that the EU is beginning to make important decisions using even a strong naval force in order to contribute both to the security of the both neighbouring and global seas.[33]

So, European Council decided to set up an EU-led naval force, called EUNAVFOR MED, in a joint effort by Member States to tackle illegal immigration and dismantle trafficking and smuggling networks in the wider region of the Mediterranean in May 2015. The above-mentioned operation beginned with the main mission of locating, arresting, controlling, immobilizing and seizing vessels that are used or suspected of being used by smugglers or traffickers, as well as rescuing refugees and migrants from the sea in order to prevent further loss of life in the South - Central Mediterranean.[34]

Operation SOPHIA (new definition of renamed EUNAVFOR MED)

---

[32] Pejsova, Eva. *The EU As A Maritime Security Provider.* European Union Institute for Security Studies (EUISS), 2019, pp. 1-8.

[33] EU, Global Maritime Security. https://www.consilium.europa.eu/media/24000/st10238en17-conclusions-on-global-maritime-security.pdf (Retrieved: 05.01.2021)

[34] Strauch, Paul. "When Stopping the Smuggler Means Repelling the Refugee: International Human Rights Law and the European Union's Operation To Combat Smuggling in Libya's Territorial Sea." *The Yale Law Journal*, vol. 126, no. 8, 2017, pp. 2421–2448.

had 4 phases:

* The first step was to develop the forces in order to identify the activities and methods of the smugglers in order to better understand how they operate.

* The second phase was aiming at the active and operational part of the plan with the boarding, search, seizure and diversion of smuggling vessels on the high seas in accordance with the provisions of international law of the sea. This phase may be extended to the coastal zone of the coastal states following a decision by the UN Security Council and the consent of the former.

* The third phase extended the previous phase as it is possible to seize ships and related assets suspected of being used for smuggling or trafficking in human beings, arresting smugglers and traffickers within the territory of coastal states, taking into account the mandate of the United Nations and the coastal states.

* Finally, the fourth and last phase concerned the withdrawal of forces and the completion of the operation.[35]

Operation SOPHIA, following a decision of the European Council, had undertaken additional tasks, the training of the Libyan Coast Guard and Navy as well as the implementation of the UN decisions on arms embargo in the international waters off the coast of Libya:

* Establishment of a trainee monitoring mechanism to ensure the long-term effectiveness of the Libyan Coast Guard training,

* Conducting new surveillance activities and gathering information on the illicit trafficking of oil exports from Libya in implementation of UNSC resolutions 2146 (2014) and 2362 (2017),

* Strengthening the possibility of exchanging information on trafficking in human beings with the State Police Services of all members, FRONTEX and EUROPOL.[36]

High Representative of the Union for Foreign Affairs and Security Policy, Josep Borrell, raised the issue of the use of this operation in Libya with the 27 EU Foreign Ministers, in an effort to monitoring of the ceasefire agreement as well as the UN arms embargo imposed on Libya at the Berlin Conference on 20 January 2020, but he failed. Operation currently ongoing,

---

[35] Marcuzzi, Stefano. *NATO-EU Maritime Cooperation: for What Strategic Effect?* NATO Defense College, 2018, pp. 1-4.
[36] Nissen, Christine, et al. *EU Security and Defence Policy.* Danish Institute for International Studies, 2020, pp. 25–39.

as a replacement, is IRINI. By launching a new CSDP (Common Security and Defense Policy) and military operation in the Mediterranean, the European Union has stepped up its efforts to implement the UN arms embargo on Libya and thus has wanted to contribute to the peace process in the country. IRINI (Greek "peace") to be the implementation of the UN arms embargo through the use of air, satellite and sea vehicles as its main task. The Mission would be able to inspect ships that are on high seas off Libya and suspected of carrying weapons or related supplies to Libya, in accordance with United Nations Security Council Resolution 2292. However, the neutrality of the operation, especially towards French ships while they are supporting opposition groups in Libya, is questioned. In addition, the illegal intervention of the Turkish ship by the operation command has damaged the legal basis of the operation.[37]

## Conclusion

With the end of the Cold War, the concept of security is constantly under revision, having shifted from traditional issues of military threats to a state's territorial integrity to so-called asymmetric threats such as organized crime, drug trafficking, irregular immigration and terrorism. The Mediterranean, home to three continents, the poorest, richest and most densely populated on the planet, is home to a wide range of criminal networks, including drug and arms smuggling, irregular migration and, in many cases, marketing of human life itself. The above action starts mainly in the southern Mediterranean basin, where criminal organizations are exploiting weak governments, endemic corruption and poverty, huge borders, which do not even have the basic security conditions, as well as limited regional and transnational coordination, which can not take the necessary action to combat the above activities.

As a result, the countries of the northern basin, which mostly belong to the EU, face a number of criminal acts on a daily basis, which disrupt their security systems. These should include the deep-rooted and unresolved problem of the Palestinian question and the Arab-Israeli conflict, which is a destabilizing factor in consolidating peace, security and development in the wider Middle East and, to a lesser extent, in the wider Mediterranean region. The Arab Spring of 2011, while expecting to bring more democracies to Arab countries, only succeeded in creating failed States, where human rights are violated more than ever, armed conflicts in Libya and Syria have been raging to this day. These uprisings with the direct result of all this to make the Mediterranean the main reservoir of sending and receiving migrants. The Syrian issue in particular, which has taken on a multifaceted dimension, has

---

[37] Megerisi, Tarek. *Geostrategic Dimensions of Libya's Civil War.* Africa Center for Strategic Studies, 2020, pp. 1-9.

caused the largest migration crisis since the end of World War II, displacing some 6 million people in Syria. It is noteworthy that most of the Syrian refugees are hosted inside Turkey (approximately 4 million), while most of them rejected or misbehaved by EU countries, plus, lack of appropriate EU financial assistance.

Nevertheless, on the one hand, the EU has been trying to increase its political caliber in the international arena, on the other hand it has not seem possible to consolidate growth and prosperity in the southern Mediterranean basin. Additional issues such as the Palestinian issue, Libyan and Syrian internal wars remain unresolved, proving that these policies simply remained at a declarative level.

After all, prospect of integrating the Mediterranean presents also problems:

* First, there are different economic systems and dynamics (large disparities in per capita income and exports).

* Second, there are major differences between the three major religious traditions.

* Third, the possible creation of a "Mediterranean regional identification", based on economic cooperation, will be considered suspicious by the Mediterranean partners.

* Fourth, the possibility of Mediterranean regional integration is inextricably linked to the evolution of the Middle East Roadmap.

It is clear that, in view of the above, the EU now has other priorities of greater importance, such as security and stability in this area through fight against illegal immigration, drug and arms trafficking etc. At the same time prosperity, development and advocacy of human rights in these countries are moving towards a more 'gentle' approach, of limited scope and effectiveness. So far, with the development of operations under its operational control, in an effort to protect its external borders, the EU has made a partial contribution to the security and suppression of challenges in the wider Mediterranean region.

In conclusion, the security perspective in the Mediterranean, so far, does not seem to be largely met, as the Mediterranean basin continues to be a geostrategic region with complex sources of destabilization, endangering both regional and international stability. The most important issues that need to be addressed immediately are the collapse of failed states, the rise of terrorist organizations and related activities, the dispersal of all types of weapons, the security of both energy resources and their transportation, and, of course, the perpetuating economic hardship, which in combination with the galloping demographic growth is boosting migration flows. Finally, the need to avoid regional tensions in the Mediterranean and not turn them into conflicts becomes more urgent, always taking into account the trends that are developing on the international chessboard, while the existing ones must be kept to a minimum, if not eliminated.

CHAPTER 6

# THE IMPACT OF FOOD INSECURITY ON MIGRATION AND CONFLICT IN THE HORN OF AFRICA

Mehmet Cem Oğultürk[*]

## Introduction

The Horn of Africa is a region of Somalia, Djibouti, Ethiopia, and Eritrea but it covers an area of 5.2 million square kilometers in terms of political and economic impact, reaching also to Sudan, South Sudan, Kenya, and Uganda. The biggest explanation is that the Horn of Africa is situated in the most strategic location in the East African region. At the same time, the region situated in the southwest of the Red Sea and the Gulf of Aden is acting as a corridor for global maritime transport.

The Horn of Africa can be identified in Africa, but not even in the world, as the poorest and most vulnerable region where it has been characterized by economic threats, internal conflicts, and political instability despite its potential natural resources and geopolitical strategic role. Despite the war, economic crisis, migration, refugee crisis, drought, hunger, unemployment, and infectious diseases in the Horn of Africa, the region has not lost its character as a global center of attention even after the colonial era. Both of these states share social and cultural rituals stemming from a century-old tradition of interrelationship, shared religious beliefs, and economic links. Moreover, the political fate of every state in the region has always been indissolubly related to the neighboring countries.

The majority of the population in the region does not have the most necessities of life (clean water, food, health care, and education). The Horn of Africa is among the lowest in the world with per capita income, life expectancy, and education, while mortality rates for adults and children are among the highest. The region is also vulnerable to deadly droughts that hinder agricultural and livestock production. The food deficit caused by droughts makes the Horn of Africa one of the most food-insecure regions in the world every year. In 2019, more than 15,3 million people were requesting humanitarian assistance in the Horn of Africa.[1]

---

[*] PhD, Guest Lecturer at National Defence University, Atatürk Institute of Strategic Studies, cogulturk@gmail.com, ORCID ID: 0000-0003-2619-9559.
[1] UN Dispatch, "Drought in the Horn of Africa İs Threatening 15 Million People | UN Dispatch," accessed November 16, 2020, https://www.undispatch.com/drought-in-the-horn-of-africa-is-

According to the United Nations FAO Technological Unit, the Horn of Africa is a territory of roughly 200,000 km2 with a total population of 160 million inhabitants. More than 40 percent of the population is undernourished in the region as a whole and 70 percent in Eritrea and Somalia. The states of the region have a total population of 160 million people, 70 million of whom live in areas defenseless to serious famines. Over the last 30 years, these states, which are all members of the Intergovernmental Authority on Development (IGAD), have been endangered with starvation at least once in a decade.[2]

Also, the revival of internal strife and insecurity in the region as a result of the civil war in Sudan, the ongoing instability in Somalia, and the unresolved rivalry between Ethiopia and Eritrea exacerbate the situation in the Horn of Africa in general. Climate change and global warming in the Horn of Africa have also led to a crisis in the region. Food insecurity in the region is more extreme in Ethiopia, Somalia, and Kenya, where more than 12 million people in the affected area require basic means of subsistence. [3]

The extreme drought in the Horn of Africa is due to climate change that affects the distribution of average rainfall in the region. Accordingly, the inadequacy of rainfall was the immediate and remote source of the humanitarian food crisis in the Horn of Africa. Concerning the advancement of the global economy and the increasingly evolving climate and environmental trends, food poverty will continue to have a major effect on both urban and rural poor. Besides, food security has been inextricably tied to international and national security.[4]

Another issue related to starvation and famine in the Horn of Africa is migration which has been severe for four decades and generally acknowledged to have the highest number of refugees. The region hosts and creates significant numbers of refugees as well. Development inequalities and prolonged wars lead to widespread relocation and movement of communities. The refugee flows in this region peaked during the period between 1978 and 1995. The military dictatorship of the Ethiopian Imperial Government in 1974, Eritrea's struggle for independence, the 1977-1978 war between Ethiopia and Somalia, and the civil conflict in Sudan and Somalia in the 1980s have all been identified as major catalysts for the region's large-scale involuntary movements. 70 million people live in areas that are

---

threatening-15-million-people/.

[2] The Food and Agriculture Organization of the United Nations, "The Elimination of Food Insecurity in the Horn of Africa - Summary," 2001.

[3] Ruqayyah M. Ladan, "Food Insecurity in the Horn of Africa: Challenges and Prospects" (Eastern Mediterranean University (EMU) - Doğu Akdeniz Üniversitesi (DAÜ), 2017),p.25 http://i-rep.emu.edu.tr:8080/xmlui/handle/11129/4555.

[4] Ibid, p.26.

vulnerable to severe food shortages, of the 160 million livings in the Horn of Africa. 22 million pastoralists live in 60 percent of the country. About 40 percent of the region's population is undernourished by food poverty and poor livelihoods. In the 2010-11 drought era, malnutrition was as high as 30%.[5] *"At the midpoint of 2019, the East and Horn of Africa region (EHoA) was home to 8.1 million IDPs and 3.5 million refugees and asylum-seekers. Today, the 3.5 million refugees and asylum seekers remain, but there are only 6.3 million IDPs."* [6] It is difficult, since so many agents are present simultaneously, to investigate the causes of migration in the Horn of Africa.

There is proof that climate-driven natural disasters and conflicts are growing in severity and frequency. Natural disasters now occur about five times as much as 40 years ago. Similarly, the effect on local economies, people's livelihoods, and lives have increased. It can seem unrelenting in some of the hardest-hit areas. One drought is followed by another, every time it strips off the limited assets of the poor and weak robs them of their self-reliance, and wounds their humanity and dignity.[7]

UNHCR reports refugees are affected more quickly by the spreading of organized crime, such as small weapons, trafficking in drugs, armed bandits, and cattle. Refugees and chaos typically go hand-in-hand. The conflict trend son the Horn of Africa has been deplorable because of the highly destructive conflicts in this area. However, it is also interesting because the regional dimension and the ties in the dispute system are based. Displaced people face difficult conditions in these rough communities and sometimes bring economic, environmental, and safety pressures on their host.[8]

Migration has led to shaping communities in which we live today, and as such, it is part of our common past. The reasons and effects of migration are both multifaceted and complex. Although many people flee their homes as a result of war or hardship, others are moving under conditions of security, political stability, and progress. People can also go to study, reunite with family members, or prepare to find jobs and provide financial help to their families back home.

Despite the enormous social, political, and economic variations between

---

[5] Kisuke Ndiku, "Horn of Africa: The Linkages Between Food İnsecurity, Migration and Conflict," Peace Direct, https://www.peaceinsight.org/blog/2014/11/horn-africa-linkages-food-insecurity-migration-conflict/.

[6] International Organization for Migration, "Total Number of Internally Displaced Persons in East & Horn of Africa Drastically Drops in 2019," accessed November 17, 2020, https://www.iom.int/news/total- number-internally-displaced-persons-east-horn-africa-drastically-drops-2019.

[7] FAO of the UN, "Horn of Africa | Impact of Early Warning and Early Action," 1, accessed November 13, 2020, http://www.fao.org/3/ca0227en/CA0227EN.pdf.

[8] Joel Florence Munanye, "The Impact of Refugees on Security In the Horn of Africa," 2011, A Research Project, University of Nairobi,p.2 accessed December 11, 2020, http://erepository.uonbi.ac.ke/bitstream/ handle/11295/3345/FLORENCE_MUNANYE_JOEL_M.A_ICM_2011.pdf?sequence=1.

and within the states of the Horn of Africa region, fundamental challenges and dynamics which are the focus of this study are closely related. Sustainable development and economic growth lead to safe, organized, and regular migration. In conjunction with these massive movements of people both within and across borders, the origin, traffic, and destination areas face complex challenges. Examining the dynamic connections among migration and agriculture, food security and rural growth is important to resolve the varied causes of migration and to work to ensure that people do not continue to migrate.

## Drivers of the Migration and Linkages with Conflict in the Horn of Africa

Human migration has gained scholarly interest since the drawing of artificial borders has created sovereign states. Modern states maintain control over borders to regulate the movement of people and goods. Still, there is no standard definition of immigration. When reviewing the meanings of migration, it can be seen that the common factor is displacement. Displacement can be either a short distance or a long-distance. The drivers of migration are also called the reasons that influence people to decide to migrate through both regular and irregular channels. This covers both voluntary and forced migration with temporary and permanent migration.[9]

Developments in the structures of states, economic and political turmoil, conflicts of interest between countries, civil wars, natural disasters, human rights violations forced thousands of people to leave their countries legally or illegally. Consequently, any form of cross-border or intra-border crossing carried out by individuals or groups of persons without legal documents authorizing or approving such movement has increasingly been categorized as irregular migration.[10]

Researches show the origin of the refugee problem in Africa back to the period of struggle for independence. Violent military conflicts witnessed in many African countries during the post-Independence period are therefore often the direct product of the discriminatory policies followed by the newly independent governments, which can be seen in important respects as a result of similar colonial policies. Conflicts frequently challenged ruling groups seeking to preserve the status quo, on the one hand, and marginalized groups pressing for reform, on the other. Therefore, in general, conflicts for control of economic and political power and systemic major human rights violations, including widespread brutality, are the prime source of population

---

[9] Berhane Keleta, "Outmigration from the Horn of Africa," *Ìrìnkèrindò: a Journal of African Migration*, no. 10 (July 2019): 2, p.16, http://africamigration.com/issue/july2019/KELETA_Issue_10.pdf.
[10] Ibid, p.18.

movements in sub-Saharan Africa.[11]

In 2010, African migrants reached approximately 30.6 million, more than double the 1980 population. The share of African migrants remaining in Africa has decreased steadily due to the diversification of migrant destinations, with about half of them still living in Africa in 2010. The number of African migrants living outside the African continent, on the other hand, reached 1,79 million in 2015, more than doubling in 15 years.[12]

Violent conflict is more of a rule than an exception in the Horn of Africa. Conflicts are being escalated at different stages: local, regional, and state. Conflict includes several actors: states, nationalists, religious groups, and community or identity groups with significant external support. Also, immigration in the Horn of Africa is a multidimensional fact. There is an increased rate of people crossing borders without legitimate and legal documents in the region. The states of the Horn of Africa share certain features but vary in others. It is, therefore, necessary to understand, before moving directly into the definition of migration conditions in these countries, that the circumstances of the countries concerned and the aspects of migration are mostly associated with these various situations. It is worth noting that the entire area faces challenges linked to low human and economic growth. Moreover, the key drivers of migration in many of the countries concerned are violent conflicts, state persecution, and oppression. Ecological factors also impact more and more countries in the region and affect food security, livelihoods, and migration decision. It is also a mixture of many factors leading to the migration decision. It is important to note that while there are common migration drivers in the region's countries, the particular background of the country is important.

The Horn of Africa is characterized by three distinct patterns of conflict/displacement. First, there is more or less continuous immigration from Somalia since the late 1980s and especially since the Somali state fall of 1991. Conflict, persistent instability, severe poverty, drought, and the lack of an effective central government until 2012 were and are factors driving people to leave the country. In addition to displacement in Somalia, this dynamic also includes refugees in Kenya, Ethiopia, Djibouti, Uganda, Tanzania, and irregular migration through South Sudan and Sudan. Somalia is estimated to have 1.1 million displaced persons and at least the amount of internally displaced people in 2016. Moreover, it involves displacement from the region to Yemen and the other Gulf countries across the Red Sea. [13]

---

[11] Joel Florence Munanye, "The Impact Of Refugees On Security In The Horn Of Africa", p.62.

[12] Hitomi Kirikoshi, Yasuo Matsunami, Shinichi Takeuchi, Natsuko Midorikawa, ed., *Migration Governance-Migration Within and from Africa* (2017), p.28.

[13] Katrin Marchand, Julia Reinold and Raphael Dias e Silva, "Study on Migration Routes in the East and

The second pattern is the conflict and displacement related to the South Sudan turmoil. This conflict is repeatedly realized as an internal conflict, however, it also focuses on ties with Sudan and northern Uganda, as it forces people across these borders and into Ethiopia and Kenya. South Sudanese migration is heavily affected by conflicts, the latest being the displacement of millions both within and outside the region, worsened by increased food insecurity. 1.3 million individuals have been displaced as a result of the turmoil in and around South Sudan. In addition to reasons such as the lack of secure livelihoods and job prospects and the lack of basic infrastructure and facilities and food poverty, migration from Sudan is also driven by conflict. The third basis for displacement does not emphasize a live conflict but on the steady movement of Eritreans, primarily because of continuous and indefinite national service obligations, the absence of political pluralism, and poor economic conditions. There are 270,000 Eritreans in the region, some of whom choose to live in that area. But there have been tremendous risks and thousands of Eritreans - particularly young people - have gone further to Europe, the Middle East, or to South Africa.[14]

In addition to three patterns, migration is also an important issue in other countries of the region. Ethiopia migration drivers are diverse, but they can be described as socio-economic factors along with ethnic and environmental disasters impacting the livelihoods of people. Ethiopia and, to different degrees, the other countries in the region all recently were hit by drought in 2011. It hit Eritrea, Somalia, and Djibouti the worst, in addition to Ethiopia. Similar factors, although the flows are much smaller, cause migration from Uganda. Specifically, the key factors in the Ugandan context have been rapid population increase, high youth unemployment rates and the lack of working opportunities, ecological degradation, and problematic ownership of land resources that are distorted in favor of older generations. The latter especially encourages youth emigration. Migration from Djibouti is comparatively limited in size, and it is hardly recorded that Djiboutian people leave their state irregularly. This is identified in relation to high levels of poverty, limited jobs, and opportunities for livelihoods.[15]

Some of the situations enumerated above reflect the causes of migration in the Horn of Africa. Conflicts between and within states cause the region's weakness and insecurity. The literature demonstrates the important correlation between conflict and rivalry to food insecurity. As a consequence, the conflict has become the leading cause of hunger in the region leading to the marginalization and destabilization of the people. They also had a long-term influence in the region due to their effects on food security and stability

---

Horn of Africa" (Maastricht Graduate School of Governance, 2017), p.18.

[14] Ibid. pp.3-4

[15] Ibid, p.3.

in the region.

## Linkage of Food Insecurity and Migration

Economic factors have been significant in stimulating migration. Poverty is a driver behind migration, but ecological challenges, landlessness, and inadequate rural livelihoods are equally important. Throughout the Horn of Africa, the low degree of development is triggered by frequent drought and ongoing political tensions that have created high levels of human migration and worsened poverty.

The chances of food shortages and hunger have long been high for IDPs and refugees. *"It is estimated that 80 % of people displaced by conflict live in countries with high levels of severe food insecurity and malnutrition. Nine of the ten countries with the highest number of IDPs faced global food insecurity in 2019. Displaced populations in these countries are increasingly dependent on foreign food aid for their survival."*[16] Recently, a growing number of studies have concentrated primarily on the impact of migration and food security on both relations. Food insecurity is also known as a driving force for migration. The notion of food insecurity is related to food production and is therefore examined in a larger sense of food poverty. However, as stated by the UN Food and Agricultural Organization (FAO), the threat to the food disaster in the Horn of Africa spreads to inadequate food production to other issues considered below.

It is shown that intense drought triggering starvation and serious food shortages is the main factor adversely affecting food insecurity in the Horn of Africa. This happens since arid or often semi-arid vegetation is a very important part of the Horn of Africa. The region's annual rainfall is insufficient and not evenly spread, so it is always poor for agriculture. While drought is normal in the area, the recent situation in the region suggests that climate change in the region is becoming much more serious, dramatic, and dangerous. This aspect impacts the production of food in the region in general.[17]

The crisis of food in the Horn of Africa is also related to the region's rising population, in addition to natural disasters and conflicts. This puts pressure on the region's small and scarce resources, also leading to a crisis of food insecurity. Hence in addition to the above-mentioned traditional factors of food insecurity, the food security crisis has also been linked to structural problems in the states in the Horn of Africa. These problems include compelling political-economic relations, dependency on food aid, and

---

[16] IOM UN Migration, "Populations at Risk: Implications of COVID-19 for Hunger, Migration and Displacement" (2020), p.7. https://docs.wfp.org/api/documents/WFP-0000118161/download/?_ga =2.263739076.911222198.1607615179-704849786.1607615179.
[17] Ladan, "Food Insecurity in the Horn of Africa: Challenges and Prospects", p.31.

corruption.[18]

In the Horn of Africa (Ethiopia, Somalia, and northeastern Kenya), nearly 12 million people suffered from hunger in the region, the worst famine in the past 60 years, the FAO declared on July 12, 2011. The UN World Food Programme had reported a few days earlier than 10 million people required food aid in this area. The Secretary-General of the UN called an emergency summit with all the directors of the agencies of the United Nations and demanded an extra generous approach from the Member States about their assistance to countries undernourishment.[19] In 2010, FAO emphasized that more than 40% of the people in the Horn of Africa were starved and millions are food insecure. With limited food and water resources, animals produce less milk, are more prone to diseases, and their mortality rate increases.[20]

Drought in the Horn of Africa is not unusual, however, 2011 was unlike; since the 2009 episode, repeated drought conditions were more extreme and plant growth was nearly impossible. Nomadic herders, frequently several hundred kilometers north of the region, had to look for more pastures. They have also left their homes without any money behind them. It was still too late for other cattle herders: The animals suffer from starvation, and their owners tried to market them at a very low price before they died.[21]

More than 260,000 people died over the following weeks and months, rendering this drought one of the biggest massacres of this decade. Another drought occurred in the area in 2017. This time, though governments and the international community reacted urgently to provide humanitarian aid and interventions that help stopped a repeat of the 2011 tragedy. A serious drought again hit the Horn of Africa in 2019. It impacts more than 15,3 million people in need of humanitarian aid. Drought arrives very soon after the drought that destroyed a lot of the region in 2017. It is devastating across the three countries. People are scrambling to get drinkable water and water to save their livestock. Moreover, people have to travel to urban centers so there is a lot of displacement.[22]

In 2019, about 30.2 million human refugees migrated to sub-Saharan Africa; 29% of 8.7 million people were from East Africa. 46% of these migrants migrated to the region of East Africa, while 54% migrated to other regions. Most also in pursuit of better economic opportunities, but often in order to prevent conflicts, insecurity, and climate shocks. Most of the

---

[18] Ibid, p.51.

[19] Albert Sasson, "Food Security for Africa: An Urgent Global Challenge," *BioMed Central*, 2012, 2, accessed November 10, 2020, http://www.agricultureandfoodsecurity.com/content/1/1/2.

[20] Food and Agriculture Organization ( FAO ) of the United Nations, "Food Insecurity in the Horn of Africa" (2010), 1.

[21] Albert Sasson, "Food Security For Africa: An Urgent Global Challenge," 2.

[22] UN Dispatch, "Drought in the Horn of Africa is Threatening 15 Million People | UN Dispatch"

refugees in the region come from Ethiopia, South Sudan, Eritrea, and Somalia. According to figures from the end of October 2020, the region plays host to 3.5 million migrants and asylum seekers, while the region already has 6.3 million IDPs. The largest internal migration catastrophes are in Somalia, South Sudan, and Ethiopia.[23]

For many families, remittances are an important source of income due to the reduced role of food insecurity and poverty in the region. In other words, migration is an effective way for families to deal with salary insecurity and food security threats and to add to the growth and stability of communities. To deal with seasonal starvation, impoverished households resort to seasonal migration. In general, households receiving remittances appear to have greater results in terms of food security than those lacking this source of income. *"In 2019, Kenya received USD 2.8 billion, followed by Somalia, estimated to have received between USD 1.3 billion and USD 2 billion. In Uganda, remittances reached USD 1.29 billion, and in South Sudan, USD 1.26 billion. Most direct recipients are based in urban areas where money transfer facilities are available; from there, remittances flow on into rural areas"*. [24]

A wide range of policy issues is addressed by international and local debates on the relationship between migration and growth, such as brain drain, remittance flows, circular migration, and the role of diasporas. Any systemic reflection on the relationship between migration and food security is notably absent from these discussions.[25] The current debates about migration and food insecurity in the Horn of Africa are still quite limited. Present conceptualization of the food security problem in Africa offers an insufficient structure for employed on the interaction between food security and migration. A comprehensive perspective on ensuring food security in the region will play an important role in preventing migration.

## Covid 19 and Impact on Food Insecurity and Migration

Africa, where the first death occurred in Burkina Faso on March 18, unfortunately, could not survive the Covid 19 pandemic due to its close contact with China, Europe, and the USA, despite the low number of cases detected. COVID-19, a global pandemic, has resulted in more than 69 million cases globally and contributed to 1,580,000 deaths as of 10 December.[26] The Horn of Africa is one of the most defenseless regions to the socio-economic

---

[23] IOM UN Migration, "Populations at risk: Implications of COVID-19 for hunger, migration and displacement", p.39

[24] Ibid, p.42.

[25] Jonathan Crush, "Linking Food Security, Migration and Development," *International Migration* 51, no. 5 (2013): 71, p.62 doi:10.1111/imig.12097.

[26] World Food Programme, "Impact of Covid-19 on Livelihoods, Food Security&Nutrition in East Africa: Urban Focus" (United Nations, 2020), https://docs.wfp.org/api/documents/WFP-0000118161/ download /?_ga=2.263739076.911222198.1607615179-704849786.1607615179.

effects of COVID-19. The fragileness of the region is due to many reasons, together with weak health services in several countries and low test capacity, well-timed identification, and reaction to COVID-19 cases.[27] The Horn of Africa is at a comparatively moderate pace compared to other regions around the world, where more than 270,000 confirmed cases and 5,000 dead by 10 December, while the number of new cases is on the increase more quickly than before. The fatality rate is calculated at between 0.6 percent and 3.5 percent worldwide, but in East Africa, it appears to be at the lower end so far.[28]

As mentioned above, the three major factors of food insecurity and migration in the Horn of Africa are conflict, climate change, and weather-related disasters. At the same time, with the conflict starting to worsen, the security situation exacerbated. Escalating terror in Somalia and Ethiopia impacted more and more people and public infrastructure, including health services, deteriorated the already vulnerable state's capacity to adapt to this pandemic.[29]

COVID-19 is appearing at a time when it is already known that the Horn of Africa is the epicenter of various emergencies exacerbated by repeated droughts and floods; conflict and insecurity; protracted refugee and internal migration crises; and the worst outbreak of desert locusts in years. These shocks have affected the livelihood of people and are worsening their vulnerabilities and resilience, particularly in light of the present pandemic.

From the beginning of this pandemic, since internal and cross-border border controls have been enforced, the number of people leaving the region has dropped sharply. The measures and policies for mitigation of COVID-19 have been severely reduced.[30] Latest reports indicate that migrants coming from the Horn of Africa to Yemen decreased by 69% between January and September 2020 relative to the same era in 2019. Since May 2020, unplanned return movements of migrants have been reported from Yemen towards Djibouti. 3,120 migrants have been accounted for as of September. In addition, remittances are an important source of income for many families in the countries of origin. Sub-Saharan Africa's remittance flows are projected to decline by 8.8% in 2020, followed by a further reduction of 5.8% in 2021 due to the effects of COVID-19, impacting families across the sub-region who will be pressured to limit their intake or

---

[27] Ayansina Ayanlade and Maren Radeny, "COVID-19 and Food Security in Sub-Saharan Africa: İmplications of Lockdown During Agricultural Planting Seasons," *NPJ science of food* 4 (2020), doi:10.1038/s41538-020-00073-0; IOM UN Migration, "Populations at risk: Implications of COVID-19 for hunger, migration and displacement"

[28] World Food Programme, "Impact of Covid-19 on Livelihoods, Food security&Nutrition in East africa"

[29] IOM UN Migration, "Populations at risk: Implications of COVID-19 for hunger, migration and displacement"

[30] Ibid.

find alternate subsistence strategies.[31]

However, with its impact on the diaspora, COVID-19 is also significantly impacted by its failure to sustain its households financially. Even if people can submit the money, lock-up acts and other financial hurdles discourage transactions. For example, due to containment policies, many money transfer firms were forced to close while their customers were prevented from left their homes to deter infection. The same difficulties limit the recipient's access to transfers. And even though others have been able to discover solutions by way of online networks, not all are eager to use these facilities.

In East Africa, 6.3 million IDPs already live on IDP sites. IDP sites encountered acute obstacles long before COVID-19, which hampered attempts to increase living standards. In urban and peri-urban IDP locations, repetitive displacement due to violence and environmental factors has put a massive burden on already limited resources. The new arrivals of displaced populations, meanwhile, tend to relocate into spontaneous colonies that are precariously built on private or public land. Many IDPs remain in overcrowded shelters, particularly those recently displaced, who are unable to get enough food. The underlying health problems are particularly alarming in poor urban areas and IDP camps. While no major cases of COVID-19 have been confirmed, surveillance is incredibly limited, rendering it almost impossible to assess if these regions are seeing an increase in cases of COVID-19. In addition to the danger of outbreaks, government agencies and humanitarian and development agencies have implemented comprehensive messaging campaigns aimed at instilling COVID-19-related transformation and equipping communities with the resources needed to reduce and respond effectively to the spread of the virus during population transmission times. [32]

The pandemic and its consequences have severely worsened socio-economic problems. Increased risk of infectious diseases, like COVID 19, is likely due to overcrowding, an extreme social combination between young and older people, and weak water and sanitation capability in the camps, particularly in displaced communities, who are housed in sites such as camps and camps. Returning IDPs and migrants are often at risk, frequently in cramped and unsanitary environments is critically wounded or strengthened shelters.[33]

Besides, COVID-19 has had significant effects on the supply, recruitment, affordability, and mobility of humanitarian assistance. IDPs, such as domestic

---

[31] IOM UN Migration, "Populations at risk: Implications of COVID-19 for hunger, migration and displacement", p.28

[32] Ibid, pp.42-3.

[33] IOM UN Migration, "Populations at risk: Implications of COVID-19 for hunger, migration and displacement", p.44.

workers for households in host communities who can no longer find employment, have felt the effects on their livelihoods. There are also reports, that rising numbers of children are engaged in casual work, with schools closed. Food prices in major markets jumped between March and June 2020, reaching their peaks over the last ten years, mainly due to a combination of macroeconomic conditions and supply problems. Transportation prices have since risen dramatically. Among the worst affected are agro-pastoralists, poor urban people, and foodstuff deficits who rely on the markets. Meanwhile, the nation remains concerned about the need for continuous, broad-based humanitarian food assistance. The weakened healthcare system has been put under great pressure, scarcely capable of delivering regular services. Although official supply routes benefited from an exemption from border closures, illicit trade – vital to the livelihoods of cross-border populations – did not. This affected women in particular, who had resorted to traveling through illegal border crossings, thereby exposing themselves to increased safety threats.[34]

The pandemic will have consequences for the complexities of migration and food insecurity. COVID-19 initially reduces mobility which is likely to increase food insecurity for the livelihoods of those who rely on mobility. Well-governed migration will be a crucial factor in a successful response to COVID-19.

## Conclusion

Migration in the Horn of Africa has enlarged and convert more multifaceted in recent years. Migration and food insecurity in the Horn of Africa are highly interrelated and trigger each other. The consequences of the regional mobility regime for food security in general require much more research and study. Food security threats and recurrent food insecurity can be significant reasons for income-generating migration. Conflict and violence, especially in Somalia and Sudan or Ethiopia, have led to the displacement of millions who have migrated to neighboring countries. These countries need to find ways to act together against common problems. The increases in migration from the region after 1990 are also partially due to long-term hunger and increased food insecurity. Existing conceptions of food security in Africa have an inadequate context to work on the relationship between migration and food security. "African solution to African problems" is always voiced. But the conditions need to be created for Africans to solve these problems alone. Strengthening African institutions and increasing their capacity seems to be the most basic solution.

---

[34] Ibid., p.43-4

CHAPTER 7

# MIGRATION BY SEA: LIBYA AND THE EU'S APPROACH

Burak Şakir Şeker[*]

## Introduction

One of the biggest challenges faced in the international arena in recent years is the political chaos in Libya since February 2011. Indeed, the fall of the Gaddafi regime after 42 years of continuous rule marked the beginning of fluctuations until today. Thus, the military intervention of the international coalition not only led to a change in the domestic political situation but also allowed the chronic peculiarities of Libyan society to explode in the most violent way. In these circumstances, the issue of migrant / refugee trafficking as well as that of human trafficking has become particularly large, making it, in combination with migratory flows from the eastern Mediterranean, one of the burning demands to manage the EU under the common European asylum and immigration policy. The EU members have had to deal with the management of migratory flows on the one hand, and the uncontrollable political situation in Libya on the other. Thus, the multi-layered civilian structure has turned Libya into a hub of instability in the wider region between cosmopolitan and ethnic forces, at the same time directly affected irregular migration to Europe and finally posed a threat to the EU itself with significant challenges and dilemmas.

Undoubtedly, the political crisis that has erupted in Libya has not only plunged the North African country into political, social and economic turmoil, but has also demonstrated in the most characteristic way its direct and immediate consequences both locally and regionally and internationally. At the same time, the Libyan crisis has once again demonstrated the complexity and importance of the North African regional subsystem, which has emerged on the international political scene in modern and contemporary world history as one of the most crucial and controversial one due to importance of its geopolitical and geostrategic position. Thus, Libya's vast oil and gas reserves, combined with the country's immediate proximity to the southern Mediterranean coast of Europe, as well as the relationship between the Maghreb and Mashreq and political developments in the country has led the international environment to the downfall.

---

[*] Assoc. Prof., Ankara Hacı Bayram Veli University

111

Therefore, the intense interest of the European states in the Libyan internal affairs, as well as other developments in many cases in them, can only be characterized as a logical development, since a multitude of European issues, such as energy security, illegal immigration and the fight against terrorism, are affected to a greater or lesser extent by political developments in Libya.

Indeed, the EU's interest for the countries of the Arab Maghreb, can be dated as far back as the 1970s, with the development of the "Global Mediterranean Policy" of the EEC establishing the notion that the progress and stability of its neighboring countries. Reaching the present and through the long, unifying European process, the African shores of the Mediterranean and especially for the long-suffering country of Libya remains indispensable for the interest of the EU countries.

In the framework of this work, an attempt is made to analyze the effects of the political chaos in Libya on the increase of migration flows to Europe, but also to explain the reasons and the deeper interests for the long-term continuation of this political and national crisis in local, regional and international level. At the same time, emphasis will be placed on the humanitarian impact of this crisis on migrant / refugee populations trying to reach EU countries, as well as to evaluate European actions through the framework of the Common European Asylum and Immigration Policy.

This research to analyze the geographical and demographic characteristics of Libya, as well as the historical course of the formation of its special features, which in several cases still influence domestic developments. It refers to the Libyan uprising of 2011, as well as the military intervention of the international coalition under NATO command, which led to the fall of the Gaddafi regime and the consequent emergence of new political actors. Then, the conflicting aspects of the current political situation will be examined, not only from the perspective of their actions, but also from the point of view of their emergence, their motivations and their internal and external support. The illegal immigration from Libya to be examined through its special, local historical characteristics, how it has shaped by domestic political developments from 2011 until today, as well as the attitude of internal actors towards this issue. At the same time, historical development of the Common European Immigration Policy, as well as its current configuration to be checked in order to understand the institutional framework within which European approach to Migration Issues in Libya has been implemented. Last section of the work will also address the reactions of international humanitarian organizations, as well as the ethical dimensions of European immigration policies.

## Political Developments in Libya

The Libyan inordinate political system has depended on several causes such as fierce, ethnic conflict, the geo-morphology of the country's soil and demographic characteristics. For this reason, it is necessary, before analyzing in more detail the essence of the subject of the work, to make a brief reference to them, in order to fully understand the source and the deeper causes of the current issues. It should first be noted that the short-lived history of the Libyan state begins only in 1951, with the establishment of the Kingdom of Libya under the leadership of King Idris I. The establishment of the Libyan state lies, on the one hand, in the lack of a unified national identity of its population, and on the other hand in the absence of historically established borders of the country even under colonial occupation. Indeed, Libya consists of three sub-regions, Tripoli, Cyrene and Fezzan, which were consolidated within 192 years of Italian colonialism. In fact, the first constitution of the newly established Kingdom referred to the tripartite federalization of the country, which was valid until 1958.[1]

Libya from its inception until 2011 experienced two political regimes, the pro-Western King Idris I and the revolutionary regime of Colonel Gaddafi from 1969 onwards. A common component of the two political systems was the attempt to retain power through manipulation of the Libyan tribal system, which not only prevented the creation of a common national Libyan identity but at the same time led to the marginalization of borders. Thus, despite the economic adequacy of the country, the management of state wealth was done solely for the perpetuation of their regimes.[2]

In particular, Gaddafi's rule, although initially aimed at establishing a common Arab identity and putting an end to Libya's tribal system of organization, eventually led to its institutionalization and the establishment of a "divide and rule" system. Indeed, the Gaddafi regime supported its perpetuation through a strong network of allied tribes which redeemed their support with a multitude of provisions and benefits through the fully dysfunctional and overblown public sector. Thus, state revenues from the exploitation of oil deposits were used for the benefit of only the tribes that supported the Gaddafi regime, which not only marginalized the rival tribes, but at the same time strengthened the racial weight of the tribal system in a wider range of corruption and state patronage.[3]

At the same time, the absence of functional state and supra-racial

---

[1] Ballinger, Pamela. "Colonial Twilight: Italian Settlers and the Long Decolonization of Libya." *Journal of Contemporary History*, vol. 51, no. 4, 2016, pp. 813–838.

[2] Terry, Patrick CR. "The Libya Intervention (2011): Neither Lawful, nor Successful." *The Comparative and International Law Journal of Southern Africa*, vol. 48, no. 2, 2015, pp. 162–182.

[3] Hweio, Haala. "Tribes in Libya: From Social Organization to Political Power." *African Conflict and Peacebuilding Review*, vol. 2, no. 1, 2012, pp. 111–121.

institutions created a hypertrophic and vast state mechanism, the primary function of which was to reward the members of the faithful tribes. Even Gaddafi's contradictory ideologies and growing state repression have intensified the social rifts that have already been caused. All this, combined with years of international isolation and international sanctions, has made the revolutionary regime even more vulnerable to new international developments, in which the spread of terrorism has played a major role.[4]

So after 42 years of continuous rule and with the authoritarianism of the regime constantly increasing in order to face the growing popular discontent, the echo of the Arab uprisings, as well as in the neighboring Tunisia and Egypt, open the situation that would follow until today. Indeed, Libyans, influenced by the rest of the Arab uprisings, began protesting in mid-January 2011, prompting Gaddafi to take pro-people rhetoric. At the same time, prominent Libyans at home and abroad called on the people to claim their rights and freedoms. Thus, since mid-February, a number of anti-opposition demonstrations have broken out in various Libyan cities, and especially in the Cyrenaic capital, Benghazi. The fact that the demonstrations started from there should not be surprising, because the area of Cyrenaica, although it included 2/3 of the total area of the country, was effectively marginalized by the regime, while its dominant tribes remained in political obscurity.[5]

The Gaddafi regime decided to violently disperse the demonstrations, suppressing the insurgents with iron fists, in order to avoid the fate of Tunisia's Ben Ali and Egypt's Mubarak. Gaddafi, taking advantage of the relative apathy of international public opinion over Libya's migration agreements with the EU and especially Italy, as well as Europe's energy dependence on it, tried to violently suppress the protests. The violent repression culminated with the beginning of the demonstrations in Tripoli and this stagnant attitude of Gaddafi, combined with the violent treatment of the protesters, led the Arab League to expel Libya from its ranks. Prominent insurgents, as well as former Gaddafi officials were meeting in the eastern Libya to shape the political expression of the revolution, which would be the intermediate political link until its inception. Thus, the National Transitional Council (NTC) was established, based in the stronghold of the rebels, Benghazi, under the leadership of the former Libyan Minister of Justice, Mustafa Abdul Jalil.[6]

At this point, it should be noted that despite the indifferent attitude of the

---

[4] Szczepankiewicz-Rudzka, Ewa. "Patterns of Libya's Instability in the Aftermath of the Collapse of Gaddafi's Regime." *Politeja*, no. 42, 2016, pp. 227–246.

[5] Busch, Nathan E. and Joseph F. PILAT. "Disarming Libya? A Reassessment after the Arab Spring." *International Affairs (Royal Institute of International Affairs 1944-)*, vol. 89, no. 2, 2013, pp. 451–475.

[6] McQuinn, Brian. "Assessing (In) Security after the Arab Spring: The Case of Libya." *PS: Political Science and Politics*, vol. 46, no. 4, 2013, pp. 716–720.

powerful European countries and the USA, the harshness shown by the Libyan regime, as well as the dimensions of the uprising, led them to get gradually clear position in favor of the insurgents and the departure of Gaddafi from power. Indeed, they took a number of actions that demonstrated a reversal of their previous stance following financial sanctions and recognizing the NTC as the legitimate government of the Libyan people.

In addition, an arms embargo was imposed and an explicit mention was made that the regime should be held accountable to the International Court of Justice in The Hague for crimes against humanity. However, despite the international outcry and disapproval of international organizations, such as the Arab League, the African Union and the Organization of Islamic Cooperation, the Libyan regime not only did not limit its extremist actions, but continued to move towards NTC. Thus, on 17/03/2011, the UN Security Council, on the proposal of the Lebanese delegation, adopted its Resolution 1973, which decided to take action by the international community, with a view to protecting the humans and military intervention in Libya. Resolution called for an immediate ceasefire and empowered members of the international community to a no-fly zone over Libya, on the other hand to take all the necessary means to protect civilians and residential areas. In this way, the international community responded immediately to the demands of the revolutionaries and the NTC fearing retaliation against a possible entry of government troops into Benghazi. [7]

Initially the four leading countries, France, Great Britain, Canada and the USA, responded to the UN Resolution within different operations (Harmattan, Ellamy, Mobile and Odyssey Dawn respectively) but after the start of operations NATO took full control of the operations under the name "Unified Protector". So, the international military operation in Libya was officially launched with the participation of 18 countries (14 NATO member states, as well as Sweden, Qatar, the United Arab Emirates and Jordan) under the single NATO administration with the aim of imposing a no-fly zone and a naval blockade, but mainly the protection of the civilian population. [8]

However, despite the explicit authorization of Resolution 1973 in the International Coalition solely for the protection of civilians, the NATO coordination of the operation was accused of violating and exceeding this mandate, by launching attacks on non-governmental organizations. This fact has been strongly criticized by many countries in the international community, such as Russia, China, Venezuela and other international actors such as Amnesty International as it was not aimed at humanitarian

---

[7] UNSC, S/RES/1973. https://www.undocs.org/S/RES/1973%20(2011) (Retrieved: 06.01.2021)

[8] Schinella, A. "Libya, 2011—Operations Odyssey Dawn and Unified Protector: The Value of Time and Outside Assistance for Improving a Proxy Force." Bombs without Boots: The Limits of Airpower, by Anthony M. Schinella, Brookings Institution Press, Washington, D.C., 2019, pp. 223–286.

intervention, but the overthrow of Gaddafi, in order to consolidate their interests in the country's mineral wealth in the new era that would emerge.[9]

NTC undertook its full duties, in order to prepare the country for the first time in its history to hold of national elections and to create General National Congress (GNC) consisting of 200 members. Its goal would be to move Libya to a new permanent constitutional reality despite the failed apparent unity that the NTC tried due to not having the necessary coherence between them. So in this fragile political climate, in the elections of July 2012, the Libyan citizens were called for the first time in the history of the country to elect the members of the GNC, which would prepare the country for its transition in the new, political era and would ensure the coveted democracy and stability.[10]

The establishment of the "Libya Shield" divided into three main brigades (Western, Central, and Eastern) was part of the effort of the now official Libyan government to achieve a unified command and organization of paramilitary organizations. The central organization, based in the city of Misrata, was set up by the Ministry of Defense with the aim of placing a sufficient number of armed groups under the state roof.[11]

It is understandable that the GNC did not have the capacity and independence to prepare the country for a transition to a stable, constitutional regime and therefore could not meet its objective within the 18-year period. Thus, upon the expiration of the deadline in January 2014, the GNC unilaterally announced the extension of his mandate for at least one year. This development, combined with its separatist tendencies, led the Libyan people especially in the east of the country to strong protests, which intensified the security gap in the country. At the same time, another power of the country, General Khalifa Haftar, having retired again to the USA. After the overthrow of Gaddafi, the GNC called in February to be dissolved in order for elections to be called, without overturning the declaration substantially. In mid-May, Haftar's forces declared war on militants in Benghazi as part of Operation Dignity, which was officially launching the second phase of the Libyan civil war.[12]

The absence of an organized, political, stabilization plan by the

---

[9] Amnesty International, Libya: Civilian deaths from NATO airstrikes must be properly investigated. https://www.amnesty.org/en/latest/news/2012/03/libya-civilian-deaths-nato-airstrikes-must-be-properly-investigated (Retrieved: 08.01.2021)

[10] Mezran, Karim, et al. Post-Revolutionary Politics in Libya: Inside the General National Congress. Atlantic Council, 2013, pp. 1-5.

[11] Alkaff, Syed Huzaifah Bin Othman. "Libya." *Counter Terrorist Trends and Analyses*, vol. 8, no. 1, 2015, pp. 112–115.

[12] Varvelli, Arturo. "Libya: From Uprising to War, 2011–2019." *Bustan: The Middle East Book Review*, vol. 11, no. 1, 2020, pp. 34–45.

international community after the military intervention of 2011, exacerbated the weaknesses of the newly formed political system of the country. Thus, the Libyan political scene became the "backbone" of the armed, paramilitary organizations, which represented the members and interests of the tribal organization. With the fall of the state monopoly of violence, the armed groups of the tribes tried to ensure the maximum possible benefit for their tribe by legitimizing their struggle against the Gaddafi regime. However, NTC, without the necessary institutions and international support, neither disarm the revolutionaries in the name of the common national interest nor completely reintegrate them into a just and democratic society. In this way, the political life of the country was controlled informally by paramilitary organizations, which had no aim at its progress and its effective unification.[13]

In May 2014, General Haftar, together with a group of army officers from the eastern provinces, established the self-proclaimed Libyan National Army (LNA), declaring the peace until the end. This forced the GNC to announce new elections in June 2014, from which the parties who want to distinguish between religion and politics managed to win the majority. For this reason, the previous religious majority in Congress reacted immediately, fearing that the new government would repeal the Political Isolation Law and impose strong anti-terrorist laws, especially on the issue of subsidies for armed paramilitary militias. So, Operation Libya Dawn was set up to formally prevent the return of former Gaddafi officials to political life.[14]

Having re-entered the civil war, the United Nations Assistance Mission in Libya (UNSMIL) has been working since early 2015 to bridge the gap between the two conflicting parties and facilitate negotiations between them. Indeed, the exploitation of oil fields and facilities was a deterrent to the consolidation of peace, as both opponents sought to control them. Thus, the UN-sponsored peace negotiations were concluded on 17/12/2015 in Skhirat/Morocco that including government which would consist of the members Government of National Accord (GNA) meaning Presidential Council chaired by Fayez Mustafa Al Sarraj as recognized by the majority of the members of the international community.[15]

In this way, it was proved in practice that the UN peace plan did not yield the desired results as the key factor in the failure of this operation was the limited number of politicians who negotiated the "Libyan Political Agreement". Indeed, the talks under the auspices of the international

---

[13] Feuer, Sarah, et al. *Libya: A Violent Theater of Regional Rivals*. Institute for National Security Studies, 2019, pp. 1-4.

[14] Kamouni-Janssen, Floor El, and Iba Abdo. Addressing Libya's Multiple Crises: When Violent Politics, Extremism and Crime Meet. Clingendael Institute, 2015, pp. 1-8.

[15] Vericat, José S., and Mosadek Hobrara. *The Fall of the Qaddafi Regime and the Breakdown of Libya*. International Peace Institute, 2018, pp. 3–5.

community did not involve broad sections of society and at the same time sidelined the armed paramilitary organizations, although in essence they were controlled by the two official political bodies. Thus, the representatives of the opposing parties, who in fact did not have such authorization from their political bodies, agreed on a plan which did not include the most important but informal political actors of the country, i.e. the armed groups. In addition, the newly established GNA needed the substantial and universal support of the international community in order to gain social support through the creation of strong institutions, support which was mainly sufficient only at the level of its official recognition.[16]

Therefore, Skhirat Agreement not only failed to put an end to the Libyan civil war and lay the foundations for the country's stability, but instead further divided society. Moreover, the attitude of the international community did not allow the weak GNA to impose its power and to bring under its complete control the entire territory of the country. The main reason for the lack of support from the international community was the focus of the actors on specific issues, such as the emergence of the self-proclaimed DAESH in parts of Libya and irregular migration.[17]

Thus, the priority of the Al Sarraj government was to defeat the DAESH from the Libyan territories, especially in the area of Sirte, which had been its main stronghold in the country for more than two years. So in December 2016, Libyan forces, after seven years of fighting, in the framework of the operation "Al-Bunyan Al-Marsoos" and with the decisive support of the American Air Force, managed to expel the DAESH fighters from the wider area of Sirte to the southern desert areas of the country.[18]

Apart from that, however, the main part of the weakness of GNC was the reduction of the autonomy of the armed groups, as well as their integration into the state machinery and budget. Of course, this effort focused mainly on the armed paramilitary organizations, which participated in the "Dawn of Libya" operation. This coalition provided its support to the GNC, while the most characteristic examples of this political movement were the integration of a large part of the brigades of Misrata in the Libyan army, as well as those of the particularly infamous trafficking of illegal immigrants. Nevertheless, Al Sarraj's government has achieved meager results in the area of dependence and control of paramilitary organizations, as well as in the imposition of its power throughout the country, having in fact lost its dominance over large parts of it. Also, the GNA had to face the forces of the former GNC, which

---

[16] Salyk-Virk, Melissa. *The Conflicts in Libya from 2011-2020.* New America, 2020, pp. 18–23

[17] Asiedu, Michael. *The Libyan Political Agreement - Time For Reconsideration.* Global Political Trends Center (GPoT), 2017, pp. 1-6.

[18] Comolli, Virginia. *Terrorism and Counterterrorism in Africa.* Edited by Jacinta Carroll, Australian Strategic Policy Institute, 2017, pp. 109–119.

remained loyal to its former president Khalifa Al Ghawil that they were looking for their dominance in Tripoli, apart from General Haftar's Libyan National Army (LNA), already the recognized army of the Tobruk government, and from the beginning the purpose of its creation.[19]

Despite the two camps' joint struggle against the spread of the DAESH threat, the two sides in the civil war failed to reach an agreement on a ceasefire and co-operation. On the contrary, Haftar, after the lapse of two years since the establishment of GNA declared that it no longer had any force, while at the final end of DAESH began his struggle against the government of Tripoli. Thus, from the summer of 2018, his troops advanced to the south and west of the country and specifically to the area of the "oil crescent". Very quickly, the successes of LNA pushed a sufficient number of armed groups to join Haftar's forces, thus making him the strongest man in the country. At the same time, the advance continued in the southern desert parts of the country, while in the winter of 2019 significant oil fields were captured, such as those of Sabha and Al Sharara.[20]

So in April of the same year, LNA began its advance towards Tripoli, in order to fully consolidate the sovereignty of the House of Representatives of Libya (HoR) on the Al Sarraj government. The so-called Operation Flood of Dignity, having the decisive military support of the UAE, brought General Haftar's troops very close to Tripoli. With this assault, the political situation has also been led to an ineffective end, continuing to this day with undiminished intensity of the wars inside the country.[21]

As for the peace negotiations, after the substantial failure of the Skhirat Agreement, they first focused on the Paris Declaration in May 2018 and the tripartite peace plan of UNSMIL in July 2019. Finally, members of the international community are trying to find a political solution to the bloody world under the auspices of the UN of the Berlin Conference, which is still ongoing.[22]

## Migration by Sea to the EU

Undoubtedly, most important issue the EU face is that of irregular immigration. One of its main corridors is that of the Central Mediterranean, i.e. from the Tunisian and especially from the Libyan coast to the European

---

[19] Trauthig, Inga Kristina, and Amine Ghoulidi. "Looking into Libya: Contextualizing Khalifa Haftar's Advances on Tripoli in April 2019." *Atlantisch Perspectief*, vol. 43, no. 3, 2019, pp. 12–15.

[20] Edwards, D., Cromwell, D., & Pilger, J. "Libya: 'It Is All About Oil.'" Propaganda Blitz: How the Corporate Media Distort Reality, by David Edwards et al., Pluto Press, London, 2018, pp. 76–96.

[21] Ibrahim, Azeem. *Rise and Fall?: The Rise and Fall of ISIS in Libya.* Strategic Studies Institute, US Army War College, 2020, pp. 12-18.

[22] Newlin, Cyrus, et al. *U.S.-Russia Relations at a Crossroads.* Center for Strategic and International Studies (CSIS), 2020, pp. 1-8.

coasts of Italy and secondarily Malta. At the same time, Libyan society shaped the special characteristics of the migration, while the peculiarities of the domestic and political scene prevented the negotiations and the conclusion of agreements between the EU and the country itself.[23]

Libya's historical relationship with immigration can be considered quite extreme, even under different circumstances and conditions in each period of time. Libya was one of the poorest countries in the world after independence, with a population of less than two million at least by 1970, having almost doubled in the last 20 years. However, the discovery of huge oil fields in the late 1950s highlighted the need for an influx of labor into the country in order for the new branch of the economy to function effectively. Thus, Libya became a destination for hundreds of thousands of migrants, the vast majority of whom came from other Arab countries, such as Tunisia, Algeria, Mauritania, etc. At the same time, these migratory flows were a powerful tool in the hands of Gaddafi in the context of the Pan-Arabism that he himself wanted to promote. But opening of the borders with the rest of the Arab Maghreb in mid-1990s led to an increase in the number of migrants from Sub-Saharan Africa and a simultaneous decline of the Arabs.[24]

In the beginning Libya was basically a destination country and not a country of origin or intermediation for the immigration. Besides, the issue of irregular migration had already begun to be of great concern to European countries due to both the creation of the Schengen area and increase in illegal immigrants from sub-Saharan Africa and the Maghreb. Thus, since the mid-1990s, EU member states decided to adopt a broader approach to externalization to Mediterranean Third Countries in order to contribute to their overall development and stability. This includes the actions of the Euro-Mediterranean Partnership or Barcelona Declaration of 1995 within the countries of Tunisia, Morocco, Egypt and Algeria.[25]

Libya was absent from these Agreements, which was already in the spotlight of the international community due to its connection to terrorism. Thus, the international isolation of the country, combined with the sanctions imposed on it by the international community, resulted in the deterioration of the economy which caused the emergence of new data on immigration. Thus, Libya's absence from the European agreements, as well as the stricter migration framework in force in the other Mediterranean countries of Africa, made it the new intermediate country to Europe. At the same time, its

---

[23] Rolando, Francesco, and Paolo Naso. "Humanitarian Corridors to Italy" *Harvard International Review*, vol. 39, no. 2, 2018, pp. 64–67.

[24] Nachmani, Amikam. "The Mediterranean Studies Association: The East Mediterranean as a Laboratory." *Mediterranean Studies*, vol. 28, no. 2, 2020, pp. 253–261.

[25] Vallelersundi, Ana Palacio. "The Barcelona Process: A Euro-Mediterranean North-South Partnership." *Georgetown Journal of International Affairs*, vol. 5, no. 1, 2004, pp. 145–151.

particularly difficult border management, due to the desert, facilitated the arrival of immigrants in the country, which was also favored by the marginalization of certain tribes, such as the Tebu and the Tuareg, who, knowing the desert routes and being in the political and economic margins from the regime itself, developed illegal but highly lucrative migrant trafficking networks.[26]

Nevertheless, the rise of international terrorism with the attack of 9/11/2001 led the Libyan leader to a complete reversal of his positions, in order for the country to be re-admitted to the international community. Libya sought to re-establish relations with the West and certainly one of the main problem came to the forefront of the debate was that of illegal immigration to Europe. In this way, the Gaddafi regime tried to cooperate on the issue with both the UN High Commissioner for Refugees (UNHCR) signing a Memorandum of Understanding (MoU) as well as with the EU itself, obviously seeking economic benefits, but mainly support for its power. Friendship and cooperation agreements with Italy and France provided tool with combating irregular immigration that decreased arrivals of irregular immigrants in 2010 from 39,000 to 4,500.[27]

The outbreak of the civil war and the subsequent foreign intervention, in addition to being the beginning of the Libyan chaos, caused the departure from the country of about 800,000 thousand migrants who were living in Libya, as well as about 1,000,000 Libyans. That is why it is understandable that the mass return has caused many problems both in the countries of origin and in post-conflict Libya, since there has always been a country that relied on foreign labor and therefore its reconstruction still had to face one.[28]

It is estimated that in 2011, about 260,000 migrants arrived in Egypt, 345,000 in Tunisia, 36,000 returned to Bangladesh and 208,000 to Nigeria. Given the overall migration flows and displacement, Europe has faced the least possible pressure, always compared to Libya's neighbors. Indeed, about 64,000 migrants arrived from the Libyan to the coasts of Italy and Malta, apparently a consequence of the Arab uprisings and the subsequent fall of the Ben Ali and Gaddafi regimes.[29]

Thus, the official outbreak of the second phase of the Libyan civil war, combined with the rise of the DAESH in Syria and Iraq, caused a fourfold

---

[26] Kah, Henry Kam. "'Blood Money', Migrants' Enslavement and Insecurity in Africa's Sahel and Libya." *Africa Development / Afrique Et Développement*, vol. 44, no. 1, 2019, pp. 25–44.

[27] Richey, Mason. "The North African Revolutions: A Chance to Rethink European Externalization of the Handling of Non-EU Migrant Inflows." *Foreign Policy Analysis*, vol. 9, no. 4, 2013, pp. 409–431.

[28] Parkes, Roderick, and Annelies Pauwels. *The EU Migration Crisis: Getting the Numbers Right*. European Union Institute for Security Studies (EUISS), 2017, pp. 1-4.

[29] Tausch, Arno. "Migration from the Muslim World to the West: Its Most Recent Trends and Effects." *Jewish Political Studies Review*, vol. 30, no. 1/2, 2019, pp. 65–225.

increase in migration flows to European shores. The migration flows until May 2017, followed increasing trends compared to the immediately preceding year, a fact which is connected with the inadequacy of GNA to control the action of armed paramilitary organizations. However, the signing of a Memorandum of Understanding between the Italian government and the GNA, in conjunction with the Malta Declaration a day later, was the turning point for the reduction of migratory flows as a sharp decline from 108,409 arrivals from the Libyan coast in 2017 to 12,977 in 2018.[30]

Their further deterioration was reinforced by the prevalence of the conservative coalition in Italy, the Northern League and the Five Stars in March 2018, which implemented a harsh anti-immigration policy in the target of which were the boats belong to NGOs, who rescued illegal immigrants off the Mediterranean and then transported them to Italian territory. Thus, this policy resulted in the still largest decrease in arrivals in Italy in 2019, 10,938 illegal immigrants have arrived to date, while at the same time there has been an increase in numbers of migrants, 1,445 in 2018 and 3000 in 2019, to Malta.[31]

It is widely accepted that the issue of smuggling and trafficking of illegal immigrants in Libya is one of the biggest risks posed by the country's almost ten-year political instability. Before further addressing this issue, it would be useful, mainly for conceptual and substantive reasons, to make a semantic separation of these two terms.

Trafficking in human beings means the recruitment, transport, relocation, accommodation or reception of persons; attendantly includes the threat or use of force or other forms of coercion for abduction, deception, taking the advantage of vulnerable position or acceptance of benefits in order to obtain the consent of a person in control of another person for the purpose of exploitation. Exploitation may include sexual exploitation, forced labor or the provision of services, slavery or practices similar to slavery, servitude or the removal of organs. Respectively, smuggling is defined as the achievement of the unlawful entry of a person into a State whose person is not a national or permanent resident, for the purpose of obtaining, immediately or directly, an economic or other material benefit.[32]

Thus, with regard to illegal immigration from Libya, there is a

---

[30] UNHCR, Mixed Migration Routes and Dynamics in Libya. https://reliefweb.int/sites/reliefweb.int/files/resources/impact_lby_report_mixed_migration_routes_and_dynamics_in_2018_june_2019.pdf (Retrieved: 07.01.2021)

[31] UNHCR, Mediterranean Situation-UNHCR data portal. https://data2.unhcr.org/en/situations/mediterranean (Retrieved: 08.01.2021)

[32] UN, The definition of trafficking in persons and the mandate for the Global Report. https://www.unodc.org/documents/data-and-analysis/glotip/Annex_II_-_Definition_and_mandate.pdf (Retrieved: 06.01.2021)

phenomenon that migrants are not simply smuggled to Europe, but in many cases fall victim to sexual or economic exploitation by trafficking networks operating in the country. Still, the inhuman treatment of migrants by their traffickers is a common phenomenon, which is not limited to the use of force, but sometimes even leads to their abduction in order to pay large sums of money from their families. The victims of trafficking networks are usually sub-Saharan Africans who travel alone to Libya, either to work there or to continue their journey to Europe.[33]

There are also many examples of corruption of government officials, although in most cases they come from members of armed groups, who have been absorbed through their group in the state payroll and therefore remain more loyal to it than to the state itself. Thus, there are a growing number of complaints from international humanitarian organizations, such as Amnesty International, which speak of the inhumane conditions experienced by illegal immigrants in Libya, throughout their journey until their arrival in target country.[34]

Armed paramilitary organizations play a very important role in shaping the internal political situation. Respectively, in the issue of irregular immigration, the armed groups play a dominant role, while many of them have been turned into organizations for the illegal trafficking and exploitation of migrants. Indeed, the fall of the Gaddafi regime has caused not only radical changes in the country's political landscape, but also a series of chain reactions with social and economic impact. Thus, the emergence of chronic, interracial disputes and their subsequent competition for political power, made it necessary to find as many financial resources as possible. At the same time, the Libyan war had a direct impact on the country's economy, as hostilities and foreign military intervention resulted in a sharp drop in oil production, which was the country's main source of revenue as about 95% of GDP, as well as the sharp outflow of migrants as Libyan economy relied on foreign labor, accounting for about 30% of the total.[35]

Thus, the collapse of the Libyan economy combined with the emergence of local, armed groups and their selfish pursuits, led them to turn to the illegal trafficking or smuggling of migrants in order to secure a source of income. Thus, taking advantage of migration / refugee flows due to the war in neighboring countries, as well as the difficult economic situation of almost

---

[33] Robert Press. "Dangerous Crossings: Voices from the African Migration to Italy/Europe." *Africa Today*, vol. 64, no. 1, 2017, pp. 3–27.

[34] Amnesty International, What makes refugees and migrants vulnerable to detention in Libya? https://reliefweb.int/sites/reliefweb.int/files/resources/082_determinants_of_detention.pdf (Retrieved: 07.01.2021)

[35] Hamad, Mahmoud. "A Law of Diminishing Returns: Transitional Justice in Post-Revolutionary Libya." *AlMuntaqa*, vol. 3, no. 1, 2020, pp. 23–37.

all the countries of sub-Saharan Africa, they created networks of due to the "bio-industrialization" of the distribution system. The absence of effective state control, but also the need for local guides to cross the desert, created a new, highly profitable "sector" of the domestic economy, which according to EU figures, brought in more than 300 million Euro per year to the groups controlled by the networks. Of course, smuggling is not limited to illegal immigrants, but includes, among other things, the smuggling of weapons, fuel, drugs, etc.[36]

It seems that the operation of the armed groups is more specific to a criminal than to a paramilitary organization for political purposes. Thus, the connection of the local armed forces with the illegal immigration is more than obvious, while the absence of state control and the agreements with the EU. In connection with the suppression of the phenomenon and the perpetuation of economic difficulties, it also increases the percentages of human trafficking cases, reaching the point of the sale of African immigrants as slaves. In the same context, there is the phenomenon that these armed groups are fighting among themselves for dominance in a certain area (e.g. Tuareg and Tebu), or a dispute which to some extent also shapes the choice of side in the civil city. [37]

On the other hand, the official Libyan political actors, despite their direct dependence on the armed groups and especially the weak GNA, have both realized that the fight against illegal immigration to Europe is one of the main issues that concern the EU member states. Given that both the GNA as well as the Tobruk government, seeking international assistance, have taken a clear stand against illegal immigration and organized trafficking networks, even at a theoretical level. However, their dependence on the power and support of heterogeneous armed groups is also a brake on reducing the illegal actions of these groups. Still, the absence of a unified, central administration and the consequent existence of a political vacuum, not only does not limit the criminal activities of the paramilitary organizations, but on the contrary it multiplies them.[38]

After examining the issue of irregular migration within the borders of Libyan territory, as well as the involvement of domestic, official and informal actors in it, it is necessary to analyze the corresponding European attitude in order to examine its work in general. However, in order to draw effective

---

[36] Mangan, Fiona. Drug Trafficking, Drug Use, and Libya's Conflict Dynamics. US Institute of Peace, 2020, pp. 3–6.

[37] Ahmida, Ali Abdullatif. "Social and External Origins of State Collapse, the Crisis of Transition, And Strategies for Political and Institutional Reconstruction in Libya." *The Lure of Authoritarianism: The Maghreb after the Arab Spring*, edited by Stephen J. King and Abdeslam M. Maghraoui, by Hicham Alaoui, Indiana University Press, Bloomington, Indiana, USA, 2019, pp. 236–263.

[38] Tossell, Jonathan. *Libya's Haftar and the Fezzan: One Year On*. Clingendael Institute, 2020, pp. 2-7.

conclusions, it is necessary to consider, first and foremost, the theoretical framework on which these actions are based, namely the legal framework of the Common European Asylum System (CEAS), as well as how they evolved within the "European construction".[39]

Under the Lisbon Treaty, the EU tried to ensure its stability through the externalization of its actions, which it tried to implement with less or more success in the Libyan crisis. Although the general attitude of the European members has developed a considerable number of initiatives, it has focused mainly on the issues of irregular immigration from Libya ignoring the root causes and problems of the country in particular. Thus, despite the European rise in Libyan politics, as well as the apparent success of these operations, the EU's significant interest on the one hand, it did not help the progress of the Libyan political dialogue, on the other hand, it provoked strong reactions from international bodies for its approach.[40]

More generally, the EU approach to the issue of irregular immigration from Libya can be examined in the light of the CEAS, as it has developed over the years. Thus, the primary objective of ensuring the free movement of persons within the Schengen area through the external security of the European borders, but also by the adoption of a common immigration framework, meets the fullest possible protection of beneficiaries of international protection which is the cornerstone of the value system of the whole of European culture.

For this reason, since the outbreak of the Libyan uprising, EU has already taken a clear position in favor of changing the Gaddafi regime, aiming at the democratization of the country, in order to ensure cooperation between the two sides. The interest in stability in the region remained undiminished due to Libya's proximity to the European coast. Therefore, the progress and development of Libya were an element for the EU, because through them not only was it easier to achieve its internal stability, but at the same time it would give the international impression that EU was now able to exercise effective common foreign policy. Nevertheless, the EU approach to the Libyan crisis could be described at least as cautious, while the immigration policy that followed, still falls into contradictions between its programmatic and real goals. The most typical example of this effort is the EU Border Assistance Mission (EUBAM) in Libya, which aimed to support the Libyan authorities in achieving the necessary for their European partners, effective border management. But, the conflicting stance of some member states

---

[39] EU, Glossary:Asylum applicant. https://ec.europa.eu/eurostat/statistics-explained/index.php/Glossary:Asylum_applicant (Retrieved 04.01.2021)

[40] The Treaty of Lisbon on The Functioning of The European Union, https://eur-lex.europa.eu/LexUriServ/LexUriServ.do?uri=CELEX:12012E/TXT:en:PDF (Retrieved 08.01.2021)

prevented the adoption of a common effective immigration policy.[41]

Thus, in the context of the European Agenda on Migration, but also of the EU Global Strategy on Foreign and Security Policy (EUGS), the EU set the goal of achieving stability and growth not only in Libya, but in all African countries through the development of various forms of cooperation. To accomplish this, emphasis was placed on training Libyan border guards, increasing the country's capacity to ensure its internal security, and cracking down on migrant trafficking and smuggling networks. Finally, EU had realized that irregular migration had to be tackled from its roots before it reached European shores, with a particular focus on combating trafficking networks.[42]

The first organized reaction came from the Italian initiative to launch the Search and Rescue Operation (SAR) the name "Mare Nostrum", just a few days after the tragic event and the second shipwreck in 2013. The operation was carried out by the Italian Navy and was a military-humanitarian operation in order to prevent similar shipwreck incidents. But the operation received a lot of criticism from international humanitarian organizations, due to the militarization of the immigrants. , in practice it proved to be very effective in rescuing about 100,000 irregular migrants in one year of operation. However, the cost of running the operation as well as the meager external assistance from EU forced the Italian government to shut down it in October 2014.[43]

Then, Operation Triton was set up under the control of Frontex, was a joint operation of 15 member states with the main objective of border surveillance and secondarily conducting SAR operations. Indeed, the limited "range" of the operation combined with its low budget (around 1/3 of Mare Nostrum) caused concern to international humanitarian organizations even before its launch. Later, the new multi-fat shipwrecks of April 2015, pushed the European institutions to triple the budget of Frontex, while at the same time the scope of action of the operation was extended.[44]

However, the increase in the number of irregular immigrants which peaked after the summer of 2015, combined with the resumption of the Libyan war, pushed the EU to carry out another operation, this time of a purely military nature. In the context of the renewed Common Foreign and Security Policy (CFSP), which included the achievement of stability in Libya,

---

[41] Parkes, Roderick. *Libya: Expanding the EU's 'Neighbourhood Watch.'* European Union Institute for Security Studies (EUISS), 2017, pp. 69–80.
[42] EU, Shared Vision, Common Action: A Stronger Europe. https://eeas.europa.eu/archives/docs/top_stories/pdf/eugs_review_web.pdf (Retrieved: 03.01.2021)
[43] Brady, Hugo. *Mare Europaeum?: Tackling Mediterranean Migration.* European Union Institute for Security Studies (EUISS), 2014, pp. 1-4.
[44] Follis, Karolina S. "Vision and Transterritory: The Borders of Europe." *Science, Technology, & Human Values,* vol. 42, no. 6, 2017, pp. 1003–1030.

it was decided to carry out a military operation. Thus, in August 2015, European Union Naval Force Mediterranean (EUNAVFOR Med) started its operations in order to combat the trafficking and smuggling of illegal immigrants in the Mediterranean, but also to protect human lives. Operation Sophia, as it was named, differed substantially from the previous two because, in addition to Search and Rescue it also focused on combating illegal immigration through a total of four phases. At the same time, the EU Council gradually entrusted it with more responsibilities, such as training the Libyan Coast Guard, overseeing the implementation of the arms embargo in the country. Also, in its work from November 2016, it would have the support of the NATO naval operation called "Sea Guardian".[45]

Operation currently ongoing, as a replacement, is IRINI. By launching a new CSDP (Common Security and Defense Policy) and military operation in the Mediterranean, the European Union has stepped up its efforts to implement the UN arms embargo on Libya and thus has wanted to contribute to the peace process in the country. IRINI (Greek "peace") to be the implementation of the UN arms embargo through the use of air, satellite and sea vehicles as its main task. The Mission would be able to inspect ships that are on high seas off Libya and suspected of carrying weapons or related supplies to Libya, in accordance with United Nations Security Council Resolution 2292. However, the neutrality of the operation, especially towards French ships while they are supporting opposition groups in Libya, is questioned. In addition, the illegal intervention of the Turkish ship by the operation command has damaged the legal basis of the operation.[46]

Naturally, the extreme anti-immigration stance of the Italian government, as well as the EU, which largely recognized Libya as a safe third country in the "Malta Declaration", provoked strong reactions from international humanitarian organizations such as Doctors without Borders, Amnesty International, etc. Through their announcements, they blasted on the one hand the Italian immigration policy, on the other hand the corresponding European one, which did not hesitate to conclude agreements with "failed states" to reduce migration flows, although it is aware that the Libyan State is not in a position to offer effective international protection to refugees and migrants.[47]

Even international organizations, such as the UN High Commissioner for

---

[45] Marcuzzi, Stefano. *NATO-EU Maritime Cooperation: for What Strategic Effect?* NATO Defense College, 2018, pp. 1-4.

[46] Megerisi, Tarek. *Geostrategic Dimensions of Libya's Civil War.* Africa Center for Strategic Studies, 2020, pp. 1-9.

[47] Doctors without Borders, European policies continue to claim lives at sea. https://www.doctorswithoutborders.org/what-we-do/news-stories/story/european-policies-continue-claim-lives-sea (Retrieved: 07.01.2021)

Refugees and IOM, who are officially active in Libyan detention centers, speak not only of the inhumane living conditions of migrants there, but also of the inability of the central administration to exercise effective control over the armed forces. Therefore, the reactions and accusations of international humanitarian organizations can be judged as completely realistic, given that the EU and its member states are essentially deaf to their visibility. Thus, through announcements, complaints and legal appeals to the competent bodies, they try on the one hand to raise the awareness of the civil society about the inhuman conditions in the Libyan detention centers, and on the other hand to put pressure on the European institutions to protect regardless of nationality and effectively safeguard the rights of those entitled to international protection.[48]

## Conclusions

It can be seen that the issue of irregular migration to Europe through the Central Mediterranean corridor is one of the most complex issues that the EU has to deal with, not only because of the complexity of the issue itself but also because of the peculiarities of Libyan society and the domestic political situation. Indeed, the social pathogens of Libya, which have been greatly exacerbated by Gaddafi's 42-year-old totalitarian rule, have manifested themselves in the most obvious and violent way, in the wake of the fall of the regime.

Thus, the traditional system of tribal organization, which was a deterrent to the acquisition of a common Libyan national consciousness, has excluded the certain races from the regime. The consequent racial disputes which artificially disguised mainly due to the relentless state repression and as well as the absence of functional state and institutions of the Gaddafi regime, were the cornerstone of the political chaos that prevails to this day in Libya.

At the same time, the military intervention of the international coalition of NATO-led states in March 2011 has contributed significantly to the widening of the security gap, given the absence of a future peace plan under the auspices of the international community, which could lead to in a new political situation through effective external assistance.

So, the internal conditions and the attempts of the internal actors to exploit the huge mineral wealth of the country for their own benefit, created an explosive combination, where rival paramilitary organizations of cities and tribes sought each other essentially for the power and weakening the central government as a part of their demands. Despite domestic and international efforts to find a commonly accepted political solution, the interests of other

---

[48] Mangan, Fiona, et al. *Managing the Secure Release of Sensitive Detainees in Libya*. US Institute of Peace, 2019, pp. 4-16.

actors has not allowed the situation to normalize, but instead created a fertile ground for the development of extremist ideologies.

Following these, the current situation, as shaped by the Skhirat Agreement in December 2015, includes not only the internationally recognized GNA of Tripoli and the rival government LNA of eastern Libya, which is substantially supported by the General Haftar, but also the Muslim Brotherhood of the former GNC, the rebels of the DAESH fighters and other powerful armed groups, as well as EU, UAE, Turkey, Egypt, Italy and France.

In this war scenario, it is understandable that each opposing side is looking for ways to increase its economic power in order to be able to impose itself on its opponents. As a consequence of this disorder, illegal activities such as fuel and arms smuggling are on the rise, which is reinforced by the inability of the central government to exercise effective control. The same framework includes the trafficking networks of illegal immigrants, as well as human trafficking, which are controlled by local armed groups.

Indeed, the rise of armed paramilitaries and the continuation of many years of civil war in a country with ineffective institutions and a strong government have been a major factor in increasing the number of irregular immigrants in Europe and abroad. At the same time, the armed groups, taking advantage of Libya's historical relationship with immigration, as well as the difficult living conditions of the populations in neighboring or other African countries, have managed to establish extensive networks of long-distance traffic to Europe. Of course, the lack of security and control in the country and the need for more and more income due to the civil war, allowed the migrant smuggling networks to carry out blatant violations of immigrants' human rights, such as torture, rape, kidnapping, slavery, etc.

Thus, the international community, and in particular the EU, which has been directly affected by the operation of trafficking networks, not only have had to deal with the ever-increasing number of migrants, but also to effectively defend universal human values and principles, except the Greek ones.

Having thus incorporated the issue of irregular migration into the core of common European policies and the focus of the Member States' interest, the EU focused on conducting joint operations and concluding agreements with the internationally recognized Libyan government on the one hand to limit the number of arrivals, on the other hand to guarantee and protect the rights of those entitled to international protection. And if for the first part of its actions, the results are considered sufficiently satisfactory, since the arrivals of migrants and refugees have skyrocketed for the first time since 2013. So, its effectiveness and determination to achieve the second part is unquestionable due to the increase in incidents of human rights violations and trafficking.

Besides, the EU is faced not only with complaints from international humanitarian organizations, but also with a great deal of moral dilemma. It can be said that it is not a good policy to immediately acknowledge human rights violations in third countries to conclude agreements with them in order to strengthen its cohesion and security and consequently reaching the European interests. Because the evolution of the EU itself has shown that its enlargement was a result of solidarity and respect for the principles of justice, equality and democracy. Therefore, the purpose of the EU should not be the adoption of policies aimed at isolating the problems, but the transcendence of common European principles across the world. In order to tackle the migration issue effectively, but also to respect human rights worldwide, it is necessary to engage more actively and creatively in Libya's humanitarian situation as well as cooperating with other countries.

In summary, the fragile political situation in Libya and the civil war that has been raging since 2011 have greatly affected the issue of irregular migration to Europe via the central Mediterranean corridor. At the same time, it has influenced the wider EU immigration policy which being confronted with the phase of Euroscepticism, seems to fall into contradictions in many cases. That is why the EU institutions but also, in particular, its Member States must advance procedures and focus their actions on ending the bloody Libyan civil war and then stepping forward for the democratic political process. Thus, EU' support can lay the foundations for the country's unity, stability and development, which will not only have a positive impact on the management of immigration issues and the protection of human rights, but on the whole process of promoting the common European principles.

## CHAPTER 8

# DEMOGRAPHIC, ECONOMIC, POLITICAL AND LEGAL DIMENSIONS OF MIGRATION POLICY IN THE RUSSIAN FEDERATION

Neziha Musaoğlu[*]

## Introduction

The phenomenon of migration has existed since ancient times, and briefly, it means the displacement of individuals or leaving their living spaces and settlements for other places. The oldest known migration in history is the "Migration of Tribes", which started from Eurasian steppes and significantly affected the future of civilizations during the centuries. The main reason that pushed people to migrate in the past was the desire to access more fertile soils and more favorable climat. Great geographical discoveries have not only changed the perception of borders and the lands of the countries but also directed the attention of people to untouched lands all over the world. First these intact lands were approached for commercial purposes, then with the development of imperialism, these lands were wanted to be seized for colonialism. In time migration movements have diversified and gained more complex dimensions. Nowadays migration became one of the most important issues of globalized world.

The objective of this chapter is to analyse the change and continuity trends in the migration policies of Russian Federation in a historical perspective. On the one hand, the study will emphasise the driving forces of the migration processes and factors that affect its management and practices; the strategies and policies developed, and instruments used in order to implement them. On the other hand, it will focuss on the problems such as illegal migration, which arise from the lack of efficent mechanisms and measures in the regulation of the migration problems. The migration policies of the Russian Federation will be examined with multidimentional aspects: political, economic and juridic.

## Migration in Russia

Both the public opinion, the scientific community and the government started to focus more on immigration in Russia starting from 2012. It has

---

[*] Prof Dr. Kirklareli University, Turkey, neziha.musaoglu@klu.edu.tr

been a huge proliferation of researches and digital materials on migration. A Board of Expertise was established under the Presidency of the Russian Federation, responsible for projects on demography at national level and policies to be developed as a result.

In the post-Soviet period, many scientific resources have accumulated on Russia's migration policies.[1] Most of the studies in this field discusses migration in terms of management and decision-making.[2] Some studies focus on refugees[3]; some others focus on secyrity issues[4] and illegal immigration.[5]

In fact the migration is a complicated phenomenon having both economic, demographic, social, geopolitical and national security dimensions. The management of migration processes on national level is defined by three

---

[1] Andrienko, Y. and S. Guriev, 2005, Understanding Migration in Russia, CEFIR Policy Paper Series, No.23, November, Center for Economic and Financial Research at New Economic School, Moscow; Zayonchkokaya (2007), Zayonchkokaya, Zh.,2007, Russia's Search for a New Migration Policy, European View: A Journal of the Forum for European Studies, Vol. 5, Europe and Immigration: 137-145; Korobkov, A., 2007, Migration trends in Central Eurasia: Politics Versus Economics, Communist and Post-Communist Studies, 40 (2): 169-189; Heleniac, T., 2008, An Overview of Migration in the Post-Soviet Space, in Cynthia J. Buckley and Blair A. Ruble, with Erin Trouth Hofmann (eds.) Migration, Homeland, and Belonging in Eurasia, Woodrow Wilson Center Press, Washington DC, with Johns Hopkins University Press, Baltimore, MD: 29-68; Robarts, A., 2008, the Russian State and Migration: A Theorethical and Practical Look at the Russian Federation's Migration Regime, in Cynthia J. Buckley and Blair A. Ruble, with Erin Trouth Hofmann (eds.) Migration, Homeland, and Belonging in Eurasia, Woodrow Wilson center Press, Washington DC, with Johns Hopkins University Press, Baltimore, MD: 99-122; Ivakhnyuk, Irina, Russian Migration Policy and Its Impact on Human Development, Department of Population, Lomonosov Moscow State University, Munich Personal RePEc Archive, 1 April 2009,1; Light, M., 2010, Policing Migration in Soviet and Post-Soviet Moscow, Post-Soviet Affairs, 26 (4): 275-313; Schenk, C., 2016, Assessing Foreign Policy Commitment Through Migration Policy in Russia, Demokratizatsiya, The Journal of Post-Soviet Democratization, 24 (4): 475-499; Turuknova, E., N. Mkrtchyan and Zh. Zayonchkovskaya, 2014, Russia's Immigration Challenges, in Tsuneo Akaha and Anna Vassilieva (eds.) Russia and East Asia: Informal and gradual integration, Routledge, New York: 200-243; Malakhov, V., 2014, Russia as a New Immigration Country: Policy Response and Public debate, Europe-Asia Studies, 66 (7): 1062-1079

[2] Nonini, D. M., 2002, Transnational Migratns, Globalization Processes, and Regimes of Power and Knowledge, Critical Asian Studies, 34 (1): 3-17; Rudnyckyj, D., 2004, Technologies of Servitude: Governmentality and Indonesian Transnational Labor Migration, Anthropological Quarterly, 77 (3): 407-434; Hoang, L. A., 2016, Govermentality in Asian Migration Regime the Case of Labor Migration from Vietnam to Taiwan, Population Space and Place, 23 (3): http://doi.org/10.1002/psp.2019

[3] Agier, M., 2006, The Chaos and the Camps: Fragments of a Humanitarian Government, in Ursula Biemann and Brian Holmes (eds.) The Magreb Connection: Movements of Life Accross North Africa, Barcelona: 260-283

[4] Bigo, D., 2002, Security and Immigration: Toward a Critique of the Governmentality of Unease, Alternatives 21 (1, supplement): 63-92; Truong, T.-D., 2011, The Governmentality of Transnational Migration and Security: The Making of a New Subaltern' in Thanh-Dam Truong and Des Gasper (Eds) Transnational Migration and human Security, Springer: 23-37

[5] Inda, J., 2006, Targeting Immigrants: Government, technology, and Ethics, Blackwell, Oxford; Fassin, D., 2011, Policing Borders, Producing Bounderies. The Governmentality of Immigration in Dark Times", Annual Review of Antrophology, 40: 213-226; Fassin, D., 2011, Policing Borders, Producing Bounderies. The Governmentality of Immigration in Dark Times", Annual Review of Antrophology, 40:213-226; Malakhov, V., "Us" and "Them": Post-Soviet Migration in Russia and (re)making Symbolic Boundaries, Eurozine, 2016, http://eurozine.com/us-and-them-2

different goals: economic, state security and human rights.[6]

According to these goals and aspects of migration, there are different definitions for the migration policy. For exemple, the migration policy definition of L. L. Rybakovsky is one of the wide-ranging definitions. It corresponds to "a system of generally accepted governance ideas and conceptually related means with the help of which the state above all, as well as social institutions, observing certain principles corresponding to the concrete historical conditions, seek to achieve certain goals corresponding to the current and the future stage of social development."[7]

Different types of migration policies can be distinct in line with this definition:

- migration policy as the product of the political system;

- migration policy is worked out and implemented not only by the state, but also by social institutions;

- different social institutions may have different ideas concerning the goals, tasks and means of migration policy;

- migration policy as the process coordinating the interests of the political and economic elites of the state, political parties, non-governamental organizations and migrants in the sphere of migration reguşlation at the federal and regional levels;

- migration as the process of interaction between states involving a change of juridiction because migrants leaving one society enter another.[8]

## Migration in Tsarist Russia

Within the historical perspective, the phenomenon of migration policies and strategies on migration in Russia passes through three different stages: Tsarist Russia, the USSR and the Russian Federation periods. Although some trends changed in this long evaluation process of migration, it is important to note that many similarities exist between each stage. In this chapter, only the post-Soviet period will be examined in details.

One of the main factors that fundamentally determines the phenomenon

---

[6] Ivakhnyuk, I., 2011, Prospects of Migration Policy in Russia: Choosing the Right Path, Maks Press, Moscow, p.32 cited from: Gasparishvili, A., Narbut, N., Onosov, A., Zhanna Puzanova, 2017, Russian Migration Policy in The Last 25 Years, Ananele Universitatii din Oradea, Seria Relatii şi Studii Europene, Tom IX, pp. 213-223, p.215

[7] Рыбаковский Р.Л., 1987, Миграция населения, Москва p.167

[8] Volosenkova, E., P. Kabachenko, E. Tarasova, Migration Policy. Managing Migration Processes, Methodology and Methods of the Study of Migration Processes, ed. Zh. Zayonchkovskaya, I. Molodikova, V. Mukomel, Moscow, 2007, p. 219

of migration in Tsarist Russia is the lack of homogeneity of the people living in the territory of the empire. The ethnic diversity appears as a direct result of the imperial expansion of the Tsarist Russia. The ethnic diversity of Russian empire, which was taken over by the USSR, constitutes the historical legacy of today's Russian Federation. Today's "Russia is a federal state which is comprised of more than 200 nationalities and people of different cultures who are accustomed to cohabiting for centuries with each other and especially during the Soviet era of internal migration between the Soviet states. Many religions are rooted in Russia's hybrid culture. It is important to note that in Russia the "host" society and those are now referred to as "migrants" were, until recently, part of the same political and cultural community: they were all compatriots. This unity of socio-cultural space and identity makes Russia distinct from other post-colonial/ post-imperial contexts which are largely alien to the population of the former metropolitan centers."[9]

The expansionist policies of the Russian state towards strategically important lands started with the invasion of Kazan Khanate and Siberia by Ivan the Terrible and then continued with the occupation of Sant Peterbourg by Peter I. During the rule of Ekaterina II, the lands around Volga River joined the empire's territory. Increasing the population in the occupied lands and especially in the central European territories of the empire around the Volga coasts, which were poor in population, and thus ensuring regional development in agriculture, was the main factor that shaped the foreign migration policies followed by the Russian administration. In 1763, the State Migration Management Directorate, possibly the first in the world history, was established in order to direct immigrants from Europe to the internal regions of the empire with low population. An important feature of these migrations from Europe to Tsarist Russia is that immigrants consisted of people with high qualifications.

"In the middle of the 18th century, among 107 members of the Saint Petersburg Academy of Sciences only 34 were Russians. Since then, Russia has had numerous Diasporas of Germans and Deutch. By the end of the 19th century, 1.8 million Germans lived in the Russian Empire, of whom 77 percent were farmers. Between 1764 and 1866, 549 colonies were founded by foreign resettlers in Russia with over 200,000 male migrants alone."[10]

## Migration during the Soviet period

After the first wave of migration during the Tsarist Russia's period, the

---

9 Malakhov, 2016 cited from: Malfait, Milka, "Russia's and EU's Migration Challenges in 2019: Comparative Analysis, DLA Piper, Sravnitel'naya Politika i Jeopolitika, 2010, T. 11, N0: 1, pp. 104-110, DOI: 10.24411/2221-3279-2020-1008, p. 106
10 Brockhaus & Efron Encyclopedic Dictionary, 1890-1907, vol. XXIV, p. 672

second biggest migration wave was experienced in the Soviet period. The immigration policies followed by the Soviet governments were also contradictory as were the policies followed by the tsarist administrations. "The Soviet period can be characterized as contradiction between strict limitations on the freedom of movement provided by the propiska system, and large-scale population movements, both voluntary and involuntary, that were inspired by economic and administrative policy measures to meet labor demand of an industrializing economy."[11]

Since the aim of the nationalities policy followed by Lenin in the early years of the USSR, which was established in place of the Russian Empire that collapsed because of the 1917 October Revolution, was to gain the non-Russian environment without fear provoking. The existing demographic and ethnic structure was tried to be preserved. The redrawing of ethnic and cultural boundaries with the effect of forced immigrations because of the Soviet nationalities policy, which were put into practice with Stalin's coming to power, led to the emergence of an even more complex and intertwined demographic structure. As a result, the frontiers of the newly created Soviet republics did not coincide with the ancient ethnic and cultural boundaries of the peoples living there. "Strategies for suppressing and assimilating this ethnic diversity initially appeared to be successuful —but by the 1980s the Soviet "family of nations" was unravelling and the reasons can be located in the strategies them-selves."[12]

In the Soviet period, internal migration was very limited and subject to strict rules. "In addition to the above limitations of internal migration, it should be said that international migration was an exception rather than a rule in the Soviet Union. For decades of the Soviet regime the USSR was a 'closed' country where international migration was strictly limited by the State. The entry and departure rules, granting and revoking citizenship and deportations were regulated by decrees and ministerial instructions issued in 1918, 1925 and 1959 that reflected the restrictive stance of the State."[13] In the Soviet period, the migration policy was focused exclusively on internal migration. Inter-republican migrations during this period were external by form, although internal by nature. This means that migration from Russia to Kazakhstan or from one Russian oblast (province) to another were regulated by the same rules. Crossing administrative borders between the republics had no special regulation.

---

[11] Ivakhnyuk, 2009, p. 1

[12] Herd, Graeme, 2000, Russia and the "Near Abroad", eds. Trevor C. Salmon, Issues in International Relations, Routledge, London and New York, p. 227

[13] Тюркин, М. , 2005, Миграционная система России : монография / М. Л. Тюркин. - М. : Стратегия, 2005 (Липецк : ОАО Полигр. комплекс Ориус). - 367 с. : ил., табл.; 22 см.; ISBN 5-9234-0051-0 (в пер.) pp. 21-22 cited from: Ivankhnyk, 2009, p. 11

## Transformation of the immigration policy in the Post-soviet period

Immigration to Russia was a key outcome of the Soviet Union's collapse which has had deep impacts on Russia's society over 25 years later. In the evolution of the Russia's immigration policy, Ivankhnyuk (2011) distinguishes 3 periods since the dissolution of the Soviet Union. "Russia over the past 25 years has seen a succession of periods when migration policy was determined by humanitarian considerations of human rights (the first halp of the 1990s), the period when national security interests were paramount (2000-2007) and the period when economic and business interests came to the fore."[14]

In a similar way another specialist of Russian migration, Meilus argues that "…the history of migration policy can be broken up into five distinct periods: 1991 to 1996, 1996-2000, 2002 to 2005 and 2006 to present. The changes in periods reflect both events inside the Russian Federation such as the transition from Yeltsin to Putin's presidency, and events outside the Russian Federation such as the 2001 September Eleventh terrorist attacs, and the 2008 economic collapse."[15]

The period of 1991-1996 was caracterised by reactivist efforts of newly formed Russian Federation to deal with the refugees entering Russia from other newly independent Post-Soviet States.[16] "…the main problem in the 1991-1996 period was a lack of state capacity and resulted in an influx of irregular, undocumented migrants"[17] "The confusion of the authorities at that time seems quite natural if one takes into account the incredible complexity and chaos that accompanied the transition from socialism to capitalism.[18]

A Federal Migration Program was accepted by the Russian Federation's Presidency in August 1994. The program classified migration into five types: forced migration, emigration, illegal immigration and internal migration.[19] The main purpose of the Federal Migration Service (FMS), which was established in 1992, was to regulate the arrival of refugees and ethnically Russians returning from newly independent Post-Soviet States. The wars and conflicts emerged in the near abroad of Russia (Armenia, Azerbaijan,

---

[14] Gasparishvili, a., Narbut, N., Onosov, A., Zhanna Puzanova, 2017, Russian Migration Policy in The Last 25 Years, Ananele Universitatii din Oradea, Seria Relatii şi Studii Europene, Tom IX, pp. 213-223.215, cited from: Ivakhnyuk, 2011, p. 33

[15] Meilus, Lina, Challenges in Migration Policy in Post-Soviet Russia, 2013, Honors Projects. Paper 17, http://digitalcommons.iwu.edu/institu_honproj/17, p. 16

[16] Meilus, 2013, p. 18

[17] Ibid.

[18] Malakhov, V., 2014, Russia as a New Immigration Country: Policy Response and Public debate, Europe-Asia Studies, 66 (7): 1062-1079, p. 1065

[19] Тавровский А. В. , 2020, Вызовы и противоречия миграционной политики России. " Исследование выполнено при поддержке РГНФ по проекту № 15-03-00805, p. 165

Tchikistan and Chechna) in the first half of the 90's caused one million refugees and 2, 2 million displaced persones.

Mihaylova draws attention to specific trends in the migration process since the beginning of this century: "First, regional CIS migration became by far the most common (93% of the 2013 total migration balance). Second, concentrations of single ethnicity communities of immigrants from Central Asia have formed. In the net balance of migrants, men of working age predominate. Secondary general education is the most frequent level of qualification of CIS migrants. Only 12.77% of the CIS immigrants and 14.40% of the immigrants from the rest of the world have a degree of higher education."[20]

## The 1996-2001 period

It is caracterized by the rise of irregular migrants; by the stabilization of some political and economic institutions; by the reelection of Boris Yeltsin; Russian Financial Collapse of 1998; by the spice in oil prices; by the end of many conflicts in the post-Soviet space.

In this period, important mesures are taken in order to institutionalise the current migration practice. The first "Concept of the State Migration Policy of the Russian Federation" was drafted in 1996 but it was not implemented until 2002.[21]

## The 2002-2005 period

It was marqued by two major events, the election of Vladimir Putin in 2000 and the 2001 September Eleventh terrorist attacks. Putin's administration put pressure on law agencies to uphold immigration policy. In this context, the 2002 Federal Law on the Legal Status of Foreign Citizens of the Russian Federation[22] was adopted and the FMS was trasformed from an independent agency to being placed under the Ministry of Interior[23]. The new law on citizeship which came into effect in 2002, overturned the previous, relatively easy procedure for obtaining Russian citizenship for former citizens of the USSR.[24] Together, both of these changes resulted in the policy of the

---

[20] Mihaylova, I., 2017, Russia's New Concept of the State Migration Policy Until 2015: A Reform Towarrds Effective Policies for International Economic Migrants, 182, Geopolitics, History, and International Relations 9 (1), 2017, pp. 176–214, doi:10. 22381/GHIR9120178, p.180

[21] Meilus, 2013, p. 21 cited from: Ivanchnyk, 2009, p. 35

[22] Federal'nyi zakon o grazhdanstve Rossiskoi Federatsii', available at: http://www.rg.ru/2000/06/05/zakon-gragdan.html

[23] Ivanchuyuk, I., 2009, rossiiakaia migratsionna politika v kontekte chelovecheskogo razvitiia: istoria i sovremennost, Issue N0: 22, Faculty of Economics of the Lomonosov Moscow State University, Moscow, p. 38

[24] Malakhov, V., 2014, Russia as a New Immigration Country: Policy Response and Public debate, Europe-Asia Studies, 66 (7): 1062-1079, p. 1065

2002 to 2005 period becoming more restrictive and leading to a flow of illegal migration.[25]

The 2002 law and institutional revisions increased xenophobia against Central Asian labor migrants.[26] Immigrants from Central Asia have been approached as a threat to national security due to the September 11 terrorist attacks executed by Elqaida, a radical Islamist organization. The 2002 Immigration Act introduced serious restrictions, making it almost impossible for immigrants from Central Asia to register officially. As a result, migrant workers have turned to the "underground" market, and the number of illegal migrants increased rather than decreased.

## 2006-2012 Period

In 2006 the Russian Federation implemented a new migration reform in order to make migration policy more liberal and less restrictive.[27]

The global economic crisis in 2008 had significant negative effects on Putin's administration, the Russian society and labor immigrants. "The economic crisis of 2008-2009 destroyed the semblance of prosperity (…) Migrant labor quotas were cut, xenophobia encreased in Russia; companies laid off migrants or in some cases simple stopped paying them."[28]

## 2010-2012 period

As the negative effects of the 2008 economic crisis on the economic stability were not serious, most of the workers who returned to Central Asia has come back to Russia since 2010. According to the Organization for Economic Cooperation and Development (OECD) report of 2010, 960,000 temporary labor migrants entered Russia legally and this number has continued to increase.[29]

The fourth period was marked by a significant liberalization of approach that some experts have called the "liberalisation turn.[30] "The liberal measures went alongside conservative measures, and while the new immigration law simplified the rules governing residence registration and the using of work permits, the authorities at the same time adopted a law which prohibits

---

[25] Meilus, 2013, p. 21

[26] Meilus, 2013, p. 23

[27] Meilus, 2013, p. 24

[28] Bishkek, Brussels, Central Asia: Migrants and the Economic Crisis. Rep.no. Asia Report 183, N.p.: International Crisis Group, 2010, p. 1

[29] Anichkova, D., Central Asia's Migrant Headache, International Economics Bulletin, Washington DC, Moscow, Beijing, Brussels, 21 June 2012:1-4, p. 1

[30] Gradirovski, 2010, Politika repatrriatsii v sovremennom rossiyskom gosudarstve, Doklad, Moscow, Vsemirnyi bank, Fond "Migratsiya: XXI vek; Zaionchkovskaya& Tyuryukanova, 2010, Migratsiya i demokraficheskii krizis v Rossii, Moscow, Tsentr migratsionnıykh issledolanii, RAN

foreign citizens from trading in markets."[31]

The reasons for such discrepancies, according to Malakhov (2014) are:

1.   Conflicts of interest between liberals and "siloviki";

2.   Differences between economic and political approaches;

3.   Differences in legal regulations and implementation"[32]

Russia in the post-soviet period experienced a succession of periods when migration policy was determined by humanitarian considerations of human rights (the first half of the 1990s), the period when national security interests were utmost (2000-2007) and the period when economic interests were paramount.[33]

### Immigration wave from the "Near Abroad"

12 new republics gained their independence with the collapse of the Soviet Union in 1991 and the internal borders that they previously share with Russian Federation turned into external borders and the citizens who whishes to leave the country of residence were made easy to change the country or to cross borders by establishing visa-free migration regimes. The creation of the Commonwealth of Independent States in 1991 faciliated the application of this regime.[34] With the agreement signed in Bishkek, the capital of Kyrgyzstan, on October 9, 1992, it is aimed that citizens of Armenia, Belarus, Tajikistan, Moldova, Russian Federation, Tajikistan, Turkmenistan and Uzbekistan are members of the Commonwealth of Independent States to travel without a visa. Uzbekistan signed the agreement in 1995 and became a member of the Community. Ukraine and Azerbaijan signed bilateral agreements with Russia on free travel with Russia instead of being included in the Agreement. After the withdrawal of Turkmenistan in 1999 and Russia in 2000 from the agreement, the Bishkek regime was abolished. Instead of a joint agreement, Russia preferred to make bilateral agreements with most of the post-Soviet republics on visa-free transition.[35] Through this visa-free transition regime between 1992-2002, 4.6 million people (1.7 million from outside Russia and 2.9 million from Russia) acquired Russian citizenship.[36]

Various immigration waves towards Russia are taken place in the post-Soviet period. At first, it is necessary to differentiate the group of immigrants

---

[31] Malakhov, 2014, p. 1067

[32] Malakhov, 2014, p. 1068

[33] Gasparishvili et al., 2017, p. 215 cited from: Ivakhnyuk, 2011, p. 33

[34] Kuznetsova, İrina, Postcolonial migrations in Russia. The racism, informality and discrimination nexus, IJSSP, 39, ½, 2019,52, pp. 52-67, p. 52

[35] Tavrovsiy, 2020, p. 166

[36] Чудиновских О. О политике и тенденциях приобретения гражданства Российской Федерации в период с 1992 по 2013 г., Демографическое обозрение, 2014, pp. 3–12

who migrated to Russia from the former Soviet republics, as the most intense domestic migration wave and consist of the so-called "nationals". "With the sudden collapse of the Soviet Union approximatively 25 million Russians were found to live beyond the borders of the newly created Russian Federation. In some newly independent former republics, for example Kazakhstan (37 per cent), Estonia (30 per cent), and Latvia (34 per cent) the propotion of ethnic Russians constituted a high minority."[37] Non-Russian immigrants from Post-Soviet geography who constitute the most compatible group for Russia in terms of ethnic belonging, common language and cultural values, are included to this category.

In order to encourage citizens, who want to return to their homeland Russia, the Russian government arranged programs like the returning program which was planed and implemented by the Russian Federal Immigration Administration. According to the statements of the President of the Russian Federal Immigration Administration, Maniatkin, the first year (2007) when the program was implemented, 50 thousand people arrived. It was planned that 100 thousand people in 2008 and 150 thousand people in 2009 would migrate to Russia. However, while the number of those who declared their willingness to come in 2007 was around 35 thousand, the real number of arrivals was 400. [38] The reason for falling below the planned figures is that the 14 administrative districts of the Russian Federation did not agree to participate in the program, and some legal restrictions are shown especially for Moscow and Saint Petersburg.

These mass migrations have a distinct ethnic character. In addition to ethnic Russians returning to their country, the peoples who were exiled during the Soviet period had the opportunity to return to their new republic, mostly from their own ethnic group, years later.[39]Apart from the ethnic Russians, people involved in second wave of internal migration consisted of citizens of the CIS, China and other countries in the Russian Federation. Most of the immigrants in this category are non-Russian citizens from the former Soviet republics. In 2009, 93% of the immigrants on the territory of the Russian Federation involved CIS citizens.[40] About half of this number consists of citizens of Ukraine, Uzbekistan and Kazakhstan.[41]

According to the statistical data for the years 2010-2011, although the countries with the highest immigration did not change, the number of

---

[37] Herd, 2000, p. 237

[38] www.online.zakon.kz

[39] Мукомель, В., 2006, Социокультурные факторы миграционной политики постсоветской России Москва, p.12

[40] Каламанов, В.А, 2013, Время преодоленя, Практическая Философия Российской Идеи,Весь Мир, Москва, p. 391

[41] www.demographia ru / articles_N / index? idR = 21 & idArt = 1901

immigrants from the CIS decreased. However, it should be noted as a remarkable development that the number of immigrants from Kyrgyzstan increased during this period. In 2013, officially, 422,738 people arrived from CIS countries, with 59,503 arriving from other countries.

The conflict in Ukraine in 2014 led large numbers of Ukrainians to cross into the Russian Federation. "More than 267 000 persons applied for temporary protection in 2014, almost 100 times more than in 2013. Russian migration policy in 2014 was focused mainly on the management of this inflow, classified by the Russian Federation as humanitarian migrants. A decree facilitated support for this group, and asylum applications from Ukrainian nationals were fast-tracked with a three-day processing limit instead of thre months. An obligation to undergo medical clearance within ten days of admission was introduced. Changes to the repatriation programme allow for the participation of persons classified as refugees from Ukraine."[42]

Asians and Africans, who use Russia as a transit station on their way to the more developed industrial democracies of the West, represent another group of migrants. According to some estimates, Moscow Oblast alone has become a temporary place of residence for more than 180,000 refugees from Iraq, Iran, Somalia, Sudan, China, etc.[43]

The different migration waves experienced in the post-Soviet period made Russia one of the important migration centers of the world. (USA; England, as well as Germany). The number of people located in the territory of the Russian Federation for less than a year is 489 thousand according to the 2010 official censuses (The number of Russian citizens permanently residing Russia abroad was 239 thousand in 2002.)[44] In 28 years since the opening of the borders, Russia has received a minimum of 24 million immigrants.[45]

## The "Brain Drain" problem

As a concept, emigration refers to the movement of a person from her/his own country to another country in order to settle permanently or temporarily reside. As a result of the widespread access to transportation means and the opportunity to travel from country to country in a way that reduces intercontinental distances, the expansion of the diameter and geography of international migration has ed to an increase in the number of immigrants at

---

[42] Country notes: Recent Changes in Migration Movments and Policies", Chapter 4, International Migration Outlook 2015, OECD

[43] Gavrilova, İrina, Migration Policy in Modern Russia: To Be or Not to BE, perspectives on European Politics and Society, 2:2, Koninklijke, Brill NV, Leiden, The Netherlands, 2001, p. 267

[44] Ob İtogah Vserossiiskoi perepisi naselenia 2010 goda, http: // www. Prepis2010.ru/results_of_the_census/results-inform. Php

[45] Kalamanov, 2013, p. 361

international level. According to the UN assessment, while the number of immigrants in the world was 175 million in 2000 (3% of those living outside their own country), this number reached 214 million in 2010.[46] According to ILO data only half (105 million) of 214 million immigrants is actively involved in working life.[47] As a result, there is a need for foreign workers in developed countries, as only the local population cannot meet the labor shortage.

With the influence of globalization, political and economic interdependence between states has increased in the international system especially after the end of the Cold War. According to the Russian researcher Ivahniuk, an expert on international migration, the interdependence on labor force exchange between states on a global level arises when economies in developed countries are met with immigrant labor from underdeveloped countries. This interdependence is largely due to the supply of foreign workers brought from outside of the labor deficit[48] and industrial activities on foreign labor. It is observed that the industrialized and post-industialized countries are not only acceptors but also donor countries that supply labor to other countries. "Replacement migration", which emerged as a new concept in the 90's, is a general term used to express the potential of international migration to meet this deficiency when the problem of demographic deficiency tendency of the accepting countries is experienced.[49]

The Russian Federation is one of the countries, which not only accept, but at the same time supllies labor force to other countries. Naturally, the CIS states established on the post-Soviet area were the region where the most immigrants received, while Russia is giving a serious "brain drain". The phenomenon of immigration of human resources from Russia was experienced most strongly in the early 90s when the USSR collapsed. Although the number of people who migrated abroad between 1990-1996 is not certain, it is recorded as 90-110 thousand per year. [50]

During the Soviet period, Russian citizens did not have the right to go abroad. However, after the collapse of the USSR, the situation changed: the borders were opened and Russian citizens started to migrate abroad for various reasons, including "brain drain".

---

[46] International Migration Report 2002, New York, United Nations Population Division Department of Economic and Social Affairs, 2002, p.1; http://www.unic.ru/bill/?ndate=2011-12-7

[47] http://ilo.org/public/russian/region/europro/moscow/info/index.htm

[48] Ivaniuk, İ., V., Mejdunarodnaya migratsia kak resurs razvitia, Vek Globalizatsii, 2011, Viipusk No: 1 (7), http://www.socionauki.ru/journal/articles/132578

[49] Alechkovskii, İ., A., Iontsev V.A., 2008, Tendentsii mejdunarodnoi migratsii v globaliziruuchemsia mire, Vek globalizatsii, Vipusk No: 2, p. 86

[50] "Uchetka umov" iz Rassii, http://www.rhr.ru/index/jobmarket/russia/6267.html Verhoturov, D., Nelaskovaia Rus, http://online.zakon.kz/Document/?doc_id=30158784

Two decades after ratification of the International Covenant on Civil and Political Rights 'freedom of everyone to leave any country, including his/her own' was realized in the 1993 Federal Law 'On regulation of departure from the Russian Federation and entry into the Russian Federation'.[51] Russian citizens received also the right for employment in other countries. Article 10 of the Law entitled 'The Right of Russian Citizens to Work Abroad' declared, "The citizens of the Russian Federation have the right to seek job and get employed outside the Russian Federation at their own will". The need for a legal framework for overseas employment of Russian citizens was a result of the socio-economic crisis challenged Russia that pushed people to look for alternative sources of income, including international labor migration.

Liberalization of internal and international movements of Russian citizens in the 1990s, have increased their mobility and made them part of the global community. However, impoverishment resulting from the economic recession made those benefits inaccessible for a significant part of population.[52]

According to Rossotrudniçestvo data, around 30 million Russians live abroad, 1/5 of them are young people. The number of Russian-speaking people is around 4 million.[53] It is one of the largest diasporas in the world in terms of numbers. The majority of people of Russian descent live in the CIS countries and the Baltics: according to data, this rate was 88.6% in 2018 (the largest diasporas are in Ukraine, Kazakhstan, Belarus and Uzbekistan). 11.4% of Russians living abroad are outside the post-Soviet geography. The most numerous Russian diasporas are located in Germany, the USA and Israel.[54]

"Brain drain" cannot be conceived only as a negative fact. According to Zerchaninova, it has positive effects in terms of "advantage to increase Russia's prestige in the world and to attract more workforce to the country."[55]

The wish to emigrate remains a subject that is not out-of-date for citizens of the Russian Federation. Almost 1/3 (31%) of the urban population living in the Russian Federation would like to migrate abroad. According to the results of the survey conducted by ROMIR in 2012, "Do you want to emigrate from Russia?" The rate of those who answered "Yes" to the question increased by 12 percentage points compared to a similar survey study conducted in 2005. The number of people who wanted to continue living in the country also decreased compared to the previous study. While

---

[51] Tiurkin, 2005

[52] Ivakhnyuk, 2009

[53] Popov, DS, Migratsionnaia policy kak component gosudarstvennoy strategii Rossii, Novaya Evraziya, N0: 3 (4), 2010 p. 35, cited from: Pal'nikov, www.perspektivy.info

[54] Сколько у нас соотечественников за рубежом // Коммерсантъ. 2006. 11 сентября, p.4

[55] Зерчанинова А. С. Никитина, Государственная Политика Поддержки Молодых Соотечественников За Рубежом, Management Issues. 2019. № 4 (59), p. 27

the rate of citizens who wanted to stay in Russia in 2005 was 66%, this rate decreased to 55% in 2012.[56] In the meantime, the countries preferred by Russian citizens for immigration changed in the period after the Eurozone crisis. It became Australia rather than European states.

## Demographic crisis, need for workforce and illegal migration

One of the important strategic goals of both the Tsarist Russia and the Soviet administrations was to rise the population of the Siberian region, which was poor in terms of population density, with the reforms of the public official Stolipin. In the period after the dissolution of the Soviet Union, Stolipin's plan to change the demography of Siberia failed. According to the data of the State Federal Statistical Office, the number of immigrants from the Khabarovsk region was about ten times the number of arrivals. In this context, while 220.8 thousand people (13.6%) migrated to the region between 1992-2007, the rate of immigrants from the region reached 72%.[57]

The relative decline of the population is not only a current demographic trend for Russia's Far East region, but also a problem for the whole country that the governments have been trying to solve since the serious demographic crisis in 1990. Regardless of the increase in the number of immigrants, according to estimates, the tendency of Russia's population continues to decrease in the 21st century. Based on the 2002 census, the estimation of ROSSTAT is that the population in Russia will increase to 137 million by 2026.[58] In case the current trends regarding population growth continue, in the first quarter of the 21.century,

Russia's population may drop to 125 million.[59] If the increase in immigration towards the middle of the 21st century is low, the population of Russia may drop to 100 million depending on the birth and life expectancy. Due to the decrease in fertility and the increase in mortality, the population that makes up the labor force is decreasing. Labor loss in Russia in 2007 was not great. (Around 300 thousand people). However, between 2010 and 2018, this number exceeded 1 million people per year. In 2026, the loss of workforce is predicted to be 67 million people.[60] In the light of these predictions, it can be said that the most important deficiency in Russia's economic life in the near future will be its labor force. According to Zayonçovskaya, a Russian expert on immigration, the most important

---

[56] Kalamanov, 2013, p. 377 cited from: Ofitsialnii sait İsledovatelskogo holdinga ROMİR, 20.09.2012, http: // romir.ru/studies/390_1348084800

[57] Statistical Bulletin, "Migration Data of the General Population", www.fedstat.ru/indicator/data.do, 28.11.2012

[58] Kalamanov, 2013, p. 362

[59] ibid

[60] Kalamanov, 2013, p. 365

conditions of success in Russia's next economic, political and demographic development is the influx of immigrants to this country. As Zayonçovskaya states "Migration is the lifeblood of Russia."[61] In a speach given in 2012, Romondanovsky, the director of the FMS also pointed that "regrettably, our economy cannot do without foreign workers."[62]

The demographic crisis in Russia does not only mean the loss of work force that the economy needs. At the same time, the loss of control over Siberia and Far East Russia, which are already low in population, carries geopolitical risks.[63] According to Popov and Mamontova, measures such as granting permanent Russian citizenship to Russian citizens living in the post-Soviet geography as well as Ukrainian and Belarusian citizens should be taken to close the population and economic power deficit of Russia. According to Galas, Russia's pursuing a transparent foreign and internal migration policy should be used as an important "soft power" instrument in solving immigration, social adaptation and integration problems.[64]

Many negative factors in the post-Soviet space like difficult economic situation, low living standards, military and ethnic conflicts led to the growth of immigration waves to Russia.[65] Most of the immigrants in Russia are immigrants in the labor market. There are three types of regimes applied to immigrants in the Russian labor market according to geopolitical interests and economic priorities. Immigrants from the republics in the Eurasian Economic Area in the first category are required to fill in only an immigrant card when entering Russia, to provide information on residence registration and the duration of their employment contract to the Immigration Administration. The second category includes immigrants from the five former Soviet republics (Azerbaijan, Moldova, Tajikistan, Uzbekistan and Ukraine) with visa-free entry. The immigration regime applied to them is almost the same as the regime applied to immigrants in the first category. Here, only a visa replacement immigration card is not required. The third category of immigrants includes immigrants from other countries. Their immigration in Russia depends on the immigration quota set by the Russian government each year.[66]

---

[61] Zayçovskaya, J.A., http://academia.info/news/15340

[62] Romondanovsky, K., Russia's New İmmigration Policy Targets Quality Not Quantity", RIA Novosti, Moscow, 28 January 2011, Features ed., 1-2 web, p. 1

[63] Popov, A. M., E.A. Mamontova, Novie prioriteti migratsionnoi politiki Rossii, Vestnik Sankt-Petersburkogo universiteta MVD Rossii, N0:1 (85) 2020, DOI: 10.35750/2071-8284-2020-1-183-188, p. 184

[64] Popov and Mamontova, 2020, p.185

[65] Pismennaya, E., Ryazantsev, S., Bozhenko, V., Central Asian Diasporas in the Russian Federation: migration channels and their contribution to socio-economic development of sending communities, Central Asia and Caucasus, Journal of Social and Political Studies, 2016, Vol. 17, Issue 4., pp. 87-94

[66] Ryazantsev, S.V., Integratsia migrantov v kontekste vnechnei migratsionnoi politiki Rossii, Demografia. Migratsia, Sotsiologicheskie issledovania N0:1, 2018, 105-111, p. 106

"According to the United Nations Development Program Report on the Russian Migration Policy, 90 percent of migrant workers are irregular.[67] "Illegal migrants working in the informal sector substantially outnumber the officially allocated quota. According to data of the Federal Migration Service, 5 million foreign nationals work illegally, according to the Ministry of Health of the Russian Federation– 8 million, while according to the Fund "Migration 21 Century" – approximately 10 million, or 12–13% of the whole working population of the country."[68] As stated by the direct evaluations of the Federal Immigration Administration as well as different approximate evaluations, 3 million to 5 million foreign citizens participate in the working life in the Russian Federation every year without official permission. Illegal immigration, which feeds the illegal sectors of the economy with labor, is the reason why some of the people of the Russian Federation have increased negative attitudes towards immigrants."[69] According to the official data of the Federal Immigration Administration, the number of people residing in Russia as immigrants and working officially registered is 1.7%. This ratio has doubled compared to the 2006 rate (3.2%).[70] Accordingly to Russian Federal Migration Management data, 630 thousand foreign nationals were banned from entering Russia in 2014 and 124 thousand people were deported. [71]

Inconsistencies of Russia's migration policy like "corruption, informal rules, nationalism, and problems in state capacity all contribute towards the inconsistent migration policy and allow illegal migration to flourish."[72]

In other words, the rise of illegal immigrants causes consequences such as violating the rights of immigrants, worsening working conditions and exploitation of their labor.

Illegal immigration is one of the new threats shaped by globalization, which includes migration processes. The migration alongside food, health, environment, population growth, disparities in economic opportunities, drug trafficking and terrorism figures in the UNDP's conceptualisation of Human Security.[73]Althoug the space of security has been narrowly expanded into these new security threats the state remains the main player in ensuring its

---

[67] Meilus, 2013, p. 15 cited from: Ivakhnyuk, 2009, p. 16

[68] Mihaylova, 2017, p. 180 cited from: Gasparishvili, A., Narbut, N., Onosov, A., Zhanna Puzanova, 2017, Russian Migration Policy in The Last 25 Years, Ananele Universitatii din Oradea, Seria Relatii şi Studii Europene, Tom IX, pp. 213-223

[69] Смирнова В.А., Нелегальная миграция как угроза национальной безопасности РФ // Миграционное право. 2009. №1.

[70] Chterbakova, E., Na konets tretevgo kvartala 2011 goda razrechenie na rabotu v Rossii imeli 1032 tiysiach innostranniih grajdan, http://www.demoscope.ru/weekly/2012/0501/barom05.php, 373

[71] http://www.fms.gov.ru/ about / statistics / details / 4281 / 14.08.2014

[72] Meilus, 2013, p. 14

[73] Buzan, Berry and Lene Hansen, 2009, The Evolution of International Security Studies, Cambridge, p. 203

national security while performing its essential duties.[74] Illegal immigration has negative effecst on many areas of social life: It poses one of the main threats to national security, geopolitical interests and international prestige in the political field. Economically, it leads to the enlargement of the size of the illegal economy, the situation in the labor market, and the withdrawal of Russian firms and workers from the market; it causes social tension in the social field, which aggravates the criminogenic situation in the country as a whole.[75]

The fact that most of the immigrants do not have "registered status" and also take part in the "dirty" and "black" economy, fear, creates an unstable situation and creates a "transience syndrome", leading to a negative attitude towards the employer, society and Russia. This situation poses a negative obstacle to the adaptation and integration of immigrants into Russian society."[76]

One of the most essential problems of today's immigration policy is the harmonization of the interests of indigenous people and immigrants. The integration of the immigrants to the society is important and as Hocaoğlu Bahadır notes in integration both the immigrants and the host country should make an effort. [77] There are two basic models known in the world for this. The first one is assimilation regardless of ethnic identity. The second model is the protection of ethnic and cultural identities and the multicultural model.[78] In this context, one of the big problems in Russia is the escalation in inter-ethnic conflicts. Mostly, the problem of immigration has been perceived by associating it with the security and protection of the state. Therefore, the security, political, economic and cultural dimensions of the migration policies to be followed should be addressed, formulated and implemented as a whole.

The solution of such complex immigration problems requires the state to have a consistent and resolute political stance. However, for a long time, political governments did not give enough importance to immigration problems. This situation brought with it the aggravation of the migration crisis: problems such as the strategic use of labor resources within the country, the withdrawal of the needed workforce to the country, the

---

[74] Сковиков А.К., 2010, Современные проблемы национальной безопасности России // Управление мегаполисом.. №5.

[75] Бурда, М.А., PolitBook, 2015 -1, Риски Нелегальной Миграции, Как Угроза Национальной Безопасности России

[76] Virkkunen, J., Economic Aspacts of Migration from Central Asia in Russia, RUND Journal of Economics, 2017, Vol. 25, No:1, pp. 102-111, DOI: 10.22363/2313-2329-2017-25-1

[77] Hocaoğlu Bahadır, N., 2018, "Avrupa Birliği Entegrasyon Politikalarında Dil Boyutu", Uluslararası İlişkilerde Göç: Olgular, Aktörler, ve Politikalar, Der Kitapevi Yayınevi ve Dağıtım Paz. Ltd. Şti., eds. N. A. Şirin Öner and S. G. Ihlamur Öner, p. 144

[78] Ryazantsev, 2018, p. 105

reduction of conflicts between immigrants and indigenous people, and inter-ethnic tensions. The adaptation and integration of immigrants with the society of the host country constitute the weakest point of that country's immigration policies. Russia, which was closed to the outside world during the Soviet period, lacks serious experience in this regard. However, the immigration problem was first included in the official regulations with the regulation and implementation of the Russian Federation Official Immigration Policy Concept, which was adopted in 2012 and covers the period until 2025. In the Concept it is pointed out that "…the important element of the Official Immigration Policy of the Russian Federation is the adaptation and integration conditions of immigrants".[79] Later in 2014, federal law studies on the adaptation and integration of immigrants were initiated.

Some experts point out the need to be cautious about accepting immigrants from post-Soviet geography as an effective additional labor force. Especially foreigners, who work as seasonal workers, send their earnings to their families in their countries instead of using them in Russia. According to the data of the Russian Central Bank, Tajikistan citizens working in Russia in the period up to the economic crisis in 2007 sent 1.6 billion dollars to their families.[80] Increasing possibilities of money transfer in electronic environment accelerated the money transfer process even more. In order to limit the people who immigrated to Russia from sending their earnings to their families, it can be considered as a solution to migrate because of family rather than individual. However, the ghettoization of immigrants with their families by concentrating in the same districts and especially in Moscow strengthens the possibility of tensions between the locals and immigrants.[81]

## Russia's legal migration regime

Based on universal values of international law, series of legal regulations have been made in order to manage the internal and external migration processes in the Russian Federation since 1991. The migration as a human right and freedoom is guranteed under the Constution of the Russian Federation. Article 27 of the Constitution establishes the right of citizens to freedom of movement, choice of the place of stay and residence and the right of to free return to its territory. Foreign citizens and stateless persons enjoy the same rights that are garanteed by the Aricle 62 of the Constitution.[82]

The Federal Law of May 31, 2002 N0: 62_FZ On Citizenship of the Russian Federation and Federal Law of June 25, N0:115-FZ On the Legal Status of Foreign Citizens in the Russian Federation; The Federal Law of July

---

[79] Ryazantsev, 2018, p. 107
[80] Delovoi Ejenedelnik "Kompania", 2008, No21. pp. 23-31
[81] Mukomel, 2006, p.3
[82] Gasparishvili, 2017, p. 215

23, 2013 N0: 203-FZ On Introducing Amendments to the Law on the Legal Status of Foreign Citizens in the Russian Federation[83] and some legislative acts of the Russian Federation are the main key legal regulations made in order to menage the current imigration processes in Russian Federation. But it is important to note that the most progressive step in the conceptualisation process of the migration in the Russian Federation is the new Concept of the State Migration Policy of the Russian Federation until 2025.[84] The Concept was developed as response to the problems that mount up in the post-USSR period, such as illegal, lower-skilled, non-diversified CIS migration and social tension. The first Russian Federation Immigration Concept (2003) focused on the national security dimension of migration by pushing socio-economic development and demographic problems to the second plan. In 2005, it was decided to update the Concept, but due to the 2008 economic crisis and the differences of opinion between liberals and conservatives within the FMS, studies on the issue were delayed. In 2009, the Migration Policy Commission was established, and the 2012 Concept was published instead of the revised 2003 Concept.

With the 2012 Concept, the adaptation and integration of immigrants into the society has entered the agenda of the Federal government. "The emphasis of the CSMP is on the coordination of new, modernized, and reformed migration policies that help achieve its central goals: to sustain the country's economic competitiveness, to alleviate the negative effects its demographic decline, to combat the deficiencies of its domestic labor market, to attract and retain talented foreign workers, and to facilitate its modernization and innovative development"[85]

As it is well known xenophobia and racism are factors that generally accompany immigration throughout the world. The possibility of encountering these negative consequences of immigration in the Russian Federation, as well as at the international level, seems strong. One of the most important legal regulations made in this context is the "Immigration Policy of the Russian Federation until the 2025 Period", which was approved by the President and entered into force on June 13, 2012. The following measures are envisaged in the first phase covering the period between 2012-2015: "A) preparing the infrastructure for the "residence" of labor migrants on the basis of public-private cooperation; b) establishing infrastructures that will ensure the integration and adaptation of immigrants, including information and legal support centers, courses that teach the language, history and culture of the

---

[83] Federal Law No. 182 of 12.11.2012 on the amendment of Federal Law No. 62 of 31.05.2002 "On Citizenship of the Russian Federation" and of 12.11.2012, http://www.consultant.ru/popular/civic/34_2.html= p173; p.368
[84] Mihaylova, 2017
[85] Ibid.

Russian Federation; c) conducting specific studies including internal and external migration issues."[86]

## Conclusion

Despite the proliferation of legal regulations on immigration, there are still problems in practice and opportunities to develop Russia's migration policies. Russia needs new approaches and instruments in modernizing its migration policy and regulating these policies. According to the assessment of the Russian expert Tishkov, "policy based on non-expert evaluations and daily phobias is in conflict with the development interests of the country. (This policy) has a restrictive detective quality and these features are getting stronger. Meanwhile, immigration policy should be aimed at encouraging and rationally managing internal migration, especially from former USSR countries to Russia."

The Russian Federation has appreciated that it cannot achieve complete and permanent solutions to the migration problem, which has become one of the important international trans-border issues due to globalization, with its own policies implemented at national level, has begun to care about implementing the international migration regime in cooperation and coordination with the international actors specialized in this field. In this regard, the approach of the Russian administration vis-à-vis the International Organization for Migration (IOM) is stated on the web page of the Ministry of Foreign Affairs as follows: "We note the relevance of the International Organization for Migration (IOM). We welcome the strengthened constructive interaction between the UN and the IOM. We trust it would enhance both organizations' capacities so that the international community can successfully respond to emerging migration challenges. We view migration not merely as a current challenge, but also as an important driver for social and economic development. We assume that a key development objective in the migration area shall be finding mechanisms for optimizing and controlling migration processes in order to enhance their positive contribution to the socio-economic sphere while taking into account national interests and priorities. We attach great importance to strengthening international cooperation in the area of migration. Russia supported the adoption of the Global Compact for Safe, Orderly and Regular Migration. It should be noted that the Compact's principles and objectives echo a number of provisions of the updated Concept of the State Migration Policy of the Russian Federation. Our country participated actively in the consultation process to develop modalities of the first International Migration Review Forum to be held in 2022."[87]

---

[86] Kontseptsia gosudarstvennoi migratsionnoi politiki Rossiiskoi Federatsii herb 13 iunia 2012 g., Http://www.grant.ru/hotlaw/federal/402320/

[87] "Russia's Position at The Seventy-Fifth Session Of The Un General Assembly 1133-23-07-2020 (https://www.mid.ru/en/web/guest/general_assembly/-/asset_publisher/lrzZMhfoyRUj/content/id/4252717

CHAPTER 9

# CENTRAL ASIAN FIGHTERS AND THEIR FAMILIES IN SYRIA: REFUGEES OR TERRORISTS?

Ainur Nogayeva[*] and Dana Akhmedyanova[**]

## Introduction

The Syrian crisis is a global conflict that involve such multiple stakeholders as the Syrian government, groups of the armed opposition, Islamist groups and jihadists from around the world (including fighters from Central Asia), regional powers and global superpowers. At the same time, the Syrian crisis is a part of the Arab Spring. Formation of the so-called "Islamic State" (ISIS, or IS) and its expansion in the region complicated the situation even more.

The international community is actively trying to resolve the Syrian crisis through the Geneva Peace Talks on Syria and the Astana peace process. From January 2017 to August 2019, Astana hosted thirteen meetings on a Syrian settlement where participants negotiated observance of the ceasefire in Syria, cooperation against the ISIS and al-Nusra Front, establishment of de-escalation zones.[1]

The 14th round of Syria peace talks in the Astana format in December 2019, as the *Special Representative of the President of the Russian Federation* for *Syria, Alexander Lavrentiev* noted, took place in the context of the transfer of significant territories in northeast Syria under the control of government forces, as well as the launch of the Syrian constitutional committee.[2]

Gradual settlement of the conflict is associated with addressing the issues of reintegration into civilian life. These concerns are also essential for the Central Asian countries, particularly since combatants from the region took part in hostilities. Problems of their returning are inextricably linked to such

---

[*] Assoc. Prof. Dr, L.N. Gumilyov Eurasian National University, IR Dep. (Kazakhstan); Erzincan Binali Yıldırım University, Political Science & Public Administration (Turkey), ainur_nogay@hotmail.com

[**] Assoc. Prof. Dr, L.N. Gumilyov Eurasian National University, IR Dep. (Kazakhstan), ahmedyanova_dk@enu.kz

[1] "Astaninskij Protsess. Posol'stvo Respubliki Kazakhstan v Rossiiskoi Federatsii", https://www.kazembassy.ru/ rus/sotrudnichestvo/mnogostoronnee_sotrudnichestvo/astaninskii_process/ (Accessed on 08.09.2020).

[2] "Diskussii Byli Ochen Polezny – Spetspredstavitel' Prezidenta RF o 14-m Raunde Astaninskogo Protsessa", 11.12.2019, https://www.inform.kz/ru/diskussii-byli-ochen-polezny-specpredstavitel-prezidenta-rf-o-14-m-raunde-astaninskogo-processa_a3593756 (Accessed on 15.08.2020).

issues of great importance as preventing and countering violent extremism and radicalization, deradicalization, rehabilitation and reintegration.

Scholars mark very rear manifestations of violence in the region, although the Tajik civil war and war in Afghanistan caused formation of networks of Central Asian jihadists.[3] The Arab Spring also raised wave of political extremism, because Islamists came to power in the Middle East and North Africa.[4] As a result, we have witnessed more often cases of involvement of nationals from Central Asia into terrorist activities (the 2017 attacks in New York, Stockholm, Saint Petersburg and Istanbul, foreign fighters in Syria and Iraq).[5] After the beginning of the war in Syria, the Central Asia fighters moved there from Afghanistan; the first Central Asia fighters came to Syria in 2012.[6]

## Central Asia: Internal Security Challenges

The current security leadership continues to focus on combating and preventing extremism and terrorism, which have posed a serious threat since 2011. On May 17, 2011 for the first time in Kazakhstan there was a terrorist attack in the city of Aktobe[7]. Then, terrorist attacks were recorded in such large cities and regional centers as Aktobe, Atyrau, Astana, Almaty and Taraz. From the beginning of 2012 to September 21, 5 anti-terrorist operations were carried out in Kazakhstan to neutralize the alleged terrorists, most of whom were killed. The previously unknown Islamist group "Soldiers of the Caliphate" (Jund al Khalifah), which had connections with "Al-Qaeda" and trained fighters for this international terrorist organization, claimed responsibility for the terrorist attacks. Sources in Afghanistan and Pakistan have reported that in recent years they have been actively sending fighters – usually ethnic Kazakhs – to Kazakhstan to recruit new members and pressure the authorities.[8]

By August 2015, the National Security Committee of the Republic of Kazakhstan claimed it had prevented five Daesh/ISIS-related terrorist incidents since the beginning of 2014 and in 2015 alone prosecuted 45 people

---

[3] Raffaello Pantucci, Mohammed S. Elshimi, "Introduction", **Understanding the Factors Contributing to Radicalisation Among Central Asian Labour Migrants in Russia**, RUSI Occasional Paper, Royal United Services Institute for Defence and Security Studies, April 2018, p. 1.

[4] Erkin Baydarov et al., "Kazakhstan in the Arab Spring Context", **Central Asia And The Caucasus**, Journal of Social and Political Studies, Volume 20, Issue 1, 2019, Sweden, https://www.ca-c.org/online/2019/journal_eng/cac-01/07.shtml (Accessed on 30.10.2020).

[5] Raffaello Pantucci, Mohammed S. Elshimi, ibid, p. 1.

[6] Erkin Baydarov et al., ibid.

[7] Ainur Nogayeva, "Central Asian States' Security Policies", **The Changing Perspective sof Central Asia in the 21st Century,** Murat Yorulmaz, Serdar Yılmaz (eds.), Istanbul: Kriter Yayınları, 2020, p.44-66

[8] Dina Malysheva, "Vyzovy bezopasnosti v Central'noj Azii," **Challenges to Security in Central Asia**, Moscow, IMEMO RAS, 2013, p. 15.

and was investigating 40 others for recruiting related to the Syrian conflict.[9]

Figure 1 presents data on deadly terrorist attacks in Central Asia between 2008 and 2018.

**Figure 1.** Terrorist Attacks in Central Asia (2008–2018)

| Date | Country | Location | Type | Deaths |
|---|---|---|---|---|
| 19 April 2009 | Tajikistan | Isfara | Murder of police officers | 1 |
| 26 May 2009 | Uzbekistan | Khanabad/Andijan | Armed attack/suicide bombing | 2 |
| 3 September 2010 | Tajikistan | Khujand | Suicide bombing | 4 |
| 19 September 2010 | Tajikistan | Kamarob | Armed attack | 25 |
| 17 May 2011 | Kazakhstan | Aktobe | Suicide bombing | 1 |
| 23 May 2011 | Kazakhstan | Astana | Bombing | 1 |
| 1 July 2011 | Kazakhstan | Aktobe | Armed attack | 3 |
| 31 October 2011 | Kazakhstan | Atyrau | Suicide bombing | 1 |
| 8 November 2011 | Kazakhstan | Almaty | Armed attack | 1 |
| 12 November 2011 | Kazakhstan | Taraz | Armed attack | 7 |
| 21 July 2012 | Tajikistan | Khorog | Assassination | 1 |
| 30 July 2012 | Kazakhstan | Almaty | Mass murder | 14 |
| 23 May 2014 | Tajikistan | Khorog | Armed attack | 1 |
| 19 May 2015 | Kyrgyzstan | Bishkek | Suicide bombing | 1 |
| 4 September 2015 | Tajikistan | Dushanbe/Vahdat | Armed attack | 39 |
| 5 June 2016 | Kazakhstan | Aktobe | Armed attack | 21 |
| 18 July 2016 | Kazakhstan | Almaty | Armed attack | 10 |
| 30 August 2016 | Kyrgyzstan | Bishkek | Suicide bombing | 1 |
| 29 July 2018 | Tajikistan | Danghara | Attack with car/knives | 4 |

**Source:** Edward Lemon, Talking up Terrorism in Central Asia, 2018, p. 3

## Central Asia as an Exporter of Foreign Fighters

There are different estimations of foreign fighters. The Soufan Group reported in 2015 about approximately 2,000 people,[10] the International Crisis Group reported the same year about 2,000-4,000 people.[11]

---

[9] Noah Tucker, **Public and State Responses to ISIS Messaging: Kazakhstan**, CERIA Brief No. 13, Washington, DC: Institute for European, Russian, and Eurasian Studies, February 2016, p. 4.

[10] Foreign Fighters: An Updated Assessment of the Flow of Foreign Fighters into Syria and Iraq, Soufan Group, New York, December 2015, p. 15.

[11] **Syria Calling: Radicalisation in Central Asia**, Europe and Central Asia International Crisis Group, 20 January 2015, Briefing No. 72, p. 1.

Central Asians, as a group, have been disproportionately represented as foreign fighters in Syria and Iraq, with close to 20 percent of all foreign fighters originating from Central Asia, while this region accounts for less than 5 percent of global Muslims. According to the International Centre for the Study of Radicalization and Political Violence (ICSR), Central Asia is the third largest source of foreign fighters for ISIL and other VEOs in Iraq and Syria. This sparked a heated debate in society about the reasons for radicalization and to the problem of fighters from Central Asia.[12]

In 2017, according to an Afghan government official, the number of fighters from the region at the end of 2016 was approximately 3,000 to 4,500. However, no one can say the real number, because of people left with families and children.[13]

According to some estimations, at least 800 of Central Asian fighters at the Middle East were killed.[14]

As Professor Kuat Rakhimberdin said in an interview, according to the intelligence services of the United States and Russia, more than 4.2 thousand people went to fight in Syria and Iraq from the countries of Central Asia. In the first place, among the countries of the region in terms of the number of militants fighting in ISIS is Uzbekistan with 1,500 people. It is followed by Tajikistan, from where there are 1,300 militants in Syria and Iraq, and almost 3,000 more of them were stopped in Turkey and/or deported to their homeland. About 500 people went to war from Kazakhstan and Kyrgyzstan, and 400 from Turkmenistan.[15] Currently, the countries of the region are taking steps to return home, punish, rehabilitate and adapt the fighters.

In 2011-2016, the number foreign fighters from Kyrgyzstan increased 20 times over and has reached 811.[16] As of June 2019, according to the Anti-Terrorism Center of the State Committee for National Security of the Kyrgyz Republic, there were 850 citizens of the Kyrgyz Republic in the war zone in the Middle East, 150 of them are considered dead.[17]

---

[12] Thomas F. Lynch III et al., "The Return of Foreign Fighters to Central Asia: Implications for U.S. Counterterrorism Policy", **Strategic Perspectives,** Institute for National Strategic Studies National Defense University, Vol. 21, October 2016, p. 3.

[13] Moheb Spinghar, "Radikalizacija Molodezhi: Prichiny Radikalizacii i Sposoby Bor'by s Nej," **Novye Vyzovy i Podkhody po Regional'noj i Global'noj Bezopasnosti v Central'noj Azii: Materialy Mezhdunarodnoj Konferencii,** (Nur-Sultan, 26 October 2018), Nur-Sultan, 2020, p. 128.

[14] Edward Lemon, "Talking Up Terrorism in Central Asia", **Kennan Cable** No. 38, 1 December 2018, p. 6.

[15] Nargiza Muratalieva, "O Tehnologijah i Njuansah Radikalizacii v Gosudarstvah Central'noj Azii", 14 October 2019, **Central Asia Analytical Network,** https://caa-network.org/archives/18256 (accessed on 28.06.2020).

[16] Mirgul Karimova, Sheradil Baktygulov, "USDOS-CTB Project: Social Media for Deradicalization in Kyrgyzstan: A Model for Central Asia. Making Deradicalization Work: Case Study – Kyrgyzstan", **Search for Common Ground**, 2017, p. 6.

[17] "Vozvrashhency iz Sirii: v Kyrgyzstane Eshe ne Reshili", 11.07.2019, //http://prevention.kg/?p=4016

Approximate evaluation of the number of militants from Central Asia is presented in Figure 2.

**Figure 2.** Estimated Number of Foreign Fighters from Central Asia

| Country | Open Source Data | Data of Intelligence Agencies | Murdered | Returnd | Convicted for Taking Part in hostilities in Iraq and Syria |
|---|---|---|---|---|---|
| Uzbekistan | 3000-3500 | 300 | 900 | - | 11 |
| Turkmenistan | 500 | - | 2 | 6 | - |
| Tajikistan | 2000 | More than 1000 | 300 | 100 | 16 |
| Kazakhstan | 500 | 200 | 80 | 33 | 33 |
| Kyrgyzstan | 500-600 | More than 600 | 70 | 40 | 47 |

**Source:** Bahtier Ergashev, Vyhodcy iz Uzbekistana – Chleny Terroristicheskih Organizacij v Sirii i Irake: Sovremennoe Sostojanie i Perspektivy, 2020, p. 237.

Afghanistan is also a source of threat: according to the Center for Strategic Studies (CSS), Ministry of Foreign Affairs, Islamic Republic of Afghanistan, today over 20 terrorist groups from different countries operate in Afghanistan, taking advantage of instability, high unemployment and poverty in the country and are trying to use the Islamic Republic of Afghanistan as a springboard for destabilization in other countries of the Asian region.[18]

## Domestic Discourses on Terrorism and Returnees: the Cases of Kazakhstan and Kyrgyzstan

The securitization of issues of terrorism and extremism in Kazakhstan's foreign policy course is expressed by its relevance within the framework of international organizations and at the bilateral level (e.g. the *Congress* of Leaders of *World* and Traditional *Religions*).[19] In contrast to other Central Asian nations, which overstate popularity of ISIS and unnecessarily politicize the threat, Kazakhstan provides a realistic threat assessment. The government does not deny facts of recruiting citizens.[20]

Representatives of religion attempt to separate true faith from terrorism and extremism.[21] The media discourse in Kazakhstan can be estimated as rather restrained: most often, the notion of "terrorism" is characterized by such concepts as "threat", "attack", "conflict", "struggle".[22]

The level of securitization in the expert discourse seems to be high, there is little evidence of using hate speech, the positions are well-documented: the

---

(Accessed on 28.06.2020).

[18] Moheb Spinghar, ibid, p. 114.

[19] Anastasiya Reshetnjak, Terrorizm i Religioznyj Ekstremizm v Central'noj Azii: Problemy Vosprijatija. Kejs Kazahstana i Kyrgyzstana. – Astana, KISI, 2016, s. 11.

[20] Noah Tucker, Public and State Responses to ISIS Messaging: Kazakhstan, p. 3-4.

[21] Anastasiya Reshetnjak, ibid, s. 13.

[22] Ibid, s. 17.

most frequently used term is "religious extremism" and such characteristics as "threat", "problem", "conflict", "struggle", "exacerbation" , "confrontation".[23]

As for public responses, very often they doubt the authenticity of extremist videos with participation of ethnic Kazakhs and explain them by conspiracy theories.[24]

In Kyrgyzstan, the level of interest in Daesh begins to manifest itself steadily only in July 2015 (according to Yandex, the affinity index for Kyrgyzstan is 232%, that is more than one and a half times higher as compared to Kazakhstan).[25]

In 2015, according to the report of the Head of Kyrgyzstan's Interior Ministry, approximately 200 citizens (among them 30 women) went to Syria, 22 citizens were killed there.[26]

In general, the degree of securitization of the problem of terrorism and extremism in Kyrgyzstan at the domestic political level is estimated higher than in Kazakhstan (meetings with representatives of power structures and national security bodies, theologians).[27]

Article 35 of the Constitutional Law of the Kyrgyz Republic "On Citizenship" provides among conditions for loss of citizenship the following:

- training outside the Kyrgyz Republic to commit a terrorist or extremist crime,
- participation in terrorist organizations recognized as such in the Kyrgyz Republic,
- participation in an armed conflict or hostilities on the territory of a foreign state.[28]

The official discourse in Kyrgyzstan is free from conspiracy theories in contrast to the public reaction, however, it is restricted to external cultural markers and explains radicalization by foreign influence.[29]

Religious leaders also consider religious extremism and terrorism as a threat to "traditional" Islam.[30]

---

[23] Anastasiya Reshetnjak, ibid, s. 31.
[24] Noah Tucker, Public and State Responses to ISIS Messaging: Kazakhstan, p. 6.
[25] Anastasiya Reshetnjak, ibid, s. 40.
[26] Thomas F. Lynch III et al., ibid, p. 13.
[27] Anastasiya Reshetnjak, ibid, s. 35.
[28] "Konstitutsionnyi Zakon Kyrgyzskoi Respubliki O grazhdanstve", http://minjust.gov.kg/ru/content/625 (Accessed on 10.09.2020).
[29] Noah Tucker, **Public and State Responses to ISIS Messaging: Kyrgyzstan**, CERIA Brief No. 14, Washington, DC: Institute for European, Russian, and Eurasian Studies, February 2016, p. 9.
[30] Anastasiya Reshetnjak, ibid, s. 37.

Kyrgyzstan's media explain terrorist activities predominantly by narratives about the "Island of Democracy" and the "Center of Geopolitics".[31] It is notable that media coverage of the issues is less politically correct than political discourse (the harsh tone the titles of articles, emotional stress and presentation style).[32]

As for Kyrgyzstani expert discourse, the problem of religious extremism is more relevant than the terrorist threat; also, there are examples of aggressive language in relation to non-traditional religious movements and their representatives, as well as to the authorities.[33]

Although Kyrgyzstan is considered as the most democratic and free country in the region, young people promote a paternalistic attitude regarding the most preferable religious policy.[34]

In general, the level of religiosity in Kazakhstan and Kyrgyzstan is quite high, however, the percentage of those who consider adherence to religion as the main factor, is relatively low (only one fifth of the believers in Kazakhstan and one sixth in Kyrgyzstan).[35] It is noteworthy that in Kyrgyzstan the level of awareness of such organizations as the Turkestan Islamic Party (48,5%), Hizb ut-Tahrir (43,2%), Jaysh al-Mahdi (19,6%) is much higher than in Kazakhstan, where 30,1%, 23,8%, and 3,1% of respondents heard about them; in Kazakhstan, a larger number of respondents know about such organizations as Soldiers of the Caliphate (15,3%), the Salafiyya Movement (16,3%), Tablighi Jamaat (11,8%) and Senim. Bilim. Omir (9,3%).[36]

Since there is a little response from religious institutions and the authorities, reflection in the media and the expert environment dominates, while both the former and the latter allow the formation of a negative narrative about representatives of certain ethnic and religious groups.[37]

As a result, there are different attitudes towards returning of ex-fighters in all the Central Asian communities. Individuals who returned to their home countries are called officially "returnees", "combatants," but mass media use emotional descriptions due to differences in public opinion.38

The issue of the return of Kyrgyz citizens from Syria and Iraq began to

---

[31] Noah Tucker, Public and State Responses to ISIS Messaging: Kyrgyzstan, p. 4.
[32] Anastasiya Reshetnjak, ibid, s. 39.
[33] Ibid, s. 50.
[34] Ibid, s. 43.
[35] Ibid, s. 56.
[36] Ibid, s. 56-57.
[37] Ibid, s. 52.
[38] "Vozvrashhency. Chetyre Raznyh Suzheta Pro Vernuvshihsja iz Sirii i Iraka", 01.10.2020, http://prevention.kg/?p=8380 (Accessed on 07.09.2020).

be actively raised after similar special operations in neighboring countries, when the authorities of Kazakhstan, Tajikistan and Uzbekistan began to actively engage in the return of their citizens.39 Before the Ministry of Foreign Affairs of the Kyrgyz Republic did not even have information about this category of citizens besides the official number of 140 Kyrgyz women who joined the ISIS.40

The turning point was in December 2018, when information about natives of Kyrgyzstan looking for an opportunity to return home appeared; there is an opinion that impact of international organizations to provide with support and the example of neighboring Kazakhstan, Uzbekistan, and Tajikistan catalyzed taking a corresponding decision.41

The participants of the first large-scale press conference of parents of Kyrgyz citizens in the Middle East held in Bishkek, on May 14, 2019, appealed to the authorities with a request to assist in the return of their relatives[42], including minor children in penitentiary institutions of Iraq.[43] The polarity of opinions in the society about returning has manifested itself during international conference entitled "Rehabilitation and Reintegration of Returners in Central Asia" (Bishkek, 2019) to which representatives of state bodies and law enforcement agencies of Kyrgyzstan, specialists from Kazakhstan, Uzbekistan, and Tajikistan participated. There were sharp divisions among the participants over estimations of decision to return as state's duty or a pressure on the state, ways of disengaging from the extremist ideology, the duration of rehabilitation due to both successful and unsuccessful cases of rehabilitation and other issues.[44]

## Drivers of Violent Radicalization and Extremism

It is necessary to put a greater emphasis on drivers of radicalization, since they determine ways of deradicalization and successful integration.

Radicalisation is defined as *"a complex, multidimensional phenomenon, emerging from the interaction of micro-individual, enabling environment (socio-cultural) and macro-structural factors: it cannot be predicted by one variable alone"*.[45]

According to findings of "Making Deradicalization Work: Case Study –

---


[39] "Vozvrashhency iz Sirii: v Kyrgyzstane Eshe ne Reshili", ibid.

40 "Kyrgyzstan Zhdet Svoikh "Geroev" s Blizhnego Vostoka. Sebe na golovu?", 19.06.2019, http://inozpress.kg/news/view/id/54222 (accessed on 29.06.2020).

[41] Ibid.

[42] "Vozvrashhency iz Sirii: v Kyrgyzstane Eshe ne Reshili", ibid.

[43] "Vozvrashhency iz Sirii i Iraka: Pravitel'stvo KR Prizyvaet ne Politizirovat' Etot Vopros", 11.09.2019, http://prevention.kg/?p=4844 (Accessed on 29.06.2020).

[44] Svetlana Lapteva, "Vechernij Bishkek: Vozvrashhency iz Sirii: Fobija ili Real'naja Opasnost'", 02.09.2019, http://prevention.kg/?p=4781 (Accessed on 18.11.2020).

[45] Raffaello Pantucci, Mohammed S. Elshimi, ibid, p. 8.

Kyrgyzstan" survey in the framework of the "Social Media for Deradicalization in Kyrgyzstan: A Model for Central Asia" pilot project, funded by the US State Department's Counterterrorism Bureau in 2016, among main causes of radicalization are:

- a lack of extracurricular activities,
- a lack of critical thinking skills,
- a lack of opportunities,
- the politicization of religion,
- an ideological vacuum,
- gaps in religious education,
- a lack of understanding of the key problems,
- a lack of communication between actors at different levels, as a result young people have to consult online resources with *violent extremist content*.[46]

Young people worry about corruption, a lack of access to government, low income, their future and prospects.[47]

Many researchers highlight the critical role of online communications and social media as a key enabling factor (conducting information campaigns and recruiting young people by the Islamic State and the Islamic Movement of Uzbekistan) and an important tool to ensure the sustainability of preventing and countering violent extremism activities, but its potential is not sufficiently implemented.[48]

Results of the survey conducted by the Search for Common Ground in 2017 showed varied reactions from the respondents to narratives leading to violent extremism:

- 61% of participants supported the information and searched for interactions to get answers,
- 20% of respondents sympathized to the messages to join the war in Syria,

---

[46] Mirgul Karimova, Sheradil Baktygulov, ibid, p. 3-4, 10.

[47] Anastasiya Reshetnjak, ibid, s. 56.

[48] Raffaello Pantucci, Mohammed S. Elshimi, ibid; Syria Calling: Radicalisation in Central Asia, ibid, p. 6; Inga Sikorskaya, Analytical Report on Action Research. Messages, Images and Media Channels Promoting Youth Radicalization in Kyrgyzstan, Ed. Ikbalzhan Mirsaiitov, Mirgul Karimova, Search for Common Ground, January 2017, p. 5, 7; Mirgul Karimova, Sheradil Baktygulov, ibid, p. 2; Noah Tucker, Central Asian Involvement in the Conflict in Syria and Iraq: Drivers and Responses, Management Systems International, January 23, 2015, p. 5; Sarah Lain, "Labour Migrants from Kyrgyzstan", Understanding the Factors Contributing to Radicalisation Among Central Asian Labour Migrants in Russia, RUSI Occasional Paper, Royal United Services Institute for Defence and Security Studies, April 2018, p. 39; Tat'jana Dronzina, "Boeviki Kyrgyzstana: Pochemu Oni Uezzhajut na Chuzhuju Vojnu", Novye Vyzovy i Podhody po Regional'noj i Global'noj Bezopasnosti v Central'noj Azii: Materialy Mezhdunarodnoj Konferencii, (Nur-Sultan, 26 October 2018), Nur-Sultan, 2020, p. 226.

- 19% of participants expressed moderate views.[49]

In general, such narratives as a just war in Syria, "Islamic State as apocalyptic utopia," and "striking back at Western oppression"[50] are the dominant motivations.

Naturally, abilities of religious leaders to resist extremist ideas, including digital literacy, are very vital.[51] For example, over 90% of Aravan's (district in Kyrgyzstan) imams do not have Internet literacy skills.[52]

It is notable that that labour migration is linked to radicalization and recruitment into extremists. According to Noah Tucker, "migration – primarily economic migration – may be the single most important factor for Central Asian recruiting to the Syrian conflict".[53] In 2015, the Head of Kyrgyzstan's Interior Ministry reported about uncovered 83 cases of people trying to recruit citizens to fight in Syria.[54] Although, we have seen cases when Central Asians came to Syria and Iraq directly from the region, it is notable that a significant number of foreign fighters came from outside Central Asia (for instance, from Russia) and were economic migrants or studied abroad, so the authorities are unable to control the outflow of citizens to the countries of the Middle East.[55] It may be explained by such factors as:

- structural motivators ("push factors" as repression, corruption, unemployment, discrimination, etc.),
- individual incentives ("pull factors" as a sense of purpose, identity, status, coercion, etc.),
- enabling factors ('radical' mentors, social networks, identity politics, an absence of familial support, etc.),
- resilience (personal experience, beliefs and values, religion, education, ties between families and friends, the rule of law, etc.).[56]

Vulnerabilities related to the administrative and legal challenges (failures of migrant workers in legalizing the status after arriving), economic reasons and discrimination, stigmatization and securitization may cause radicalization; however, it should be stressed that only a small percentage of labor migrants in Russia are being radicalized and vulnerable to radicalization (it is assumed

---

[49] Inga Sikorskaya, ibid, p. 6.

[50] Noah Tucker, Central Asian Involvement in the Conflict in Syria and Iraq: Drivers and Responses, p. 13-14.

[51] Mirgul Karimova, Sheradil Baktygulov, ibid, p. 10; Anastasiya Reshetnjak, ibid, s. 50.

[52] Mirgul Karimova, Sheradil Baktygulov, ibid, p. 10.

[53] Noah Tucker, Central Asian Involvement in the Conflict in Syria and Iraq: Drivers and Responses, p. 11.

[54] Thomas F. Lynch III et al., ibid, p. 13.

[55] Raffaello Pantucci, Mohammed S. Elshimi, ibid, p. 2; "Vozvrashhenie iz Sirii i Iraka: Pregrady i Vozmozhnosti", 04.06.2019, http://prevention.kg/?p=3444 (Accessed on 18.11.2020); Tat'jana Dronzina, ibid, p. 226.

[56] Raffaello Pantucci, Mohammed S. Elshimi, ibid, p. 7.

that among them are young people, illegal migrants, uneducated migrants, and lonely people).[57]

There is a debate over an interaction between economic exclusion and violent extremism because only the respondents without experience of radicalization pointed out financial motives. As a result, the research discourse has shifted from absolute poverty to relative poverty.[58]

## Profile/ Portrait of the Central Asian Fighters and Their Families

Many militants left the country with their wife (or wives) and children (a sign of the permanent migration), mostly in groups from certain localities (it most likely that recruiters are operating there) and did not inform their relatives about this decision.[59]

Findings of the UN Women survey showed that many women followed their husbands, and this was not their choice.[60] Women who went to hostilities can be conditionally divided into four groups:

1) women who followed their husbands, they were recruited by them,

2) women who left on their own free will without men and with children; there are also such cases when women left their husbands voluntarily,

3) women who, at the time of the war, were already in the Middle East (in Waziristan, Iraq) and just joined the terrorists,

4) non-religious women (a small group) who left in search of love, family building, etc.; surprisingly, there are women who began their religious practice already in Syria.[61]

Scientists shape the profile of identifiable Kyrgyzstanis fighters in Syria as "primarily politically and economically marginalized ethnic Uzbeks from southern Kyrgyzstan whose messaging, recruiting, and social media activity is primarily in the Uzbek language and largely ignored by the Kyrgyzstani media" (according to independent statistics, in 2015 there were from 500 to

---

[57] Raffaello Pantucci, Mohammed S. Elshimi, ibid, p. 3, 4; Mohammed S. Elshimi, "Analysis", **Understanding the Factors Contributing to Radicalisation Among Central Asian Labour Migrants in Russia**, RUSI Occasional Paper, Royal United Services Institute for Defence and Security Studies, April 2018, p. 63, 66.

[58] Mohammed S. Elshimi, ibid, p. 63.

[59] Edward Lemon, ibid, p. 6; Tat'jana Dronzina, ibid, p. 215.

[60] Obzor Situacii po Polozheniju Zhenshhin i Nasil'stvennomu Ekstremizmu v Stranah Evropy i Central'noj Azii, OON-Zhenshhiny, June 2017, p. 6; "Vozvrashhenie iz Sirii i Iraka: Pregrady i Vozmozhnosti", ibid.

[61] **Obzor Situacii po Polozheniju Zhenshhin i Nasil'stvennomu Ekstremizmu v Stranah Evropy i Central'noj Azii**, ibid, p. 6; "Zhusan: My Dostigli Tol'ko Remissii Ekstremizma", 11.01.2020, http://prevention.kg/?p=5893 (Accessed on 17.11.2020).

1,000 ethnic Uzbeks in Syria).[62]

Perceptions of the ideal among young people vary depending on region, for instance in Kyrgyzstan:

- in Bazar-Korgon and Nookat districts, the ideal is the image of a Muslim who is doing jihad and enter paradise after dying,
- in Suzak district, respondents have a similar image, but a caliphate should be built by peaceful means,
- in Kara-Suu district, the ideal image is similar to image created by the inhabitants of Suzak, war is considered as not appropriate,
- in Uzgen district, the ideal image is similar to the image perceived by the residents of Kara-Suu (a traditional understanding of Islam),
- in Aravan district, the ideal image is an individual who has good religious education and evaluate the real situation,
- in Zheti-Oguz district, the ideal image is a martyr who embarks on the path of jihad,
- in Kara-Balta town, the ideal image is a Muslim for whom jihad is a way of life.[63]

It is remarkable that, according to surveys' findings, youth, a marital status, the economic situation and the degree of religiosity are not determining factors; an individual decision to join foreign terrorist organizations can be viewed in the context of religious illiteracy (it creates conditions to mislead potential recruits) and a certain social and educational immaturity, but the fighters who left the country cannot be considered as illiterate, at the same time, they have no professional education.[64]

## Threat of Returnees

On the one hand, some analysts assume that a mass return to Central Asia is unlikely.[65] On the other hand, *other scientists suggest that a mass return to the Central Asian region coincided with the expansion of the IS contingent in Afghanistan at the beginning of 2019 because it is a part of the ISIS strategy to regenerate and create the support center in Central Asia.*[66]

*In connection to that, the priority concern is the growth of radicalism due to returning of Kyrgyz women and their minor children from penitentiary institutions in Iraq and Syria.*[67] By the time of their departure, Kyrgyz fighters were radicalized in varying degrees, so it can be assumed that at the time of arrival they are more

---

[62] Thomas F. Lynch III et al., ibid, p. 13.
[63] Inga Sikorskaya, ibid, p. 6-7.
[64] Tat'jana Dronzina, ibid, p. 226.
[65] Edward Lemon, ibid, p. 6.
[66] "Kyrgyzstan Zhdet Svoikh "Geroev" s Blizhnego Vostoka. Sebe na golovu?", ibid.
[67] Ibid.

radicalized (but varying degrees of radicalization may remain).[68]

According to statistics, a third of IS women are recruiters; moreover, the other risks are related to uncertain behavior of individuals after returning to the environment that pushed them out before, disagreement of some relatives to accept children and women who find themselves in Syria and Iraq.[69]

Experts believe that it is necessary to return people only after preliminary rehabilitation from the state's security perspective; meanwhile, this group of people does not have the status, rights and obligations to undergo a rehabilitation in Kyrgyzstan.[70]

To prevent a risk of secondary radicalization for returned women rehabilitation has gone in three directions:

- towards women who gave up religious practice, took off their hijabs and conduct a secular way of life,
- towards women who accepted the Abu Hanifa madhhab and already confidently read namaz together with the ustaz of mosques,
- towards women who are partially deradicalized and continue to follow Salafism (the main group).[71]

Mental changes in the consciousness of women

– understanding that Salafism was the real reason for their departure
– are already a sign of successful deradicalization, but not desalafitization, because not all women moved away from its ideology.[72]

There must be an individual approach to each returner to find out the reasons why they went off to the zones of military conflicts; in addition, returners may express their opinion in the media, and tell about the real situation.[73]

## Conclusion

The return of foreign fighters is closely linked to the security of the countries of origin. In this regard, the governments of these countries faced the challenge of leaving these people or returning them, treating their family members as terrorists or forced migrants and refugees. The countries of Central Asia also have encountered difficulties in reaching such decisions. Ambiguity regarding this problem and divisions in society are emerging in

---

[68] Tat'jana Dronzina, ibid, p. 227.
[69] Svetlana Lapteva, ibid.
[70] Ibid.
[71] "Zhusan: My Dostigli Tol'ko Remissii Ekstremizma", ibid.
[72] Ibid.
[73] "Vozvrashhenie iz Sirii i Iraka: Pregrady i Vozmozhnosti", ibid.

debates in academic communities, media and social networks.

Going from one extreme to another from a dominantly rigid approach to forgiveness for everyone is equally dangerous. Tackling this problem requires differentiated treatment policies and the study of best practices.

CHAPTER 10

# DETERMINING THE SOCIO-ECONOMIC AND SECURITY IMPACTS OF ROHINGYA REFUGEES ON NEIGHBOURING COUNTRIES: BANGLADESH AND INDIA


Murat Pınar[*] and Soyalp Tamçelik[**]


## Introduction

Migration and refugee movement, affecting most parts of the modern world in a direct or indirect way, are among the top issues that require a global responsibility and burden sharing. More and more people are leaving their homes, lands, jobs, workplaces, habits, cultural heritage, relatives, loved ones and eventually their countries. While migrants mostly relocate due to factors such as underdevelopment, climate change and natural disasters, refugees are subjected to forced migration due to factors such as wars, discrimination, human rights violations and genocide. Therefore, it can be said that migrants opt to relocate, whereas refugees are forced to do so.

Although the situation of refugees is often referred to as *"refugee crisis"*, many people believe that this term is not appropriate. Because the crisis is not caused by the refugees, in fact, they are themselves the victims of it. The term *"refugee crisis"* emphasizes the risks and threats posed by refugee movements while neglecting the problems, difficulties and pains refugees are suffering from. Therefore, it would be better to call it *"solidarity crisis"*[1] or *"reception crisis"*[2] instead of the term *"refugee crisis"*. Bundling migration and refugee movement as a crisis is highly denigrating. No one can deny that media plays a major role in building such a perception. The media illustrates

---


[*] Ankara Hacı Bayram Veli University, Faculty of Economics and Administrative Sciences, Department of International Relations, Middle East and Africa Studies Master Program. ORCID ID: 0000-0001-8110-7157, E-mail: muratpinar18@yahoo.com

[**] Prof. Dr.; Ankara Hacı Bayram Veli University, Faculty of Economics and Administrative Sciences, Head of International Relations Department, ORCID ID: 0000-0002-2092-8557, E-mail: soyalp@hotmail.com


[1] Ban Ki-moon, "Refugees and Migrants: A Crisis of Solidarity", United Nations University, 09 May 2016, https://unu.edu/publications/articles/refugees-and-migrants-a-crisis-of-solidarity.html (Access: 27.09.2020).

[2] Andrea Rea, Marco Martiniello, Alessandro Mazzola, Bart Meuleman, **The Refugee Reception Crisis in Europe Polarized Opinions and Mobilizations,** Éditions de l'Université de Bruxelles, Belgium, 2019, p. 16.

165

refugees as a problem for the global North, in fact, the majority of refugee movements and their impacts occur in the global South.[3]

People had to leave their lands for centuries due to political, religious, ethnic and administrative pressures. However, mass migration movements affecting the modern world come in abundance in the 20th century. An estimated 20 million people were displaced due to forced migration between 1944 and 1951, in the wake of World War II. Over time, refugee movements have evolved into a journey of hope from developing countries to developed or other developing countries.[4] Colonial activities, dictatorial governments, coups and economic crises have had an important share in rising it to a global scale.[5] Since refugees do not feel safe and secure in their countries of origin, they move to other countries or are displaced within the same country.

The Copenhagen School and Barry Buzan extend the concept of securitization from a military-only aspect to political, economic, social and environmental domains.[6] This new approach broadens the scope of threats as well. Threats are not anymore limited to states, but different threats arise, such as rapid population growth, mass migration, cultural imperialism, economic challenges, climate change, environmental risks, and pandemics.[7] New threats bring forward new methods to be applied in order to ensure security. However, many cases show that very inhumane measures and practices violating human rights are put into use by states to ensure security. People are killed, tortured, raped, imprisoned, forcedly displaced, and prevented from access to basic services such as health and education.[8] These actions taken to ensure a group of people's safety threaten the security of another group of people. Basically, what has been done under the name of security is causing insecurity.

Without any forcing reasons, people would not abandon their ancestors'

---

[3] Anna Lindley, **Crisis and Migration - Critical Perspectives**, New York, Routledge, 2014, p. 6.

[4] Countries that had not undergone the Industrial Revolution were described as *"underdeveloped"* or *"undeveloped"* countries in the period before the development economy and theories emerged. With the implementation of the development economy in the 1950s, the term "underdeveloped country" was used both in German and English languages in order to comply with the rules of diplomatic courtesy. The term *"country close to development"* was used in the 1960s, lately this term was abandoned and the term *"developing"* was used in political and official speeches. (Oswaldo De Rivero, **Kalkınma Efsanesi: 21. Yüzyılın Bağımsız Yaşayamayan Ekonomileri,** çev. Ö. Karakurt, İstanbul, Çitlembik Yayınları, 2003, p. 88.).

[5] Yakup Bulut, Soner Akın, Sedat Karakaya, "A Memoir Upon How the Refugee Problem is Looked At". **International Congress of Management Economy and Policy Proceedings**, Volume I, 26-27 November 2016, pp. 3016-3018.

[6] Barry Buzan, Ole Weaver, Jaap de Wilde, **Security: A New Framework for Analysis,** London, Lynne Rienner Publishers, 1998, pp. 21-25.

[7] David Skidmore, "Security: A New Framework for Analysis", **The American Political Science Review**, 93(4), 1999, pp. 1010-1011. doi:10.2307/2586187.

[8] Hossain Ahmed Taufiq, "Rohingya Refugee Crisis and the State of Insecurity in Bangladesh", **Genocide and Mass Violence**, Chapter VI, 2019, p. 146, https://www.researchgate.net/publication/328103777 (Access: 26.08.2020).

lands where they were born and raised, leave the societies they have lived together, and set about long, arduous journeys to places where they are mostly not welcomed. In this chapter, the reasons why the Rohingyas have been subjected to forced migration and the impacts of this migration on neighbouring countries, Bangladesh and India are discussed. International refugee protection in international law, the responsibilities of actors, what can be done to alleviate the burden on host countries and sharing the responsibilities are also elaborated.

The main purpose of this study is to evaluate the socio-economic and security impacts of Rohingya refugees on neighbouring countries Bangladesh and India, and to put forward recommendations about what can be done to alleviate this burden. The theoretical framework of the study is grafted on the international legal framework for refugee protection. This legal framework consists of international human rights law, humanitarian law, refugee law and criminal law. The migration and refugee related terms used in the study have been cross-checked with International Migration Law-Glossary on Migration by International Organization for Migration (IOM). The main hypothesis of the study is that the extant situation of refugees poses a big burden to the host nations. From this point of view, the study is also based on the assumption that the host nations need local, regional and international support in order to overcome the burden. Although the study aims to define the refugee impacts on both India and Bangladesh, the main focus of the study shifts more to Bangladesh. This is mainly because of the relatively more academic and field studies found in literature about Rohingyas in Bangladesh. One reason for this can be the fact that due to a huge number of refugees in Bangladesh than in India, there are more field studies with Rohingyas settled in refugee camps in Bangladesh. Another reason could be that India does not allow studies to be done with the Rohingyas living on its soil. In each case, more studies are needed about Rohingyas in India.

In the next section, the conceptual framework and terminology used in the study as well as the legal structure for the refugee rights and the protection are discussed. The following section elaborates on the situation of Rohingyas and the conflict in Myanmar. This section also talks about the persecution and human rights violations the Rohingyas suffered. The fourth and the fifth sections of this chapter are dedicated to socio-economic and security impacts of Rohingya refugees on Bangladesh and India. Finally, the chapter concludes with some suggestions for easing the burden on the host countries.

## Migration, Emigration and Immigration

Quite a few words with slight differences are used to define the movement of people from one place to another. This might be confusing for non-native English practicers. To begin with, migration is a common term for people changing their places of usual residence, either within the same country or to another. These moves could be either temporary or permanent. Migration could be linked with various reasons, including work, education, health, or family reunification.[9]

From the departure country's perspective, the act of people leaving out is called emigration and they become emigrants.[10] From arrival country's view, the act of people coming in is called immigration and they become immigrants.[11] In fact, immigration is more than just a physical displacement activity; it is a social entity that has continuous effects on individuals and society, both on the immigrants' side and on the host community side. While internal displacement of people is mostly seen as an internal problem of the country, immigration is not national anymore as it affects the societies of other countries.

## Forced Migration

Forced migration is a result of force, compulsion, or coercion. The term covers the movements of refugees, displaced persons, and victims of human trafficking.[12] It is a global problem arising from many different root causes. Among these, totalitarian regimes, political crises, international interventions, people's security and economic requirements are the most prominent ones. In most cases, intertwined causes feed each other and turn into an inextricable spiral.[13]

## Refugee

A refugee is a person who is deemed to be eligible for the United Nations' refugee protection. Recognition of people by the host country as refugees is not a requirement. The host country does not need to be a signatory of 1951 Convention or the 1967 Protocol as well.[14] According to Article 1 of the 1951 Convention, in order to gain refugee status, a person has to;

- have a reasonable fear that he will be persecuted because of his religion, race, nationality, membership of a certain political opinions or social group,

---

[9] International Organization for Migration (IOM), **International Migration Law-Glossary on Migration**, No. 34, pp. 132, 137. https://publications.iom.int/system/files/pdf/iml_34_glossary.pdf (Access: 03.11.2020).
[10] ibid., pp. 63-64.
[11] ibid., p. 103.
[12] ibid., p. 77.
[13] Bulut, op.cit., pp. 3016-3018.
[14] IOM, op.cit., p. 170.

- be outside the country of his/her citizenship and be not able to or unwilling to benefit from the protection of his/her country because of this fear,
- be outside the country of usual residence if he is not a citizen, and be unable to or unwilling to return there because of this fear.[15]

The 1951 version of the definition had a time restriction referencing to the events before 1 January 1951, however, it was removed by the 1967 Protocol Relating to the Status of Refugees, and a more comprehensive definition was accepted.[16] The 1951 Convention and 1967 Protocol are the two fundamental documents for protecting refugees' rights and providing solutions to their problems. The definition of refugee can also be found in other international conventions such as the 1969 Organization of African Unity Refugee Convention[17] and the 1984 Cartagena Declaration.[18] These two definitions have very similar features to that of the 1951 Convention.

The 1951 Convention imposes regulations on the signatory countries. For example, parties should not discriminate refugees according to their race, religion or country of origin (Article 3). However, not all parties willingly or unwillingly fulfill the responsibilities with the same level of sensitivity due to their socio-economic conditions. Refugees are not only under the 1951 Convention and the 1967 Protocol protection today. They are protected by a broader legal framework which consists of international human rights law, humanitarian law, refugee law and criminal law. The *1948 Universal Declaration of Human Rights* and the *1949 Geneva Conventions* are the forerunners of the international legal framework for the protection of refugees. The 1948 Universal Declaration of Human Rights states that everyone has the right to seek asylum. United Nations General Assembly, having the experiences of World War II, founded UNHCR in 1950. UNHCR defines refugee protection as the commitment to secure access to a country of asylum, granting asylum and refugee status, ensuring the protection of human rights and non-refoulement.[19]

---

[15] UNHCR Turkey, **1951 Geneva Convention**, Article 1, Para 2, http://www.multeci.org.tr/wp-content/uploads/2016/12/1951-Cenevre-Sozlesmesi-1.pdf (Access: 04.10.2020).

[16] Cemile Çelik, Hazar Kaan Özkonak, Osman Karaarslan, "Mülteci Hukuku-Doç. Dr. Ülkü Halatçı Ulusoy ile Röportaj", **Hukuk Gündemi**, 2015/2, pp. 30-33.

[17] African Union, **Convention Governing the Specific Aspects of Refugee Problems in Africa**, https://au.int/sites/default/files/treaties/36400-treaty-0005_-_oau_convention_governing_the_specific_aspects_of_refugee_problems_in_africa_e.pdf (Access: 29.10.2020).

[18] UNHCR, **Cartagena Declaration on Refugees,** https://www.unhcr.org/about-us/background/45dc19084/cartagena-declaration-refugees-adopted-colloquium-international-protection.html (Access: 29.10.2020).

[19] Chiara Merritt, "Protection in Protracted Refugee Situations: The Case of Rohingya Refugees in Bangladesh", **BRAC Institute of Governance and Development (BIGD) Working Paper**, No. 43, September 2017, BRAC University, Dhaka, p. 2.

There are also other international instruments and conventions that provide human rights protection and security for refugees. For example, the *1984 UN Convention Against Torture and other Cruel, Inhuman or Degrading Treatment or Punishment* attaches great importance to the principle of non-refoulement. The *1989 Convention of the Rights of Child* requires the provision of help and protection to children and women. The *"non-refoulement"* is a principle of international law. According to this principle, asylum seekers and refugees should not be forced to return to the country where they may face persecution or any threat to their lives.[20]

There were around 18 million refugees worldwide in 1992. By 2010 the number almost doubled and reached to 34,4 million. By the end of 2019, a total of 79,5 million people around the world have left their homes. Approximately 26 million of them are refugees and 50% of the refugees are under the age of 18. 68% of the worldwide refugees come from Venezuela, Syria, South Sudan, Myanmar and Afghanistan. 73% of refugees have sought refuge in neighbouring countries; respectively, Turkey,[21] Colombia, Pakistan, Uganda and Germany are the countries that host the refugees most.[22] But this crisis is not about numbers; it is about solidarity and reception.

The popular movements known as the *"Arab Spring"* that affected almost all of the Arab countries in North Africa and the Middle East were attempted to be suppressed by force in Syria. This caused a civil war that has ended up with millions of refugees. While 6.6 million[23] Syrians were displaced in their own country, another 5.5 million[24] Syrian refugees fled to neighbouring countries. Although many of them seek refuge in neighbouring countries, a good number of them do not stop there and continue their long journeys to reach other countries with the hope of more promising economic and social conditions. Thus, there are demographic, socio-economic, and cultural impacts on countries of origin and host countries and transit countries. The interaction between the host nation and the immigrants affects the codes of both sides, and the socio-economic problems turn into global-scale problems that all states have to deal with.

---

[20] D., L., Marshilong, "Refugees Status in India: A Special Reference to Rohingya Refugees", **International Journal of Science and Research (IJSR)**, Volume 8, Issue 7, July 2019, pp. 1359-1361.

[21] Turkey is Party to 1951 Geneva Convention. (Republic of Turkey, Prime Ministry Acts and Decisions Study Department, (1/125)", 5.5.1961, Number: 71-1448/1444.)

[22] UNHCR, **Figures at a Glance**, https://www.unhcr.org/figures-at-a-glance.html (Access: 28.09.2020).

[23] UNHCR, **Syria Emergency**, https://www.unhcr.org/syria-emergency.html?gclid=EAIaIQobChMIs OOX8PzU6wIVTOd3Ch0oPAIdEAAYASAAEgJzI_D_BwE (Access: 06.09.2020).

[24] There are 3,6 million Syrian refugees in Turkey, 880 thousand in Lebanon, 658 thousand in Jordan, 244 thousand in Iraq, 130 thousand in Egypt. (Last updated 27 Aug 2020). https://data2.unhcr.org/en/situations/syria#_ga=2.237893440.1530870373.1599410959829198539.1598905479&_gac=1.41036438. 1599410959.EAIaIQobChMIsOOX8PzU6wIVTOd3Ch0oPAIdEAAYASAAEgJzI_D_BwE (Access: 06.09.2020).

## Protection of Refugees

Despite the international legal framework, not enough protection can be assured for refugees. Their problems do not wither when they cross into another country. Due to economic recession, heavy tax burden, high unemployment and precarious employment, tensions rise between the host and the refugee communities, consequently polarization and anti-refugee actions increase. The opposing discourses and actions are encouraged by some political parties which aim to increase their popularity and votes. Being confined to uncertainty, helplessness and poor conditions makes refugees an easy target for pro-racist actions. This situation can be seen frequently not only in Asian or African countries but also in Western countries. In 2018, on the island of Lesbos,[25] a customer attacked violently a Bangladeshi man working in a market just because he tried to suggest the customer not to park in a disabled people parking place.[26] In another example, a camerawoman deliberately tripped a refugee who was running with his child in his arms and kicked them on the ground in front of the eyes of the whole world. These are not good examples of refugee protection.

More steps need to be taken on national and international scale to provide better protection. The responsibility, capacity and power are main factors for both the international community and the host nation in providing refugee protection. Every one of these factors contributes closely to the provision of refugee protection. According to international law, the responsibility to protect refugees belongs to the host country. However, this theory does not always apply to real-life conditions. For example, host countries advocating that the burden of global refugee movements is disproportionately shouldered by them might tend to ignore their responsibility to protect refugees. On the other hand, the international definition of refugee is not always accepted by the host countries that treat the refugees as illegal immigrants. Host countries, which view refugees as a disproportionate burden, try to transfer their responsibilities to other actors, especially UNHCR. Even though UNHCR takes the lead to help the refugees, the responsibility to protect refugees still rests with the host countries. Even though it is the responsibility of the host nation, the responsibility of the international community to protect refugees cannot be overlooked. Within the scope of Responsibility to Protect (R2P), the international community should be involved in responsibility and burden sharing. This sharing should not be merely for short term and financial support; it should be intended for

---

[25] Turkish name used for Lesvos.

[26] Theodoros Fouskas, "Unravelling Solidarity and Hostility: Mobilizations Concerning Migrants, Asylum Seekers and Refugees in Anti-Migrant Times in Greece", **The Refugee Reception Crisis in Europe Polarized Opinions and Mobilizations,** Andrea Rea, Marco Martiniello, Alessandro Mazzola, Bart Meuleman (Ed.), Éditions de l'Université de Bruxelles, Belgium, 2019, p. 139.

the long term and covering all areas of requirements.[27]

Accepting the responsibility to protect refugees alone is not enough, the capacity to realize it also is required. Funding is the most prominent factor affecting the capacity to protect refugees. Developing countries that host refugees often have low capacity since they have excessive debt, high population growth and high unemployment rates. Low capacity creates impediments for the protection of refugees, and host countries are therefore becoming more hesitant about granting asylum. Since there is no international standard on how to accommodate refugees in international refugee law, the practices of nations differ. Direct and indirect foreign aid is provided to host countries by international organizations and donors. However, the burden of the host country is not limited to meeting the needs of the refugees, but there are also other costs such as environmental pollution, contamination of water resources and destruction of forests in the areas where refugees are settled. Insufficient funding by the international community, the emergence of donor fatigue and reduced financial support have direct negative consequences on refugee protection capacity and quality. The international refugee regime relies heavily on voluntary donations. For example, 98% of UNHCR funding is provided by voluntary donations, mostly from donor countries, only 2% comes from the UN.[28]

Unsatisfactory financial support reduces the capacity of organizations such as the IOM and the UNHCR, who are acting on behalf of the international community to provide protection to refugees. In the first six months immediately after the mass influx of refugees (September 2017 - February 2018), a total amount of US $ 517.78 million, and US $ 882 million for the rest of 2018 were required for the needs of 1,2 million Rohingya refugees living in Bangladesh. While calculating these financial needs, the daily expenditure per refugee was taken as 2.45 dollars, which is only the amount required to provide basic demands.[29] The EU provided 36 million Euros in 2018 for Rohingya refugees. The total financial support provided by the EU for Rohingya refugees in Bangladesh since 2007 has exceeded 86 million Euros.[30] EU authorities might be feeling happy because of donation. However, as it can be calculated easily, sufficient international financial support could not be provided. The donations by international donors stay far below the amount required to meet even the daily needs of refugees.

---

[27] Merritt, op.cit., pp. 4-6, 23-25.

[28] ibid., pp. 6-7.

[29] Kudrat-E-Khuda (Babu), Michael William Scott, (reviewing editor), "The Impacts and Challenges to Host Country Bangladesh Due to Sheltering the Rohingya Refugees", **Cogent Social Sciences**, Volume 6, 2020 - Issue 1, https://www.tandfonline.com/doi/full/10.1080/23311886.2020.1770943 (Access: 18.10.2020).

[30] European Commission, European Civil Protection and Humanitarian Aid Operations, "The Rohingya Crisis", **ECHO Factsheet,** August 2018, https://ec.europa.eu/echo/factsheets_en (Access: 11.11.2020).

## Rohingyas and Forced Migration

Due to the discriminatory policies implemented by Buddhist-dominated Myanmar since the 1960s, hundreds of thousands of Muslim Rohingyas were forced to leave their lands. Many human rights violations, including rape, murder and arson, were reported during the campaign by Myanmar security forces.[31]

## Background

Rohingyas have been living in the lands where they have been forced to abandon today for centuries. The first Muslim settlements in the region commenced by the Arab merchants as of the 9th century and the number of Muslims increased over time. Tensions between ethnic groups erupted during the British colonial period in the 19th century.[32] Rohingyas had to suffer forced migrations in 1942, 1978, 1991, 2012, 2016 and the latest in 2017. From 1948, when Myanmar gained its independence until the military coup in 1962, the Rohingyas had full citizenship rights and were able to serve in the Myanmar Parliament. However, during the military rule, the civil, political, educational and economic rights of the Rohingyas were gradually taken away. With the 1982 Citizenship Law, the Rohingyas were removed from the list of officially recognized minorities, and were deprived of many fundamental rights, including citizenship, freedom of movement, access to health and education, marriage rights and voting rights. Thus, they have become the world's largest stateless group.[33]

The identity cards, also known as white cards, were issued by the military junta in the 1990s to many Muslims, both Rohingya and non-Rohingya. White cards ensured some limited rights such as the right of temporary residence, however full citizenship was not granted. White card holders were allowed to vote in the 2008 constitutional referendum and in the 2010 general elections. Nevertheless, discriminatory activities led by the Buddhist extremist nationalists continued against the Rohingyas. In the 2014 census conducted by the Myanmar Government, the Rohingyas were only allowed to register as Bengali, not with their ethnic identity. In the constitutional referendum held in 2015, the Rohingyas' white cards were nullified and so were their rights to vote. In addition, no Muslim MP candidate could attend the 2015 general elections. The Myanmar Government went further and forced the Rohingyas to carry the cards that identify them as foreigners, not

---

[31] Eleanor Albert, Lindsay Maizland, "The Rohingya Crisis", **Council on Foreign Relations**, 23 January 2020, https://www.cfr.org/backgrounder/rohingya-crisis (Access: 17.10.2020).
[32] Stefan Bepler, "The Rohingya Conflict: Genesis, Current Situation and Geopolitical Aspects", **Pacific Geographies**, Number 50, July/August 2018, p. 5. (DOI: 10.23791/500410).
[33] Burma/Bangladesh, Burmese Refugees in Bangladesh: Still No Durable Solution, Human Rights Watch, May 2000, Vol 12., No. 3 (C), pp. 9-11.

citizens.[34]

In August 2017, an armed rebel group named Arakan Rohingya Salvation Army (ARSA) attacked some police stations in Rakhine State. Thereupon, the Myanmar Government ordered disproportionate military force without distinguishing between civilians and the rebel group. A major operation was initiated by the Myanmar army, the houses and villages of the Rohingyas were systematically burned down, and thousands of people lost their lives as a result of the acts of violence. Due to this disproportionate and excessive use of force by the Myanmar army, ignoring the distinction between civilian and rebel, a massive influx began.[35]

Myanmar's military operations against the Rohingyas have been described as *"ethnic cleansing"* by many senior UN officials, including the UN Secretary General.[36] More than 700 thousand Rohingyas have taken refuge in neighbouring country Bangladesh, and some others in Pakistan, Malaysia, India, Saudi Arabia, Indonesia and Thailand. Neither of these countries is a party to the 1951 Convention or the 1967 Protocol.[37] It is not known exactly how many Rohingyas are still in Myanmar. In IDP camps in the central part of Rakhine state, at least 120 thousand Rohingyas are considered struggling to survive in overcrowded shelters and very poor conditions.[38] Despite the fact that more than three years passed since hundreds of thousands of Rohingyas fled from Myanmar and took refuge in Bangladesh, the humanitarian situation and human rights violations in the region still persist. According to UNHCR, there are 860 thousand Rohingya refugees in Cox's Bazar today. In Rakhine state, approximately 600 thousand Rohingyas are being exposed to ongoing violence and discrimination. India, Malaysia, Indonesia and other countries are hosting 150 thousand Rohingya refugees.[39]

## Reasons for the Dispute

Religious, political and economic reasons stand behind the conflicts between Myanmar and Rohingyas. The Buddhist majority population of Myanmar perceives Muslim Rohingyas as a threat to the Buddhist culture and

---

[34] Albert, op.cit.

[35] Alvin K., Tay, et al, Culture, Context and Mental Health of Rohingya Refugees: A Review for Staff in Mental Health and Psychosocial Support Programmes for Rohingya Refugees, UNHCR, Geneva, Switzerland, 2018, pp. 11-12.

[36] Dorothy Sang, "One Year on Time to Put Women and Girls at the Heart of the Rohingya Response", **Oxfam International**, September 2018, p. 3, (DOI: 10.21201/2018.3194).

[37] UNHCR, **States Parties to the 1951 Convention and its 1967 Protocol**, https://www.unhcr.org/protection/basic/3b73b0d63/states-parties-1951-convention-its-1967-protocol.html (04.10.2020).

[38] Tay, op.cit., pp. 6-12.

[39] UHNCR, **Conference on Sustaining Support for the Rohingya Refugee Response 22 October 2020,** Joint Closing Announcement by Co-Hosts, 22 October 2020, https://www.unhcr.org/news/press/2020/10/5f915c464/conference-sustaining-support-rohingya-refugee-response-22-october-2020.html (Access: 22.10.2020).

people in Myanmar. Myanmar sees not only the Muslim Rohingyas, but also Muslim Bangladesh as a threat.[40] Despite this perception, Rohingyas refrain from making any separatist demands and stay away from violent groups or organizations.[41]

Not only religious and ethnic tensions, but also geopolitical and economic interests lie behind the conflict between Myanmar and the Rohingyas. Although Rakhine state has rich natural resources, it is one of the poorest states in Myanmar. Myanmar nationalists see the Rohingyas as an economic burden and a rival for a small number of job opportunities. The low level of trade and economic relations between Myanmar and Bangladesh has worsened due to the refugee incident.[42] Many international observers and experts believe that the conflicts are the result of the geopolitical interests of global players. Rakhine state has strategic importance for the countries neighbouring Myanmar. India sees Myanmar as a gateway to Southeast Asia for its regional goals and related *"Look East"*[43] or *"Act East"*[44] policies. Indian companies operate at the Shwe Gas field off the coast of Rakhine state.[45] India has been in cooperation with Myanmar also on military subjects.[46] On the other side, China aims to reach the Bay of Bengal through the Rakhine state as a part of the *"One Belt One Road"*[47] project. In order not to endanger the economic relations between the countries of the region, ensuring and maintaining the internal security of Myanmar overlaps with the interests of China in the region.[48] India's geopolitical interests necessitate its struggle against Chinese presence and domination in the region. For this reason, India is reluctant and ineffective in putting pressure on Myanmar.[49] Otherwise Myanmar could move to the side of China.

---

[40] Brian Gorlick, "The Rohingya Refugee Crisis: Rethinking Solutions and Accountability", **Working Paper Series** No. 131, Refugee Studies Centre, University of Oxford, December 2019, pp. 15-18.

[41] Carol Christine Fair, "Arakan Rohingya Salvation Army: Not the Jihadis You Might Expect", **Lawfare**, 09 Dec 2018, https://www.lawfareblog.com/arakan-rohingya-salvation-army-not-jihadis-you-might-expect (Access: 20.09.2020).

[42] Bepler, op.cit., pp. 8-10.

[43] Rohan Mukherjee, David M., Malone, "Indian Foreign Policy and Contemporary Security Challenges". **International Affairs**, 87:1, The Royal Institute of International Affairs, Oxford, p. 90.

[44] KV Kesavan, "India's 'Act East' Policy and Regional Cooperation", **Observer Research Foundation,** Feb 2020, https://www.orfonline.org/expert-speak/indias-act-east-policy-and-regional-cooperation-61375/ (Access: 05.11.2020).

[45] Khriezo Yhome, "Examining India's Stance on the Rohingya Crisis", **ORF Issue Brief**, July 2018, Issue No. 247, p. 3. https://www.researchgate.net/publication/326317165 (Access: 08.10.2020).

[46] Kiran Sharma, Yuichi Nitta, "With an Eye on China, India Gifts Submarine to Myanmar", **Financial Times**, 04.11.2020, https://www.ft.com/content/5aa36fac-7686-4067-ad1a-46a0f4c0d3ea (Access: 05.11.2020).

[47] Nazirul Islam Sarker, Altab Hossin, Xiaohua Yin, Kamruzzaman Sarkar, "One Belt One Road Initiative of China: Implication for Future of Global Development", **Modern Economy**, 09(04), January 2018, pp. 623-638. (DOI: 10.4236/me.2018.94040).

[48] Bepler, op.cit., pp. 8-10.

[49] Gorlick, op.cit., pp. 15-18.

## Persecution and Human Rights Violations

Hundreds of documents, reports and proofs have been prepared by international organizations that the Myanmar army systematically and structurally conducted violence against Rohingya men, women, girls and children because of their ethnic origins and religious beliefs, and they did these actions deliberately as a part of military strategy. In the researches conducted by human rights organizations, it was found that rapes were very common, massive and mutilating, very young girls were raped by more than one Myanmar soldier, often in front of their relatives, even pregnant women were attacked and fetuses were taken out from their bodies. These findings may reflect only part of the real situation, as there are victims of rape who were murdered or who concealed that they had been raped. Two-thirds of the rape victims interviewed by Human Rights Watch had not reported their rape to a humanitarian organization. However, it was diagnosed that these people had symptoms of post-traumatic stress disorder as well as some obvious symptoms such as injuries and infections during the checkups performed by health clinic personnel.[50]

An international independent Fact Finding Mission (FFM), consisting of prominent lawyers and human rights experts, was created by the UNHRC to examine the events in Myanmar and the situation of refugees. FFM officials conducted field visits and interviews with victims, government officials, UN and NGO workers. Moreover, forensic evidence was collected and analyzed by a team of experts on sexual violence in war, international criminal law and military operations. In the FFM reports containing the findings of all these studies, it was stated that serious crimes were committed against Rohingya men, women and children, and added detailed information with the names of those who violated human rights. The FFM also reported that despite the tripartite agreement between UNHCR, the UN Development Program, and the Myanmar government, the Myanmar government did not take the necessary steps to create the conditions for the return of the refugees.[51] The government of Myanmar prevents international humanitarian aid delivery to Rakhine state, makes it difficult or even prohibits the entry of aid organizations, especially organizations with a Muslim identity, into the region. A share of incoming aid deducted as tax, and only the remaining part was distributed among Muslims and Buddhists.[52]

---

[50] **Bangladesh and Burma: the Rohingya Crisis**, House of Commons International Development Committee, Second Report of Session 2017–19, January 2018, pp. 29-31.

[51] Gorlick, op.cit., p.1-5.

[52] **Sığınma Hakkı Perspektifinde Arakan Raporu**, International Refugee Rights Association, May 2018, p. 40.

## The Burden on Bangladesh

Bangladesh has a long history of hosting Rohingya refugees. Before 2017, there were approximately 32,000 registered refugees in the two camps, Kutupalong and Nayapara in Bangladesh. With the refugees arrived in August 2017, Kutupalong has become the world's largest refugee camp. The issue of granting assistance to such a large number of refugees has caused a major humanitarian emergency.[53] Bangladesh society embraced hundreds of thousands of Rohingya refugees with the empathy they had gained as a result of the refugee experience they survived during their struggle for independence in 1971. However, this hospitality brings a heavy burden to Bangladesh. Myanmar, the other side of the problem, despite the UN's attempts, does not show the necessary interest in creating the conditions that will enable the refugees to return safely and voluntarily. Almost no progress has been made especially in the scope of ensuring human rights in Myanmar.[54]

Having a huge population and a low level of development, Bangladesh has undertaken a heavy socio-economic burden. This situation has exceeded the current capacity of Bangladesh and has created enormous pressure on infrastructure, services, resources and the environment. The continued economic challenges associated with these pressures create tension between the host community and refugees in Bangladesh. It does not seem possible to realize a short term solution to reduce the burden caused by the refugee influx, including the refoulment. Rohingya refugees do not want to return to Myanmar because of vital reasons such as the substandard living conditions imposed on them, the lack of legal and human rights protection, political exclusion, and hopelessness about what they will encounter Myanmar if they return.[55] Although three years have passed since the great influx, the majority of Rohingyas currently rely on the international community's assistance and the hospitality of the Bangladesh Government.

Bangladesh Foreign Minister Shahidul Haque made a speech about Rohingya refugees at the UN Security Council on 28 February 2019. He expressed that Bangladesh was approaching a breaking point. He added that long-term hosting had been causing negative impacts on Bangladesh's economy, environment, social fabric, and security. He also stated that even if a group of 300 Rohingyas return on a daily basis, it would require a total time of 12 years to complete the entire return.[56] However, the UN Security

---

[53] Tay, op.cit., pp. 13-15.
[54] Gorlick, op.cit., pp. 6-8.
[55] ibid., p. 1.
[56] United Nations Meetings Coverage and Press Releases, Crisis in Rakhine State, Violence Could Derail Gains in Myanmar's Peace Process, Special Envoy Warns Security Council, Calling for Unimpeded Humanitarian Access, Security Council 8477th Meeting (PM), SC/13727, 28 February 2019,

Council's not taking a decisive step regarding this forced migration caused great suffering. The permanent members, China and Russia, did not accept the idea of taking any action against Myanmar. Despite the fact that countries on a global scale theoretically support the 1951 Convention, the 2016 New York Declaration and the R2P regime, in practice, not an equivalent response has been given to alleviate the pressure on Rohingya refugees and to share the burden of Bangladesh. Countries such as Japan and India have also been among the countries that abstained from voting the UN General Assembly and UNHRC decisions on human rights in Myanmar due to various geopolitical interests that apply to them.[57]

Bangladesh's approach to Rohingya refugees has been shifting between two polarised positions since the 1970s. The Bangladesh Nationalist Party (BNP), having a religious-nationalist ideology, sees refugees as religiously Muslim brothers and embraced them. On the other side, the Bangladesh Awami League (BAL), which advocates for language-nationalism, shows less tolerance towards Rohingya. The socio-economic conditions of the local people are also effective in changing political approaches to the Rohingya issue.[58] Bangladesh encounters many difficulties in economic, demographic, social and environmental impacts due to Rohingya refugees.

## Economic Impact

In the Joint Response Report 2020 prepared by the UN, UNHCR and IOM, a total of US$ 877 million required aid was predicted to meet the critical needs of Rohingya refugees and local Bangladeshi people. Requirement for food ranks first with US$ 254,6 million, followed by cleaning and sheltering. Health and education could only find a place in the fifth and sixth places. The number of people in need is 1,3 million, including 855 thousand Rohingya refugees and 444 thousand local Bangladeshi people. The Joint Response Plan has four strategic goals: strengthening the security of Rohingya refugees, providing life-saving and high quality assistance, increasing the quality of life of the communities in Ukhika and Teknaf, and finally working towards achieving sustainable solutions in Myanmar.[59] In another study, *"Bangladesh-Rohingya Crisis Response Plan 2020"* by IOM, it is stated that a fund of more than US $ 125 million is needed in 2020 for IOM to be able to provide assistance to Rohingya refugees in Bangladesh. Of the US $ 136 million

---

https://www.un.org/press/en/2019/sc13727.doc.htm (Access: 15.09.2020).

[57] Gorlick, op.cit., pp. 15-18.

[58] Meghna Guhathakurta, "Understanding Violence, Strategising Protection Perspectives from Rohingya Refugees in Bangladesh", **Asian Journal of Social Science**, 45 (2017), pp. 639–665, (doi: 10.1163/15685314-04506003).

[59] Humanitarian Response, **2020 Joint Response Plan Rohingya Humanitarian Crisis, January - December 2020**, Bangladesh, pp. 7-11. http://www.humanitarianresponse.info/en/operations/bangladesh (Access: 24.10.2020).

demand made for 2019, only US$ 54,4 million could be met. The turn rate is 40%, even below half of what is required.[60] The figures imply that international organizations and donors are reluctant to provide the demanded financial support. As the refugee situation extends over a longer period, it is highly likely that the attention of international donors and the amount of donations will decrease. Just the opposite, the population and needs of refugees will increase. This means that greater economic burdens await Bangladesh.

Agriculture, a grave component of Bangladesh economy[61] despite its declining share in the GNP in the last two decades, has been adversely affected by many factors. These factors include loss of land, pollution, water scarcity, theft, and the fall in market prices due to the entry of aid supplies. Local people are becoming more concerned about worsening the economy, increasing unemployment, falling wages due to undocumented working, increasing transportation costs, house rent, and fuel, damaging roads by heavy vehicles belonging to aid organizations.[62] The economic conditions in the camps deteriorate, poverty is increasing, and daily working wages are falling, whereas the prices of daily need goods are increasing at high rates. Lack of training opportunities and lack of legal jobs in the camps have led to an illegal camp economy.[63] Small and medium-size merchants of the host community may be benefitting economically from the presence of refugees.[64] The fact that the Rohingyas and the local people living in Cox's Bazar speak a similar language makes it easier for them to merge. The similarity of language helps many local unemployed youths to find work with aid organizations in refugee camps. However, this job opportunity causes labour shortage on the local side, and local farmers have difficulties in finding workers. In addition, the arrival of Rohingya refugees results in a decrease of tourists visiting Saint Martin Island of Cox's Bazar, thus a decrease in tourism income.[65]

Large-scale and abrupt refugee movements culminate in big impacts on the economy of the host countries. In order to turn these impacts, which have negative repercussions in the short term, into positive contributions, long-term plans and policies are needed for refugees and host nations. The sound integration of refugees' work power into the host society will induce a

---

[60] International Organization for Migration (IOM), **Rohingya Refugee Crisis Joint Response Plan 2019**, https://humanitariancompendium.iom.int/appeals/bangladesh-2019 (Access: 27.09.2020).

[61] For 2016-2017, the share is 14,79%. (Minhazur Rahman Rezvi, "The Factors of Declining Agricultural Growth in Bangladesh and Its Impact on Food Security", **South Asian Journal of Social Studies and Economics**, 2018, Article No. SAJSSE.42080, p.4).

[62] Bepler, op.cit., p. 9.

[63] Rudabeh Shahid, **Assessing the Treatment of Rohingya Refugees in Bangladesh**, Atlantic Council South Asia Center, September 2019.

[64] Tay, op.cit., pp. 13-15.

[65] Kudrat-E-Khuda op.cit.

double-sided benefit both for the host nation and the refugees. The refugees will increase their economic well-being and their confidence in the future. If harmony is achieved between the two sides, refugees will cease to be a burden and commence contributing to the economy of the host nation. However, this adaptation may not be as easy as described. There is a requisite for policies and joint studies, which must be followed decisively for a long time.

All the steps to be taken, as stated in the 1951 Convention, aim at the successful functioning of the global refugee regime and providing the necessary protection for refugees. In this context, all actors should feature fair responsibility sharing. On 20 December 2018, the UN General Assembly approved *The Pact on Migration and Asylum,* which focuses on a balanced sharing of responsibilities for refugees and providing more assistance to reduce the burden on the host countries. Accordingly, all other countries have a responsibility to reduce the burden of a host country. In order for the global refugee regime to function properly, each country must put hands under the rock[66] and help lift it together. The inclusion of refugees in the labour force is a major approach to support the development of host countries.[67]

## Demographic Impact

The arrival of refugees has caused a significant population burst in the Cox's Bazar region. Rohingya refugees constitute 76% of the total population in Ukhia, where the Kutupalong camp is located, and 26% in Teknaf. The vast majority of Rohingyas live in camps, with an estimated segment of less than 10% living within the host community.[68] Due to the low awareness of Rohingya refugees about family planning, more population growth is expected in the camps. Population growth implies that the demand for food, clothing, shelter, work, health and other basic needs will increase in the near future.[69] The people of Bangladesh, a very high population, are one of the poorest communities in the world in terms of GDP per capita income.[70] That is why local people who cannot benefit from the assistance provided by humanitarian aid organizations feel ignored, and this situation creates tensions between Rohingya refugees and Bangladeshi people. For this reason, the Government of Bangladesh wants the Bangladeshi people to be helped

---

[66] Turkish idiom, *put one's hands under the rock,* means to take responsibility, https://sozluk.gov.tr/ (Access: 01.11.2020).

[67] Maegan Hendow, **Bridging Refugee Production and Development**, ICMPD, Jan 2019, Vienna, pp. 11-18.

[68] Tay, op.cit., pp. 13-15.

[69] Kudrat-E-Khuda, op.cit.

[70] Bangladesh GDP for 2019 is US $ 302,5 billion and GDP per capita is US $ 1,855. (The World Bank, https://data.worldbank.org/indicator/NY.GDP.PCAP.CD?locations=BD&most_recent_value_desc=f alse (Access: 15.10.2020)).

by the civil society organizations which help the refugees. Although it does not comply with the law of protection of refugees, due to its desperation and socio-economic situation, the Government of Bangladesh tries to benefit from the aid provided by NGOs.[71]

## Environmental Impact

Refugees living in overpopulated campsites in Bangladesh consume up the natural resources and ecosystem around them. Increasing environmental degradation, which is the outcome of refugees' activities, has been causing a dangerous spiral cycle that threatens the health of refugees in return. The need for land and firewood results in constinuation of cutting trees, loss of forests and biodiversity. If necessary, precautions are not taken in time, potential threats such as the destruction of vegetation and forests, decrease and pollution of water resources, and the spread of human waste to the environment may arise. Although humanitarian organizations have been building shelters in cooperation with Bangladeshi authorities, these are not abundant, and therefore, refugees construct their own shelters using wood. Refugees cut trees not only for building shelters but also for fire fuel. This significant amount of consumption of wood induces deforestation and loss of vegetation, weakening of infrastructure, damage to wildlife, and rapid depletion of Bangladesh's natural resources. The destruction of forests in the regions where refugee camps are located also affects wildlife, which is a part of the ecosystem. Elephants, for example, feel stressed as refugees build their shelters within their habitat. Because of this stress, an elephant attack near the Kutupalong refugee camp resulted in the deaths of several refugees.[72]

Cutting trees and losing the vegetation cover of the region causes the soil to become vulnerable to rain and strong winds and increases the risk of landslides.[73] Temporary shelters located on the slopes face landslides' danger, especially when heavy raindrop during the monsoon season.[74] Shelters and roads are flooded in refugee camps because of heavy rainfall. The camps don't have sufficient roads, and access to refugees becomes almost impossible as extant dirt roads turn into mud. This situation slows down the logistics support to refugees.[75]

---

[71] International Refugee Rights Association, op.cit., p. 40.
[72] Michael Honeth, et al, "An Investigative Environmental Impact Assessment for Kutupalong Refugee Camp and Surroundings, Bangladesh", **Investigative EIA – Kutupalong Refugee Camp**, University Centre of the Westfjords, Iceland, October 29, 2017, pp. 3-7.
[73] Kudrat-E-Khuda, op.cit.
[74] Bepler, op.cit., p. 9.
[75] Honeth, op.cit., pp. 6-7.

## Security and Social Impact

Rohingya refugees faced physical security threats such as landmines, military violence, arson, rape and murder while fleeing Myanmar. However, the security concerns of the refugees did not end when they crossed the border into Bangladesh. Rohingyas living in refugee camps try to survive very unfavourable conditions. Adverse conditions such as excessive heat, malnutrition, and dehydration are common in the camps. However, the physical threats experienced in the camps are not limited to these. Refugees live in makeshift shelters built from bamboo branches, use the well water, and try to make a hilly land usable. They wait in long queues to receive humanitarian aid. In the overcrowded camps, which are located in a limited space, physical security concerns, various crimes, inadequate services, serious protection difficulties, especially faced by women and girls, are reported to be quite prevalent. The intra-group or inter-group conflicts, as well as dangers from wildlife and the environment also affect the lives of refugees in terms of physical security. Intergroup and intragroup conflicts can often stem from religious disputes, resource sharing, and overcrowding.[76] Living conditions are deteriorating for hundreds of thousands of refugees stuck in the Cox's Bazar region of Bangladesh. Widespread poverty and tensions with local people raise security concerns in the Rohingya camps. Kidnapping is a major security problem. The IOM detected 420 human trafficking cases between December 2018 and June 2019. It is alleged by international organizations that some Bangladeshi border guards, military officials, and police officers take bribes from traffickers. Mass demonstrations were held in August 2019 to protest inadequate security and disorder in refugee camps.[77] Despite all these unfavourable conditions, refugees prefer to stay in Bangladesh rather than returning to Myanmar. The biggest and perhaps only reason for this instinct is that people are happy to be alive and safer.[78]

As a result of many Rohingyas taking refuge in Bangladesh, local people also face multi-dimensional problems. As an example, Bangladeshis who were able to move freely in their own lands now have to carry their ID cards to prove their identity. Pastures, where they used to graze their animals, are now filled up with the Rohingyas. Rohingya refugees often try to leave the camps and cross into local villages. The local people do not feel safe and do not know what to do if the Rohingyas resort to violence. Local people previously benefitted from many opportunities such as free medical check-ups, health services, subsidies and counselling are now provided by NGOs and international organizations. However, with the massive influx of refugees, such services ended; therefore local people started feeling

---


[76] Gorlick, op.cit., pp. 6-8.
[77] Shahid, op.cit.
[78] Gorlick, op.cit., pp. 6-8.

discontent with the Rohingyas' presence. The Bangladeshi, thinking that the Rohingya would return to Myanmar in a short time, dedicated their lands to refugees' use. However, as time passed, the lack of progress on the return of refugees started worrying locals about the future of their own lands.[79] Lack of enough teachers, mainly due to the preference of charity jobs that pay better fees, and limited access to schools have negative impacts on the education of children including both Rohingya and local children.[80] School buildings have been used as military barracks. Some of the children left their education and started working in Rohingya camps.[81]

Drug trafficking and addiction constitute another detrimental security problem for Rohingya and local people. It seems very likely that Rohingyas who cannot find employment opportunities fall into the network of drug traffickers. Since Rohingya youth are not legally allowed to work in Myanmar, they opt to illegal ways of earning their lives. Rohingyas, who have been involved in the drug trade, possibly continue this trade when they come to Bangladesh. Drug trafficking is not limited to camps; it also finds its way to local settlements and cities.[82] Drug sales in camps increase the number of drug use and addiction. Those who are drug addicts but do not have enough money to buy it, become subjected to all kinds of abuse by criminal networks in exchange for drugs.

**Gender-based Impact**

More than 50% of the population in the refugee camps in Bangladesh consists of women and girls. 16% are mothers without husbands. This means one in every six families is mother-governed. Rohingya women live with great security threats. In fact, women and girls have to struggle with the greatest difficulties and risks in camp life. Due to cultural and social traditions, they are kept away by strict rules from leaving home, going from one place to another, and participating in decision-making mechanisms. In a survey, more than one-third of women responded that they did not feel safe or comfortable when going to refill water, toilets or showers. Since women, girls and children are the most vulnerable ones to physical threats in the camps, safe areas are required to prevent harassment and attacks.[83]

Half of the women and three-quarters of the adolescent girls stated that they could not have the sanitary materials they needed during their menstrual

---

[79] Kudrat-E-Khuda, op.cit.

[80] Bepler, op.cit., p. 9.

[81] Kudrat-E-Khuda, op.cit.

[82] ibid.

[83] UN Women, **Gender Brief on Rohingya Refugee Crisis Response in Bangladesh,** January 2018, https://asiapacific.unwomen.org/-/media/field%20office%20eseasia/docs/publications/2017/10/gender-advocacy-paper-for-rohingya-refugee-crisis-response-in-bangladesh-r10.pdf?la=en&vs=2521 (Access: 27.09.2020).

periods. Many women also stated that they do not want to leave their shelters because of dignity and security concerns as well as the lack of appropriate clothing. The outcomes of the survey show that women's gender-specific needs are not adequately met and women cannot access to basic services. Humanitarian aid should focus not only on infrastructure, premises and services, but also meeting the needs of women and girls, ensuring their safety and securing their rights.

Women and girls witnessed and became the victims of rape, torture and deaths in Myanmar. The trauma, stress and pain they suffered in Myanmar did not end when they passed to Bangladesh. Numerous assessments, media reports and testimonies of the Rohingya refugees reveal the prevalence of gender-based violence in camps, including sexual harassment and assault, child marriage, forced marriage, and the presence of criminal networks abducting women and girls for prostitution.[84] There are hardly any police in the camps at nights, and this adds up more to security concerns already being experienced due to the increased trafficking of women, prostitution and drug trafficking.[85]

According to UNHCR, women and girls face security risks even when they are collecting firewood from the forest and lining up at distribution points. The deficiency of sufficient lighting-up in the camps further increases such risks and aggravates security concerns. Human trafficking gangs entering the camps especially hunt for widows and orphans. Research has revealed that human trafficking is not limited to Bangladesh. Rohingya women are also sent to India and Pakistan. Another source of concern in the camps is the increase in child marriage. Rohingyas enforce their children to marry at a young age to make a decent income and prevent the child from falling into an embarrassing situation. Bangladesh has the highest rate of child marriage in Asia, with 59% of girls getting married at the age of 18 and 22% at the age of 15. Therefore, Rohingya refugees' practice of child marriage is not seen as an anomalous situation by locals.[86]

## Healthcare Services

The main health problems refugees are encountering include poor sanitation, malnutrition, and pandemics. The interviews with the refugees revealed that the biggest problem in the camps was sanitation. Only one toilet is allocated to every 10 families, and a water tube to every 50 families. Since toilets are clogged in a very short time, the use of the open area as a toilet leads to the risk of epidemic diseases such as diarrhoea and cholera. There is

---

[84] Sang, op.cit., pp. 3-8.
[85] Bepler, op.cit., p. 9.
[86] House of Commons International Development Committee, op.cit., pp. 35-37.

a shortage of drinking water due to insufficient water lines and water wells. It has been found out that some of the drinking water wells are drying up, and some of them are mixed with toilet drains. Children walk around barefoot in the camps because they do not have shoes to wear. Since there are no windows in the shelters where the refugees live, there is no ventilation, and the smoke and polluted air inside invites respiratory system diseases. As refugees are so busy finding food and clothing to sustain their lives, they cannot pay enough attention to health issues.[87]

Healthcare services in and around the camps are provided by different organizations, including the Government of Bangladesh, UN agencies, and national and international NGOs. Healthcare units consist of primary centres and secondary facilities. Healthcare units provide service to both refugees and the host community. The government of Bangladesh cooperates with WHO, UN agencies and NGOs in areas such as emergency aid, and prevention of epidemics. In the refugee camps, babies, children under the age of 5, pregnant and breastfeeding women, and young girls composes the ones who are in need of nutrition most. In Cox's Bazar, 24,3% of refugees in a camp were diagnosed with acute malnutrition. As a result of long-term malnutrition, 40% stunting or chronic malnutrition, and over 30% anaemia is seen. Moreover, there are some depreciating factors such as high disease rate, poor sanitary and sheltering opportunities, and the heavy rain season.[88] Lack of clean water and inadequate toilet and shower facilities increase the risk of contagious diseases such as cholera and malaria for refugees who already have weak immunity. Furthermore, measles, mumps, rubella and polio outbreaks are potential risks in case of insufficient vaccination. Sexual intercourse without adequate protection and hygiene occurs to be also a potential risk for the transmission of HIV/AIDS. Refugees suffer not only physical ailments but also experience psychological disturbances. Psychological support is necessary, especially for children who lost their families and witnessed deaths.[89]

As the COVID-19 epidemic outbreak spreads globally, the situation in the Rohingya camps worsens. It is not possible to ensure isolation and social distance in overcrowded camps where even healthcare personnel are deprived of personal protective equipment. The Government of Bangladesh reduced the access of humanitarian aid personnel to the camps by 80% in April 2020. Due to this measure taken to prevent the spread of the virus, basic services have become more difficult to be provided in the camps, the shortage of food and water has increased, and hygiene and cleaning facilities have further reduced. The epidemic has created both physical and moral

---

[87] Kudrat-E-Khuda, op.cit.
[88] Tay, op.cit., pp. 21-22.
[89] Honeth, op.cit., pp. 7-9.

influences on the refugees, including the prevailed fear that the virus would spread to the whole camp and cause a great massacre. A total of € 64,8 million has been allocated by the EU to reduce the impact of COVID-19 on Rohingya refugees and Bangladeshi host communities around Cox's Bazar. Although such short-term solutions are needed and helpful, a fast, comprehensive, coordinated and long-term solution should be provided by the international community in order to resettle refugees, prevent congestion in camps and help the people recover.[90]

## India's Burden and View about Rohingyas

India, having accepted refugees since its independence in 1947 and hosting more than 200,000 refugees today, has been widely praised for this benevolent behaviour. However, she has not shown this welcoming policy towards the Rohingya refugees. The Muslim identity of the Rohingyas seems to have an earnest impact on this attitude. India sees the Muslim Rohingyas as a potential threat to its national security due to its internal dynamics and problems with Pakistan. As a reflection of this stance, India abstained from the UN Resolution on the *"Situation of Rohingya Muslims and other Minorities in Myanmar"* in 2017.[91] Officially, there are 40,000 Rohingya refugees in India, according to UNHCR's records.[92]

The quest for life and freedom of the Rohingyas in India started with their immigration to India after the violent conflicts in Myanmar in 2012. India regarded the conflicts as a domestic issue in the first place and pledged to aid US\$ 1 million to Myanmar.[93] When Rohingya refugees first came to India, they did not encounter any opposing reaction. In many states, they were allowed to set up camps and work for a small amount of fee. Although they did not have adequate health, education and housing facilities, they were happy to be away from the violence in Myanmar. However, after a while, the Government of India and the intelligence service started to closely monitor the refugees for security concerns. The Government of India started viewing Rohingya refugees as 'illegal' immigrants, engaged in robbery, smuggling and human trafficking. The government seem to have the opinion that due to Rohingya refugees, Indian citizens were deprived of medical, professional, housing, and educational provisions. Another concern of India has been that Rohingya refugees may be related to radical groups and this situation may

---

[90] Felix Heiduk, Antje Missbach, "Risking Another Rohingya Refugee Crisis in the Andaman Sea", **SWP Comment**, No. 30, June 2020, German Institute for International and Security Affairs, p.1-4.
[91] Yermi Brenner, "Rohingya Migration to India: Patterns, Drivers and Experiences", **Mixed Migration Center Brief Paper**, April 2019, p. 9.
[92] Gorlick, op.cit., pp. 15-18.
[93] Yhome, op.cit., p. 3.

threaten national security, especially in Jammu and Kashmir regions.[94]

As a result of this perception, India decided and commenced deporting Rohingyas. India's expulsion of refugees is a violation of international refugee protection law and a violation of the principle of non-refoulement. The act of deporting is also against the Article 21 of the Indian constitution, which allows people to live freely in India. Identity documents issued by UNHCR are not recognized by Indian authorities, and Rohingyas are prevented from using health and education services, and finding employment. Refugee groups in India are treated differently, divided as legal and illegal. Rohingya refugees are the group that suffers the most from this unequal and discriminative practice.[95] The Government of India does not grant them refugee status. This view of India, which sees the Rohingyas as a threat to national security, is also reflected by the Indian media, allegedly showing that Rohingya refugees are associated with radical groups.[96] The fact that India is not a party to the 1951 Geneva Convention and 1967 Protocol does not mean that it has no responsibility to protect refugees. The Rohingya people were not granted the rights provided to other refugee groups in India and were subjected to different treatment and discrimination. The Supreme Court of India stated that a balance should be established between national security and human rights.[97]

## Geopolitical Interests

Despite being considered a regional power, India voided the expectations that it would take an active role in addressing the situation of Rohingya refugees. Therefore, she has been criticized by the international community and UNHCR for his decision to send refugees back to Myanmar. However, geopolitical, security and economic interests play a key role in India's approach to Rohingya refugees. India has been in favour of establishing a diplomatic balance between Bangladesh and Myanmar. By doing so, India aims to create a role for herself in finding a solution to the crisis. Because India is highly concerned that other regional opponents will gain significant geopolitical gains if she remains ineffective on the refugee matter.[98]

India's high-level political expression of support to Myanmar overshadowed the bilateral relations between Bangladesh and India. Upon the reaction of Bangladesh, India softened her approach towards the issue

---

[94] Carol Christine Fair, "Rohingya: Victims of a Great Game East", **The Washington Quarterly**, 41:3, Fall 2018, pp. 63–85.

[95] Monika Verma, "Struggle for Life and Liberty: Rohingyas In India". **International Center for Cultural Studies**, Dec 2019, https://www.researchgate.net/publication/338194048, (Access: 11.10.2020).

[96] Yhome, op.cit., p. 4.

[97] Marshilong, op.cit., pp. 1359-1361.

[98] Yhome, op.cit., p. 5.

and initiated a program called *"Operation Insaniyat"* to help Rohingya refugees in Bangladesh. In September 2017, India delivered 53 tons of humanitarian aid consisting of basic supplies such as sugar, rice, salt, pulses, tea, cooking oil, instant noodles, mosquito nets and biscuits. India sent another 373 tons of humanitarian aid to Bangladesh in May 2018.[99] By this operation, India acted in line with its geopolitical and strategic interests rather than sincere humanitarian concerns and sympathy. India does not want Myanmar and Bangladesh to fall under China's control and China to have a bigger influence in the region. Otherwise, this situation will cause India to lose power and reputation in the region. In great accordance with this strategy, India aims to eliminate the discontent that rose against herself in Bangladesh. By taking into consideration that India has not been treating well the Rohingyas living on her soil, it can be concluded that India is approaching the refugees not with humanitarian concerns, but with cold strategic interests and realistic policies.[100]

## Socio-Economic Impact

The main reason behind the movement of Rohingya refugees into India is the unfavourable living conditions in Bangladesh. Some of the refugees who first took refuge in Bangladesh preferred to transfer to India due to the adverse conditions in the camps, difficulties in finding a job and the reactions from the local people. According to the research and surveys conducted by the Indian authorities, the Rohingyas' preference of India as a country of refuge grafts on better living conditions and a safe environment, the hope of higher economic opportunities and the desire to reunite with the family. Some refugees preferred India because of its large Muslim population. However, Rohingyas travelled to India under very difficult and dangerous conditions. They were exploited for reasons such as not having official identity documents, not knowing Indian languages and not having money. In addition to the hunger and thirst, it was reported that there were robberies by smugglers and sexual assaults on Rohingya women by Indian border guards. There are also statements that Rohingya girls were kidnapped and sold in India for prostitution or forced marriages. Rohingya refugees mostly settled in Hyderabad and Jammu cities where the Muslim population is predominant. Refugees have been facing many obstacles in India, where they came with hope of a better life. However, they live in difficult conditions in all areas of life, such as finding shelter and food, and accessing education and health services. They often live in poor, shantytowns, in scarce hygiene with

---

[99] Mudasir Amin, **Nobody's Children, Owners of Nothing': Analysing the Indian State's Policy Response to the Rohingya Refugee Crisis**, Policy Report No.24, The Hindu Centre for Politics and Public Policy, February – May 2018, pp. 71-74.
[100] Niranjan Sahoo, "India's Rohingya Realpolitik", **Carnegie Rising Democracies Network**, October 2017.

limited access to water and sanitation. They pay rent to live in illegally built slums. They are always face to face with the risk of being forced to evacuate these homes where there are not enough cleaning facilities. In the interviews with the refugees, it was stated that the income they earn is not enough to survive, and food shortages are pervasive.[101] Since most Rohingya refugees in India do not have a handcraft skill, they can only find low-skilled jobs in the informal market.[102]

Child labour is widespread in poor Rohingya families who are large in numbers and do not have sufficient income. Some families live only on children's earnings. Most children do not attend school, despite the fact that they are at school age. Families do not opt to send their children to school due to the distance of schools from Rohingya residential areas, security concerns and lack of language skills. Those who attend school generally attend only primary school and only a small number of students go to secondary school. There are almost no high school or college students. Since Indian authorities do not accept identity documents issued by UNHCR to refugees, Rohingya children are expelled from public schools. One fourth of the Rohingya refugees stated in their interviews that they were intimidated and harassed by Indian police and intelligence services. It was determined that the refugees who were arrested by the police on fraudulent charges in Hyderabad were defended by lawyers cooperating with the police, and the lawyers shared the fees they received from Rohingya refugees with the police. There are interviews by local Indians that the refugees are beaten and their phones stolen, Rohingya women are harassed, they are not allowed to fill water, and the local governments are not taking any action against all these.[103]

According to World Bank data, the Indian economy has had the highest growth rates all over the world, higher than the world average in the last 25 years. In 2035, India is expected to be the third largest economy in the world.[104] India's GDP is US$ 2,875 trillion as of 2019, which corresponds to approximately nine times the GDP of Bangladesh. Due to India's population of 1.366 billion, its GDP per capita is US$ 2.104. This figure corresponds to 13% more of Bangladesh's GDP per capita.[105] Although India is at a much higher level than Bangladesh in terms of economic development, it can be inferred that India is not as hospitable as Bangladesh in terms of refugee acceptance.

---

[101] Brenner, op.cit., pp. 4-12.

[102] Tay, op.cit., p. 15.

[103] Brenner, op.cit., pp. 7-10.

[104]Sumit Roy, China and India, "Rising Powers" and African Development: Challenges and Opportunities, The Nordic Africa Institute, Uppsala-Sweden, pp. 6-7.

[105] The World Bank, https://data.worldbank.org/indicator/NY.GDP.PCAP.CD?locations=IN(Access: 27.10.2020).

## Suggestions for Easing the Burden

The developing countries host 85% of the refugees worldwide. However, this hospitality puts colossal charges on them. Therefore, the solutions suggested for easing the burden need to be multi-domain and multi-dimension. The domains may be economic, social and environmental, while the dimensions should be short, medium and long terms. The stakeholders of the solutions are the international community, host nations, originating nations and the refugees.[106] Unconventional solutions are required and these solutions, based on lessons learned from previous international responsibility-sharing efforts, need to be supported by the international community.[107] First of all, a fair and long-term burden sharing is required to alleviate the load of host countries that have undergone a tremendous socio-economic strain. Secondly, the root causes of forced migration need to be identified and eliminated. In order to achieve this, substantial duties fall on UN, international organizations, states and NGOs. Next, the international system handling mass human movements needs to be strengthened to enforce human rights and provide protection for refugees. Despite additional and even disturbing burden, it is the responsibility of the host nation's politicians and community leaders to avoid discrimination and intolerance against refugees and to build bridges, not walls, between the host and the refugee communities. Should the refugees properly integrated, they will contribute to the growth and development of the host country rather than being a pain.[108]

Medium and long-term solutions are expected to prioritize what is more significant to both refugees and the host country. While focusing on medium and long-term solutions, solutions to everyday problems should also be sought; otherwise, minor daily problems will prevail and pose major challenges in the future. These problems include meeting the urgent needs, which directly affect the living conditions of the refugees, such as sheltering, heating, health services, clean water, sanitation, and food. Moreover, refugees generally face problems in the areas of education, marriage and livelihoods. Rohingya refugees believe that their living conditions and their ability to stand on their own feet will improve in the medium and long term through education and employment. However, refugees focus more on short-term needs and assistance and pay less attention to medium and long-term needs, aspirations and plans. Refugees need to be able to integrate their short-term perspective into longer-term expectations. Refugees, believing that

---

[106] Ki-moon, op.cit.
[107] Caitlin Wake, Veronique Barbelet, Marcus Skinner, "Rohingya Refugees' Perspectives on Their Displacement in Bangladesh Uncertain Futures", **Humanitarian Policy Group Working Paper**, June 2019, pp. 1-3.
[108] Ki-moon, op.cit.

humanitarian aid will not last forever, work unregistered or voluntarily. Because of the living conditions in the camps, more women are forced to work to provide a living for their own household. This fact makes some changes to stereotypes and opinions about gender and work norms in the camps. It is necessary to provide sufficient funds to improve living conditions in refugee camps. Providing adequate and open communication about the government's intentions and refugees' options will alleviate the refugees' concerns and tensions. Government officials and employees of humanitarian organizations have a significant role in communication. If possible, home visits and face-to-face meetings with women who cannot leave their homes will increase communication effectiveness. During these interviews, surveys should be administered to determine the medium-and long-term expectations and needs of refugees. Establishing trust between refugees and camp management will contribute to the protection of social life and order. For this purpose, it is of great importance that refugees and especially women are represented in the administration and decision-making mechanisms. Relevant stakeholders, including UNHCR, IOM and refugee-focused NGOs, have to do their part to ensure that refugees' voices are heard loud enough by the international community and are represented at high-level political and policy discussions.[109]

Alternative policies should be put forward in accordance with host countries to overcome this burden. These policies, defined by national and international actors, are aligned with the priorities and needs of host countries and focus on promoting socio-economic development. Short-term approaches that rely solely on humanitarian aid have both poor returns and substantial financial burden. Since host countries and neighbouring countries are mostly developing countries, adopting a long-term development approach and including not only the host country but also other countries in the region will yield more effective results. For successful long-term development planning, it is necessary to establish a horizontal and vertical coordination mechanism between all actors in order to evaluate the needs, determine the responsibilities and prevent unnecessary duplication and deficiencies.[110]

In order to ease the burden of countries, the international community should support these countries. This burden is too heavy to be handled alone, especially by a developing country. The international community should provide enough support not only in the initial phase of the influx of refugees but also as long as the refugee situation continues. In this context, all national and international actors are expected to act in harmony. A high level of preparedness and cooperation is required in order to be able to intervene in

---

[109] Wake, op.cit., pp. 1-3.
[110] Hendow, op.cit., pp. 20-22.

imminent and emergency situations. For this purpose, before any crisis begins, necessary capacity building and cooperation activities should be carried out with the participation of both international and national actors.[111] The UNHCR asks the international community and regional countries to provide support not only for the basic demands but also for critical needs that arise according to changing situations.[112] A donor conference on *"Sustaining Support for the Rohingya Refugee Response"* was held on 22 October 2020, hosted by UNHCR together with USA, UK and EU. During the video teleconference, UNHCR called for the increase of international support and doubling the efforts.[113]

Regional and global organizations such as the UN Security Council, ASEAN or the Organization of Islamic Cooperation (OIC) have failed to assure the necessary political developments for the return of Rohingya refugees. Many of the Rohingya refugees do not want to return because of what they suffered. In order to conduct a voluntary return, refugees first wait for their requests to be fulfilled. For a voluntarily return to their lands in Myanmar safely and dignified, Rohingyas' reasonable demands include fair trials for crimes committed against them and compensation for damages, full human rights assurance in Myanmar, and civil rights including Myanmar citizenship. The biggest responsibility for a transparent, safe and sustainable return falls on the country of origin, Myanmar. Myanmar's responsibility calls for clear political commitments and adherence to these commitments. A solemn question that needs to be answered is who, in practice, and under what conditions will check if the Myanmar authorities act in accordance with their commitments. Another condition for voluntary returns is that Rohingya refugees, especially women, should be included in the negotiations, and a commonsense that refugees should be allowed to make a free choice to return or not. Otherwise, the reliability of the process will be weakened.[114]

Rohingya refugees and local people should be assured to have access to employment opportunities and their demands for food, drinking water, health and education are met. Surveys with refugees and local people put forward different priorities. Among the priority needs of refugees are food, clean water, shelter, electricity and fuel, and tea. On the other hand, water, health services, roads and infrastructure and employment are among the top

---

[111] Sally Shevach, Kate Sutton, Josie Flint, Nadiruzzaman, "When the Rubber Hits the Road: Local Leadership in the First 100 Days of the Rohingya Crisis Response", **Humanitarian Exchange**, Number 73, October 2018, pp. 18-19.
[112] UNHCR, UNHCR Calls for Solidarity, Support and Solutions for Rohingya Refugees ahead of an Urgent Donor Conference, 20 October 2020, https://www.unhcr.org/news/briefing/2020/10/5f8 d7c004/unhcr-calls-solidarity-support-solutions-rohingya-refugees-ahead-urgent.html (Access: 23.10. 2020).
[113] UHNCR, Conference on Sustaining Support, op.cit.
[114] Gorlick, op.cit., pp. 19-28.

priorities of the local people.[115] Employment opportunities need to be created for refugees so that they can stand on their own feet. For this purpose, a labour market assessment by the host country is required at national, regional and local levels. This assessment will be a significant source that can be used to guide the studies on the labour market, employment strategies, and vocational training programs. Moreover, the skill levels and special abilities of all refugees, including newborns, should be recorded. In accordance with these records, appropriate workforce-employment matching can be made by the host country. Finding a job is not easy in developing countries where employment is low. Refugees in Bangladesh can find only a limited amount of jobs even in the informal economy, and in most cases, they become vulnerable to exploitation due to the lack of legal protection. Refugees often have to work in sectors that are not desired by the local population. Allowing Rohingya refugees to work in areas with labour needs, including seasonal work, is considered a positive approach for both refugees and local communities.[116]

Humanitarian needs and development demands vary in protracted refugee situations. Refugee children need to be included in the host country's national education system. This will enable children to participate fully and actively in social life, learn the language of the host community, and contribute to the host country's economy in the upcoming years. Refugees should be provided with services within the existing service structure of the host country, and new structures specific to refugees should be avoided. Citizens of the host country should also be included in projects and programs related to refugees, and an inclusive approach should be followed. These approaches will reduce tensions and vulnerabilities and make significant contributions to the development of social cohesion. Good and healthy communication between refugees and the local community needs to be established. In this direction, raising awareness in both the refugee group and the host community will prevent information pollution while contributing to the development of social cohesion between the two parties. The inclusion of credible local actors as well as media tools will be beneficial. Countries hosting refugees need moral support as well as financial support. Their good practices need to be appreciated by the international community. National institutions working to ensure social cohesion need to be supported and strengthened by donors. Basic education and vocational training should be provided to different refugee groups such as women and youth, and different skills in areas where the host country has labour shortage. These trainings constitute a grave step in improving the employment of refugees in the host country. If the refugees cannot be provided with registered employment

---

[115] Humanitarian Response, op.cit., p. 16.
[116] Gorlick, op.cit., pp. 19-28.

opportunities, they will be seeking for working illegally. This situation will cause both the enforcement of refugees to work under inhumane conditions and loss of tax income. Refugees should be allowed to use not only their workforce potential but also their investment and entrepreneurial skills should be given a chance.[117]

Providing the resettlement of Rohingya refugees to developed countries may be a solution that will ease the burden of Bangladesh. Currently, the refugees' moving to third countries is usually through limited, irregular channels, paying high costs and facing personal risks. The provision of the settlement by UNHCR, IOM and related governments could make it more streamlined, and prevent or reduce factors such as fraud and human trafficking. With this practice, several thousand refugees have settled from Malaysia to Canada, USA, Japan and New Zealand. Canada also accepts refugees from Bangladesh. Resettlement in third countries not only benefits a few thousand lucky minorities, but also supports those who are left behind. Refugees, settled in third countries with more work opportunity, send some of their income to family members and relatives left behind. Incoming money contributes to the improvement of the lives of refugees in Bangladesh. It is imperative to provide a reliable resource so that the situation of refugees does not turn into a humanitarian crisis. In case the interest of the international community and donors for Rohingya refugees decreases, disappears or the priority shifts to another issue, there is a risk that the resources provided to the refugees will fade away. If this risk comes into life, the situation will worsen for Bangladesh. If the Government of Bangladesh decides to manage the prolonged refugee problem with limited external support, then she may be exposed to political criticism and anger from its own public.[118]

## Conclusion

Countries use their security concerns as an excuse and engage in harsh interventions that amount to human rights violations against different religious, ethnic, and political groups they see as a threat. Due to persecution, people set out dangerous travels to take refuge in other countries. Many new threats and risks await those who can overcome all these difficulties and reach refugee camps in the host country. Rohingyas living in camps in Bangladesh experience difficulties in all domains of life. Women, girls, and children are the most vulnerable ones. However, Rohingyas still prefer to live in these camps rather than return to Myanmar as they feel safer in Bangladesh than in Myanmar.

Rohingyas human rights in Myanmar have been violated for many years.

---

[117] Hendow, op.cit., pp. 24-62.
[118] Gorlick, op.cit., pp. 19-28.

They were subjected to various inhumane persecutions as reflected in the reports prepared of the UN and other international organizations, and it was even claimed that ethnic cleansing was executed by the Myanmar army. Despite these reports, the international community did not take effective measures to stop Myanmar, and the countries seemingly prioritised their geopolitical interests over human cost. While countries unanimously agree upon the discourse that human life is valuable 'in theory', they do not show the same sensitivity and unity in practice. Unfortunately, this contrast between the discourses and behaviours of the international community in Myanmar was not a first. In the past, in Nagorno-Karabakh, Rwanda, Bosnia and Kosovo experienced the same.

It seems that the number of refugees in the world will continue to increase; more people will leave their lands and become refugees. However, in most cases, it is difficult to find the desired solutions to the refugees' problems because the countries they take refuge in are developing countries and the socio-economic conditions they live in are not strong enough. These countries don't have adequate capacity and power to shoulder the burden alone. The hospitality of Bangladesh with hundreds of thousands of refugees, brings burden in economic, demographic, social, security and environmental domains. It is very difficult for Bangladesh to overcome this burden alone. Therefore, financial and moral support of the international community is a must.

This support should be planned and implemented not only in the form of short-term financial support, but also in the medium and long term to cover all areas of need. This solidarity crisis or reception crisis needs to be dealt with by the whole world, not just the regions where the impacts are directly felt. Unfortunately, solutions to the problem cannot be found on a global scale. Not even an outstanding success is achieved in collecting the funds in order to meet the most basic needs of refugees, such as shelter, food, sanitation and health. Responsibility for protecting the refugees falls into host country. In this context, governments should try to meet the socio-economic and security needs of refugees in cooperation with international institutions. Of course, the capacity and power of the host country may not be enough to realize this ideally. However, what is important here is to act with a good sense of intention and responsibility. Host countries and communities should not view refugees as a source of the problem, and stop hostility and discrimination against them. While meeting the basic needs of refugees in the short term, steps should also be taken to ensure their integration into the host society in the medium and long term by providing them with opportunities such as education and employment.

The biggest common responsibility among the international community, the host country and the country of origin is to create the necessary conditions for the return of refugees. In order to resolve existing conflicts, international cooperation should be ensured and the voices of refugees should also be heard in these efforts. However, Myanmar is so slow to take the necessary initiatives for the return of Rohingya refugees. There is almost no progress on this matter. Rohingya refugees do not want to return to Myanmar because they do not feel safe and do not know what is waiting for them when they return. In fact, this seem to suit Myanmar's aims. The ongoing acts of violence against the Rohingyas in Arakan show that the Rohingya refugees will continue to stay in Bangladesh in the near future. In order to ensure justice and accountability, the international community should put the necessary pressure to investigate allegations of human rights violations and bring those responsible to justice. In this way, criminals will be punished and the victims will be compensated. Compensation to be given to refugees will not erase what they lived, and bring back their lost and loved ones. However, it will facilitate their financial and moral recovery. Failure to exhibit this determination may pave the way for similar events in the future and encourage criminals.

Today, Bangladesh is home to over one million Rohingya refugees. For a developing country, this burden is quite heavy. Bangladesh needs constant financial and moral support. It does not seem that the refugees' stay in Bangladesh will end soon. On the contrary, the number of refugees and their needs will grow. If the necessary measures are not taken, this increase will cause bigger socio-economic and security problems in the future. International donations are not sufficient, and it is likely that international interest will decrease further in the future due to what is called 'donor fatigue'. This means that the burden on Bangladesh will increase even more. Compared to Bangladesh, India's economic conditions are better and the number of refugees hosted is smaller. It means India's burden is lighter. However, the Rohingya refugees in India also experience difficulties due to India's own internal dynamics and approach to Rohingyas because of its strategic interests.

In conclusion, the international community, states, donors, host nation, originating country and refugees themselves share the responsibility. This is a big burden on the host nations. They need global assistance and continuous support to provide refugees smooth and seamless transition to normal life.

CHAPTER 11

# IMMIGRATION AND BELONGING ON THE AMERICA - MEXICO BORDER

Ferdi Güçyetmez[*]

## Introduction

Throughout history, humanity is in the records as a living being in continuous motion. Although migration is an ancient phenomenon historically, it has played an essential role in industrialization and modernization processes. It has been an essential aspect of social life and political economy since the 1650s. In the history of international migrations, primarily due to capitalism and labour mobility, the years between 1850-1914 witnessed mass migrations in Europe and North America. Although xenophobia and economic stagnation, which increased after 1914, led to a significant decrease in immigration, the migration situation continues. Especially in the last quarter-century, when globalization and regional conflicts that started after the second world war continued, migration movements accelerated due to many reasons. Besides, migration conditions are improving due to the developing technical progress.

The most critical phenomenon that determines immigration policies is identity. In other words, immigration policies are shaped under the understanding of the nation-state and the determination of international regulations. While international actors are trying to create a standard immigration regime, extreme-right movements that have risen significantly through xenophobia and anti-immigration are taking place. Identity problem stands out in the cultural dimension of the globalization process. This problem, expressed with the phenomenon of multiculturalism in the global process, is related to the recognition of minority rights and identities within the nation-state. In this respect, does the United States of America care so much about the rights and identities of minorities within nation-states? This question is not easy to answer, but the emphasis is on minorities in nation-states. In this study, we will guide our study from the perspective of the history of immigration between Mexico and the USA and the identity of immigrants.

---

[*] Lecturer at University of Neuchatel and İstanbul Kent University.

## Migration and World Systems Theory

The basic patterns of human migration have changed over the years, but the underlying rationale for human migration has been substantially consistent. People who migrate have one thing in common: going to a place they never know about these directions constitutes leaving their home and country to go to a place with a different language and culture. Some immigrants migrated to areas where the population is sparse, while other immigrants migrated towards the centres of the population.[1]

Scientists tell us that our global story, our migration adventure, began in eastern Africa, and they date back to about 50,000 or 60,000 years ago.Based on archaeological, genetic and linguistic evidence, it is believed that the first intercontinental movement of Homo Sapiens migrated to what we now call the Middle East, the Arabian Peninsula, the Indian periphery, South Asia, and possibly Australia. Later, it was passed to Northern and Southern Europe, Central Asia and then North and South America through the Bering Strait.[2]When we look at the history of human migration, the pre-modern human takes us back millions of years.[3] It started to spread from East Africa to various parts of the ancient world and caused the formation of substitute species in Africa, Europe and Asia.[4]

**Figure 1.** Migration map of humanity[5]

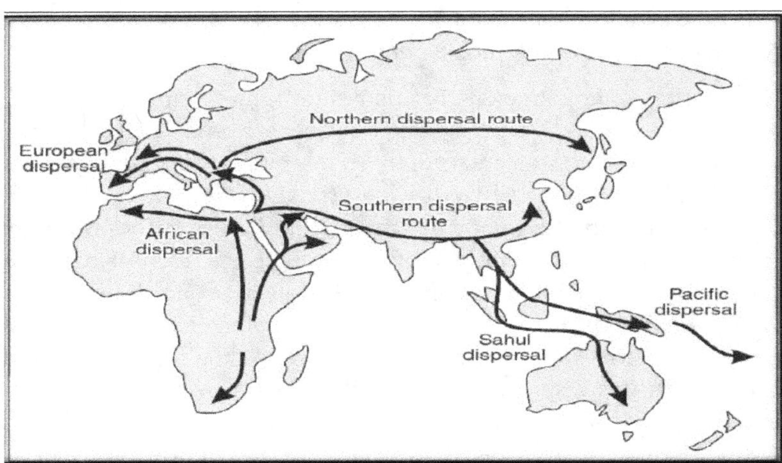


---


[1] Mannıng Patrick, **"Migration in Human History"**, D. Christian (Ed.), The Cambridge World History,Cambridge: Cambridge UniversityPress, 2015, pp. 278

[2] Brıan Keeley, **International Migration,** OECD Publishing, 2009, p. 29.

[3] Sayın, Hüdayi (2017). **"Uluslar Arası Güvenlik Ve Göçmen Kaçakçılığı"**, İktisadiyat, 1(1), s.137.

[4] Manning, ibid, p. 279

[5] Hıscock Peter, Early Old World Migrations Of Homo Sapiens: Archaeology. **The Encyclopedia of Global Human Migration,** Edited by Immanuel Ness, 2013.p.2.

In the 300 years from 1550 to 1850, when 10 million people crossed the Atlantic as slaves, almost 50 million Europeans crossed the Atlantic from 1840 to 1940. Another mobility is that 80 million immigrants are moving from India and China. Sparsely populated regions of North America and Southeast Asia absorbed more than 30 million immigrants. North and Central Asia included more than 20 million immigrants in their regions ruled by China and Russia.[6]

We can say that 55 to 58 million immigrants from Europe immigrated to Continental America until 1940. In addition to these, we can add 2.5 million immigrants from China, India, Japan and Africa to the group immigrating to America. In light of the information revealed, America, one of the leading countries that accepted immigration, had a population of 59 million in 1850 and reached 325 million in the 1950s. As the migration movement continues throughout the world, the United States of America is the leading country, with approximately 50 million immigrants. The top sending (origin) countries in the immigrant population are India, which sends more than 16 million people, followed by Mexico with 13 million.[7]

As we mentioned about the distribution of immigrants, 50 million immigrants are in the United States of America. As the excess of international immigrants in America causes many problems with it, its effect on the population, social and cultural structure of the country is indisputable. For this reason, although America's international migration policies are always on the American agenda, they are becoming more stringent for new immigrants every day. Trump made controversial statements regarding immigrants during his election campaign. He then signed two presidential decrees regarding the wall on the Mexican border and cities protecting illegal immigrants. So historically, the United States of America has been receiving immigrants continuously for over a century.

When we examine the migration flow between America and Mexico, theoretically, it will be correct first to examine it in terms of world systems. World-systems theory is based on Wallerstein's "modern world-system" study. In this study, Wallerstein conducted comparative analyses on the global expansion of the European-dominated capitalist system, which has been shaping since the 16th century. He reassessed and made sense of the mechanisms and historical processes in which unequal political and economic structures were created, spread throughout the world, and that included non-capitalist or pre-capitalist regions into the global market economy. This system mentioned by Wallerstein consists of three areas connected to the

---

[6] Manning, ibid, p. 304.

[7] Mckeown Adam, Global Migration 1846-1940, Journal of World History, Vol.15, No.2, 2004, pp. 155-189.

same centre, which are the areas formed by the centre, periphery and semi-peripheral states.[8]

According to the world-systems theory, the main reason of migration is the spread of the capitalist mode of production from the centre to the periphery countries, and subsequently the inclusion of new regions in the world economy, which has become increasingly integrated. At the same time, colonial regimes in the past provided this, today "neo-colonial" regimes, multinational corporations and foreign direct investments. Central states penetrate neighbouring countries in search of raw materials and cheap labour in order to gain additional profits without being affected by the rise of workers' wages in the domestic market. This influence usually comes with the process of "modernization" and "commercialization" in agriculture and requires the replacement of capitalist techniques with traditional processes, especially in the agriculture and manufacturing sectors.[9]

He classified other countries according to the degree of dependence on the dominant capitalist powers, which he defines as core nations. In this classification, periphery countries are named as the most dependent countries on the global market, and semi-periphery countries are named as fewer dependent countries compared to the periphery countries. The nations in the external arena, on the other hand, remained isolated from the global capitalist system. According to the world-systems theory, the main reason for migration is the spread of the capitalist mode of production from the centre to the periphery countries, followed by the inclusion of new regions in the world economy, which has gradually become integrated.[10]

The widespread use of the languages, cultures and modern consumption models of the central countries, together with the development in transportation and communication infrastructures, open a door for immigrants to the major countries. Migrants "invited" to countries are well-educated migrants who are needed not only to be employed in unskilled labour but also to be employed in skilled jobs. These immigrants are increasingly needed in global cities, which have become centres of activities such as banking and finance.[11]

The management and education system established by the central

---

[8] Wallerstein, Immanuel. The Modern World-System: CapitalistAgriculture and the Origins of the European World-Economy in the Sixteenth Century. New York: Academic Press. 1976, p. 232

[9] Arango, J. **"Explaining Migration: A Critical View"**, International Social Science Journal, Vol. 52, Issue. 2000, p. 291.

[10] Massey, D. S. **"Why Does Immigration Occur? A Theorical Synthesis"**, C. Hirschman, P. Kasinitz, J. DeWind(eds.), The Handbook of International Migration: The American Experience, Russell Sage Foundation:New York. 1999, p.40.

[11] Massey, D. S.,Arango, J., Hugo, G., Kouaouci, A., Pellegrino, A., Taylor, J. E. (september) **"Theories of International Migration: A Reviewand Appraisal"**, Populationand Development Review, Vol. 19, No. 3. 1993, p.447.

countries has formed a reflection of the centre in the surrounding countries, and the management and exploitation of the surrounding countries have been made possible with this system. In countries without colonial ties, the effect of economic influence is prominent: the fact that Mexicans increasingly turn to American universities, speaking English, and closely follow the American consumer style is a sign of this. The advertising campaigns also reinforce these cultural and ideological connections established with neighbouring countries and mass media carried out by the central countries.[12]

For 300 years, Europeans settled in America, Africa, Asia and most of Oceania, thus guiding the migration movements of the period.[13] Although the exact number of "colonizing" immigrants is not known, it is possible to say that there has been enough out-migration in other parts of the world to establish European domination. In this process, immigrants are generally divided into three classes: the relatively large number of farmers, the smaller group of managers and craftsmen, and an even smaller group of entrepreneurs who set up plantations to produce raw materials for Europe's growing mercantilist economy. Although the share of Europeans in participating in plantation production is low, the direct impact of this sector on the size and composition of the American population does not go unnoticed. With pre-industrial technology, plantations required sizable cheap labour. East Asian indentured workers partially met this demand, but the most crucial source of the workforce was African slaves who were displaced. For 300 years, about ten million Africans were "imported" to America and, together with the European colonies, took part in the social and demographic formation of America.[14]

While industrialization and urbanization were provided by internal migration in the European continent with the capitalist process, America and Australia continents experienced the industrialization and urbanization process based on capitalism thanks to external migration. Europeans who immigrated to America and Australia played an active role in the economic development and social changes of the countries they went. With the support of the European bourgeoisie, capitalism has significantly developed in the migrated continents; an urbanized and industrialized society has been created. Complementary to these European immigrants, the first leg of American immigration, the second pillar is African immigrants. Africans were used as slaves of the continent. Therefore, the history of capitalism is the history of

---

[12] Abadan-Unat, N. **Bitmeyen Göç: Konuk İşçilikten Ulus-Ötesi Yurttaşlığa**, İstanbul Bilgi Üniversitesi Yayınları: İstanbul. 2002, p.17.

[13] Weiner, Myron, The Global Migration Crisis: Challenge to Statesand to Human Rights, HarperCollins: New York. 1995, p.21

[14] Massey, Douglass S. **"Why Does Immigration Occur? A Theorical Synthesis"**, C. Hirschman, P. Kasinitz, J. De Wind(eds.), The Handbook of International Migration: The American Experience, Russell Sage Foundation:New York, 1999, p.34.

exploitative migration.[15] While the slave trade was experienced in the international arena, the major countries also experienced intense immigration movements within themselves. The expropriation of small farmers from their lands caused them to migrate to the city and become workers in the workshops. The masses who could not find a job in the city preferred to immigrate to America or the countries determined as colonies.[16]

The first period of migration movements, called transatlantic, was followed by the "Great Migration" period between about 1800 and 1925. More than 52 million people left the industrializing countries of Europe in search of new life in America as well as Australia.[17] 85% of these immigrants preferred to go to only five countries. Although 60% of it goes to America, other preferred countries are Argentina, Australia, Canada and New Zealand; the main emigration nations are Britain, Italy, Norway, Portugal, Spain and Sweden. Not all international migrants are European, but they have the majority (about 88%).[18]

The rapid increase in transatlantic migration as of the middle of the 19th century is closely related to the developments in transportation facilities. Although there were high population movements in pre-industrial Europe, economic and technological development increased both the scale and types of migration. Especially the construction of railways on both sides of the Atlantic and the construction of more advanced sea vehicles have accelerated the migration processes.[19]

This large-scale immigration wave from Europe came to a halt with the outbreak of the First World War and initiated the limited migration period that would last for about forty years. During this period of immigration, countries that previously immigrated and gave immigrants started to raise their borders against immigrants; Hostility towards non-citizens - "foreigners" has been observed, especially in North America and Europe. Moreover, for the first time in this period, wide and official differences among immigrants were emphasized, and it was felt that "refugees" should be defined as a particular immigrant category.[20]

## America's transformation into the United States

Since 1492, the American continent has been under European colonialism. Spain gained profit with the first arrival of Christopher

---

[15] Peköz, Mustafa, **Avrupa Birliğinde Göçmenler Almanya'da Türkler/Kürtler,** Gün Publishing: İstanbul, 2002, p.16.
[16] Toksöz, Gülay, **Uluslararası Emek Göçü**, İstanbul Bilgi UniversityPublish: İstanbul, 2006, p.13.
[17] Skeldon, Ronald (1997), **Migration and Development,** Longman: England. Stark, 1997, p.65.
[18] Ibid, Douglass, p. 34
[19] İbid, Skeldon, 67.
[20] Marfleet, Philip, **Refugees in a Global Era**, Palgrave Macmillan: New York. 2006, p.71

Columbus in America in 1492.[21]The Portuguese came to the continent in 1500, the French in 1534 and the British in 1603. Those who came to the area first founded the town of Jamestown. The first colonial period in America started in 1608 when a group of 100 people from England settled in the Virginia region.[22]All colonies in America have become a major colony of England. In time, England expanded its right of sovereignty over the colonies and tried to strengthen its hegemony in the region with the migration movements it supported. However, in 1780, three out of every four Americans were either English or of Irish descent. "This situation has ensured the dominance of the English language and culture in the American continent throughout history. America's population was approximately 1 million 600 thousand people in only 13 colonies in 1760."[23] Many people who fled political persecution and wanted freedom were coming to America from Europe, crossing the ocean. The Irish were on the run from famine. Why did these people see America as a devotee? Partly because this land does not belong to anyone. A mobile border was moving west every year. Every human being became his own master by going to the extreme.[24]

In 1750, several tribes and small colonies established their rule in the American continent, especially in the plains, but their impact on the outside world was negligible. On the other hand, a large part of the continent was under the influence of Europe. The population and wealth of these colonies were snowballing, and by 1750 the total economic power of the colonies was more remarkable than most of the states on the European continent. Britain's victory in the Seven Years' War had pulled the pin of the American independence movement. Nevertheless, if the British Royal Navy and army did not exist, "Americans would have already severed the ties that bind them to Great Britain." The colonies, whose economic power increased day by day, expressed their grievances more and more strongly.[25] The 2nd American Congress convened in Philadelphia in 1775, and the struggle for independence officially started with a declaration published. After nearly six years of hard war, the Americans prevailed and declared their independence on July 4, 1776. The delegation headed by Thomas Jefferson adopted the Declaration of Independence on July 4, 1776.[26] This document is essential for the history of democracy and political science. At the end of the declaration, it was declared that an independent state named "The United States of America" was established, provided that the states are free in

---

[21] Charles McLean Andrews, The Colonial Background of the American Revolution: Four EssaysIn American Colonia lHistory, Yale UniversityPress, London, 1978, p.93.

[22]Richard Middleton, **Colonial Amerika: A history 1607-1760,** Cambridge Mass.,Blackwell, 1992, p.12.

[23] Thomas L.Purvis, Colonial America to 1763, Facts On File, Inc., USA, 1999, p.19.

[24] Andrea Maurois-Louis Aragon, **America-Russia, Vol:1,** New York, 1968, p.9.

[25] Marc Ferro, Colonization: **A Global History,** 1.st Edition, Routledge, London, 2005, p.350

[26] James Stuart Olson-Robert Shadle, **Historical Dictionary of European Imperialism,** GreenwoodPress, New York, 1991, p.245.

internal affairs. The Paris Peace was signed on September 3, 1783, and Britain recognized the independence of the United States. Then, with the "The Treaty of Alliance" signed on February 6 by establishing an alliance between America and France in 1778, France recognized the independence of the American colonies.[27] The northern border of the USA is today's Canadian border, the western border is the Mississippi River, and the southern border is Spain's Florida. France took the island of Tobago in the Antilles. Spain took Florida and Menorca. The Netherlands turned out to be harmful because he lost the Negapotam in South India to England. Thus, the British gained the right to trade with the colonies of the Netherlands.[28]

While in 1782, the USA consisted of 13 federal states with a population of 3.5 million, within half a century, it expanded rapidly through war and purchases. In 1803 Louisiana was bought from France for 80 million francs, Florida in 1819 from Spain for 5 million dollars, Texas from Mexico for 15 million dollars. Oregon was bought from Spain in 1846. In 1846 the 49th north parallel became the border with Canada. In 1867 Alaska was bought from Russia for 7.2 million dollars. The Hawaiian archipelago was purchased in 1893. The USA captured Puerto Rico and the Philippines because of the war with Spain in 1898. In 1917, the USA bought the Virgin Islands, which are very important in the Caribbean Sea and consist of 50 islands, from Denmark for 25 million dollars.[29] As a result of these initiatives made by America, European culture and civilization have found a new spreading area. It is true that America, which received more than 66 million immigrants in the period from 1820 to the 2000s, was an immigrant society. As a result of migrations, unemployment has decreased in Europe, and political and religious fights have lost their importance. The USA has now been a balancing act against Europe. Thus, the United States of America appears as the first country in the world with the highest ethnic diversity.

## Immigration integrations and identity formation in America

National identity crises can be seen in almost every country in the world today. America is a society founded by 17th and 18th-century settlers, almost all of them from the British Isles. These early settlers defined America in terms of race, culture, ethnicity, and most importantly, religion. Americans gained independence in the 18th century; It was a homogeneous society with a majority of whites, British and Protestants. However, today the homogeneous structure has disappeared. A heterogeneous character has emerged from Black, Hispanic, Asian, Catholic, Jewish and many identities.

---

[27] George Ticknor Curtis, History of the Origin, Formationand Adoption of the Constitution of the United States: With Notices of Its Principal Framers, Vol:2, Harper&Brothers, New York, 1865, p.156.
[28] Fahir Armaoğlu, **Siyasi Tarih**, TTK publisher, Ankara, 2003, pp.24-25.
[29] Claude Julien, **American Empire**, VintageBooks, France, 1973, p.58.

Immigration and familiar spirit are key elements of American national identity. Being a nomadic society, Americans did not attach importance to space, but rather values and principles. According to Huntington, these two assessments of identity are correct; but it is missing. Expressions that do not give us information about the culture that created the soul. When evaluated historically, the content of American identity has been related to four main components: These are race, culture, ethnicity and ideology. America associated with race and ethnicity is no longer even possible. From a cultural point of view, Protestant culture is under severe siege by the threat of Hispanization. If we evaluate it from the perspective of the Soviet example, ideology can no longer be considered as a unifying element.

In the early twentieth century, President Theodore Roosevelt believed that immigrants were the most critical force in American society and had the right to expect something from them. Accordingly, President Roosevelt deemed himself permissible to ask that the immigrants, who are the incredible power of America, express their full loyalty to America and not keep their ties with their former countries above their ties with America.[30] The main factor that gives America this ethnic diversity has emerged with the international migration movement. Predominantly, the wave of immigration started in Western and Northern Europe and then continued to include Southern and Eastern Europe. The great waves of immigration that started in the 19th century left us with a mixture of races that the world has not witnessed before. Few nations on earth have the heterogeneity of America. Everyone has an immigrant background, including American Indians. America is the Nation of Nations in Walt Whitman's phrase. As a result of all these migrations, a synthetic new ethnic structure and a new nation will begin to rise in America. This new nation has always been aware of the ethnic diversity that it harbours deep within its own ethnic identity.

In the studies conducted on the American society, the difference between the assimilation of the European-origin populations that make up the ethnic groups and the assimilation of the blacks and Asians who constitute the racial groups, that is, they are immediately perceived to be different, have been revealed. Accordingly, while people of European descent are truly assimilated into American society, in the case of groups of different races, the cycle is defined not by assimilation but by the formation of two separate social systems. Stating that it is essential to distinguish between cultural assimilation and structural assimilation, Fraizer pointed out that although blacks have acquired American culture, they are not assimilated into American culture to

---

[30] Nathan Glazer, **We Are All Multiculturalists Now,** Cambridge, MA: Harvard UniversityPress, 1997, p.67.

the same extent.[31]

According to Huntington, the assimilation of different groups into American society has taken place in various ways and has never been completed. The following statements by Huntington about America's Anglo-adaptation model are remarkable: "Historically assimilation in general, and cultural assimilation, is the greatest and even the greatest American success story. This gives him millions of devoted, energetic, talented, capable of expanding its population, occupying a continent, and its economy, largely dependent on America's Anglo-Protestant culture and values of the American faith, and supporting America to become a great power in global affairs. It has provided the opportunity to develop together with ambitious people"[32]. As can be understood from here, the Anglo-adaptation model has been realized by integrating large immigrant communities into an already existing cultural framework.

Huntington stated that World War II increased the importance of the ideological content of American identity and prepared the way to the end of ethnic and racial definitions of this identity on the legal level. Huntington, who included Philip Gleason's testimony on this issue, stated that the war increased common sense regarding national unity and national belonging; That the American people have one primary goal; He stated that even though it is not shared equally, the difficulties and dangers of war are shared by all, and as in all great wars, economic inequalities are minimized. He stated that World War II was a great shared experience that shaped Americans 'understanding of national identity for the next generation. Therefore, during World War II, Americans' identification with their country reached its peak.[33]

When we look at the emphasis made by the former American President Kennedy on the fact that the USA was nationalized as a community of immigrants on the first immigrants to America, we can see certain parallels with Huntington's analyses we have just quoted:" The British, who constituted the majority of the first settlers in America, determined the basic principles of American institutions; our form of regime, our laws, our language, our tradition of religion and freedom of worship. As the nation grew, some of these concepts were changed, but the basic elements remained. Those who came later built everything on these basic principles. However, immigrants from many countries and different social, national and ethnic backgrounds have settled in America".[34]Throughout American history, English has been essential to American national identity. We can say that it is

---

[31] Dominique Schnapper, **Relationship WithThe Other,** Gallimard, Paris, 1999, pp.281-290.
[32] Huntington, P. Samuel.,**Who We Are?, The Challenges to American's National Identity,** Simon&Schuster, New York., 2004 p.330.
[33] Huntington, ibid, p.136.
[34] Kennedy, John, F.;Harper&Row (1964) *Anation Of Immigrants*, HarperCollinsPublishers, 1964, p.11.

the foundation of American society. Immigrant groups have from time to time tried to make use of another language. However, they have not been successful in the long run. Asian and Hispanic immigrants, who have come heavily since the 1980s, have tended to oppose English to a large extent. This has led to Spanish being spoken in some states of America. America, an immigrant nation, remained an immigrant nation to some extent. However, what is most important is a nation that combines immigrants with their society and culture. Immigrants were assimilated over time and gained an Anglo-Saxon and Protestant structure and joined the society. In a way, they were fully int

## Crisis between America and Mexico

The driving force was the immigration of Latin Americans, especially those of Mexican origin. This process, which introduced Americans to an entirely different culture, reflected the rise of a blended society and culture, half American and half Mexican in some areas. Mexican immigration differs from immigrants who come thousands of miles away and accept American values. Because the neighbouring country is Mexico, and more importantly, the situation of protecting heterogeneity by dispersing the immigrants to the country, as envisaged by the Founders for assimilation, has not been achieved in Hispanic immigrants. No immigrant group in American history has claimed any historical claims from American soil. However, Mexicans can do that. As a result, Mexicans, along with other Spanish-speaking populations, are causing a bifurcation in the sociological structure of the United States, creating a bifurcation situation. In this process, definitions such as Mex-America and Mexico were made for the region, which is the southwest of the USA and the north of Mexico.[35]

Although the land size of the United States doubled with Thomas Jefferson's purchase of Louisiana in 1803, in 1845, the country was much smaller than it is today. The Rocky Mountains formed the western border of the country. On the southwestern border was Mexico, which gained independence from Spain in 1821. Mexico was much bigger in those years than it is today. Its territory covered Texas, New Mexico, Vlach, Nevada, Arizona, all of California, Colorado, and parts of Wyoming. In 1836, Texas left Mexico with the help of the USA and named itself the "One Star Republic".

US President William Henry Harrison passed away on April 4, 1841, exactly one month after he took office. Later, John Tyler replaced Harrison. Tyler left Mexico in 1836 and demanded the annexation of Texas, which

---

[35] Howard Zinn, A Young People's History of the United States:Columbus to theWar on Terror, TriangleSquare 2009, p. 75.

declared its independence. This understanding, which includes the annexation of the land piece, has been defined as "Manifest Destiny" by John L. O'Sullivan, editor of The Democratic Review Magazine. In his article, O'Sullivan used the expressions "Our experience of freedom and ensuring our self-management gives us the right to spread and own the entire continent, which is our obvious destiny.".[36]

In 1845, the US Congress included Texas within its borders. Texas approved the annexation of the USA on July 4, 1845, and was accepted as a slave state on December 29, 1845. At that time, many Americans believed their country needed to expand further westward. President James Polk was also one of the enlargement parties. He told his secretary that one of his primary goals as president was to get California into the United States.

Indeed, President James Knox Polk was not satisfied with Texas. He stated that his aim was the whole of "Hispanic North America". It wanted to annex California, which is a crucial port, especially in the Pacific Ocean and is strategically located to develop trade with the east. In the presidential campaign held in 1844, Democratic Party members wanted not the only land from Texas to the Rio Grande, but also Oregon and California, which stretched as far as the Pacific Ocean. For many years there has been an agreement that the border between Mexico and the USA is the Nueces River, 150 miles north of the Rio Grande. In the spring of 1846, the army was ready to start the war Polk wanted. US President Polk ordered the commander of the 3500-man troops, Zachary Taylor, deployed on the Nueces River, to advance to the Rio Grande, the neutral zone between the US and Mexico. This action invited the Mexican attack as expected on April 25 1846. The Mexicans ambushed the American expedition of 63 soldiers, killing six and taking the others hostage.[37]

All we needed was an excuse. Indeed, one of Taylor's officers disappeared while riding a horse along the river. The skull was later found crushed. Everyone thought that Mexican guerrilla fighters crossed the river and killed him. The next day, the Mexicans attacked a patrol and killed sixteen soldiers; Taylor then sent to Polk a message that the war had begun. The Mexicans were the first to shoot, but the American Government's request was also fulfilled. Congress declared war. Only a handful of lawmakers voted against the war. These MPs were those against slavery and believed that war was an excuse to create new slave states.

Many Americans welcomed the war news. They held rallies in cities across the country to support the war. Thousands of people volunteered to join the

---

[36] Remini, Robert, **The House: Short History of United States.** Harper Collins e-books. London, 2006, p.122.
[37] Ibid, Remini, p.127.

army. Many members and leaders of the church made anti-war speeches. Over time, others joined them. Volunteers also slowed down after the first wave of excitement. The army had to pay to recruit enough soldiers. Besides, the volunteers were offered land if they served throughout the war. Some of those who were enlisted were shocked by the bloody face of the war. Others switched to the Mexican side to get more money. The war itself has won military after victory for the United States. General Taylor defeated a significant force of Mexicans in Buena Vista in February 1847.

As a result of the Mexican-American War, the Treaty of Guadalupe Hidalgo, which included the annexation of 1 million square kilometres of Texas, the sharing of the Oregon Country of 750 thousand square kilometres, and the waiver of Mexico's rights, was signed. A total of 1.4 million square kilometres of land was transferred to the United States. Thanks to the Treaty of Guadalupe Hidalgo, the US gained new territory one-third of its current territory. Today, the 78 thousand square kilometre region, which covers the south of the state of Arizona and the southwest of New Mexico, was bought from Mexico by the USA for 10 million dollars. Thus, the current border of the USA and Mexico was determined. The Mexicans, who had to give more than half of their land to the USA in return for a compensation of 15 million dollars, learned this annexation as a US occupation since their primary school education. In US primary schools, this event was taught in a more diluted form as the US-Mexico War.

In the first two decades of the 20th century, Asian and European immigrants received more attention in the USA. US immigration restrictions were not an issue for Mexicans until 1929. With the Great Depression, Mexican immigrants were scapegoated, and many were repatriated. It is explained by the fact that Mexicans have not been a subject of debate until this time, and they are not sufficiently recognized in the country. On the other hand, Mexicans, who returned to their countries, could not belong to either community. After their relatively better living conditions in the USA, their desire to live in Mexico decreased. Also, their societies have begun to look at them from a different perspective.

## Immigration between America and Mexico and the problem of national identity

A stable immigration system has formed between Mexico and the United States, which started in the 1950s. He theorized very well this system, which became the usual situation, and its outputs shaped by social and economic conditions. However, after 1986, this immigration system has changed radically. The mobility ceased to be the cyclical migration of male workers to a limited number of states and cities, and the net migration rate rose sharply. Immigration became a nationwide feature where families came and settled.

This transformation was not the result of changes in social, economic or political factors, as the dominant theories claim, but as a result of dynamic processes in the public opinion that brought about the militarization of the Mexico-USA border. Established in 1977, the US-Mexico Border Program works to ensure the self-determination of border communities by facilitating leadership development, accompanying immigrant communities' organizational processes, providing them with technical support and providing resources.

The Mexico-USA border is an important transit point for illegal immigrants who want to go to the USA. Although it does not make people feel special, Mexico, which is on the route of many immigrants, has been the most important transition point since the 19th century when the border was established. In the 20th century, more stringent follow-up of border crossings began in 1924 with the establishment of the Border Patrol. The presence of troops at the border and the strengthening of the border, especially in urban areas, has increased in recent years. In 1990, fences were strengthened, three layers of steel were used, high-tech motion detectors and military drones were used on the borders of two major urban areas, San Diego / Tijuana and El Paso / Juarez. Immigrants and human smugglers tried to change their routes at border crossings in response to these measures of the USA. For example, these people tried to cross the border in a new road in the Sonoran Desert in central Arizona that they call the Devils Highway. Small towns such as Sonoita on this road have turned into accommodation centres thanks to immigrants. Providing rooms, food and services to migrants and smugglers, this town has become an outpost. For these reasons, people who wanted to migrate had to pay more money by taking more significant risks.[38]

The Hispanic population in the USA reached approximately 70 million in 2020. Hispanics have been a significant driver of US demographic growth, accounting for half of the national population growth since 2000. While the Hispanic population living in the USA consists of a mixture of various countries, people of Mexican origin constitute 63.3% of the Hispanic population. According to 2015 data, 36 million Mexicans live in the USA.[39]

In his book "Who Are We?" Samuel Huntington stated that America's Anglo-Saxon culture faces some challenges. He stated that one of these challenges is that immigrants from Latin America with a massive immigration wave cannot be separated from their countries of origin and are not

---

[38] Cravey, Altha J. **"US-Mexico borderlands: Violence and the Politics Of Exclusion"**. Placing Latin America, Contemporary Themes in Geography. F. Bosco, F. ve E. Jackiewicz (Ed.). Maryland: Rowman&Little field Publishers, Inc.,pp. 2012, 205-218.

[39] Flores, A. (2017). **"How the U.S. Hispanic Population is Changing"**. Pew Research Center. Erişim: http://www.pewresearch.org/fact-tank/2017/09/18/how-the-u-s-hispanic-population-is-changing, 19.04.2020.

assimilated in the USA. He noted that the immigrants' mostly speaking Spanish made Hispanics empowered. Huntington thinks that this situation will have significant effects on American national identity.

## Conclusion

Throughout history, immigrants have created and changed societies. However, in the examination we have done here, we see that immigrants are assimilated in an order. At this point, we are talking about not a society that creates its own identity and belonging, but a structure that tries to build an identity on the identity of another society. Immigrants threaten national identity by creating or trying to create a supranational or sub-national identity. However, it is difficult to claim that the identity desired to be created sufficient in providing a haven for the society and the individual, amid the uncertainties brought by the modern world. It seems that the discussion that globalization will create a world culture / (identity) that will accommodate all cultures or, on the contrary, will continue to be destroyed by only imposing certain cultures.

Identity policy approaches to immigrants have often tended to be explained as assimilation, integration and multiculturalism. However, today it is possible to argue that these approaches have diversified beyond assimilation and integration. Today, the perception of identity has developed within the framework of some new problematic issues. The answer given to the question of whether the identities emerging as a result of the encounter of differences as a result of migration are hybrid identities or radicalized parallel identities is the determining factor of identity politics in the context of migration.

It is observed that the perspective on the immigration movement from Mexico to the USA changes according to the political environment and years. With this study, it was understood that the historical background of the immigration between Mexico and the USA, the US government's focus on border controls over time, and the policies implemented by the USA, immigrant rights are based on an increasingly ignored framework. Migration is a phenomenon that has survived with human history. Today, it will continue to continue in different parts of the world for different reasons. The phenomenon of immigration that has turned into a cultural practice and the immigrants who realize this important phenomenon should be seen as a cultural wealth with the humanitarian policies of the governments instead of being seen as illegal people that countries are trying to prevent by building concrete walls. In this study, based on the Mexico-USA border, the course of immigration from Mexico to the USA, the historical background of the border and the geographical features of the region that affect the migration; The violence experienced by immigrants in crossing the border, the discrimination and acceptance that immigrants face after crossing the border and living in the US are discussed.

The study focuses on migration and identity connection as the last of the basic categories that will be the source of the discussions on identity and identity politics today. Millions of people around the world leave their habitats for various reasons and encounter different cultures. During these encounters, it is possible for identities to radicalize or to hybridize by influencing each other. As a result, the cultural hybridization approach included in the study handled the relationship between migration and identity based on irreversible cultural change. Intercultural and multicultural approaches are evaluated in the context of immigrant identity, and it has been determined that they have some limitations.

CHAPTER 12

## THE DEFERRED ACTION FOR CHILDHOOD ARRIVALS (DACA)

Zekeriya Alperen Bedirhan[*]

**Introduction**

Persons born outside the United States and immigrated into the country as children without valid federal approval are likely to find provisional work permission and avoid deportation. As the name implies, Deferred Action for Childhood Arrivals (DACA) was an American policy, which prevented the ejection of undocumented migrants brought into the country illegally by their parents. Rescinded by President Trump in 2017, DACA asserted that eligible migrants were free from deportation for two years, but were not conferred formal legal statuses.[1]

A large number of policies in the United States are multifarious and highly asymmetrical. This is a reflection of the complex and fractured nature of policy making in the country; considering the numerous levels of governance, with powers to make policy decisions split among various informal and formal actors. The same applies for DACA, which despite being created by executive action instead of than legislation, was regulated by different federal and state agencies.[2]

Prior to the policy, the DREAM Act bill, was presented in the US Senate and House as a means of offering guidance on ways of dealing with children who immigrated into the country illegally as kids but had completed military service and college. The bill was contested, but brought before the Congress in 2007 where it also faced numerous impediments.

Various obstacles the bill faced in the earlier years are credited for inspiring the then President Obama to ratify DACA. The policy was officially established in 2012 by a memo from the Secretary of Homeland Security with applications getting verified by the US Citizenship and Immigration Services (CIS).[3] DACA was denounced overwhelmingly by Republican Party leaders

---


[*] Istanbul University

[1] Zatz, Marjorie S., and Nancy Rodriguez. *Dreams and nightmares: Immigration policy, youth, and families*. University of California Press, 2015, p.86.

[2] Gonzales, Roberto G., Veronica Terriquez, and Stephen P. Ruszczyk. "Becoming DACAmented: Assessing the short-term benefits of deferred action for childhood arrivals (DACA)." *American Behavioral Scientist* 58, no. 14 (2014): 1852-1872.

[3] Nowlin, Matthew C. "Theories of the policy process: State of the research and emerging trends." *Policy*

who mentioned that it was an infringement of executive power by the president. In their view, the president lacked the power to reform immigration rules or create one.[4] Overall, DACA was enforced by different department of the American government including the Immigration and Customs Enforcement and Customs and Border Protection besides the CIS who were required to exercise enforcement discretion when dealing with persons who met the policy's requirements.

During his tenure, Obama sought to expand DACA, but his efforts were countered by 26 states and Republican governors. The states and governors sought an injunction regarding the expansion and requested the court to merge DACA and Deferred Action for Parents of Americans (a comparable project).[5]

As outlined in previous sections, there were numerous players involved in the execution of the policy. For instance, in a case filed by an agent of Immigration and Customs Enforcement at a Texan District Court, the presiding judge mentioned that DACA was characteristically unlawful.[6] In totality, DACA's use in the immigration field was supported and dismissed in equal measure by different government department, agencies, and politicians who mentioned that failure to involve the public in the process was tantamount to a violation of the US immigration law.

DACA is a critical matter because it outlines how children immigrants who might have never known any other country other than the US since their birth are treated in the country. This essay explores DACA through the lens of three policy theories (multiple streams analysis, advocacy coalition frameworks, and democratic policy design) and offers a critical review of the American immigration policy and changes that have occurred over the years.

## Stage Heuristics Model

The model posits that public policy involves numerous processes that proceed sequentially and consist of more than one decision. The stages mentioned in the model include agenda setting, formulation, legitimation, implementation and evaluation, which policy must follow before it is espoused in the public domain.[7]

The policy has numerous flaws, it is time consuming and requires input

---

*studies journal* 39 (2011): 41-60.

[4] Singer, Audrey, and Nicole Prchal Svajlenka. "Immigration facts: Deferred action for childhood arrivals (DACA)." *The Brookings Institution* (2013).

[5] Gonzales and Terriquez, op.cit, p. 1852).

[6] Wadhia, Shoba Sivaprasad. "In Defence of DACA, Deferred Action, and the DREAM Act." *Tex. L. Rev. See Also* 91 (2012): 59.

[7] John, Peter. *Analyzing public policy.* Routledge, 2013, p.80.

from numerous sources in addition to its difficulty to use which therefore makes it ineffective in understanding DACA. Even though the stage heuristics model offers a comprehensive way of analysing policy, the model has numerous flaws, which makes it largely ineffective.[8]

In fact, the model has been criticised by numerous scholars as incapable of offering efficient solutions that can influence public policy. In view of the authors, the stages model is unsuitable, difficult to apply, inefficient, non-appealing, and unstable framework in the analysis of public policies.[9]

As such, alternative theories of the policy procedures are required to help in the analysis of federal policies. Concepts that can be used in place of the heuristics theory include multiple streams analysis, advocacy coalition frameworks, and democratic policy design.

## Advocacy Coalition Framework of the Policy Process

The Advocacy Coalition Framework remains one of the most prominent models to understanding public policy that emerged during 1990s. The approach is highly acclaimed and has been referenced in more than 80 research papers on public policy, specifically in the United States, but also in other developed nations.[10] It is one of the few major approaches crafted in the United Stes after Heclo's renowned assertion of a shift from the clubby periods of Washington politics to complicated relations among a large and constitutionally active populace.[11]

Within this framework, aspects that were previously managed discreetly by a small fraction of insiders have now become politicised and controversial. Admittedly, the focus of this model is to enable people make sense of complicated policy making systems containing numerous agents and government departments. Furthermore, it aids in processing policy in numerous new ways, from largely politicised disagreements involving various actors in different areas, to problems that are perceived as specialist or technical and handled regularly, mostly by policy specialists beyond the public domain.[12]

Additionally, it sheds light on systems that create decisions using inadequate information and involves extreme ambiguity and uncertainty and

---

[8] Peters, B. Guy. American public policy: Promise and performance. Cq Press, 2018, p.48.

[9] Sabatier, Paul A., and Christopher M. Weible, eds. *Theories of the policy process*. Westview Press, 2014.

[10] Leifeld, Philip. "Reconceptualizing major policy change in the advocacy coalition framework: A discourse network analysis of German pension politics." *Policy Studies Journal* 41, no. 1 (2013): 169-198.

[11] Weible, Christopher M., Paul A. Sabatier, Hank C. Jenkins-Smith, Daniel Nohrstedt, Adam Douglas Henry, and Peter DeLeon. "A quarter century of the advocacy coalition framework: An introduction to the special issue." *Policy Studies Journal* 39, no. 3 (2011): 349-360.

[12] Sabatier, Paul A., and Christopher M. Weible, eds. *Theories of the policy process*. Westview Press, 2014.

requires considerable amounts of time to transform decisions into results.

Advocacy coalition involves individuals from different positions (agency officials, elected, interest groups, scholars) who have a mutual belief system and without a trivial extent of coordinated activity over time. ACF concentrates on the interactions among conflicting advocacy coalitions in a policy subsystem that, in turn, functions in a larger political system. The concept's depiction of subsystems portray an open, multi-tier policy making structure.[13] Here, the perception of policy substructures are widened from the conventional notions of iron triangles restricted to governmental agencies, legal commissions, and interest groups to incorporate actors at divergent levels of government, in addition to reporters, scholars, and policy experts who play star roles in the creation, dissemination, and appraisal of policy ideas.[14] Moreover, the model focuses mostly on the significance of belief systems: most actors might be influential since they have similar views as others; converting those principles into policy outcomes and decisions is a mutual goals. Overall, beliefs are the "adhesive" that ensures a large number of actors stays together.

In view of the concept, DACA was influenced by different beliefs held by various actors in the policy making system. According to the coalition framework, the likely belief that influenced the policy was deep core beliefs. The beliefs concern an actor's "basic personal attitude," often perceived as a point on the right/left wing continuum. [15]

Illustrations of such philosophies include perception that some individuals are malicious and socially unredeemable or whose welfare need count the most. This is particularly true for the defenders of the DACA who mentioned that children assimilated into the society under the act were innocent and ought not to be deported. The implication was that such children have only known the United States as their home and English as their language and might have already enlisted in colleges and the military.[16]

Therefore, kicking them out will be malicious since such a move would have insignificant impact on the problems facing ordinary Americans such as unemployment, taxation, and wages. Other aspects that were involved in the establishment of DACA were policy core beliefs and secondary aspects. Core beliefs are important policy positions that govern the appropriate balance and

---

[13] Jenkins-Smith, Hank C., Daniel Nohrstedt, Christopher M. Weible, and Paul A. Sabatier. "The advocacy coalition framework: Foundations, evolution, and ongoing research." *Theories of the policy process* 3 (2014): 183-224.

[14] Weible, Christopher M., Paul A. Sabatier, Hank C. Jenkins-Smith, Daniel Nohrstedt, Adam Douglas Henry, and Peter DeLeon, op.cit, p.352

[15] Leifeld, Philip, op.cit, p.172

[16] Sabatier, Paul A., and Christopher M. Weible op.cit, p.108

distribution of power among levels of government.[17]

This was typified by the numerous government branches that were involved in defending or refuting the program. Secondary aspects, on the other hand, refer to the delivery, funding, and adoption of policy goals, which in this case was the issuance of temporary stay orders to eligible children brought into the US illegally.

Even though the ACF was established on a critique of the stages heuristic, it still concentrates on improvements over a long period, usually a decade or more to permit (though theoretically), for a full policy cycle. Such a long term focus is likely to the main limitation of the model if the policy was meant for a short period like the DACA.[18] The main advantage of the concept is that encourages easy interaction of actors, decision-making, creation and modification of institutions, and evaluation of previous decisions in line with that external events and new information. Presently, there are few policy models that offer a comprehensive overview of the policy procedure like ACF. The theory explicitly explains the connection between ideas, institutions, socioeconomic factors, networks, and choices.[19]

For instance, though the concept remains influential in the American political sphere, it has proven effective in other policy subsystems in nations like the United Kingdom witnessing immobility of policy networks.[20] Besides, whilst the first framework explores the importance of ideas, it minimises the possibility of critics suggesting that ideas are given illustrative value separate from their use and acceptance by actors. It is problematic to get this equilibrium right, but ACF does so fairly well.[21]

## Multiple Streams Analysis of the Policy Process

Multiple streams framework, pioneered by John Kingdon, has been used numerous times since the publication of his manuscript *Agendas, Alternatives and Public Policies*. Although the book exclusively focuses on the United States, the theory offers a clear way of understanding public policy using secondary and primary appraisals of agenda procedures in the fragmented American political system. [22]

In view of this concept, there are three variables; political, problem, and

---

[17] Jenkins-Smith, Hank C., Daniel Nohrstedt, Christopher M. Weible, and Paul A. Sabatier, op.cit, p.183

[18] Weible, Christopher M., Paul A. Sabatier, Hank C. Jenkins-Smith, Daniel Nohrstedt, Adam Douglas Henry, and Peter DeLeon, op.cit.

[19] Sabatier, Paul A., and Christopher M. Weible, op.cit, p.72.

[20] Jenkins-Smith, Hank C., Daniel Nohrstedt, Christopher M. Weible, and Paul A. Sabatier op.cit, p.186

[21] Weible, Christopher M., and Paul A. Sabatier. "A guide to the advocacy coalition framework." *Handbook of public policy analysis: theory, politics, and methods* (2007): 123-136.

[22] Zahariadis, Nikolaos. "Ambiguity and multiple streams." *Theories of the policy process* 3, no. 1 (2014): 25-59.

policy streams that work in sync to create "windows of opportunity" for agenda setting. To begin with the problem stream focuses on the opinions of problems which are perceived as "public" in the sense that federal input is required to solve them.[23]

These issues often reach policy makers owing to dramatic incidents like crises or feedback from programmes that appeal to the public. Policy stream entails the involvement of specialists and analysts who explore the issue and recommend solutions. Here, possibilities for policy inaction and action are isolated, evaluated, and reduced to practical options.[24]

Lastly, political stream encompasses aspects that affect the body politic like changes in the national attitude, legislative or executive turnover, and interest group activism crusades. According to the concept, the mentioned streams run along dissimilar conduits and are independent of each other until a policy window opens; this is the only time the streams intersect.

Multiple stream analysis is applicable in the DACA and can be useful in understanding actor interactions, policy outcomes, and the application of different rules in the policy process. In case of DACA, the window opened due to the existence of a compelling problem; the possible deportation of children who had lived in the united states all their lives because their parents immigrated illegally.[25] In this case, there is a possibility that policy entrepreneurs are willing to push their proposals and finding solutions to political problems.

In this situation, the policy entrepreneur was likely the president who perceived the issue of deportation and somehow inhumane and likely to destroy the lives of people who had invested their time, emotions, and resources in living the American dream.[26] What is more, the concept posits that in some situations, the window might be opened by certain actors in the policy subsystem to advance the issues they care about. This might have been what happened with the establishment of DACA under president Obama's tenure, whose presence as a policy entrepreneur played a critical role in the adoption of the DACA immigration policy.

As outlined in the previous section, multiple streams analysis asserts that the opening of windows might also be occasioned by apparently isolated external incidents like accidents and crises. While the United States has a large

---

[23] Weible, C.M., Heikkila, T. and Sabatier, P.A., Understanding and influencing the policy process. Policy Sciences, 45(1), 2012, pp.1-21.

[24] Herweg, Nicole, Christian Huß, and Reimut Zohlnhöfer. "Straightening the three streams: Theorising extensions of the multiple streams framework." *European Journal of Political Research* 54, no. 3 (2015): 435-449.

[25] Weible, C.M., Heikkila, T. and Sabatier, P.A. op.cit.

[26] Zahariadis, Nikolaos. op.cit. p,25

number of immigrants, most of them are staying in the country illegally. The immigrant influx into the country has been perceived as a crisis in waiting by numerous individuals, therefore, the intervention through DACA might be viewed as a means of averting the pending crisis.[27] However, the program might have been impossible to effect without the presence of "policy entrepreneurs" within and outside the government. Still on the policy, the theory posits that the divergent streams of politics, policies, and problems often come together at critical times. Resolutions become enjoined with problems, and they both get entangled with advantageous political forces. Only then, does the issue metamorphose into a discernible issue on the institutional or official agenda and the public policy begins to tackle it.[28] From previous literature, the issue of immigrants getting stay permits in the United States began in 2001, but the issue became problematic, thereby necessitating the adoption of DACA in 2012.

The multiple streams framework has proven valuable in aiding in the explanation of policy dynamics while envisaging the merging of various communal phenomena to propel an "idea whose time has come" into fruition. The application of the theory of multiple streams is becoming prevalent in policy sciences and comparative analysis,[29] which implies that the model is somewhat advantageous. For instance, the model was used in the late 1990s as part of the United States' foreign policy, in the privatisation of public enterprises in Germany, Britain, and France, and America in combating illegal drug use.[30] The model has also been applied in cooperative pollution control ventures among environmental groups and companies in Europe and the US as well as far-reaching dynamics to improve policy changes and reformations in Eastern Europe.

## Democratic Policy Design of the Policy Process

Democratic policy design is a public policy theory put forward by Anne Schneider and Helen Ingram in 1997. Focusing on the process of policy formation in democratic nations, with special stress on the United States, the model asserts that policy makers often divide the community into target groups, which are either punished or rewarded depending on their location on a four-quadrant web.[31] The four quadrants according to the model are: Advantaged, which comprises people who are influential politically and

---

[27] Herweg, Nicole, Christian Huß, and Reimut Zohlnhöfer, op.cit. p,446.

[28] Weible, C.M., Heikkila, T. and Sabatier, P.A. op.cit.

[29] Zahariadis, Nikolaos. op.cit. p,25

[30] Herweg, Nicole, Christian Huß, and Reimut Zohlnhöfer. op.cit, p.442

[31] Mayer, Igor S., C. Els Van Daalen, and Pieter WG Bots. "Perspectives on policy analyses: a framework for understanding and design." *International Journal of Technology, Policy and Management* 4, no. 2 (2004): 169-191.

viewed positively; Dependents, these are politically weak groups, but perceived positively; Contenders are powerful politically but viewed negatively; and Deviants who are politically fragile and are seen negatively.[32] Founded on this assessment, the immigrant children might be perceived as dependents since thy lack political influence, but are seen as beneficial in the American economy.

Founded on the model, politicians often strive to implement public policies, which profit the Advantaged, while issuing punishments and sanctions to Deviants as a way of guaranteeing their future political success. In most instances, the Contenders and Dependents are nearly always disregarded by the policy makers.[33] Any attempts to chastise the contenders might be put off by their political power while attempts to castigate dependents might be negated by the affirmative public perception they have in the community. On the flip side, policymaking, which profits contenders is problematic owing to their bad public reputation whilst that which helps dependents is not valuable for legislators since the group does not political power with which to "recompense" such programmes via campaign donations or voting.[34] The process is known as "degenerative policy design" according to the model and speculated as a dominant and lasting aspect in the American political system.[35] DACA was meant for the dependents as a means of elevating them in the society despite the fact that they would not repay the good that was done to them. However, in subsequent years, the government perceived the program as worthless leading to its rescinding by the Trump administration.Conclus

The United States has always had problems grappling with the issue of illegal immigration. Most of the immigrants often cross the American borders to pursue the American dream with varied levels of success. However, there is no guarantee of permanent stay in the country with a large number of immigrants facing deportation or opting to stay in the country illegally. This situation is not special for only DACA. Recent development under the rule of Trump presidency showed us, immigrants are not welcomed and populist movements support this anti-immigration rhetoric. For children who have known the US as their home country, such moves can be very dangerous. It is for this reason that the Obama administration established DACA to offer temporary work permits to people who immigrated into the country as minors. However, the policy was faced with various setbacks leading to its

---

[32] Birkland, Thomas A. An introduction to the policy process: Theories, concepts, and models of public policy making. Routledge, 2019, p.174.

[33] Ingram, Helen, and Steven Rathgeb Smith, eds. *Public policy for democracy*. Brookings Institution Press, 2011, p.164.

[34] Mayer, Igor S., C. Els Van Daalen, and Pieter WG Bots, op.cit, p,41

[35] Birkland, Thomas A. op.cit, p,75

ultimate termination in 2017. The immigration policy failed to work due to the US's fragmented political system, which requires input from numerous parties with dissimilar opinions and attitudes.

In its entirety, this essay bridges various empirical and theoretical models to evaluate and invigorate public policy issues that warrants more focus as opposed to fragmentary conceptual perceptions. By combining and comparing DACA with current policy models and with prominent bodies of research, this exposition endorses the usage of the multiple streams framework in understanding policy issues in the United States. However, it suggests that the model needs amending or merging with elements of other models to offer a more powerful and accurate portrayal of American policy-making reality.

CHAPTER 13

# THE ISSUE OF IMMIGRATION IN THE UNITED STATES ELECTIONS: A LOOK AT TRUMP-ERA


Akın Sağıroğlu[*] and İlhan Aras[**]


## Introduction

In the 1870-1880s, the main targets of the American people were Chinese immigrants who were a threat to Americans' jobs, wages, and lifestyle. Therefore, the first law enacted to prevent a certain ethnic group in America was the Chinese Exclusion Act of 1882. In the following century, there were different migrant targets. In 1942, in the aftermath of the Pearl Harber bombing, Executive Order 9066 was signed by President Roosevelt which led to the displacement and detention of more than 110.000 Japanese Americans from 1942 to 1946. Towards the end of the 20th century, Latin Americans and Muslims were more on the agenda. After the September 11 attacks, Muslims were seen as a potential threat to America's security.[1] Nearly 150 years later, the same issue has been heavily debated in American politics.

Today, there are about 47 million immigrants living legally or illegally in the United States (US). The US has the largest immigrant population in the world. In the US, immigrants make up 14 percent of the total population.[2] The US has always attracted attention as a country that has received immigration from the past to the present. While immigration was an important issue in the establishment and development of the US, it is noteworthy that today it is a threat in the election campaign.

Immigration has always been an important issue in American politics. Besides being seen as an important issue for the US, it was also seen as a threat in economical, security and cultural terms. In the 2016 elections, the issue of immigration was frequently used by Donald Trump. Trump maintained his harsh rhetoric about the negative effects of immigration not only before the election but also after the election.[3] Two groups were

---


[*] Lecturer, Adıyaman University.

[**] Assoc. Prof. Dr., Nevşehir Hacı Bektaş Veli University,


[1] Laura Finley, Luigi Esposito, "The Immigrant as Bogeyman: Examining Donald Trump and the Right's Anti-immigrant, Anti-PC Rhetoric", **Humanity & Society**, Vol. 44, No. 2, 2020, p. 181.

[2] Ronn Pineo, "Immigration Crisis: The United States Under President Donald J. Trump", **Journal of Developing Societies**, Vol. 36, Issue 1, 2020, p. 8.

[3] James C. Garand, Dan Qi, Max Magaña, "Perceptions of Immigrant Threat, American Identity, and Vote Choice in the 2016 U.S. Presidential Election", **Political Behavior**, 2020, https://link.springer.com/

particularly prominent in Trump's anti-immigrant discourse, *"terrorists, specifically Muslim terrorists, and refugees, especially from Syria"*. These two groups came to the fore in the anti-immigrant discourse.[4] Also, Trump's Mexican wall promise has been one of the most talked about topics in the elections.

As Garand, Qi and Magana point out, *"Americans who perceive high levels of immigrant threat will translate their negative immigrant attitudes into political behavior, including casting votes for presidential and congressional candidates who express support for restrictive immigration policies."*.[5]

This chapter mainly deals with the anti-immigration in American politics by only focusing on the Trump era. First of all, the discourses against immigrants before the 2016 elections were outlined. In the following section, practices and discourses within the scope of anti-immigration in the Trump era are discussed.

## Before 2016 Elections

Trump stated that there are 3 basic principles to make a real immigration reform in the immigration system[6]:

*1. A nation without borders is not a nation. There must be a wall across the southern border.*

*2. A nation without laws is not a nation. Laws passed in accordance with our Constitutional system of government must be enforced.*

*3. A nation that does not serve its own citizens is not a nation. Any immigration plan must improve jobs, wages and security for all Americans.*

Trump has continued his anti-immigrant rhetoric in each platform. In September 2015, there was a dialogue on CBS's comedy program Late Show: *"(…) We have to have a wall. We have to have a border. And in that wall we're going to have a beautiful big fat door where people can — they come into the country, and they come — listen to me."*[7]

Trump answered the murder of a suspect trying to cross the Mexican border as *"this is merely one of thousands of similar incidents throughout the United States. [...] In other words, the worst elements in Mexico are being pushed into the United*

---

article/10.1007/s11109-020-09644-z (Access 07.08.2020).

[4] Massimiliano Demata, "A great and beautiful wall" Donald Trump's populist discourse on immigration", **Journal of Language Aggression and Conflict**, Vol. 5, No. 2, 2017, p. 280.

[5] Garand, Qi, Magana, **op.cit**, p. 2

[6] Donald J. Trump, "Immigration Reform that Will Make America Great Again", 2015, https://assets. donaldjtrump.com/Immigration-Reform-Trump.pdf (Access 28.09.2020).

[7] The Late Show with Stephen Colbert, "Donald Trump Has Nothing to Apologize for." 23 September 2015. https://www.youtube.com/watch?v=Ns7ocpRhDD8(Access 07.08.2020).

*States by the Mexican Government*" [8]

Throughout the election campaign, Trump regularly visited the families of Americans killed by Hispanic illegal immigrants. These visits were seen as messages that portray immigrants as a threat to the American people and security.[9]

According to Trump, immigration is an important obstacle to making America great again, which is also the election slogan. Making America great again means going back not only to the 1990s but also to the 1950s. It is noteworthy that there was less ethnic and racial diversity in this period.[10]

Trump frequently mentioned about Mexican immigrants in his statements in 2015[11]:

*"When Mexico sends its people, they're not sending their best. They're not sending you. They're not sending you. They're sending people that have lots of problems, and they're bringing those problems with us. They're bringing drugs. They're bringing crime. They're rapists. And some, I assume, are good people."*

- "I can never apologize for the truth. I don't mind apologizing for things. But I can't apologize for the truth. I said tremendous crime is coming across. Everybody knows that's true. And it's happening all the time. So, why, when I mention, all of a sudden I'm a racist. I'm not a racist. I don't have a racist bone in my body."
- "What can be simpler or more accurately stated? The Mexican Government is forcing their most unwanted people into the United States. They are, in many cases, criminals, drug dealers, rapists, etc."

These statements showed that the election campaign of Trump was based on anti-immigration. The anti-immigration manifested itself in two ways: Mexican immigrants and immigrants came from Muslim countries. Thus, "Mexico" and "Muslim countries" statements come to the fore in Trump's anti-immigration statements.

Sanders and Clinton, the Democratic candidates of the elections, defined immigrants as "immigrants," "families" and "workers", while Trump defined immigrants as "illegal aliens" and "criminals". In addition, in the Hillary for America 2016 campaign, Democratic candidate Clinton considered the

---

[8] Jesse Byrnes, "Trump: 'Infectious disease is pouring across the border'", https://thehill.com/blogs/ballot-box/ 246982-trump-infectious-disease-is-pouring-across-the-border (Access 11.07.2020).
[9] Finley, Esposito, **op.cit**, p. 187.
[10] Jamie Winders, "Immigration and the 2016 Election", **Southeastern Geographer**, Vol. 56, No. 3, 2016, p. 295.
[11] Michelle Ye Hee Lee, "Donald Trump's false comments connecting Mexican immigrants and crime", https://www.washingtonpost.com/news/fact-checker/wp/2015/07/08/donald-trumps-false-comments-connecting-mexican-immigrants-and-crime/ (Access 15.08.2020).

immigration issue "a family issue".[12]

Trump claimed that he would prevent the immigration problem with a 10-step immigration plan. According to Trump, the plan will do more to prevent migration than has been done in 50 years. The content of the plan is as follows[13]:

- one: the wall
- two: end "catch and release"
- three: zero tolerance for criminal aliens
- four: block funding for "sanctuary cities"
- five: cancel Obama executive orders on immigration
- six: suspend visas from certain countries with inadequate screenings
- seven: ensure countries take back immigrants the United States deports
- eight: complete the biometric entry- exit visa tracking system
- nine: turn off the jobs and benefits magnet
- ten: reform legal immigration

Republican candidates' interest in immigration has not been at the same level. Trump used the issue of immigration more than any other Republican candidate during the election process.[14]

### After the Elections

Although immigration is not the most important factor in the people's choice of the US presidential candidate, it has been a polarizing issue for American people.[15] There is no doubt that immigration was the only issue that hit the 2016 elections. In fact, previous US presidents also aimed to prevent illegal immigration entry into the US. However, Trump has pursued stricter policies than previous presidents in terms of both rhetoric and practice in the fight against irregular immigration. Therefore, Trump's immigration reform has been criticized for the following reasons, *"deterrence policy of family separation, incarcerating migrant parents and treating their children as unaccompanied minors."*.[16]

Trump's victory has also been seen as a logical response to the fears and concerns that have been going on for decades in most people.[17] "Make

---

[12] Winders, **op.cit**, p. 294.

[13] Richard Ruelas, "Here's what's in Donald Trump's 10-point immigration plan", August 31, 2016, https://www.azcentral.com/story/news/politics/elections/2016/09/01/heres-whats-donald-trumps-10-point-immigration-plan/89685816/ (Access 13.09.2020).

[14] Winders, **op.cit**, p. 291.

[15] Jessica De Alba Ulloa, Rodolfo Reta Haddad. "Immigrant Politics. Analyzing U.S. Presidential Elections through Immigration and Hispanics", **Revista Mexicana de Análisis Político y Administración Pública**, Vol. 5, No. 1, 2016, p. 155.

[16] Hugh Hutchison, "Continuity and Change: Comparing the Securitization of Migration under the Obama and Trump Administrations", **Perceptions**, Vol. XXV No 1, 2020, p. 83-94.

[17] Finley, Esposito, **op.cit**, p. 179

American Great Again" and "America First" which discourses in Trump's election campaign have a nationalist character and combine with anti-immigration discourses.[18] In addition, Trump's harsh anti-immigrant rhetoric and promises led to the strengthening of xenophobia in American society.[19]

One of the most important events in the 2016 elections had been the Mexican Wall. Trump claimed that *"I would build a great wall, and nobody builds walls better than me, believe me, and I'll build them very inexpensively, I will build a great, great wall on our southern border. And I will have Mexico pay for that wall.".*[20] This statement was one of the most memorable discourses of the 2016 elections. Trump's wall promise aimed to prevent immigration to the US. Building walls to prevent immigration has been a visible measure for anti-immigrant voters.

On May 7, 2018, Attorney General Jeff Sessions announced that, "I have put in place a "zero tolerance" policy for illegal entry on our Southwest border. If you cross this border unlawfully, then we will prosecute you. It's that simple."[21] Trump Administration argued that the zero-tolerance policy was important to prevent immigrants from coming to the US and to protect the judiciary from many asylum cases.[22]

Kocher noted three executive orders in the first week of the Trump administration[23]:

- Border Security and Immigration Enforcement Improvements
- Enhancing Public Safety in the Interior of the United States
- Protecting the Nation from Foreign Terrorist Entry into the United States

These executive orders[24] basically signaled that the stricter measures to be taken after the immigration management of the Obama era and the entry to the US will be subject to more difficult conditions.[25] These orders can be considered as the implementation of the "Make America Safe Again"

---

[18] Garand, Qi, Magana, **op.cit,,** p. 6.

[19] Marc Hooghe, Ruth Dassonneville, "Explaining the Trump Vote: The Effect of Racist Resentment and Anti-Immigrant Sentiments", **PS: Political Science and Politics**, Vol. 51, No. 3, 2018, p. 528.

[20] Time Staff, "Here's Donald Trump's Presidential Announcement Speech", https://time.com/3923128/donald-trump-announcement-speech/ (Access 3.10.2020).

[21] The United States Department of Justice, "Justice News", https://www.justice.gov/opa/speech/attorney-general-sessions-delivers-remarks-discussing-immigration-enforcement-actions (Access 12.10.2020).

[22] William A. Kandel, **The Trump Administration's "Zero Tolerance" Immigration Enforcement Policy,** Congressional Research Service Report, 2018, https://fas.org/sgp/crs/homesec/R45266.pdf p. 2.

[23] Austin Kocher, "The New Resistance: Immigrant Rights Mobilization in an Era of Trump", **Journal of Latin American Geography**, Vol. 16, No. 2, 2017, pp. 165-166.

[24] For detailed information see Maryellen Fullerton, "Trump, Turmoil, and Terrorism: The US Immigration and Refugee Ban", **International Journal of Refugee Law**, Vol. 29, Issue 2, 2017, pp. 327–338.

[25] Kocher, **op.cit**, p. 166.

discourse for Trump.[26]

Trump effectively used the murder of a US citizen named Kate Steinle by an immigrant with a criminal record in 2015 during the election process. Trump gave the name of the murdered Kate Steinle to an illegal immigration law proposal. The law referred to as Kate's Law was prepared regarding heavy penalties for immigrants involved in serious crimes in the US.[27]

Trump's initiatives have had the potential to create a radical break from the policies of past administrations, including past Republican administrations.[28] The Trump administration has taken up many issues related to immigration after taking office. Among them[29]:

*"aggressive and large scale deportations of undocumented immigrants and legal immigrants with minor legal or criminal offences; significant to substantial reductions in almost all categories of immigrant and non-immigrant visas, including H-1B and other employment visas, student visas, and family unification visas; substantial reduction in the number of refugees accepted into the United States; officially banning immigrants from selected Muslim countries; extreme vetting of all individuals who apply for all types of visas; [...] Official presidential national emergency declaration to build a wall on the Mexican border; placing thousands of children and adults in detention facilities in what many claim are "cages" across the United States, with children separated from their parents; deporting parents while their children remain in detention in the United States; providing financial and other important resources to state and local governments who cooperate with U.S. immigration policies; threatening to punish local and state governments who try to protect the human rights of immigrants; threatening and punishing countries which refuse to cooperate with U.S. immigration policies; [...] arresting immigrants seeking refugee status or asylum at the U.S.-Mexican border; and preventing immigrants seeking asylum at the Mexican border from entering the United States."*

Trump blamed immigrants for causing US citizens to become unemployed. In addition, Trump has opposed to international programs that support immigrants.[30] Throughout the 2016 elections, Trump constantly kept the fear of the white working class becoming alien on US soil. For the white working-class, it is necessary to protect the US from foreign influence. So

---

[26] Kristin E. Heyer, "Internalized Borders: Immigration Ethics in the Age of Trump", **Theological Studies**, Vol. 79, No.1, 2018, p. 150.

[27] Whitehouse.gov., "Statement from President Donald J. Trump on House Passage of Kate's Law and No Sanctuary for Criminals Act", https://www.whitehouse.gov/briefings-statements/statement-president-donald-j-trump-house-passage-kates-law-no-sanctuary-criminals-act/ (Access 11.10.2020).

[28] Gary Reich, "Hitting a Wall? The Trump Administration Meets İmmigration Federalism", **Publius: The Journal of Federalism**, Vol. 48, No. 3, 2018, p. 372.

[29] Amadu Jacky Kaba, "United States Immigration Policies in the Trump Era", **Sociology Mind**, Vol. 9, 2019, p. 322.

[30] Chi Nguyen, Maraki Kebede, "Immigrant Students in the Trump Era: What We Know and Do Not Know", **Educational Policy**, Vol. 31, Issue 6, 2017, pp. 720-721.

much so that Americans, who believe that immigrants will damage their current situation, have tended to vote 3.5 times more for Trump.[31]

As Kaba points out, highly skilled immigrants may be discouraged from coming to the US because of Trump's anti-immigrant view. According to Trump, immigrants take on the jobs of American citizens, and immigrants are less educated and burden for American society. However, Trump's view of immigrants does not reflect the truth. Immigrants are among the most educated people in the US. Another negative consequence of preventing immigrants from coming to the US is the decrease or stagnation in the US population. These results will also have a negative impact on both the social structure and economic development of the US.[32]

Trump's harsh rhetoric against Muslim immigrants is based on the argument that Muslims pose a security threat to America. Trump has announced that he will limit and even ban immigration from Muslim countries that he sees as a threat.[33] Trump's travel ban affected Muslims the most. This ban has also been compared with some examples in history. These historical examples are the bans on Muslims and Arabs after 9/11 or Iranian students during the Carter era.[34]

As a result, the section on "immigration" on the website of the White House begins with the following text[35]:

*"The United States must adopt an immigration system that serves the national interest. To restore the rule of law and secure our border, President Trump is committed to constructing a border wall and ensuring the swift removal of unlawful entrants. To protect American workers, the President supports ending chain migration, eliminating the Visa Lottery, and moving the country to a merit-based entry system. These reforms will advance the safety and prosperity of all Americans while helping new citizens assimilate and flourish."*

## Conclusion

As is well-known, "America" and "immigrant" words are often used together. For decades, the contribution of immigrants to America's development has been consistently emphasized. However, in order to gain votes in the elections, the issue of immigration was also used like every other

---

[31] Daniel Cox, Rachel Lienesch, Robert P. Jones, "Beyond Economics: Fears of Cultural Displacement Pushed the White Working Class to Trump", 2017, https://www.prri.org/research/white-working-class-attitudes-economy-trade-immigration-election-donald-trump/ (Access 7.10.2020).
[32] Kaba, **op.cit**, p. 336-344.
[33] Nguyen, Kebede, **op.cit**, p. 717.
[34] Bill Ong Hing, "Entering the Trump Ice Age: Contextualizing the New Immigration Enforcement Regime", **Texas A&M Law Review**, Vol. 5 Issue 2, 2018, p. 261.
[35] Whitehouse.gov., "Immigration", https://www.whitehouse.gov/issues/immigration/ (Access 21.09.2020).

subject. At this point, the immigration debate in the 2016 elections had a significant impact on the voters.

The 2016 elections were an important breaking point in anti-immigration. Trump has presented this issue as a major threat to America. For Trump, immigration has been evaluated with words such as illegal, threat, terror, security. Therefore, preventing immigration has been shown as a necessary condition to protect America's security and the future. For this, the construction of the Mexican wall and sanctions against immigrants, who were seen as "dangerous", were decisive statements during and after the election process.

The solution to the problems in US immigration policy should not be in order to gain votes. Even if the US immigration policy needs reforms, these reforms should not be carried out with a populist rhetoric.[36] In the post-Trump period, the transformation of the discourses in the election process into practice will not be positive for the US.

---

[36] Anna Maria Mayda, Peri Giovanni, "The economic impact of US immigration policies in the Age of Trump", **Economics and Policy in the Age of Trump**, Chad P. Bown (Ed.), London, CEPR Press, 2017, p. 74.

CHAPTER 14

# AN ALTERNATIVE SOLUTION TO PROBLEMS ARISING IN REFUGEE CRISES: HUMANITARIAN SPACE AND HUMANITARIAN SYSTEM

Saadet Çalışkan Ciğer[*]

## Introduction

The event that shaped the lives of countries and therefore people the most in the 20th century was undoubtedly the Cold War that lasted from 1947 to 1991. In this period, security concerns came to the forefront, the realist doctrine established an indisputable dominance over all other international relations theories and the area of international relations was as in the state of nature. Therefore, this period affected all policies of states and people's lives and lifestyles with a domino effect.

The anarchy structure of international relations prevailed during this period when the world was divided into two political poles and even the states that emerged in the non-aligned movement were actually closer to either one of the world's two superpowers. Each state and, therefore, people first thought of their own interests and acted with security concerns. Even humanitarian aid was carried out only for political purposes to empower members of one's own bloc or to prevent a state from entering under the influence of the opposing bloc. One of the distinguishing features of this period from today is that due to the insufficient development of mass media, the needs of countries for humanitarian aid could not be announced by civil society, and even if they were announced, the necessary aid was not delivered due to state policies.

From the moment when the end of the Cold War deactivated many of the above limitations, the pace of globalization began to increase noticeably. As security concerns declined, states began to restore the balance between freedom and security and even to give weight to freedom on this scale. With the increase in mass media, civil society gained dynamism and the movement that began in the 1990s – combined with the introduction of social media into our lives – paved the way for the development of the idea that not only states but also humanity itself should find solutions to the problems

---

[*] Independent Researcher, E-mail: caliskan.saadet@gmail.com

231

experienced by humanity.

The biggest problems of the 21st century (including refugee crises and the prevention of these crises) have consisted of humanitarian issues, which have also been the biggest concern of civil society.

With the pressure of civil society on governments, the concept of humanitarian system has been shaped and it is aimed to deliver humanitarian aid to the regions where it is needed. however, there are two biggest obstacles to this purpose: Since non-governmental organizations enter into conflicts or crises, it is needed to ensure the life safety of NGO workers and not allow some states to involve in crisis or conflict areas in order to hide their own mistakes from the public. In order to overcome this problem, the concept of humanitarian space has emerged.

The concepts of humanitarian space and humanitarian system have represented the necessary conditions for non-governmental organizations to reach all over the world in the 21st century. In other words, humanitarian space must be established in order to establish a humanitarian system and to make humanitarian aid.

This article will begin with the introduction chapter explaining the scope of the subject matter. The second chapter of the study will investigate the concepts of humanitarian space and system as well as the conditions for the implementation of these concepts. The third chapter will provide a brief overview of the concepts of refugee and refugee crisis and the perspectives of states towards these concepts. The fourth chapter will discuss how to implement humanitarian space and system as an alternative solution to refugee crises. In conclusion, it will be explored how the concepts of the humanitarian system, space and aid can contribute to alleviating refugee crises and improving the living conditions of refugees in the short and medium term.

## Humanitarian space, humanitarian system

The Cold War is a period in which Western and Eastern bloc countries pursued policies according to static counter-wing for 47 years. With the end of this period, globalization first affected states, and as a result of globalization, power shifts occurred in these states[1]. With the impact of globalization, citizens began to challenge government authorities and the state's domination of freedoms, which were described as unwavering during the Cold War. Bringing security at the center of their domestic and foreign policies, states had to start to attach importance to the norms, traditions and social values of other states and societies apart from the concept of hard

---

[1] Jessica T. Mathews, "Power Shift: The Age of Non-State Actors", **Foreign Affairs**, No. 76, pp. 50-66.

power with the impact of globalization. Again, due to the impact of globalization, borders that had been strictly protected for 47 years began to lose importance. Many states set out to establish interstate organizations or adapt existing ones to the new order in order to keep up with globalization in this new world. Naturally, the adaptation of each state to this process was not equally easy. In this case, NGOs forced the resistant states to transform.

In this new era, the most important effect of the easy passage from borders has been on non-governmental organizations that want to bring aid to people living in conflict zones or underdeveloped areas. These NGOs have had the chance to cross borders more easily than state institutions since they are pursuing only humanitarian purposes. The most remarkable element of this period has been the creation of humanitarian space by NGOs that know no borders. NGOs have set out to establish humanitarian space with a human-centered approach rather than a state-centered approach of states to provide the necessary aid in the regions where aid is needed.

## What is humanitarian space?

Although there is no definition agreed upon by the whole world or NGOs, the first people and institutions that came up with this concept have defined what humanitarian space is. The concept of humanitarian space was first defined by Rony Brauman, the former president of Doctors Without Borders as *"espace humanitaire"*[2]. Brauman's definition of humanitarian space is based on NGOs and according to this definition, NGOs need an environment where they can assess needs, freely observe the use and distribution of donations, and communicate directly and freely with people. To further elaborate on the definition, Brauman's concept of free means that there is no political interference in the transmission of humanitarian aid from donors to recipients by NGOs. The second most accepted and used definition is by Oxfam (Oxford Committee for Famine Relief), one of the world's leading NGOs. In parallel to Brauman's definition, Oxfam also advocates that there should be no political interventions in humanitarian aid. On the other hand, humanitarian space has also been defined as the necessary working environment for providing the protection and assistance people are entitled to and for charities to respond impartially and freely to people's needs[3]. In other words, humanitarian space means that NGOs which provide humanitarian aid face no obstacles while helping people objectively and impartially[4]. Another factor that Oxfam attaches importance to when

---

[2] **Humanitarian space: A review of trends and issues**, Overseas Development Institute, London, 2012, p.1
[3] Policy Compendium Note on United Nations Integrated Missions and Humanitarian Assistance, Oxfam International, Oxford, 2008, p.1.
[4] Challenges to Humanitarian Space: A Review of Humanitarian Issues related to the UN integrated Mission in Liberia and to the Relationship between Humanitarian and Military Actors in Liberia,

defining humanitarian space is that it also references people's right to protection and assistance[5]. Thus, according to Oxfam, the creation of humanitarian space starts from individuals who need it.

As NGOs have started to be active after the end of the Cold War, the emergence of the idea that they could play an important role in preventing refugee crises, the United Nations have not been indifferent to the concept of humanitarian space. United Nations High Commissioner for Refugees has defined humanitarian space as a social, political and security environment where people for whom UNHCR feels concerned due to its nature are allowed to be protected and provided with aid.[6]

A common definition in the light of the above definitions would be that humanitarian space is the social, political and security environment required to deliver aid to people who need it as an unalterable and irrevocable right that is free of political interference.

Since every human community in the world lives under the sovereignty of a particular state, there are certain conditions for humanitarian space to be established in that environment. More comprehensively, there are three pillars needed for the creation of humanitarian space. These are: The legal pillar, the security pillar and the principles pillar.

## The legal pillar

The Geneva Convention of 1949, the 1951 Convention on the Legal Situation of Refugees[7] and the Additional Protocols to the Geneva Convention of 1977[8] have formed the basis of humanitarian aid in the world. These covenants have also given NGOS freedom of movement so that they can provide humanitarian aid. Nevertheless, the covenants do not provide the entire structure necessary to create and maintain the legal pillar of humanitarian space. In addition to these covenants, local laws and regulations set by states that have rule over their territory are also important. In other words, the role of local authorities has a critical role in creating humanitarian space since governments must allow NGOs to operate on their territory in order to create humanitarian space.[9]

---

Monitoring and Steering Group, Liberia, 2005, p.5.

[5] **Humanitarian space: a review of trends and issues**, Overseas Development Institute, London, 2012, p.1

[6] Elizabeth G. Ferris, **The Politics of Protection: The Limits of Humanitarian Action**, Washington D.C., Brookings Institutions Press, 2011, p.176.

[7] Françoise Bouchet-Saulnier, **The Practical Guide to Humanitarian Law**, çev, Brav Laura, & Michel Camille, Plymouth, Rowman & Littlefield, 2014, p. 695

[8] ibid., p. 312.

[9] Governments may have laws preventing foreign NGOs from providing humanitarian aid in order to create humanitarian space, and they may need to replace such laws. Another challenge experienced by NGOs is the disagreement between the central government and the federal government on the assistance

In consequence, although NGOs have legal grounds from international law, states are required to allow NGOs due to their right to rule over their territory and, where necessary, to change their laws preventing NGO activities. If these conditions are fulfilled, the legal pillar of humanitarian space will be established.

## The security pillar

Security is perhaps one of the most important issues for NGOs, volunteers working for NGOs and aid personnel. Many people around the world live in conflict or crisis zones and need regular help for long-term problems such as injuries, famine and thirst that these people may face. Therefore, NGOs have to enter conflict and crisis zones to bring aid to people. It has been repeatedly observed that state authority and control are lost in many crisis zones, especially in areas with refugee crises and influxes. In these cases, it becomes almost impossible for NGOs to enter the areas where there is a crisis as they need to ensure the safety of themselves and employees.

NGOs are going through a process of cooperation with the UN or with states where the crisis zone is located to overcome this problem and ensure their safety against injuries. The assistance of the UN or local authorities is essential and inevitable, especially when it comes to bringing aid to areas where refugee crises and migration floods are concentrated, in order to ensure distribution of aid to refugees without turmoil or conflict.

Consequently, it is necessary to receive support from a UN force or local authorities if a UN force is not formed in crisis environments in order to ensure the establishment of the security pillar. The safety pillar can only be formed under these circumstances.

## The principles pillar

The Red Crescent and the Red Cross, two of the oldest organizations in history that provide the necessary assistance to people in need, have basically adopted seven principles. These principles are humanity, impartiality, neutrality, independence, voluntary service, unity and universality[10]. Four of these principles, which are humanity, impartiality, independence and neutrality, are also the principles that make up the pillar of humanitarian space.[11] These principles are a must-have for forming humanitarian space in

---

of NGOs in countries with federal administrations.

[10] François Bugnion, "Guiding lights through many dilemmas", Red Cross Red Crescent, Vol 1. No. 1, 2015, p.1.

[11] Lary Minear, "The craft of humanitarian diplomacy", **Humanitarian diplomacy: Practitioners and their craft**, Lary Minear, & Hazel Smith (Ed.), Tokyo, United Nations University Press, p.16.

a region.

## Humanitarian system

Although there not a generally accepted definition, humanitarian system with its widest definition is the collection of aid by local, regional, national and international organizations to provide aid in kind, financial aid or human resources to people affected by wars, crises or emerging problems. The main purpose of local, regional, national and international organizations here is to save lives in crises such as refugee crises and to gather the necessary aid or man power[12].

The most important condition for the functioning of the humanitarian system is forming the humanitarian space[13] (Audet, 2015, pp. 142-144). In other words, the humanitarian system must be established in order to provide humanitarian aid, and humanitarian space must be formed to ensure that this humanitarian system is active.

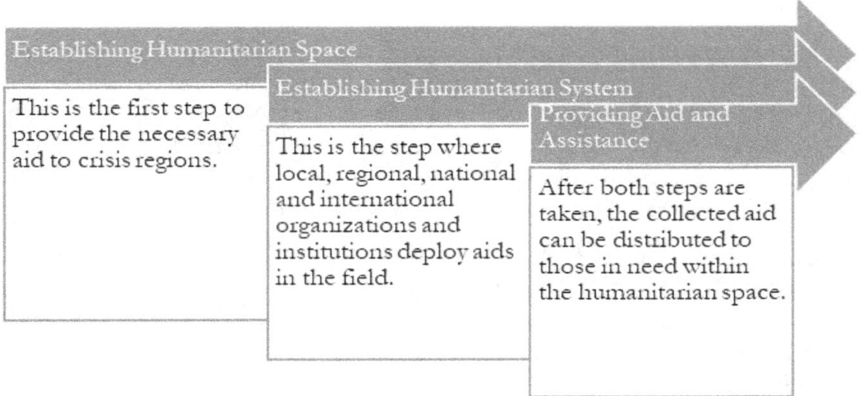


The humanitarian system has started to be established based on NGOs in the 21st century. NGOs have started to take more active roles than states in all crisis points of the world. This has been especially seen in refugee crises. States experiencing this crisis grant the necessary permissions for NGOs to prevent political interference by other states and not create security vulnerabilities, while keeping distance from state interventions in crises.

On the other hand, the intervention of NGOs in crises has advantages and disadvantages. If we take a look at the advantages, NGOs have no

---

12 John Borton, "Trends and Challenges in Measuring Effectiveness in the Humanitarian System", **Measuring What Matters in Peace Operations and Crisis Management**, Sarah Jane Meharg (Ed.), Kingston, McGill-Queen's University Press, 2009, pp. 159-169.
13 Francois Audet, "Humanitarian space", **The Routledge Companion to Humanitarian Action**, Jenny H. Peterson & Roger Mac Ginty (Ed.), New York, Routledge, 2015, pp. 142-144.

interests like states and there is no hostile state or society to NGOs, thus, they can easily access every region. Furthermore, states and societies have a more positive view of NGOs since they do not expect any interests from providing aid. This positive outlook allows NGOs to overcome bureaucratic procedures more quickly, especially in crisis areas. Another advantage of NGOs is that they collect the resources needed for their projects or assistance from volunteers. The public pressure for transparency of state administrations after the Cold War and giving more importance to freedom in the question of freedom or security have led citizens to question where their taxes are spent on. Hence, if even a small part of the citizens oppose to assistance provided by states, this might cause problems for the government since citizens pay taxes.

On the other hand, the disadvantages arise in the security problem in the establishment of humanitarian space and system. Since NGOs go to various crisis areas, the problem of ensuring the necessary security remains on the table.

Although it may seem difficult to establish and operate a humanitarian space and system, these concepts appear to be the most effective way to actively bring the necessary assistance to people at crisis points when combined with the increased activity of NGOs in the post-Cold War era.

## The concept of refugee and refugee crisis

Although article 1 of the Universal Declaration of Human Rights regulates that "All human beings are born free and equal in dignity and rights. They are endowed with reason and conscience and should act towards one another in a spirit of brotherhood," this is not the case in realpolitik.

As of 2020, 79.5 million people have been forcibly displaced and refugees make up 26 million of them[14]. The refugee issue in the 21st century is different from World War II when this problem first appeared, however, the reactions of countries to the refugee problem – which is a humanitarian crisis – have not changed much in 75 years. Rather than obvious differences, there are many similarities between the reasons and methods used by countries that tried not to accept Jews as refugees during World War II and the reasons and methods used in today's refugee crises.[15] In other words, the situation of refugees appears to be sacred when appealing to consciences, while it is considered a situation to be avoided from the point of view of countries. Refugees are excluded by countries and are deemed dangerous subjects according to the policies they follow.[16] To go further, the concept of refugee

---

[14] https://www.unhcr.org/figures-at-a-glance.html (Access 20.11.2020)
[15] Joseph Carens, **The Ethics of Immigration**, Oxford, Oxford University Press, 2013, p. 193.
[16] Giorgio Agamben, **Kutsal İnsan: Egemen, İktidar ve Çıplak Hayat**, translated by İsmail. Türkmen,

is regarded to be identical to terrorism and crime by the majority of societies and is seen as a major threat to Western culture.[17]

Human rights are a set of rights that any human being has as soon as he is born, regardless of religion, language or race. However, the situation does not progress in the same way for refugees in realpolitik. When people who have to emigrate leave their countries and cannot return, the way other states view these people changes along with their own state. Their natural human rights granted by birth begin to be ignored by states[18]. The fact that human rights can be discarded so quickly in the real world reveals the situation that rights are only on paper. As a matter of fact, for nations, refugees and immigrants mean that their culture will change and their existing jobs will be taken away by foreigners. With the continuation of this understanding, refugees lose their birth-born human rights when they have to leave their homeland.

The legal regulations and sanctions necessary to prevent this situation, on the other hand, are lost in the anarchic structure of international relations. Although international institutions (such as the UN) officially exist to prevent this situation, they remain dysfunctional in reality as these institutions do not have the power to impose sanctions on states in the anarchic environment of international relations. Hence, when a person has to leave his country, he faces a great threat of being deprived of his human rights. In case of refugees, they lose the protection of their natural human rights against other states due to the lack of their nation-state that is supposed to serve as an umbrella organization to protect individual rights.

Looking at the concept of refugee in-depth, it can be uttered that it is necessary not to define the concept only as a person who has leave his country. From the moment they are forced to leave their country, refugees lose their job, environment, the living space to which they belong and have spent their life, as well as people and places they love. Within the nation-state system, it seems very difficult for refugees to find a new homeland and replace what they have lost.[19] As a matter of fact, nation states and nations are very reluctant to provide refugees with a homeland and the necessary conditions to replace what they have lost.[20]

Evaluating the concept of refugees by a metaphor will make it easy to

---

İstanbul, Ayrıntı Yayınları, 2013, pp. 89-98.

[17] Emma Larking, "Human Rights, the Right to Have Rights, and Life Beyond the Pale of the Law", **Australian Journal of Human Rights**, Vol. 18, No. 1, 2012, p. 71.

[18] Hannah Arendt, **Totalitarizmin Kaynakları 2: Emperyalizm**, translated by Bahadır Sina Şener, İstanbul, İletişim Yayınları, 2014, pp. 256-258.

[19] Hannah Arendt, **The Jewish Writings,** New York, Schocken Books, 2007, p. 264.

[20] Serena Parekh, "Beyond the Ethics of Admission: Stateless People, Refugee Camps and Moral Obligations", **Philosophy and Social Criticism**, Vol. 40, No. 7, 2013, p. 652

comprehend the overall situation: Refugees can be considered as a cell that is part of an organ within the body but has to go to another organ since it has to leave. In this case, countries and societies act in the same way that the new organ is on the alert and wants the antibodies to act, thinking there is an anomaly. Nation states see the refugee crisis or problem as a situation that soldiers or police should deal with and want to tackle this issue through non-governmental organizations in order not to burden the budget and waste taxes.

In the current order, either various measures are taken so that refugees do not cross the border or refugees who cross the border are forced to live in camps under the control of law enforcement. The reaction of developed countries that are not neighbors to refugee giving countries in the face of this situation is usually to take preventive measures. The first of the measures taken by Western countries has been to impose various penal sanctions on transportation companies that carry people without visas. Another measure has been to prevent the applications of those who do not meet the necessary requirements for refugee status in the regions where refugee crises are spreading by sending civil servants to these regions before refugees enter their territory. Another measure taken in this area has been to patrol the sea to prevent refugees from coming by sea in illegal boats. In the case of Greece, this substance became more severe and Greek forces tried to keep refugees away from the border by sinking inflatable boats belonging to Syrian refugees.[21] Another measure has been to set a time limit for the application of refugees from the moment when the crisis broke out. The final measure has been to try to make various bilateral agreements to ensure that refugees stay in the countries where they first go, far from their borders[22].

On the other hand, others problems are waiting for refugees who can cross borders. Refugees are housed in camps or tents in isolated areas called conservation centers. In cases where camps can be established, their needs such as disease treatment, education, food and clothing are met in a limited way and law enforcement units generally avoid intervening in the problems arising from not meeting such needs in the camp.[23]

---

[21] http://www.aljazeera.com.tr/haber/yunan-teknesi-multeci-botunu-batirdi (Access 23.11.2020)
https://www.hurriyet.com.tr/gundem/yunan-sahil-guvenlik-multeci-botunu-boyle-patlatti-40016425 (Access 23.11.2020)
https://www.trthaber.com/haber/turkiye/yunan-sahil-guvenligi-siginmaci-botlarini-batirmaya-calisti-465255.html (Access 23.11.2020)
https://www.cnnturk.com/video/dunya/ege-denizine-agdan-duvar (Access 23.11.2020)
https://www.ntv.com.tr/dunya/yunanlilar-batirdi-turkler-kurtardi,kKM7VfMm20KuBaqMkUMNaQ (Access 23.11.2020)
[22] Mehmet Kocaoğlu, "Günümüz Mülteci Krizi: Arendtçi Bir Eleştiri", **Amme İdaresi Dergisi**, Volume 51, Issue 4, 2018, pp. 25-26.
[23] Giorgio Agamben, **Kutsal İnsan: Egemen, İktidar ve Çıplak Hayat**, translated by İsmail. Türkmen, İstanbul, Ayrıntı Yayınları, 2013, pp. 105-106.

Refugee camps are now used as the most common refugee sheltering system and although this system began to be used temporarily for refugees seeking asylum during World War II when almost all of Europe was at war, it has unfortunately become widespread today as the solution of the refugee problem.

While the behavior of countries on the refugee issue results from the anarchic nature of international relations, the inadequacies of international law in forcing states can also create space for them to escape the refugee problem. First of all, the Geneva Convention's acceptance of people who leave their countries for fear of arrest for their ethnic, religious, social and political membership gives the states the right not to grant refugee status to those who are outside these criteria. Thus, states are able to send the incoming person back and assume no responsibility.

Another weakness of the Geneva Convention is that it does not include a compelling provision for states regarding refugees. Coercive clauses such as minimum conditions for refugees are not included in the convention. Although the non-refoulement principle in the convention prevents sending refugees back, refugees can only stay in the country under the conditions that states consider suitable. Since the non-refoulement principle applies only to the country where refugees first reach, they can be sent back to the country where they were accepted as refugees after they pass to a second or third country.

In consequence, refugees are accepted not by economically developed countries of the world and Europe, but by medium-sized or underdeveloped countries in the current system of the international area.[24] This has been a serious problem for refugees accepted by countries with limited economic resources. Thanks to the current system, nomically developed countries are using medium-sized and underdeveloped countries as a lightning rod to prevent refugees from coming to their home countries.[25] Almost all developed country societies see refugees as a security and integration problem. At the same time, spending taxes for people other than the relevant developed country's citizens without interest is a situation that immobilizes states and decision-makers.

### Possible solution to refugee crises: Humanitarian space, system and aid

Although the prevention of refugee crises and the acceptance of refugees'

---

[24] Michel Dummet, **On Immigration and Refugees**, London, Routledge, 2001, pp. 34-35.
[25] Syrian refugees and Turkey are the best examples of this situation. EU countries have produced many projects to prevent Syrian refugees from coming to Europe and expected Turkey to accept these projects and commit to never send Syrians to Europe.

natural rights by all countries seems to be a utopian approach in the short term, creating humanitarian space and system to overcome refugee crises more painlessly and meet the needs of refugees avoided by states seems to be one of the most reasonable options.

Examining the three pillars of humanitarian space that should be established in possible refugee crises, it can be observed that some of the infrastructure required for the legal pillar was provided by the Geneva Convention of 1949, the Convention on the Legal Situation of Refugees in 1951 and the Additional Protocols to the Geneva Convention of 1977. It is also necessary for states to have NGOs to meet with refugees, to determine their needs, and to make legal arrangements for refugees to enter into camps if they are kept in camps. Another step that must be taken after states have made legal arrangements will be the creation of the security pillar. For this, the UN or if the UN is not involved in a related refugee crisis, the state involved in the crisis must ensure the security of NGOs. Ensuring the safety of NGO officers, many of them voluntarily in the crisis zone, will ensure that they can provide the necessary aid quickly and that the needs of refugees can be met. At the same time, many NGOs in the world would support a humanitarian space established on the basis of the security pillar. Finally, in order to establish the principles pillar, NGOs that help in the refugee crisis must act within the framework of humanity, impartiality, independence and neutrality principles and, if necessary, adhere to these principles even if they are citizens of countries involved in the refugee crisis.

When the pillars of humanitarian space are formed, the states involved in the refugee crisis must clearly explain the course and situation of the crisis in order for the system to take action. However, states generally block the flow of information so that they do not take responsibility for refugee crises or to prevent the world from hearing the poor conditions provided to incoming refugees. In this case, the establishment of humanitarian system is disrupted.

Given that international conventions on refugees as well as the way states view refugees and refugee crises will not change, the establishment of humanitarian space and system will offer states and refugees a solution to a reasonable extent, if not at the maximum level.

## Conclusion

The nation-state system is a system in which the interests of nations are prioritized and states put the needs and wishes of their own citizens ahead of other nations. Regular, competitive and public elections in democratic systems reflect the wishes of societies to governments as administrations. Therefore, no government prefers to spend the resources it collects from its own citizens through taxes on foreigners instead of spending it on its own citizens. Leaders of political parties and governments are afraid to take steps in this regard, considering the criticisms they will receive in the elections, and want to stay as far away from refugee crises and influxes as possible.

Hence, a system in which humanitarian space is established, the humanitarian system is functional and aid is delivered to refugees under the responsibility of NGOs seems to be the most reasonable solution for both countries and refugees in the short and medium term.

When a refugee crisis occurs in one region, humanitarian space can be created in that region, and humanitarian system can be planned to allow refugees to go to other countries and all the needs of refugees can be met in this process. When this is actualized, cases like sinking the inflatable boats of refugees and leaving them dead even in winter so that they do not set foot in their countries, as in the case of Greece, can be prevented.

It is a known solution for countries to prevent refugees from coming to their lands. The main reason for this is that these countries think that refugees will be a problem for them and that they will bring a material, cultural and social burden. If states help and allow humanitarian space and system to be established in their own countries, the rates of encountering material, cultural and social burdens for refugees will decrease, NGOs will be able to meet material needs and provide refugees with a living space within the framework of the culture and social environment of the country in which they come from.

Refugee camps were temporarily established during World War II, yet they became permanent after the war and started to be used as a solution to refugee crises, therefore, camps are viewed as an emerging environment in refugee crises. The urgent and humanitarian needs of refugees living here such as food, shelter and clothing can be met by NGOs without spending money from the state's treasury with the establishment of humanitarian space and system. Thus, the living conditions of refugee camps can be improved and a win-win solution can be used by both refugees and the country that accepts refugees.

The Geneva Convention only accepts people who leave their countries as refugees for fear of arrest for their ethnic, religious, social and political membership, leaving the choice to whether grant refugee status to others not meeting this criterion to states. In these cases, states are usually able to send the person or persons back and refuse to accept them as refugees in order not to take their financial responsibilities. In other words, states do not want to assume responsibility. In cases where states do not want to assume responsibility, the establishment of humanitarian space and system will pave the way for NGOs to assume this responsibility and for states to evaluate refugees without financial loss.

According to the UNHCR's 2019 report, refugees are mostly accepted by medium-sized or underdeveloped countries, not by economically developed countries. This situation leads these countries to deal with various economic, social and cultural problems with limited resources. If humanitarian space and system are established, on the other hand, the difficulties experienced by these states can be avoided. Since the impact areas of NGOs are not limited to the borders of a country, humanitarian space and system can reach all regions of the world as soon as they are established. Therefore, more support can be provided to countries that try to help refugees with limited resources.

Although present in many countries in the world, one of the questions citizens of every country, where the needs of refugees are met, is why their taxes are spent on foreigners. This situation does not change with the economic development of the country. In economically developed countries with current surplus, when the state allocates resources to refugees, citizens argue that if there is a surplus of resources, taxes should be reduced instead of spending the surplus on foreigners, while in a country where citizens have economic problems, citizens ask why taxes are spent on foreigners and not on themselves. With the establishment of humanitarian space and system, NGOs do not have such problems as they spend in-kind or cash resources they collect from volunteers from all over the world. Volunteers are providing aid voluntarily so that the negative perception of refugees in the eyes of communities will change with the reduction of resources allocated by countries to refugees.

In conclusion, although humanitarian space and system may not bring a permanent solution to refugee crises, they can solve at least some of the existing problems in the short to medium term. This will allow refugees to at least improve their quality of life and ensure the basic humane conditions after the traumatic process in which they are forced to leave their countries. The idea that humanitarian space and system can be used effectively by NGOs can create a new perspective in the short- and medium-term solution of refugee crises.

# CHAPTER 15

# DEVELOPING EFFECTIVE RESILIENCE BASED STRATEGIES FOR REFUGEES

Murat Koray[*]

## Introduction

According to the data of the United Nations, 70 million people around the world have been displaced by reasons such as conflict, starvation, danger of death, violence and abuse. United Nations High Commissioner for Refugees (UNHCR) stated that 30 million of them are refugees who fled their country due to fundamental human rights violations, while 40 million are those who have been forced to migrate within the borders of their countries[1]. UNHCR's latest Global Trends report shows that *"79.5 million people were forcibly displaced at the end of 2019. That's fully 1 per cent of humanity, or 1 in every 97 people on earth. Some 11 million people were newly displaced in the course of last year — fleeing wars, violence or persecution. Overwhelmingly it is low- and middle-income countries that are most affected"*[2]. Refuge, or formerly known as asylum, requires a person to leave the country of his / her nationality or residence, due to various pressures or discriminatory legal proceedings, to leave the country of a foreign state; diplomatic representation or consulate buildings, warships or state aircraft and denotes seeking protection. The regulations for the protection of asylum seekers were made especially during the League of Nations period, followed by protection measures within the auspicies of the UN organization[3]. In this context, the only universal treaty today is the UN Convention on the Status of Refugees dated 28.07.1951 and the Supplementary Protocol dated 16.12.1996. t is necessary to add some regional agreements signed within the framework of South America, Africa and the Council of Europe[4]. The 1951 Refugee Convention and its 1967 Protocol and 1969 OAU Convention Governing the Specific Aspects of Refugee Problems in Africa are the key legal documents[5]. Traditionally, the right to

---



[*] Piri Reis University, Lecturer, nmkoray@pirireis.edu.tr



[1] https://www.milliyet.com.tr/dunya/dunyanin-multeci-krizi-6196169

[2] https://www.unhcr.org/unhcr-global-trends-2019-media.html?gclid=Cj0KCQjw0rr4BRCtARIsAB0 _48OHT0x9dz7m-ktscBw7GTViLT8RQXhccwyhyw6-LJKr4ES55w2HHdwaAqvbEALw_wcB

[3] Odman, T., "Mülteci Hukuku", Ankara, 1995, s.17-48

[4] Resmi Gazete 5.9.1961, Sayı 10898 ve Resmi Gazete 5.8.1968, Sayı 12968

[5] Convention and Protocol Relating to The Status of Refugees, https://www.unhcr.org/1951-refugee-convention.html, https://www.unhcr.org/3b66c2aa10 , https://www.unhcr.org/about-us/background/45dc1a682/oau-convention-governing-specific-aspects-refugee-problems-africa-adopted.html

refuge refers to the right of a state to allow foreigners to enter and remain in their country who have escaped pressure from the state of their nationality or residence[6]. When the situation of both the state and the individual regarding the right to refuge is examined, it is seen that a state is the only authority for foreigners to enter and stay in the country according to the main principle in international law. In accordance with this main principle, whether a state grants asylum to foreigners in its country is an issue to be evaluated within the framework of the international obligations and national legislation of that state. If a state has entered into a certain obligation in this regard with a treaty, it has to recognize the right of asylum in terms of foreigners who fulfill the conditions of the relevant treaty. On the other hand, if there is no such treaty obligation, there are no international rules of procedure or general law[7]. According to UNHCR data, internally displaced persons, UNRWA and UNHCR refugees and asylum seekers are shown in Figure-1. The rate of asylum seekers among the refugees in the 10-year period is around 4% (min: 2%, max: 6%). Generally, the countries where refugees and, asylum seekers come from are Syria, South Sudan, Ukraine, Myanmar, Africa's Sahel region, Afghanistan, Iraq, Libya and Somalia, Central African Republic, Ethiopia, Democratic Republic of the Congo and Yemen. Figure 1 does not include 3.6 million Venezuelans displaced abroad.

**Figure 1.** Global forced displacement (Source: UNHCR, 2019)[8]

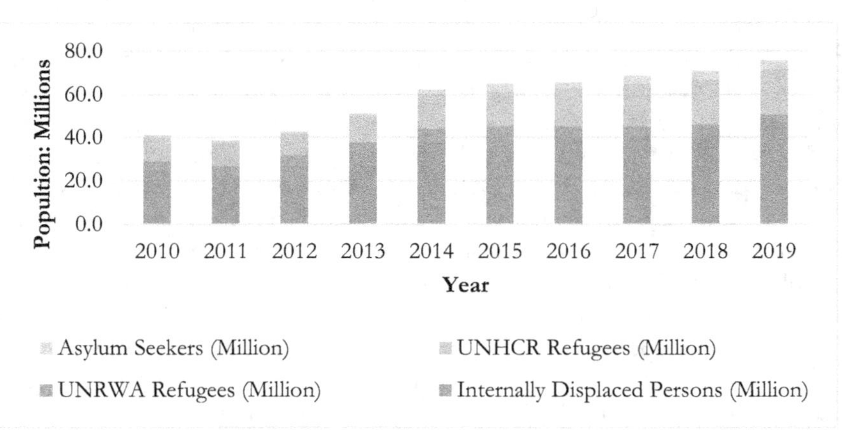


The main reasons of migration as refugees or asylum seekers are war, conflict, persecution, human rights violations and events seriously disturbing public order. The most people who have been forced to leave their homeland

---

[6] Grahl-Madsen,A., "Territorial Asylum", Encyclopedia, Vol.8, s.43

[7] Cour internationale de Justice (C.I.J, International Court of Justice), Recueil, 1950, s.286

[8] UNHCR (2019), "Global Trends: Force Displacement in 2019", pg.7 https://www.unhcr.org/statistics/unhcrstats/5ee200e37/unhcr-global-trends-2019.html

are generally citizens of the Democratic Republic of Congo (DRC), Burkina Faso, the Syrian Arab Republic (Syria), the Bolivarian Republic of Venezuela (Venezuela) and Yemen. However, considering the Nagorno-Karabakh conflict, which turned into a hot conflict between Azerbaijan and Armenia recently, the fact that 1 million Azerbaijani Turks had to leave their lands gives circumstantial evidence. So, the situation may melt the frozen conflicts leading to a greater crisis in the Caucasus than in the Middle East. Refugees somehow leave their countries and seek a safe place or moving heaven to take shelter. As a result of searching for a safe area, a refugee crisis emerges in the host countries they reached, which in turn triggers the start of an asylum seeking process in developed countries. Top international displacement situations by country of origin until the end of 2019 are shown below in Figure 2.

**Figure 2.** Top international displacement situations by country of origin until the end of 2019

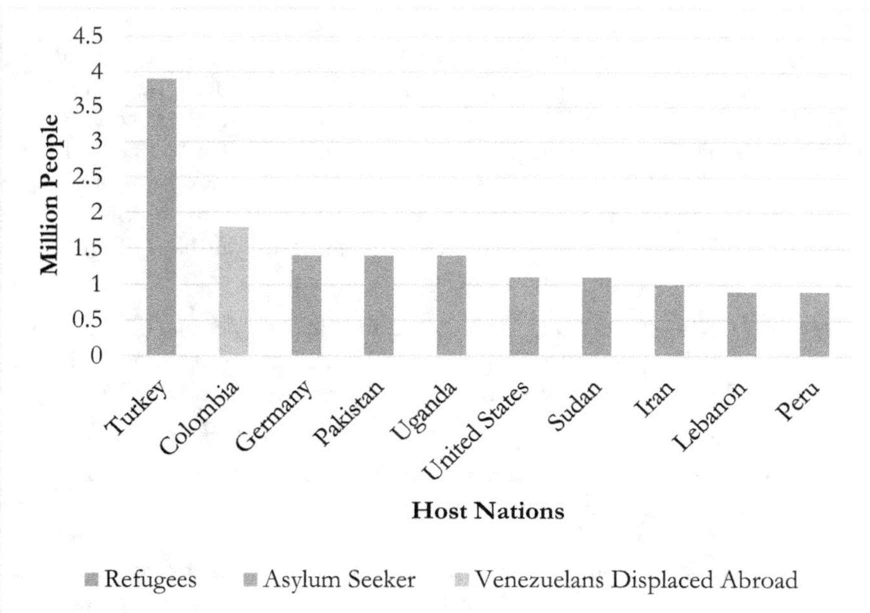


Source: UNHCR, 2019[9]

Looking at the world, it is seen that there is a migration movement from east to west. It is observed that in geographies where forced migration is intense, the final living areas that immigrants intend to reach are the USA and the EU. In addition, the strong border and coast guard mechanisms that the

---

[9] UNHCR (2019), "Global Trends: Force Displacement in 2019", pg.8 https://www.unhcr.org/statistics/unhcrstats/5ee200e37/unhcr-global-trends-2019.html

USA and the EU developed as a result of the immigration policies cause the immigrants to pile up in the countries shown in Figure-2. The rate of refugees and asylum seekers reaching the USA and the EU is around 7%. The main problem area is resilience capacity of the host countries for refugees and asylum-seekers. Therefore, there is a need to develop effective resilience based strategies for refugees and asylum-seekers.

## The Perspectives of Host Countries on Refugees & Asylum-Seekers

After the end of the cold war in 1990, the global refugee crisis indicated a marked increase between 1997 and 2002 after nearly seven years of unstable circumstances. Mass influx with an increasing rate of nearly 64% from 2005 to 2006 turned into a global migration crisis and, over 30 million people were displaced. Immigrants had been divided into some categories; such as refugees, asylum-seekers, internally displaced persons (IDPs), returnees (refugees and IDPs), stateless persons and the others of concern to UNHCR by origin. Refugees and asylum-seekers were 30% of the total immigrants in 2006[10]. After the intense mass flux increase in 2006, it was noticed that the refugees and asylum seekers increased by 14% in 2007. Therefore, it was understood that the refugees and asylum seekers should be scrutinized seperately[11]. According to the analysis of the Norwegian Refugee Council's (NRC) Internal Displacement Monitoring Center (IDMC), 80% of refugees are hosted by neighboring countries that remain in their region of origin. In addition, this analysis reveals that more than half of the refugees prefer to be located in urban centers rather than rural areas. The numbers of Internally Displaced Persons (IDPs) and Refugees are shown in Figure 3.

Although there are many displaced and stateless people in the world, legally, having refugee status requires a sui generis process and the people closest to this status are defined as asylum seekers. Some legal processes regarding refugee status may differ from country to country.

In fact, it should not be ignored that every IDP is a refugee candidate if the necessary protection measures are not taken. For example, considering that 43.3% of the total 31.7 million people under UNHCR's responsibility in 2007 were IDP, it would be an inevitable fact that If approximately 13.7 million people could not be protected in their homeland, a refugee crisis would occur especially in the neighbouring countries. When comparing UNHCR's 2007 and 2008 data, it is seen that the total number of refugees

---

[10] UNHCR, 2006 Global Trends: Refugees, Asylum-seekers, Returnees, Internally Displaced and Stateless Persons, https://reliefweb.int/report/world/2006-global-trends-refugees-asylum-seekers-returnees-internally-displaced-and-stateless

[11] UNHCR, 2007 Global Trends: Refugees, Asylum-seekers, Returnees, Internally Displaced and Stateless Persons, https://www.unhcr.org/statistics/unhcrstats/4852366f2/2007-global-trends-refugees-asylum-seekers-returnees-internally-displaced.html

under the United Nations High Commissioner (UNHCR) mandate and, the United Nations Relief and Works Agency for Palestine (UNRWA) mandate, asylum seekers and conflict-based IDPs did not change[12].

**Figure 3.** Number of IDPs and Refugees[13]

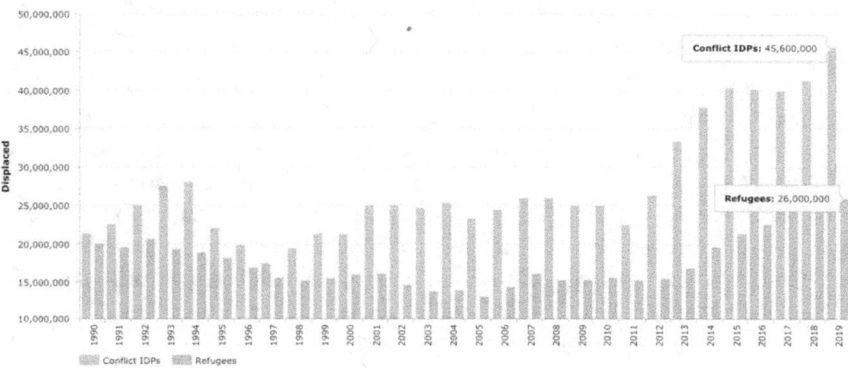

However, while millions of people were resettled in their homeland, so many people had to leave their insecure settlements. Therefore, the focus should be on the number of circulating people, not the total number of refugees only. While developing countries host five-fourths of the world's refugees, it is thought-provoking that developed countries hesitate to take responsibility. Regardless of whether refugees reside in cities or camps, it is seen that increasing instability slows the pace of progress of developing countries, considering that each choice creates its own problems and imposes a serious financial burden on society. UNHCR has defined the following population categories shown in Figure 4, referred to as "persons of concern".

**Figure 4.** UNHCR's Population Categories referred to as "persons of concern"

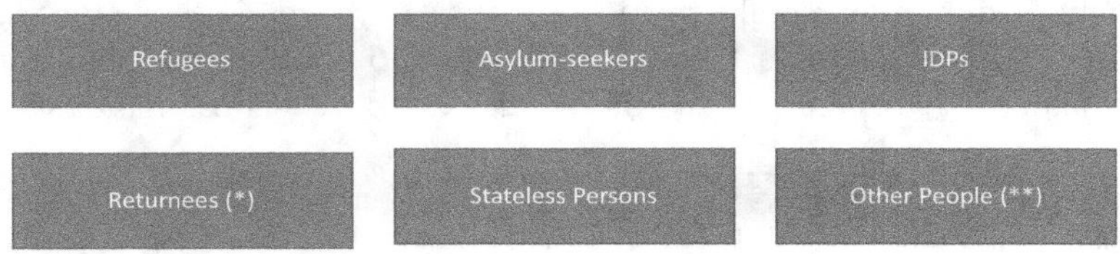


(*) refugees who have returned home (returnees) and IDPs who have returned home

(**) Other People: People in refugee-like situations (included under refugees); and people in IDP-like situations (included under IDPs).

Aside from the burden of the refugee crisis on host states, it is an

---

[12] UNHCR, 2008 Global Trends: Refugees, Asylum-seekers, Returnees, Internally Displaced and Stateless Persons, https://www.unhcr.org/4a375c426.pdf

[13] Source: IDMC, Global Internal Displacement Database, https://www.internal-displacement.org/database/ displacement-data

inevitable fact that the living conditions of people outside the refugee category are much direr. Despite all the measures taken, their being alone with their destiny brings with it a potential human rights problem. Although it is generally given a lesser value than those vital part when "the others" are mentioned, it will not be wrong to think that they will be exposed to more difficult conditions than refugees, due to the fuzzy status of the others (e.g. refugee-like situation).

According to UNHCR data (2008), 1.4 million of 10.5 million people under the auspieces of the UNHCR were located in the Bolivarian Republic of Venezuela, Ecuador and, Pakistan in refugees-like situations. Although a total of 6.6 million stateless people from 58 countries have been identified by UNHCR around the world, it is stated that the number is almost twice as high. In fact, refugees and asylum seekers are also stateless, nevertheless, they are given a separate category, the rest qualify as stateless. For more than 30 years, Afghanistan was the main country of origin for refugees in 69 asylum countries around the world. However, Syria was the main country of origin for refugees in 126 asylum countries since 2014. Thus, while one in four refugees in the world was from Afghanistan[14], one in three refugees came from Syrian.[15,16]

## The Birth Pangs of The New World Order and The Tragedy of Forced Migration

Migration is a phenomenon as old as human history. Throughout history, whoever seizes power has forced others to migrate. Migration events, which have become the tragedy of humanity, mostly emerged as a result of a crisis, and sometimes they have been the harbinger of a new world order as a result of birth pangs experienced at the intersection of each era. In fact, even the immigrants who fled to America for the sake of freedom, after getting power where they went, tried not only to forced migrate the locals, but also other groups who had immigrated like them from where they were[17]. Since forcing to migrate is a crime against humanity, those who should undertake the responsibilities of this crime cannot be expressed as states, nations or

---

[14] UNHCR Statistical Yearbook 2016, 16th edition, pg.12, Table-2, Total Population of Concern: 5,166,269,file:///Users/demo/Desktop/UNHCR%20Statistical%20Yearbook%202016,%2016th%20edition.pdf

[15] According to UNHCR Statistical Yearbook 2016, 16th edition, pg.15, Table-2, Total Population of Concern: 12,643,356, file:///Users/demo/Desktop/UNHCR%20Statistical%20Yearbook%202016,%2016th%20edition.pdf

[16] Amnesty International (2020), "The World's Refugees In Numbers", https://www.amnesty.org/en/what-we-do/refugees-asylum-seekers-and-migrants/global-refugee-crisis-statistics-and facts/#:~:text=Refugees%20around%20the%20world%20%2D%20facts%20and%20figures&text=Syria%20has%20been%20the%20main,hosted%20by%20126%20countries

[17] Richard F. Mollica (2019), Violence toward Immigrants as the "Other", S. Megan Berthold and Kathryn R. Libal, Editors, Refugees and Asylum Seekers: Interdisciplinary and Comparative Perspectives, Praeger, pg.10.

empires, or terrorist organizations. This phenomenon can be best expressed by considering the laws of physics. Because neither the moral understanding created by the history of mankind nor the divine orders from the skies could correct the wild creature called human. While the vast universe seems to be stable from the outside, it can be seen that the balance of imbalances is formed in an endless war as you get to the details at the micro level. Even when looking at seas, dynamically changing temperature, salinity, pressure, and density changes can be easily observed. When one of the factors changes, the reflexive reactions of all the remaining factors prove that the world is a living being. This is also the case with migration movements. Somewhere the economy deteriorates, crisis looms, regional conflicts arise, someone recovers to their origins to survive, and maintains its survival like a wild animal, the weak dies or runs away, natural selection always works in its own nature. This situation is very cruel and is not explained by any code of ethics. A man who loses his mind will become superior to the wildest animal. This is the painful truth of life that is filled with majestic illusions. As a result, when the balance of the world changes due to economic reasons, technological leaps, political wars, global warming or any other reason, natural selection works and migration begins. Obviously, those who profit from chaos have to carry the can, but unfortunately paying the price of the felony is made primarily by the neighbouring countries around the country where the chaos originated. If there is a category called developed, developing and failed states in the world, it means that someone has broken the balance in their favour. Encouraging smart and talented people in the world to brain drain because they cannot find value in their own country, and then step aside after achieving the title of hosting the most immigrants in the world and, leaving others to their fate like a human pulp, to remain indifferent to people dying on the open seas, condemn them freezing to death on the mountains in the middle of the winter, remain indifferent to their deaths on a minefield, not to prevent terrorist organizations from falling into their hands, keeping silence for their being sold in human markets and being forced into prostitution, not to prevent them from paying a bitter prescription for their choice to live instead of fighting and, not to care about dying for their honour, has zeroed the ration cards of humanity. Putting the blame on humanity, the rich, terrorists, illiteracy, population density, religions or any other subject will not provide a solution that will hinder unwanted human mobility in the world. Looking at the economic cycles, the world income inequality turns into a sinusoidal wave whose oscillations gradually narrow when considering the last 5000-year period, and the 60-year cycles in the last 300 years are reduced to 30 years as in Figure 5 and Figure 6.

**Figure 5.** Power Centers in History from 3000 BC to 1735[18]

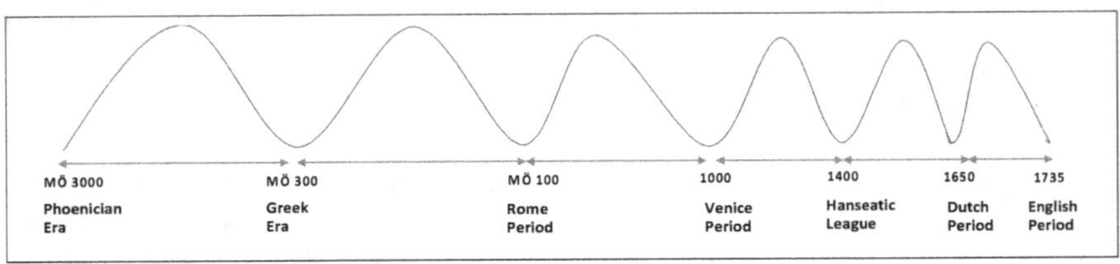



Schumpeter made a prediction by 2020. A simulation was made until 2050, since it is highly probable that it would be a 30-year cycle due to technological leap. In this case, as in 1856, 1900, 1950 and 1990, long waves are expected to reach the deepest point at the beginning of 2020[19].

**Figure 6.** The waves of Kondratieff that Joseph Schumpeter worked (Revised by the author)[20].

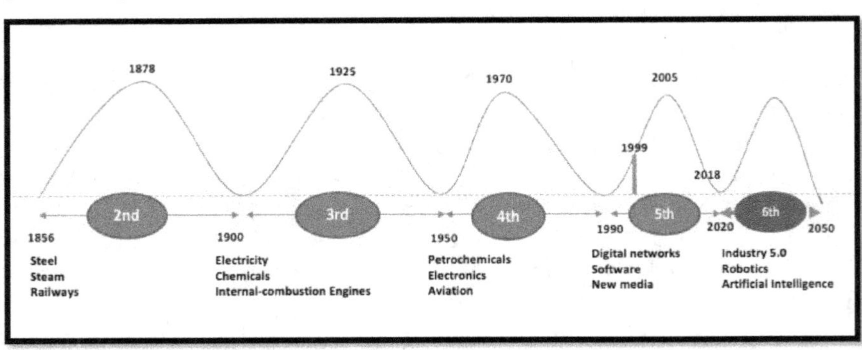



Economic reasons have disrupted the game in every periodic cycle and the center of gravity has always shifted westward at a certain speed. A few centuries later, the center of gravity will likely shift towards Africa, where humanity began. Wherever the center of gravity of world trade shifts along with the economic cycles, the unbalanced situation on the other side triggers the crisis in those regions and causes unwanted human movements. If this fled of people, which is very difficult to control, is not managed well, it can create a destructive effect just like a flood disaster. Therefore, the issue of what kind of strategy should be followed should not only fall on the exposed states, the crisis that has occurred should be internationalized and turned into a problem of humanity and all states should take responsibility.

---

[18] Stopford, M. (2009). Maritime Economics. New York, USA: Routledge, pg.6

[19] Koray M. (2020), Developing A Combined Qualitative Ship Valuation Estimation Model, (Istanbul: Piri Reis University, Graduate School of Science and Engineering, PhD Thesis), pg.68

[20] Barnett, V. (1998), Kondratiev and The Dynamic of Economic Development, New York, USA: Mc Millan Press, pg.6

## Assessing the Syrian Crisis in the Context of Refugees and Asylum-Seekers.

Although the tragic events continue in various crisis regions of the world, since the biggest number of immigrants in the last 5-6 years originates from Syria, it would be beneficial to consider this study as an example. Throughout history, whoever wanted to control the Syrian sovereignty ended in frustration and even disappeared from the scene of history. Since the Syrian region has a commercial appeal and it is difficult to secure this region, it is an inevitable fact that global and regional actors are sneakily waiting for an opportunity to seize this region. However, when a regional or global actor intends to seize this region, other dynamics come into play and a weary conflict begins in the focus of a great tension. This regional tension triggers great human mobility. Due to the recent internal turmoil in Syria, life-threatening escapes began primarily to neighbouring countries. This flow, which is far above the official figures, has brought along vital risks and responsibilities. Thanks to the Turkish people's nomadic origins and their compassionate nature stemming from their understanding of Islam, they embraced the refugees regardless of who they were. Just as it is a physical reality that liquids cannot be compressed, the flow of a mass of people in panic is not blocked by any wall. The strategic direction of the world will accelerate a greater flow of people in the future and the crisis management plans implemented today will be insufficient. The example of Syria has given the signs of this danger today. Although the migrants are categorized only as people in need to help, the resume of each person adds another link to the chain of measures to be taken. In addition, apart from innocent people, terrorists, smugglers, illegal organizations, intelligence agencies, money launderers, etc. are penetrating into the interior of the target country. Therefore, on the one hand, innocent people should be protected, on the other hand, malicious people or organizations should be weeded out. However, when the number of people exceeds millions, it is not easy to classify these people. Moreover, there is a risk of innocent people falling into the hands of these illegal organizations and incurring their threat, and forcing these people to illicit activities. Among those refugees and asylum seekers, there are women, children, the elderly as well as the sick, disabled and the poor. In the first step, these have board and lodging problems. Immediately after, health, education and security needs must be completed without delay. Health, education and security needs must be fulfilled without delay immediately after entering into a country. Meeting the language barrier, communication problems, religious needs, psychological traumas, and rehabilitation needs of incoming people requires high performance and cost. For a country to deal with so many problems alone, it could cause damage to that country in the medium and long term dramatically. If those who succeeded in establishing a peace zone around their country by applying the right strategy on time have enabled to shift the threat to other countries and these countries have been exposed to the influx of refugees, their advantage cannot be explained by ethical values. Because as much as the fact that the principle, liquids cannot be compressed, the principle of compound containers is just as accurate. When a country is overwhelmed with such big problems, the victims, who were taken care of in the early days, are left alone with their own destiny and move from the camps to the city centers. These people can find employment in the city or town where they arrive, at best as cheap workers. Of course there are exceptions. Businessmen, traders, congregation leaders, in short, financially strong people and individuals with know-how, including scientists, can easily find a place in any country, including citizenship. If we look at UNHCR's data on the Resettlement of Syrian Refugees in 2019 shown in Figure 7, it will be seen that only 53% of the need could be met.

**Figure 7.** UNHCR Data on Resettlement of Syrian Refugees in 2019[21]

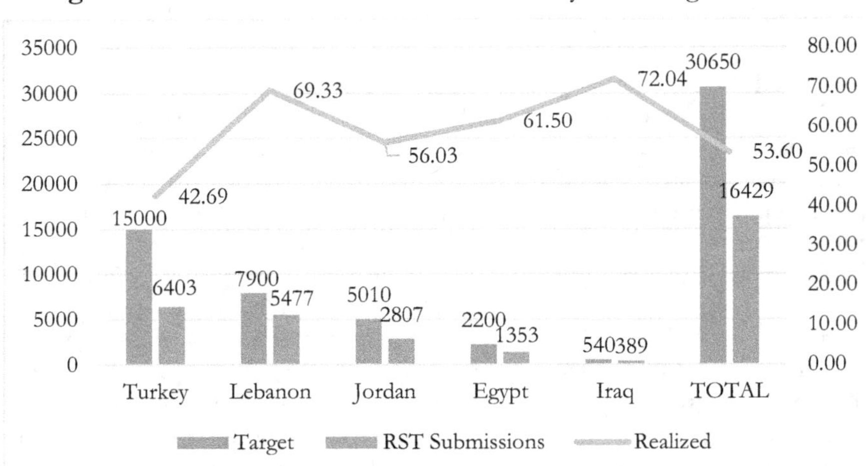


The number of refugees registered between 2014 and 2020 is 5,570,382 (last update, 14.10.2020). However, Resettlement Submissions of Syrian Refugees between 2014 - 2020 are realised as 176,561. Resettlement Submission Rate is only around 3%. In this case, it is noteworthy that Self-organized Refugee Returns to Syria between 2016-2020 was 250,555.[22] It would be appropriate to say that unregistered figures are not negligible. Providing accommodation is not enough alone. Education, health, a regular

---

[21] UNHCR, 2019, Update: Durable Solutions for Syrian Refugees, July-August 2019, file:///Users/demo/Downloads/Reg'l%20Durable%20Solutions%20for%20Syrian%20Refugees%20-%20July-Aug%202019.pdf
[22] UNHCR, 2020, Operational Portal Refugee Situations, Resettlement of Syrian Refugees 2014-2020. http://data2.unhcr.org/en/situations/syria_durable_solutions

job opportunity, social integration, social acceptance process, prevention of cultural erosion, food, energy, security needs and meeting the endless list of needs become such that it is an ironic situation. So, a country offers its guests the social security that it cannot recognize to its citizens. The despair of millions of poor people who cannot be served them and who are left alone with their fates creates an obstacle to return as the time gets longer. Moreover, the homeland of newborns is now the host country. Just as the gazelles with high birth rates manage to maintain their survival in the struggle for the survival of lions and gazelles, this natural selection also manifests itself in migration movements. The status of a child who has reached the age of seven and speaks the language of that country makes the problem even more complicated, as the proportion of newborns is higher than immigrant deaths. For this reason, rather than adopting a course of actions that remains on coated paper in order to preserve national interests, developing effective resilience-based strategies for refugees should be an unavoidable task for all countries of the world.

## How to Develop an Effective Resilience-Based Strategies for Refugees

In order to develop a strong and effective strategy, the meaning of the term resilience must be well understood. Because, since the term resilience has no exact equivalence in other languages, first of all, the meaning of this concept needs to be analyzed well. Resilience[23] is ***"the process of being able to adapt well and bounce back quickly in times of stress"***. Calculating the stress, and strain of a spring material or the absorbent capacity of a sponge is similar to determining how many refugees a country is capable of hosting. Stresses are of three main types, such as tensile, compressive and shear. In addition, the properties of the spring's material used such as plasticity, brittleness, malleability, hardness, fatigue and ductility are among the factors affecting its strength. A sponge's absorption capacity depends on a variety of factors such as thickness, density of the web, radius of fiber, temperature, surface tension and viscosity of fluid, all influenced the absorption rate and capacity to varying degrees. If we simulate countries to a spring, we have to look at yield point. Because irreversible structural defects may occur after this point. If we simulate the countries to a sponge, after the absorption capacity is filled, the permeability increases and that state opens the customs gates, and just as the refugees arrive in that country, this time they start to spread to the target countries. At first, the intensity of Syrian Refugees were felt in Turkey. Then, Turkey has accepted to accomodate the refugees in certain time without foreign aids. Afterwards Turkey has opened the borders

---

[23] Riopel L., PositivePsychology.com, Resilience Skills, Factors and Strategies of the Resilient Person, https://positivepsychology.com/resilience-skills/

towards the targetted countries that the Refugees intend to move. In this example, the sponge theory has worked. If Turkey did not open the borders, spring theory would have been realised. Perhaps irreversible social distortions would have occured. The establishment philosophy of Turkish Republic is against racism and discrimination. Therefore, the structure of population was devised to be homogenous. However, the large number of Syrian Refugees' arrival has changed this homogenous population design in the vicinity of Gaziantep. As the period extends, the cultural structure of immigrants also changes. In fact, newborn children grow up in a convergence, becoming like any citizen of that country. This creates a de facto situation that will hinder the return strategy. The volume of registered refugees from Syria are shown in Figure 8. Considering the national power elements of the countries where Syrian refugees migrated, it is seen that the integration and employment of so many people is very difficult and the crisis cannot be managed without foreign aids.

**Figure 8.** Registered Refugees from Syria[24] (last update: 14.10.2020)

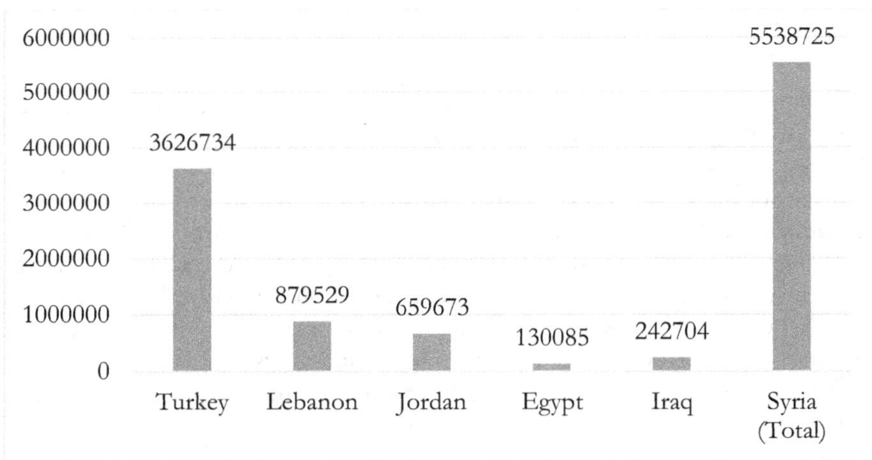


The COVID-19 pandemic has had an additional impact on the current crises in the world. Since there is no barrier that can stop the immigrants from all over the world, there should promulgate a declaration of intent by the UN for the establishment of buffer zones inside or outside of the countries exposed to crises and, the internationalization of these areas.

The main pillars of resilience strategy are shown in Figure 9. During World War I and World War II, there were great human movements and

---

[24] UNHCR, 2020, Operational Portal Refugee Situations, Registered Refugees from Syria - Breakdown by Country of Asylum http://data2.unhcr.org/en/situations/syria_durable_solutions

tragic events that cannot be described. With the experiences gained from these wars, many countries included large migration movements in their mobilization preparation plans. However, in regional crises such as Afghanistan, Syria, Rwanda, and Venezuela, these mobilization plans have remained on the dusty shelves and have not worked. Therefore, the preliminary phase to resist the regional crisis requires serious human intelligence activities and uninterrupted network-based situational awareness infrastructure. When tens of thousands of people threaten the target country and gather at the borders in a crisis, it is necessary to establish asylum centers just within the country's borders in the preparation phase to create a safe heaven for them. The harder it is to keep water in dams, the more difficult it is to keep desperate people in a safe refugee camp for longer.

**Figure 9.** The Main Pillars of Resilience Strategy

| Readiness | Resist | Absorb | Accomodate | Recover | Transform | Adapt |
|---|---|---|---|---|---|---|

Although survival is the most important goal, as long as life continues, Abraham Maslow's hierarchy of needs will eventually come to the fore. Therefore, the refugee problem should be handled in a holistic way. In this case, all problem areas such as subsistence, accommodation, education, social cohesion programs, vocational acquisition programs, employment, free movement, residence and citizenship procedures should be carried out from a single center but under the control of relevant ministries. Each country should measure its resilience capacity. Of course, when taking such measures, economic capacity will be a priority concern. Because, as monthly expenses will arise between the hunger line and the poverty line per individual, the economy, from unemployment rate to purchasing power parity (PPP) should be reviewed. In a country where the youth unemployment rate exceeds 20 percent, taking advantage of and using the refugees as cheap labour will further increase the pressure on the current unemployment rate and increase the unrest in the society. These appear as factors that determine resistance and absorption capacity. A country will be able to overcome the problems it may encounter in the short and medium term, as long as it does not exceed the maximum number of refugees previously determined. However, even if you close the doors, as long as the refugee influx continues, the target country will reach the saturation point after a while. Refugees, whose safety is guaranteed, their minimum vital needs are met, and their social adaptation processes are provided, are removed from the camps where they live. So, even their free movement in the country have been ensured, in a sense, as they are in a normalization process like 'semi-citizens', that country becomes a center of attraction for new refugees. In this case, an endless spiral process starts. In order to prevent a cycle without an exit, a mechanism should be established by the UN. The United Nations should take into account the principle of compound containers and take refugees under international protection by ensuring equitable and reasonable sharing of refugees to developed and developing countries around the world. If the unitary structure of the country in which the crisis broke out dissolves and the country is divided into more than one country, the risk of statelessness of the refugees may arise if the separated parts are recognized as independent states. In the case of Syria, approximately 5.6 million of the population of 16.91 million are refugees according to 2018 data. It is unacceptable to transform Syrian territory into a new political structure without allowing these people to return. Therefore, although the stages between "readiness and recovery" require a great struggle, "transform and adapt" stages require a delicate effort too. Since the last two stages may require a coercive operation, it may be possible to assign a peacekeeping force to be established under the auspices of NATO or the UN by the UN Security Council. A buffer zone of 20 to 50 square kilometers should be established at the border of neighbouring countries around the country of crisis and refugee camps should be established within this region. Afterwards, vital areas should be built within this area during "transformation and adaptation" phases. Until the end of the crisis, legal arrangements should be made by the UN in a way that the sovereign rights of the sovereign state within the vital or security zone are suspended. The concept that is shown in Figure 10 are related to buffer zones and vital area.

**Figure 10.** Buffer Zones and Vital Areas in a Country in Crisis

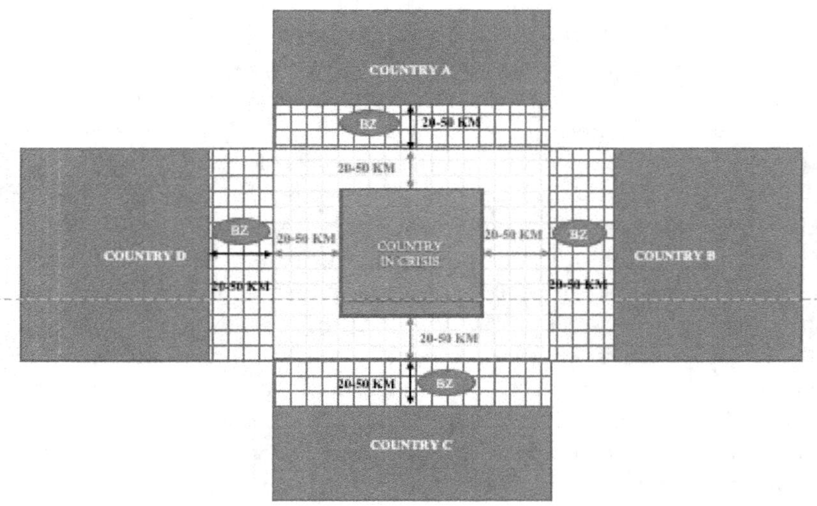

## Conclusion

Traumas arising from the refugee crisis experienced by millions of people who were forced to leave their home, homeland and migrate is a common problem that humanity should deal with regardless of their ethnic origin, gender, status, beliefs and culture. The tragedy is very different from natural disasters that cause destructive damages. Increasing freedoms towards individualization from the unitary state structure understanding that prioritizes the interests of Nations, Peoples and Societies, on the one hand, it contributes to the progress of the world with the richness brought by differences, on the other hand, it has started to melt the adhesives that bind the basic building blocks of nations. Countries that will develop resilience strategies should always consider the "Spring", "Sponge" and "Compound Containers" simulation. This simulation should be taken into account at every stage of the resilience strategy cycle as in Figure-11, and should never be brought to the overflow point with the yield point of a spring, the permeability point of a sponge, or compound containers without scale.

**Figure 11.** Resilience Strategy Cycle

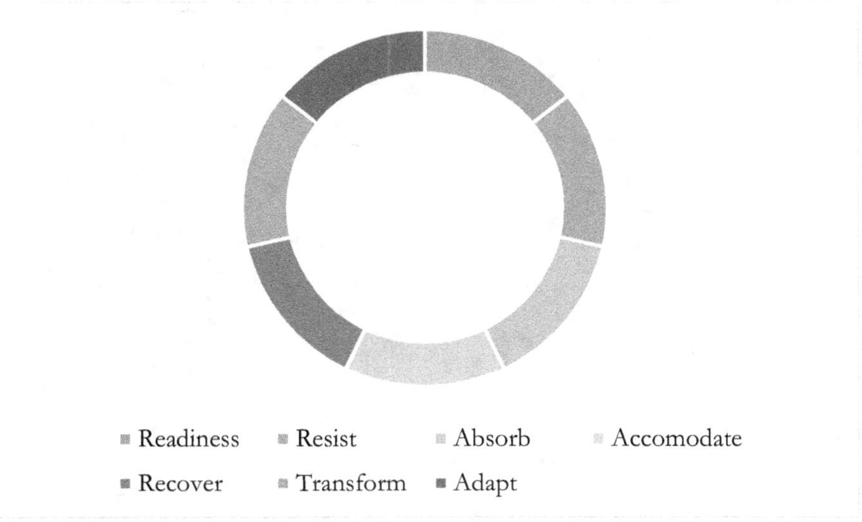


This cycle should be addressed by the UN and target countries exposed should be supported at all stages. If a country is left alone in the face of the refugee influx it is subjected to, and if that country takes care of refugees despite all difficulties, then if the unitary state structure cannot be protected, that country will lose its sovereignty. As a result of the crisis in its country of origin, the target country's claim for land on behalf of refugees and may even bring up the right to annex a part of that country's territory through a plebiscite. This situation may lead to a new jurisprudence in the law of nations. People who are stateless should not be allowed to form a commune or ghettos in the vicinity of cities. Instead, refugees should be classified as talent orientated and their employment should be ensured as soon as possible by adapting to the society they are in. Since the strategies that will be formed by countries alone will only be aimed at protecting their own survival, the UN acquis should be established in this regard and all refugees in the world should be employed in proportion to their national income, taking into account their consents. In this way, the rehabilitation, adaptation, resettlement and ultimately repatriation of the victims could be faster. As the period extends, the number of people who want to return to their country gradually decreases and changes the population of the country they live in and causes cultural changes. Also, material and moral damages are in a nature that cannot be compensated for many years. Foreign aid and grants on this issue are like a drop in the bucket. Education, health, energy, subsistence and accommodation expenditures constitute the main expense items. In light of the aforementioned discussion, resilience strategies developed by countries should be in harmony with each other. All refugee movements around the world should be monitored under the auspices of the UN. The unitary structure of the country of origin should be preserved and the triggering of regional crises should be prevented.

# CHAPTER 16

## ENCLAVITY AND REFUGEES

Tarık Demir[*]

## Introduction

Today, it is observed that large scale migration movements have increased and millions of people are crossing borders under unregistered immigrant or refugee status every year. The subject of enclave / exclave[*] country territories, which comes to the forefront in border studies emerging as an eccentric form of migration, in other words, enclavity phenomenon, is observed to be closely associated with the issue of refugees and immigration. Considering today's conjuncture, which manifests an increase in the measures taken by nation-states for controlling foreigners' access to their countries through borders, it is observed that on the part of refugees, who live within the borders of enclave/exclave countries, the attempt to enter countries surrounding these territories poses more challenges. In other words, it is observed that starting from post-colonial period, the country borders have been re-drawn and the number of enclave country territories has increased[*]. Similarly, as a result of

---

[*] Dr. Lecturer, İstanbul Gedik University Faculty of Economics, Administrative and Social Sciences, Department of International Relations.

[*] It is seen that the first international document, which mentioned the concept of enclave, is Madrid Treaty dated 1526. In political geography, enclave is the name given to a territory belonging to one country that is enclosed within the territory of another. On the other hand, exclave is defined as a territory legally attached to another country with which it is not physically contiguous. In other words, if the territory of any country, is separate from the home country and also politically enclosed within a foreign country, this territory is called exclave. It is observed that those two concepts are closely related with each other based on their premise. In other words, a geographical entity is regarded as an exclave from the perspective of a home country; while it is identified as an enclave from the perspective of the country enclosing it, and international community (Susanne Nies, **Sand in the Works: Enclaves Challenging Metropolitan States: A comparative study on the governance of Cabinda, Ceuta, Kaliningrad, Nagorno Karabakh, Nakhchivan, Melilla and Gibraltar**, Paris Institut d'Etudes Politiques, 2004, p. 19). As an example, East Berlin enclave is regarded as enclave from the perspective of both German Democratic Republic and eastern bloc countries; while it can be identified as exclave from the perspective of Federal Republic of Germany and other states (R. J. Johnston et. al., **Diccionario de Geografía Humana**, Madrid, Alianza Editorial, 1987, p. 156).

[*] As far as world history is concerned, it can be observed that enclaves were formed under the effect of four waves. The first wave corresponds to Pre-Westphalian period in Europe. In this era, since there was no such concept as state in the modern sense of the word, the states were not addressed based on a specific territory, but as the property of a lord. It can be suggested that this phenomenon paved the way for the emergence of *patchwork states*, which are established through the donations of the Church, heritage and acquisition In this context, the term "patchwork states" refers to the enclave phenomenon. The period, in which European colonial powers such as Spain, Portugal, France, Netherlands, Britain and Germany emerged in the stage of history and built their overseas empire, corresponds to the second wave. Overseas colonial territories, which were established during the period from the 16th century to the 20th century,

261

globalism, cases of immigration and number of refugees increased significantly due to adverse economic conditions or ethnic conflicts.

In daily use, the term enclave is a concept, which is used to define different social, cultural, political and economic phenomena. In other words, the existence of different social, cultural, political and economic enclaves can be suggested. For instance, the term enclave refers to rock fragments in geology, lands of a diocese enclosed by foreign lands in canon low, immigrants who are minorities among the dominant sections of the society in a country, and outward oriented dominant economies of a national economy in the field of economics. In all these examples, the state of "being enclosed" (*enclavamiento*) and "being positioned as an island" (*por efecto del aislamiento*) comes into prominence[1]. On the other hand, the study analysed only political enclaves at international level in connection with the refugee phenomenon.

In the study, among several enclaves on the face of the earth, only three groups of enclaves/exclaves were investigated within the framework of refugee phenomenon. These enclave groups are Spain's enclaves Ceuta and Melilla, which are surrounded by the lands of Morocco in North Africa, Cooch Behar (Koch Bihar), located in the West Bengal state of India, which is the largest enclave group in the world, and enclaves of Ferghana Valley, which are enclosed in the lands of Tajikistan, Uzbekistan and Kyrgyzstan. The main reason, why these enclaves were included to the study is that, compared to other enclaves, they are more on the agenda in connection with the question of refugees and borders. Finally, when considered seasonally, it must also be stated that Spanish Ceuta and Melilla enclaves emerged in the second wave, Cooch Behar enclaves emerged in the third wave and Ferghana Valley enclaves emerged in the fourth wave.

## Spain's North Africa Enclaves: Ceuta and Melilla[2]

It is observed that Spain's enclaves in North Africa are posing security threats for EU in terms of illegal migration. Ceuta and Melilla[3] (See Map-1)

---

were defined as enclave by their own imperial centers in their relations with metropole states. Several of enclaves, which had emerged in the second clave, disappeared with the collapse of the colonial system. It is observed that the third wave is directly connected with the collapse of colonial empires in Europe. This period can be called the post-colonial period. Finally, the fourth wave is connected with the disintegration process of multinational socialist states such as USSR and Yugoslavia. It is observed that nearly twenty enclaves and/or exclaves emerged in this era (Evgeny Vinokurov, **A Theory of Enclaves**, Lanham, Lexington Books, 2007, p. 89-90).

[1] Pierre George, **Diccionario de Geografía**, Madrid, Catedrático de Geografía de la Universidad Complutense de Madrid, 1991, p. 211; Evgeny Vinokurov, **A Theory of Enclaves**, Lanham, Lexington Books, , 2007, p. 9; Mark Moberg, Transnational Labor and Refugee Enclaves in a Central American Banana Industry, **Human Organization**, Vol. 55, No. 4, 1996, p. 425.

[2] For detailed information see. Tarık Demir, **Kolonyal Dönemden Günümüze Jeopolitik Bağlamda Anklav/Eksklav Ülke Toprakları-Güvenlik İlişkisi**, Ankara, Nobel Bilimsel Eserler, 2019, p. 166-178 and passim.

[3] It is seen that Ceuta enclave was conquered by Portugal in 1415, and it was transferred from Portugal to

are enclave country lands of Spain, surrounded by Moroccan territories along Mediterranean coasts with autonomous city status. Today, it is seen that Ceuta and Melilla enclaves are used as a kind of leverage and gateway for illegal migrations particularly from Morocco, the country that surrounds these enclaves, to EU countries due to a series of factors, economic reasons being in the first place. It is observed that, use of these enclaves as illegal transit routes cause certain weaknesses in terms of illegal migration between both Spain and Morocco, and EU and Morocco[4].

Although these enclaves, which are located in the transit point between Europe and Africa continents, have certain advantages in terms of ferry transport, tourism and commerce, both enclaves are not economically self-sufficient and are mostly dependent on Morocco. Also, immigration of Muslim groups from North Africa to these enclaves is also a remarkable development in the region[5]. It is seen that demographic balance in the enclave changed over the course of time due to immigration. On the other hand, as a result of this process of immigration to Enclaves, Spanish government conducted nationalist campaigns in order to reverse this process[6]. It is seen that issues of immigration and refugees were the most important factors that affected the bilateral relations between Spain and Morocco in the nineties. In other words, it can be suggested Spain, which has a GNP (Gross National Product) fourteen times more than that of Morocco, is an economic centre of attraction for Muslim groups living in enclaves on the borderline separating two different social and economic worlds. An immigration treaty

---

Spain with Lisbon Treaty dated 1668 following the dissolution of Spain-Portugal Union (Iberian Union 1580-1640). It is seen that Melilla enclave was directly seized by Spain in 1497. It can be suggested that these enclaves functioned as garrison cities (*presidio*) of Spain until the modern Moroccan state was established. Today, these enclaves are under the civil administration of Spain as autonomous cities (*las ciudades autonomias*). From a geopolitical point of view, it is seen that 15th and 16th centuries were periods, which witnessed an intense colonial rivalry between Spain and Portugal. It could be argued that the reason why Ceuta and Melilla enclaves were conquered was because they served as safe outposts for Spain against the attacks of Muslim Moors. On the other hand, towards the middle of 19th century, they acted as protective entities to prevent the region from being assimilated under the influence of France (Antonio-Miguel Bernal, **Historia de España (Monarquia e Impería)**, Vol. 3, Barcelona, Critica-Marcial Pons, 2007, p. 449). In 20th century, violent conflicts occurred as Spanish government attempted to establish order in these last colonial lands against Berber Riffian rebels in 1921, and during the Civil War in 1936 (Matthew Car, Policing the frontier: Ceuta and Melilla, **Race & Class**, Vol. 39, No. 1, 1997, p. 62).

4 Susanne Nies, op. cit., p. 57. Ceuta is located on the south of the Strait of Gilbaltar, while Melilla enclave, which is further east, overlooks the Alboran Sea and wider Mediterranean. Both cities are the products of Spanish conquest history. It is seen that a series of reinforcement attempts were made in enclaves in order to discourage the European and Non-Christian population in and around Portugal over the course of time. Today, such reinforcement attempts still continue to prevent illegal immigration and refugee influx. Since Ceuta and Melilla are on the immigration routes in Sub-Saharan Africa-Europe direction, they played a key role in wider Euro-African border zone (Polly Pallister-Wilkins, The Tensions of the Ceuta and Melilla Border Fences, **EurAfrican Borders and Migration Management: Political Cultures, Contested Spaces, and Ordinary Lives**, Paolo Gaibazzi, Stephan Dünnwald and Alice Bellagamba (Ed.), London, Palgrave Series in African Borderlands Studies, 2016, p. 64).

5 Ibid., p. 59-61.

6 Peter Gold, Europe or Africa? A Contemporary Study of the Spanish North African Enclaves of Ceuta and Melilla, Liverpool, Liverpool University Press, 2000, p. 120.

was signed in 1992 to solve the problem of illegal immigration and refugee, thus paving the way for legal immigration. However, it is observed that Moroccan authorities are not complying with the requirements of this treaty systematically. They agreed to take back only the irregular Moroccan immigrants, who were repatriated from Spain and were not sub-Saharan. However, this treaty eventually caused a decrease in the number of irregular Moroccan immigrants, but on the other hand caused an increase in the illegal immigration through sub-Saharan Ceuta and Melilla enclaves[7].

**Map 1.** Ceuta and Melilla Enclaves[8]

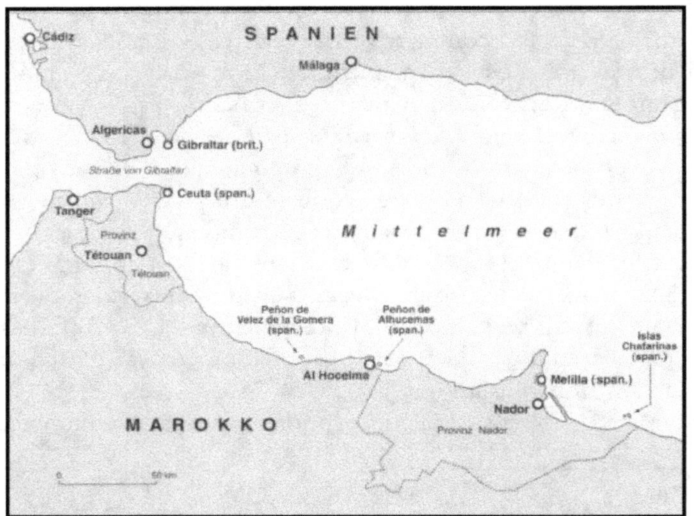


The most important problem in the issue of refugees is that Morocco does not accept these immigrants since the countries of origin cannot be determined due to the lack of documents of the immigrants who want to reach to Europe through the sub-Sahara region. It is seen that after being declined by Moroccan state, these immigrants entered refugee camps in the outskirts of Ceuta and Melilla, such as Calamocarro and La Granja[9]. In June 18, 1996, the police and refugees in Ceuta and Melilla had a violent conflict as a result of which approximately 370 million refugees were deported.

---


[7] Carmen González Enríquez, Ceuta and Melilla: Clouds over the African Spanish Towns. Muslim Minorities, Spaniards' Fears and Morocco-Spain Mutual Dependence, **The Journal of North African Studies**, Vol. 12, No. 2, 2007, p. 228.

[8] Frank Meyer, "Wer ist fremd an diesen Orten?" Zur Bedeutung von Identität, Kultur, Raum und Zeit in den spanisch-nordafrikanischen Städten Ceuta und Melilla ("Who Is Foreign in These Places?" On the Significance of Identity, Culture, Space and Time in the Spanish North African Towns of Ceuta and Melilla), **Erdkunde,** Vol. 58, No. 3, Jul.-Sep. 2004, p. 236.

[9] Peter Gold, Immigration into the European Union via the Spanish enclaves of Ceuta and Melilla: A reflection of regional economic disparities, **Mediterranean Politics**, Vol. 4, No. 3, 1999, p. 26.

Within this framework, it can be suggested that immigration process caused conflicts between local community and refugees in Ceutaa and Melilla, the last colonial enclaves of Spain[10]. As a result, it is seen that the Spanish state built 10.5 km border fences in Melilla in 1993 and 8.2 km in Ceuta in 1996 with the funds obtained from the EU in order to prevent this illegal and irregular immigration and refugee influx. It is observed that fences have been regularly raised due to the increasing human mobility since 1993[11].

## Cooch Behar Enclaves of India and Bangladesh[12]

It is observed that Cooch Behar (See Map 2) region in the state of West Bengal of India causes some problems in border crossings with its complicated enclavity phenomenon. It can be suggested that these enclaves, whose history can be traced back to 18th century, formed as a result of the conflicts between feudal lords in Bengal and Cooch Behar. Throughout the war, Mughal and Cooch Behar kings occupied each other's territories, and acquired these small pieces of land with the peace treaty signed in 1713. This enclave land cluster maintained its existence in the form of autonomous principalities also during Britain period.[13] It can be suggested that the main problem in Cooch Behar enclaves, which are a sort of a matryoshka enclave cluster, is the conflicts between Hindu and Muslim communities, and as a

---

[10] Susanne Nies, op. cit., p. 66. When Spain joined EU, the cities of Ceuta and Melilla have also been included in Schengen Area. However, it should be noted that there is flexibility in the field of control of goods and persons between Morocco and these enclaves. Although inclusion in Schengen aquis has a strong symbolic value for the local population, the necessity of this flexibility is emphasized due to obvious practical reasons, such as facilitating the commerce between Morocco's Nador and Tetuan cities and Spanish enclaves (Sara Iglesias Sánchez, EU Citizenship and Migration Law: Reshaping the Balance of Multi-National Communities? The Case of Ceuta and Melilla, **European Journal of Migration and Law**, Vol. 18, 2016, p. 262).

[11] Polly Pallister-Wilkins, loc. cit., p. 64. For Ceuta and Melilla enclaves and illegal asylum processes, see. Carmen González Enríquez and Ángel Pérez González, Ceuta y Melilla: nubosidad en el Estrecho, **Política Exterior**, Vol. 22, No. 126, Nov.-Dec., 2008, pp. 137-144; G. W. S. Robinson, Ceuta And Melilla: Spain's Plazas De Soberanía, **Geography**, Vol. 43, No. 4, Nov. 1958, pp. 266-269; Karin Von Hippel, Domestic pressures in irredentist disputes: the Spanish army and its hold on Ceuta and Melilla, **The Journal of North African Studies**, Vol. 1, No. 2, 1996, pp. 157-171.

[12] For detailed information see. Tarık Demir, **Kolonyal Dönemden Günümüze Jeopolitik Bağlamda Anklav/Eksklav Ülke Toprakları-Güvenlik İlişkisi**, Ankara, Nobel Bilimsel Eserler, 2019, p. 101-105 and passim.

[13] Reece Jones, The Border Enclaves of India and Bangladesh: Forgetten Lands, **Borderlines and Borderlands: Political Oddities at the Edge of Nation-State**, Alexander Diener and Joshua Hagen (Ed.), Lanham, Rowman&Littlefield Publishers, 2010, p. 18. Throughout a period of 300 years, Cooch Behar enclaves underwent five changes of sovereignty. The first period is the era of Mongolian rule. The second period is the period during which East India Company took over the administration of the area on behalf of British government in 1765 after Mongolian rule. The third period is the period between 1947-1949, when India and Pakistan achieved their independence, but Cooch Behar Merger Agreement was delayed for two years until 1949. The fourth period is the period when states of India and Pakistan, instead of merging, kept the enclaves on two sides of the border. It can be suggested that the final period beings in 1971, when Bangladesh, which constituted the eastern part of Pakistan, seceded from Pakistan and emerged as an independent state (Evgeny Vinokurov, op. cit., p. 49). For further readings on Cooch Behar, See also. Syedur Rahman, **Historical Dictionary of Bangladesh**, Lanham, The Scarecrow Press, 2010, p. 123.

result of this, the population's immigrating to India, and Bangladeshi people's replacing this population in the area[14].

**Map 2.** Cooch Behar's Location[15]

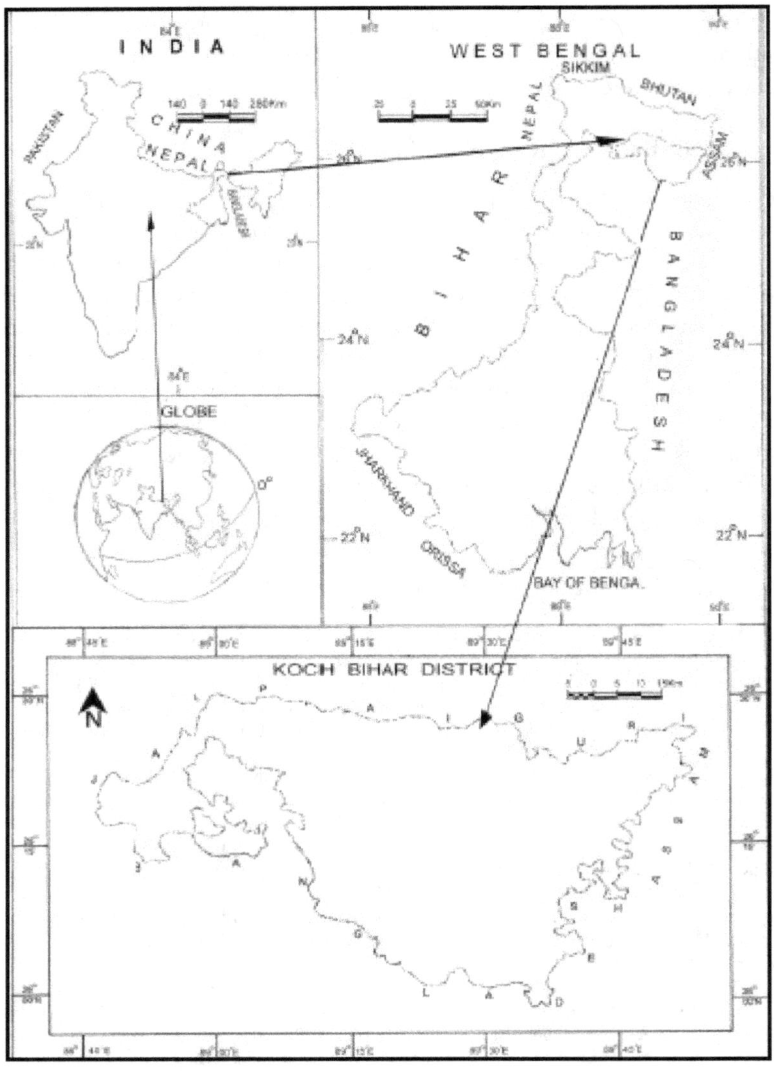


Although India and Bangladesh signed a treaty of amity and started

---

[14] Evgeny Vinokurov, op. cit., s. 138.

[15] Dulon Sarkar, Structural Analysis of Existing Road Networks of Cooch Behar District, West Bengal, India: A Transport Geographical Appraisal, **Ethiopian Journal of Environmental Studies and Management**, Vol. 6 No.1, 2013, p. 76.

negotiating important problems regarding enclave settlements, the problem could not be solved[16]. Within this framework, it is seen that immigration and refugee problem in the Berubari enclave of Pakistan (after 1972, Bangladesh), which is also located within Cooch Behar enclave and surrounded by Indian territories, was solved when Tin Bigha corridor was transferred by India to Bangladesh in 1992[17].

It is observed that enclavity and the resulting phenomena of asylum, constituted one of the important points of conflict between India and Bangladesh It is seen that the problem started in 1949 when Cooch Behar Princely joined India and included these territories by merging with West Bengal (See Map 3).

**Map 3.** Enclaves Belonging to Bangladesh and India in West Bengal[18]

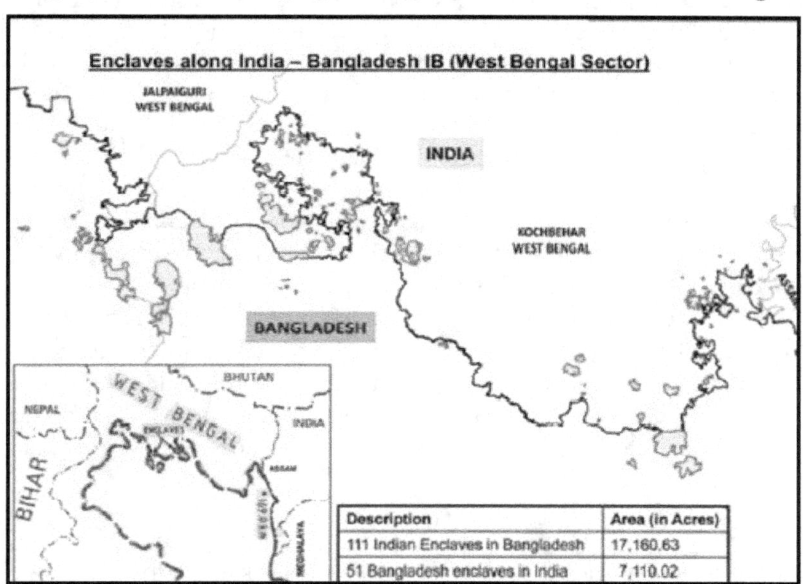


| Description | Area (in Acres) |
| --- | --- |
| 111 Indian Enclaves in Bangladesh | 17,160.63 |
| 51 Bangladesh enclaves in India | 7,110.02 |

It is observed that bilateral agreements, which could solve problems of the populations in these settlements to the interests of all parties, were not concluded until 1990's due to the deep-rooted hostility between India and Pakistan. It can be stated that those living in the enclaves live in isolation without any social and economic protection from the state. Furthermore, it is seen that persons living in India or Pakistan/Bangladesh enclaves are arrested and deported by all sides. Therefore, in 2011, India and Bangladesh

---

[16] Srinath Raghavan, **1971: A Global History of the Creation of Bangladesh**, Cambridge, Harvard University Press, 2013, p. 271.
[17] Syedur Rahman, **Historical Dictionary of Bangladesh**, Lanham, The Scarecrow Press, 2010, p. 104.
[18] Ibid., p. 141.

decided to implement India and Bangladesh Land Border Agreement for resolving these border conflicts. The agreement came into force after it was approved by Indian parliament in 2015. This agreement officially ended the decades-old regional border and related migration problems between the two countries. Both parties exchanged the enclaves under their sovereignty, and enclaves were annexed to the home country by means of corridors. However, it should also be emphasized that the tension between India and Bangladesh continues due to population mobility[19].

## Ferghana Valley Enclaves[20]

Like Cooch Behar enclaves, the enclaves in Ferghana Valley (See Map 4) also have complicated characteristics. It is seen that this enclave complex, which is enclosed in the territories of Kyrgyzstan, Uzbekistan and Tajikistan, has survived until today as a legacy of the border arrangements of the Stalin period. In other words, it is seen that a series of enclaves were created as a result of the divide and rule policy under the Stalin regime. It is seen that this enclave complex gives rise to ethnic problems and border disputes today[21]. While the enclaves in the Ferghana Valley were not an outstanding issue during the USSR period; it has become a serious problem after Soviet Republics in the region gained their independence. Central Asian states started to show extreme sensitivity to the issue of their sovereignty by the end of the 1990s. Due to this sensitivity, it is observed that the bilateral relations between the states in the Ferghana Valley, especially Kyrgyzstan and Uzbekistan, deteriorated under the influence of nationalist feelings. It is seen that those who are most dramatically affected by these developments are those living in enclaves. Especially the extreme security measures taken at the borders constitute the most important source of conflict in bilateral relations[22].

---

[19] Amit Ranjan, **India-Bangladesh Border Disputes: History and Post-LBA Dynamics**, Singapore, Springer, 2018, p. 5; 73. It is seen that one of the strangest results of the division of the Indian geography is the formation of 197 enclave settlements in North Bengal. Enclaves lived in villages, which were completely surrounded by the lands of India and Pakistan due to interesting historical reasons, which can be traced back to pre-colonial period. Thus, 123 Indian settlements surrounded by Pakistani lands and 74 Pakistani settlements surrounded by Indian lands have emerged in a 100 km corridor. What is worse, since the relations between India and Pakistan was not good, both states did not allow passage through their regions for the other to reach to its own enclaves. (Willem van Schendel, **A History of Bangladesh**, Cambridge, Cambridge University Press, 2009, p. 97-98).

[20] For detailed information see. Tarık Demir, **Kolonyal Dönemden Günümüze Jeopolitik Bağlamda Anklav/Eksklav Ülke Toprakları-Güvenlik İlişkisi**, Ankara, Nobel Bilimsel Eserler, 2019, p. 97-101 and passim.

[21] Sergey Abashin et. al., Soviet Rule and the Delineation of Borders in the Ferghana Valley 1917-1930, **Ferghana Valley: The Heart of Central Asia, Studies of Central Asia and Caucaus**, S. Frederick Starr et. al. (Ed.), New York, M. E. Sharpe, p. 105; Alaeddin Yalçınkaya and Khusan Abidzhanov, Solution Process of Enclave/Exclave Areas in Uzbekistan and Kyrgyzstan, MANAS Journal of Social Studies, Vol. 9, No. 4, 2020, passim.

[22] Nick Megoran, The Borders or Eternal Friendship? The Politics and Pain of Nationalism and Identity

**Map 4.** Central Asia and Ferghana Valley[23]

Although the Ferghana Valley, shared by Uzbekistan, Tajikistan and Kyrgyzstan, is a single-piece region geographically, economically and culturally, the region was shared between three countries after the collapse of the USSR. It is seen that ethnic conflicts that started after the collapse of USSR caused intricate and extraordinary border arrangements including enclaves (See Table 1). It is observed that three states sought safe "borders with a human face" in order to end conflicts resulting from border problems, and in this context, took important steps towards regional cooperation. Considering the intensity of the internal migration phenomenon in the Ferghana Valley, it is seen that the phenomenon of enclave makes this internal migration an important problem among states. It is seen that many seasonal workers migrate to regions where taxes are lower and it is easier to find arable land[24]. The unusual social-spatial border arrangements that emerged after independence are perhaps most evident in the eight extra-regional settlements in the Ferghana Valley. It appears that each enclave has its own history in the Soviet national-regional delimitation and subsequent

---

along the Uzbekistan and Kyrgyzstan Ferghana Valley Boundary, Cambridge, Sidney Susex College, 2002, p. 110.

[23] Nick Megoran, The critical geopolitics of the Uzbekistan-Kyrgyzstan Ferghana Valley boundary dispute, 1999-2000, **Political Geography**, Vol. 23, 2004, p. 732. For detailed information about the ethnography of Ferghana Valley, see. Nick Megoran, For ethnography in political geography: Experiencing and re-imagining Ferghana Valley boundary closures, Political Geography, Vol. 25, 2006.

[24] Baktybek Beshimov et. al., A New Phase in the History of the Ferghana Valley 1992-2008, **Ferghana Valley: The Heart of Central Asia**, S. Frederick Starr et. al. (Ed.), Armonk, M. E. Sharpe, 2011, p. 224.

changes. It can be argued that these enclaves pose challenges on the sustainability of cross-border activities such as transportation, trade and immigration. For example, it is observed that the phenomenon of immigration and asylum, especially when evaluated together with the imposition of new national ideologies, concerns of irredentism, hostility between the countries of the region and securitization phenomena, which emerges as a result of all these developments, affects the enclave residents negatively[25].

**Table 1.** Enclaves in Ferghana Valley[26]

| Enclave | Area (km²) | Population | Country | Contiguous with | Main population |
|---|---|---|---|---|---|
| Sokh | 325 | 50,000 | Uzbekistan | Kyrgyzstan | Tajik |
| Shakhimardan | 90 | 5,000 | Uzbekistan | Kyrgyzstan | Uzbek |
| Vorukh | 90 | 30,000 | Tajikistan | Kyrgyzstan | Tajik |
| Kalacha | 2 | 1,000 | Uzbekistan | Kyrgyzstan | Tajik |
| Barak | 1 | 700 | Kyrgyzstan | Uzbekistan | Kyrgyz |
| Kairagach | 1.5 | 190 | Tajikistan | Kyrgyzstan | Uzbek |
| Sarvak | 15 | 1,300 | Tajikistan | Uzbekistan | Uzbek |
| Jangy-Aiyl[a] | 1 | 300 | Uzbekistan | Kyrgyzstan | Kyrgyz |

## Conclusion

It is seen that enclaves, which are subject to extraordinary border arrangements, are closely, are closely related to migration and asylum phenomenon. Considering the mobility of today's world, where large-scale irregular migration movements are increasing and millions of people cross borders with unregistered immigration or refugee status, it is seen that as isolated lands, enclaves cause certain problems between surrounding countries. Three different enclave country territories, which come to the forefront in the question of immigration and asylum, were analysed in the study. Within this framework, Spain's Ceuta and Melilla enclaves in North Africa, Cooch Behar and Ferghana Valley enclave clusters, where the phenomenon of immigration and asylum are experienced the most, were analysed.

It is observed that people who want to immigrate or seek refuge to other regions from enclave country regions confronted with more problems due to the phenomenon of enclavity itself. In other words, it can be suggested that the processes of immigration and asylum generally creates much more pressure on immigrants and refugees in case of certain political conflicts

---

[25] Christine Bichsel, Conflict Transformation in Central: Asia Irrigation disputes in the Ferghana Valley, London, Routledge, 2009, p. 19-20.
[26] Christine Bichsel, op. cit., p. 20.

between the home country, which includes the enclave territory, and the country or countries surrounding the enclave. It is seen that this situation causes political problems between Spain and Morocco states in North Africa, between India and Bangladesh states in Cooch Behar enclave cluster, and finally between Uzbekistan, Kyrgyzstan and Tajikistan for the enclave clusters in Ferghana Valley. It is seen that political problems are resolved either with bilateral border agreements regulating the issue of immigration and asylum, or making border crossings more controllable by establishing corridors between the enclave and the lands of the home country.

# CHAPTER 17

# REFUGEES AND CLIMATE CHANGE

Sezin İba Gürsoy[*]

## Introduction

The displacement process of people depends on many economic, social, political, cultural and environmental reasons. The number of international migrants has continued to grow rapidly, reaching from 150 million in 2000 to 220 million in 2010 and 272 million in 2019. The number of refugees also increased from 14 million in 2000 to 26 million in 2020.[1]More than half of all refugees globally originate from just three countries – Afghanistan, Somalia, and Syria.

Earthquakes, floods, global warming, drought and desertification affect people directly or indirectly, causing loss of life and property, and disasters cause people to migrate to other regions. There has been growing recognition of the impacts of global environmental change on human mobility. According to statistics published by the Internal Displacement Monitoring Centre, an average of 26.4 million people worldwide have been forcibly displaced by various environmental factors or sudden or drought, such as earthquakes, each year since 2008. Large-scale displacement triggered by climate and weather-related hazards occurred in many parts of the world in 2018 and 2019, such as Mozambique, the Philippines, China, India and the United States of America.[2] Environmental change and degradation are also influencing many Pacific Islanders to migrate because of the vulnerability to natural hazards, some of which are linked to climate change.

The displacement caused by environmental problems on a global scale has been discussed since the 1970s. However both scientific / academic and political discussions on the concepts of environmental migrants or environmental/climate refugee have been increasing in the last 20 years. The process of temporary or permanent displacement due to environmental changes includes the concept of the environmental refugee. The obligation to relocate people due to the effects of global climate change has created the concept of climate refugees. Since the concepts of environmental migrant,

---

[*] Dr. Öğr. Üye. Kırklareli Üniversitesi, İİBF, International Relations

[1]International Organization Migration (IOM), World Migration Report 2020, Switzerland, 2019, s. 10. https://publications.iom.int/system/files/pdf/wmr_2020.pdf. Accessed:26.10. 2020

[2] Ibid. p.2.

environmental refugee, climate refugee are not clearly recognized, this study aims to bridge this gap. It will cover the questions of who should be accepted as climate refugees in the context of global climate change, what status should be given to climate refugees and what kind of policies should be developed for these people. In this context, this study evuluates the scope of the concept of climate refugees as evaluated through the legal regulations and practices at both a national and international level. Accordingly, in the following sections of the study; migration and climate change issues, terminology of refugees related to environment and global climate change, and lastly legal status of climate refugees will be explained.

## Linking climate change and migration

Climate change has physical effects such as increasing global temperatures, droughts, floods, extreme weather events, change of seasons, loss of coastal strips, inefficiency of agricultural lands and spread of diseases. These changes lead to the emergence of resource insecurity, increase in social unrest, the spread of poverty, and consequently, an increase in human mobility. The International Organization for Migration estimates that 200 million people will be forced to leave their homes and migrate due to rising sea levels, drought and floods in 2050.[3]

Robert McLemanclassified the drivers of migration into two ways. The first effect is climate processes, which include sea-level-rise, loss of agricultural land, desertification, decreasing water resources and drought. Climate processes include environmental changes that occur relatively slowly over a period of time due to global climate change. The second effect on migration is climate events, including floods, storms, hurricanes and typhoons. Unlike climate processes occuring over a long time period, climate events occur suddenly in a short period of time.[4]

These effects push individuals into forced migration due to environmental degredation. World Disasters Report of the Red Cross and Red Crescent Societies 2001 that focus on recovery stated that the world counted 25 million "environmental refugees".[5] Despite all these views, there is rarely a direct causal link between climate change and movement. According to Joanna Apap, climate change in itself may not trigger a human movement. In addition to this; while climate-specific events, such as a particular storm, may cause movement, the link between a particular storm and climate change is

---

[3] Oli Brown, **"Migration and Climate Change"**, International Organization for Migration ,IOM Research Series, No:31, 2008, s.28.

[4] İbid, p.17-18.

[5] 2001 World Disaster Report, International Federation Of Red Cros and Red Crescent Socities, p.11. https://www.ifrc.org/Global/Publications/disasters/WDR/21400_WDR2001.pdf. Accessed:19.11. 2020.

not necessarily easy to establish.[6]

McLeman, suggest three ways in which climate change can cause refugees. The best-known case of climate refugees is tropical storms and floods caused by rising water levels or changes in the environment. The migrations that occurred after Hurricane Mitch (Central America, 1998), Hurricane Katrina (United States, 2005), Hurricane Aila (Bangladesh, 2009) and Typhoon Haiyan (Philippines, 2013) can be given as examples of such migration.[7] The second effect is sea level rise. Countries with lands below sea level such as Bangladesh suffer from salinization of agricultural lands with the rise; and faced with issues such as pollution of water resources. It is estimated that 30 million people from Bangladesh will become climate refugees by 2050.[8]Bangladesh's environment minister has even said that 20 million 'ecological refugees' would emerge if official estimates of sea level rise were met.[9]

The most vulnerable areas in this case are the *"small island developing states (SIDS)"* in the Pacific due to their topography, low altitudes, and coastal erosion, increased drought, coral bleaching, and storm surges.[10] Studies show that the people of Maldives are migrating to habitable zones. The third effect of climate change on migration is the emergence of semi-arid and arid regions with the change of regional rainfall regimes. The shortages in these regions force people to migrate.[11] A fifth of those living in Tuvalu, the example of the SIDS countries, have been forced to immigrate for these reasons.McAdam gives Tuvalu and Kiribati as *'disappearing states'* that will be uninhabitable by 2050, and their people will become "climate refugee".[12]Similarly, Farbotko and Lazrus claim that Tuvalu is a laboratory and litmus test for the effects of climate change on Earth.[13]

Third, and more indirectly, climate change will contribute to political conflict situations that will result in countries seeking security. When climate crises coincide with economic or social tensions, the potential for forced

---

[6] Joanna Apap, **"The Concept of Climate Refugee Towards a Possible Definition"**,European Parliamentary Research Service,2019, https://www.europarl.europa.eu/RegData/etudes/BRIE/2018/62 1893/EPRS_BRI(2018)621893_EN.pdf. (Accessed: 22.09.2020)

[7] Robert McLeman, "Migration and Displacement in a Chanching Climate", **Epicenters of Climate and Security: The New Geostrategic Landscape of The Anthropocene**, Ed. Caitlin E. Werrell, Francesco Femia, The Center for Climate and Security, 2017, s. 102.

[8] Jane McAdam, "Swimming against the Tide: Why a Climate Change Displacement Treaty is Not the Answer", Vol: 23 No:1 IJRL, 2011, s. 10-11.

[9] 2001 World Disaster Report, op cit., p. 35.

[10] IPCC, AR4 Climate Change 2007: Impacts, Adaptation and Vulnerability, https://www.ipcc.ch/report/ ar4/wg2/. Access: 12.09.2020

[11] McLeman, op.cit., p.102-104.

[12] McAdam, op.cit, p. 8.

[13] Carol Farbotko, Heather Lazrus, "The first climate refugees? Contesting global narratives of climate change in Tuvalu", **Global Environmental Chance**, 2012, p. 385.

migration from rural areas increases significantly.[14] Gönenç and Kibaroglu argued that migration did not lead directly conflicts, but could increase the probability of instability and conflict by changing the existing ethnic composition and population distribution both within and between countries.[15]

## Terminology: Refugee, environmental refugee and climate refugee

The number of concepts emerging in the context of migration and the environment is quite high since the end of World War II. After the United Nations promulgated the Universal Declaration of Human Rights in 1948, the convention on the status of refugees was adopted in 1951 as a result of the intense flows of forced migration caused by the war. The Convention clearly defines the concept of refugee and limits the content of persecution to what is expressed in the definition. The Convention which entered into force 22 April 1954, defined a refugee as:

*"any person who owing to well-founded fear of being persecuted for reasons of race, religion, nationality, membership of a particular social group or political opinion, is outside the country of his nationality and is unable or, owing to such fear, is unwilling to avail himself of the protection of that country; or who, not having a nationality and being outside the country of his former habitual residence as a result of such events, is unable or, owing to such fear, is unwilling to return to it."[16]*

After the Protocol relating to the Status of Refugees was adopted 31 January 1967, and entered into force 4 October 1967. These two documents form the foundation of the international refugee regime. It is assumed that the 1951 Refugee Convention is still the main central document of the international refugee regime. It should be noted that the 1951 Refugee Convention is the most important convention still adopted on the international platform. In the definition, environmental issues such as droughts, floods, desertification, and rising sea level are not included.

Definitions of immigration and the status of refugees, which began with increased environmental awareness in the 1970s, developed through various efforts after the Cold War.At this point, the conceptual framework of migrant, environmental migrant/refugee and climate refugees will be discussed in this section.

**Migrant:** An umbrella term, not defined under international law, reflecting the common lay understanding of a person who moves away from

---

[14] Oli Brown, op cit. p.22.

[15] Defne Gönenç, Ayşegül Kibaroğlu, "İklim Güvenliği Kavramının Türkiye İklim Politikasındaki Yeri", **Alternatif Politika**, 2017, s.5.

[16] Convention relating to the Status of Refugees. United Nations, 1951, https://www.ohchr.org/Documents/ProfessionalInterest/refugees.pdf. Accessed: 21.10.2020.

his or her place of usual residence, whether within a country or across an international border, temporarily or permanently, and for a variety of reasons.[17]

**Environmental migrant:** Environmental migrant is defined by IOM as;

*"A person or group(s) of persons who, predominantly for reasons of sudden or progressive changes in the environment that adversely affect their lives or living conditions, are forced to leave their places of habitual residence, or choose to do so, either temporarily or permanently, and who move within or outside their country of origin or habitual residence"[18]*

**Environmental refugee:** This concept was initially put forward by Lester Brownin 1976. After this, in 1984, Sir Edmund Hillary included this approach in his book entitled *Ecology 2000: the changing face of the earth.* Hillary used as like"..*in Ethiopia, a new failure of the rains during the past for years has created a new class of environmental refugees..."[19]*

The concept has been further popularized by Essam El-Hinnawi. He claimed that "environmental refugees" are;

*"... those people who have been forced to leave their traditional habitat, temporarily or permanently, because of marked environmental disruption (natural and/or triggered by people) that jeopardised their existence and/or seriously affected the quality of their life".[20]*

After the cold war, in 1992, Agenda 21—the influential intergovernmental program of action agreed upon by almost all governments at the 1992 United Nations Conference on Environment and Development—has often been used the term "environmental refugees"[21]. The IOM used the following definition for its "environmental migrants" in 2007:

*"Environmental migrants are persons or groups of persons who, for compelling reasons of sudden or progressive change in the environment that adversely affects their lives or living conditions, are obliged to leave their habitual homes, or choose to do so, either temporarily or permanently, and who move either within their country or abroad."[22]*

---

[17] International Organization for Migration, Glossary on migration, IML Series No. 34, 2019.

[18] International Organization for Migration,**"Climate Change, Environmental Degradation and Migration"**, 2011, https://www.iom.int/idmclimatechange. Accessed:22.10.2020.

[19] Edmund Hillary, *Ecology 2000: The changing face of earth*, Joseph, 1984, Michael Joseph Ltd, p. 214.

[20] Essam El-Hinnawi, **Environmental Refugees**. United Nations Environment Programme, Nairobi. 1985.

[21] United Nations Conference on Environment & Development, **Agenda 21,**Rio de Janerio, Brazil, 1992, https://sustainabledevelopment.un.org/content/documents/Agenda21.pdf. Accessed: 11.09.2020.

[22]International Organization for Migration, **Discussion Note: "Migration and the Environment"**, 2007, https://www.iom.int/jahia/webdav/shared/shared/mainsite/about_iom/en/council/94/MC_IN F_288.pdf. (Accessed: 12.10.2020).

Regarding concepts, Karen McNamara has produced pioneering work in detail on the discourse of environmental refugees, especially in the UN's discourse. Indeed, McNamara tries to show how environmental refugees have been built as *"adaptable subjects"* to environmental degradation since 1996, in parallel with the climate refugee discourse discussed above.[23]

This concept has been expressed in different ways in the literature (environmental migrants/refugees, environmentally-induced displaced people, environmental displacees, etc.[24] Myers and Kent thought that there are individuals who had to leave their habitat due to unusual factors such as storms and floods.[25] Myers also examines environmental refugees as the people who feel extremely unsafe in their own territory because of climatic hazards, droughts, deforestation, and have no other option but to flee to somewhere secure.

In the midst of all this debate, the concept of environmental refugees is also used for the term *"climate refugees"*. It would be correct to note that whether there is a practical difference between "environmental refugee" and "climate refugee" remains unclear. While the term" environmental refugees " is more common in scientific publications, climate refugees have not moved too far into scientific writing, as it is a new concept.

**Climate migration:** It is considered a subcategory of environmental migration. It refers to a singular type of environmental migration caused by climate change. The concept of climate migration is defined by the IOM as follows:

*"The movement of a person or groups of persons who, predominantly for reasons of sudden or progressive change in the environment due to climate change, are obliged to leave their habitual place of residence, or choose to do so, either temporarily or permanently, within a State or across an international border."[26]*

This study underlines a special issue. Climate migrants should not be considered a problem in any binding international agreement, nor is there any international body tasked with protecting climate migrants.

---

[23] Karen McNamara, **"The Politics of 'Environmental Refugee' Protection at the United Nations",2006,** University of New South Wales, Sydney, unpublished PhD thesis, p.165.

[24] Bogomil Terminski, **"Environmentally-Induced Displacement. Theoretical Frameworks and Current Challenges"**, https://www.weadapt.org/sites/weadapt.org/files/legacy-new/knowledge-base/files/50e6b5828f417environmentally-induced-displacement-terminski-1.pdf. (Access 12.10.2020).

[25] Norman Myers, Jennifer Kent, "Environmental Exodus, an emergent crisis in the global arena", **Climate Institute magazine,** s. 18-19. http://climate.org/archive/PDF/Environmental%20Exodus.pdf. (Access:10.05.2020).

[26] Warsaw International Mechanism Executive Committee (WIM ExCom) Work Plan Action Area 6 on Migration, Displacement and Human Mobility, UNHCR, https://www.unhcr.org/protection/environment/57459e3d7/warsaw-international-mechanism-executive-committee-wim-excom-work-plan.html. (Accessed: 30.10.2020).

**Climate refugee:** The concept of climate refugee is used in international public opinion and academic research. However, the absence of a complete definition and different uses bring some drawbacks.[27] Climate refugees have a narrower meaning than the concept of environmental refugees. Bierman and Boas define climate refugees as: *"individuals who have to leave their habitats due to changes in the environment associated with the three effects of climate change (sea level rise, extreme weather events, drought and water scarcity)."*[28]

In the Encyclopedia of Global Political Geography, a climate refugee is expressed as "a person dislocated by climatic change induced environmental disasters. Such disasters are evidence of human-influenced ecological change and disruption to Earth's climatic system, primarily through the emissions of greenhouse gases."[29]

There is a very new term in this climate-induced relocation. *"Climigration"*, coined because of climate change, is described as; *"a specific type of permanent population displacement that occurs when community relocation is required to protect residents from climate-induced biophysical changes that alter ecosystems, damage or destroy public infrastructure and repeatedly endanger human lives."*[30]

RobinBronen first ride this term for forced permanent migration of communities due to climate change.[31]A 2018 study by Matthews and Potts defined this term as *"a specific type of permanent population displacement that occurs when community relocation is required to protect residents from climate-induced biophysical changes that alter ecosystems, damage or destroy public infrastructure and repeatedly endanger human lives."*[32]

It must be said that the main problem and complexity regarding climate refugees is the issue of legally defining the concept as accepted by international law.[33] Despite the presence of this concrete problem, these people are neither explicitly defined as a category nor recognized as refugees under "climate refugees" by the 1951 Convention relating to the Legal Status of Refugees.[34] Neverthless, it is debated that there may be situations in which

---

[27] Frank Laczko, Christine Aghazarm, **Migration, Environment and Climate Change: Assessing the Evidence**, International Organization for Migration, Geneva, 2009, pp. 7-40.

[28] Frank Bierman, Ingrid Boas, Preparing for a Warmer World: Towards a Global Governance System to Protect Climate Refugees, Global Environmental Politics, Volume 10, Number 1, February 2010, p. 67.

[29] M.A. Chaudhary, Gautham Chaudhary,**Global Encyclopaedia of Political Geography**, 2009, p. 43.

[30] Robin Bronen, F. Stuart Chapin, "Adaptive governance and institutional strategies for climate-induced community relocations in Alaska", **Proceedings of the National Academy of Sciences**, 110(23), 2013, s.9320.

[31] Robin Bronen, Forced Migration of Alaskan Indigenous Communities Due to Climate Change: Creating A Human Right Response, https://www.oceanfdn.org/sites/default/files/forced%20migration%20 alaskan%20community.pdf, (Access 13.07.2020).

[32] Tony Matthews, Ruth Potts, "Planning for climigration: A framework for effective action", **Climatic Change**, 2018, 148(4), 607-621.

[33] Apap, op cit, p..4.

[34] United Nations, 1951. Convention relating to the Status of Refugees. https://www.ohchr.org/

the refugee criteria of the 1951 Convention may be expanded further. For example, refugee status may expand in cases of drought-related famine, armed conflict and violence.[35] However, Biermann and Boas have seena very weak possibility of including climate refugees under the scope of the 1951 Geneva Convention. [36]

### Legal status of environmental / climate refugees

Since the early nineties, international institutions rarely use the term "environmental/climate refugees". The International Organization for Migration and the United Nations High Commissioner for Refugees (UNHCR) use the concept of environmentally displaced person (EDPs), instead of the concepts of climate refugee or environmental refugee.

Regardless of the concept, people displaced across borders due to climate change, environmental degradation and disasters may in some cases need international protection. In this context, both international organizations and NGOs on this issue are needed. For instance, The UNHCR has played a pioneering role in raising awareness about climate change as a driver of migration. Also, the Intergovernmental Panel on Climate Change (IPCC) has warned that "the greatest single impact of climate change could be on human migration".

The International Organization for Migration (IOM) usefully defines "environmentally induced migrants" as *"persons or groups of persons who, for compelling reasons of sudden or progressive changes in the environment that adversely affect their lives or living conditions, are obliged to leave their habitual homes, or choose to do so, either temporarily or permanently, and who move either within their country or abroad"*[37]

A broader definition of refugees has been adopted in two regional conferences. The first one is the 1969 Organization of African Unity Convention Governing the Specific Aspects of Refugee Problems in Africa focuses on situations that compel people to leave their countries in search of safety and sanctuary. And the other is the 1984 Cartagena Declaration on Refugees. Similarly, these two conventions provide protection to climate refugees only in the event of a serious incident affecting public order.

Among the reasons for becoming a refugee in the Convention of the Organization of African Unity, there are cases of serious deterioration in public order. The convention does not include the concepts of climate

---

Documents/ProfessionalInterest/refugees.pdf. (Access 10.10.2020).

[35] https://www.unhcr.org/climate-change-and-disasters.html. (Access 28.11.2020).

[36] Bierman and Boss, op cit, p.22.

[37] Koko Warner, Charles Ehrhart, Alexde Sher binin, Susano Adamo, Tricia Chai-Onn, **"In Search of Shelter: Mapping the Effects of Climate Change on Human Migration and Displacement"**,Care International, Columbia University, 2009,p. 2.

refugee and environmental refugee. However, the phrase *"events that seriously threaten the public order in a part or whole of their country"* allows the assessment of environmental disasters caused by climate change within this scope.

In the Cartagena Declaration, it is recommended to expand the scope of the refugee concept. The concept of climate refugee and environmental refugee is not directly included in the declaration. The reasons that must exist in order to be accepted as a refugee are expressed as general violence, external pressures, internal disturbances, violations of human rights and other factors that directly disrupt public order. It is possible to expand the scope of the refugee definition indirectly by including environmental issues among these other elements.[38]

Since 1990, America has established a status under the name of Temporary Protected Status (TPS), specifically for victims of natural disasters. Temporary Protection Status is granted in three cases. First, the existence of danger due to ongoing armed conflict. The second is the fact that the living conditions are temporarily paralyzed by earthquakes, floods, drought and similar environmental disasters, or because a foreign state is unable to cope with the return of its citizens to their country as a result of environmental disasters, and is demanding that America give temporary protection to its citizens. Third, is the presence of reasons preventing people from returning to their countries for extraordinary and temporary reasons, provided that the Temporary Protection Status does not contradict the national interests of America.[39] Ekşi claims that the temporary protection status is interpreted and applied quite narrowly in America.[40]

The amendment to the refugee law in Australia includes the definition of climate refugees and the Ministry of Immigration authorizes the issue of visas to people who have been displaced due to climate change disasters. New Zealand, on the other hand, accepts people who are displaced by climate change under the name of the Pacific Access Category in numbers determined annually. [41]

Also the EU with a significant history of immigration issued temporary protection in January 2016 which provide displaced persons from non-EU countries and unable to return to their country of origin, with immediate and temporary protection. The European Union Temporary Protection Directive states that those who are displaced due to disasters caused by climate change can also be included in the article providing protection to migration due to

---

[38] McAdam, op cit, s. 48,49.

[39] Ruth Wasemi, Karma Ester, **"Temporary Protected Status: Current Immigration Policy and Issues,"** Congressional Research Service, 2010, s.2-3, https://www.everycrsreport.com/files/20100119_RS20844_f22d31ccd4760aedc741d8213821d20a3a17b9db.pdf. (Access 24.10.2020).

[40] Nuray Ekşi, "İklim Mültecileri", **Göç Araştırmaları Dergisi**, Cilt:2, Sayı:2, 2016, s.38.

[41] McAdam, op cit, p. 102.

violence, human rights violations and armed conflicts. However, since the relevant article (Article 2 / C) does not regulate the scope of the directive in detail, climate refugees cannot be included within in this scope.

In addition to this directive, in 2011 after work on climate refugees, the European Parliament noted that; *"Because of the fact that the term 'environmental refugee' has been challenged both in the academic and political debate, we suggest to use the more general term of 'environmentally induced migration' to denote the broader phenomenon and 'environmentally induced displacement' to denote forced forms of mobility primarily engendered by environmental change"* So again he term is not literally recognized by the EU and that it is not possible to interpret existing legislation as incorporating "climate refugees" within the protection regime.[42]

## Conclusion

Climate change and environmental degradation, which are multidimensional and causal issues, are among the reasons for migration today. Indeed the relationship between migration and environmental conditions is not a new phenomenon, the concept of environmental refugees emerged in the 1970s in parallel with environmental crises. However, the concept of climate refugee is newly raising public awareness. Individuals who have to move due to long-term climatic processes such as drought, rising sea level, loss of water resources and agricultural lands and sudden climatic events such as hurricanes and floods are called climate refugees.

Also, "climate refugee" or "environmental refugee" concepts are widely used in the media and legal terminology but these terms are a misnomer under international law. It should be noted that there is no international regulation that protects individuals who migrate due to climate change and environmental reasons, and forces states to act in this direction.[43]In the current regime, most climate refugees could be conceptualized as internally displaced persons. However, the absence of a legal framework constitutes an important obstacle to the establishment of a protection mechanism for individuals fleeing environmental damage regardless of whether they are due to climate or not. This legal gap makes it difficult to deal with the issue both on a national and international level; and reveals limitations on protections available for the people affected by environmental stresses.

As a result, the rights, entitlements and protection options for people displaced by climate are uncertain in international law, and there is no

---

[42] Albert Kraler, Tatinana Cernei, Marion Noack, **"Climate Refugees" Legal and policy responses to environmentally induced migration"**, European Parliament, Brussel, 2011, https://www.europarl.europa.eu/RegData/etudes/etudes/join/2011/462422/IPOL-LIBE_ET%282011%29462422_EN.pdf, (Access 11.09.2020).
[43] Ekşi, op cit, s.18.

international agency or institutional solidarity such as the United Nations High Commissioner for Refugees (UNHCR), with a specific mandate to assist them.[44] Climate refugees whose legal status is uncertain can cause social tensions and indirectly, security problems due to resource shortages. The first thing to do to prevent the emergence of security problems that may arise due to climate change and to manage the issue of climate refugees is to determine the international legal status of refugees.[45] Another step is to establish aid funds for countries most affected by climate change. Establishing an international regime specifically for climate refugees requires the cooperation of different actors such as the United Nations, governments, non-governmental organizations and transnational companies. Through this, the international community must recognize that the human mobility occuring as a result of climate change is not a problem that can be solved by different countries unilaterally. Like climate change, the scale and severity of the problem can only be addressed by concerted international efforts.[46]

---

[44] Jane McAdam, Ben Saul,"An Insecure Climate for Human Security? Climate-Induced Displacement and International Law", p.7.https://www.peacepalacelibrary.nl/ebooks/files/3573990 72.pdf. (Accessed 29.10.2020).

[45] Fırat Harun Yılmaz, Mücahit Navruz, **"Küresel İklim Değişikliği, İklim Mültecileri Ve Güvenlik"**, ASSAM Uluslararası Hakemli Dergi , 2019, ss.255-270.

[46] Pareh, Serena, "Climate Change and Human Rights: Climate Change and Refugees", **The 2015** Paris Conference and the Task of Protecting People on a Warming Planet, 2015.